Live Like Men

Eugene Luning

Copyright © 2014 Eugene Luning

All rights reserved.

ISBN-13: 978-1495479939

ISBN-10: 1495479935

To my Jenny

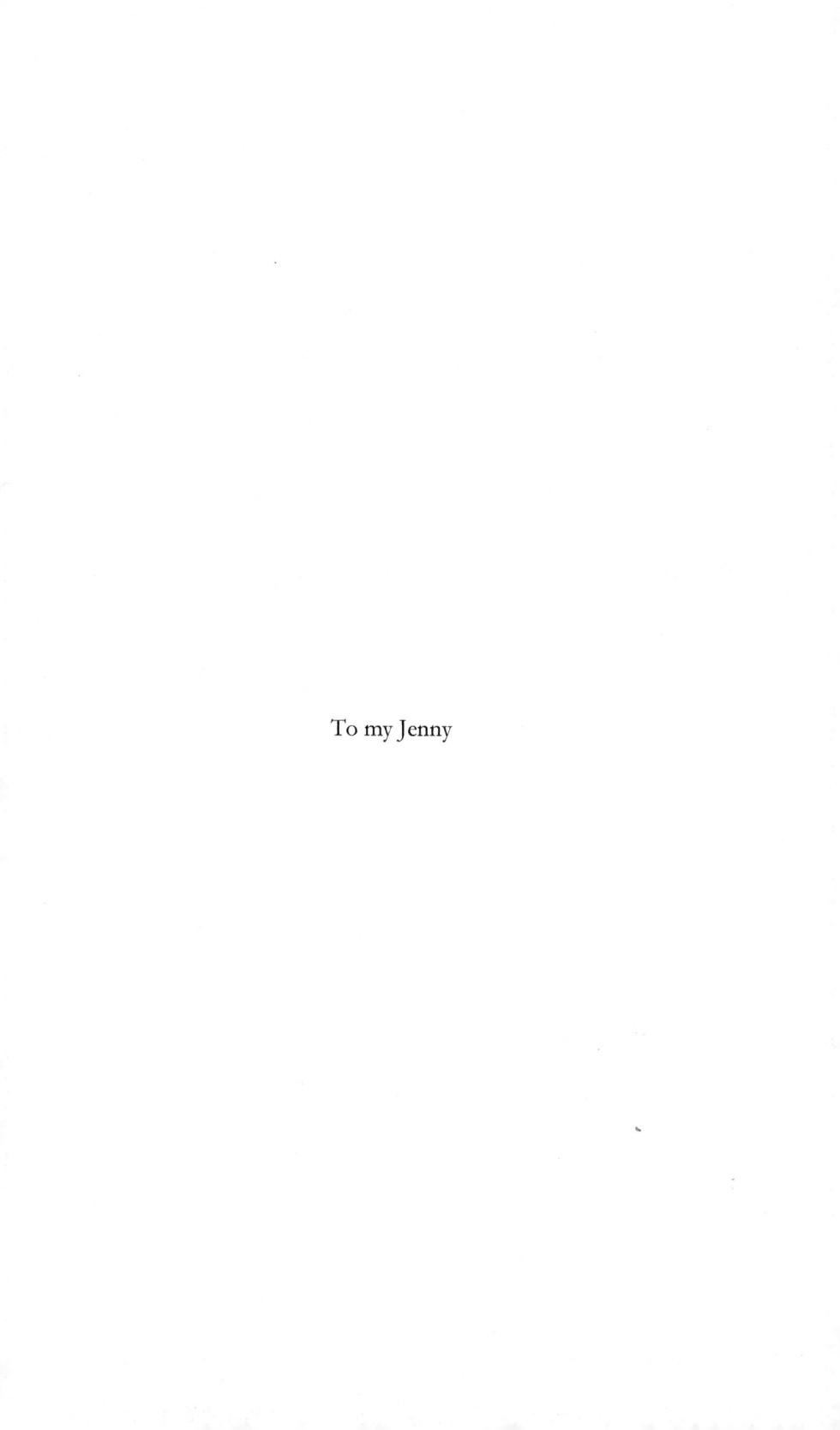

"Be on your guard, stand firm in the faith, live like men, be strong! Let everything that you do be done in love."

1 Corinthians 16:13,14 – J.B. Phillips Translation

"It is not Christian men who shape the world with their ideas, but it is Christ who shapes men in conformity with Himself. But just as we misunderstand the form of Christ if we take Him to be essentially the teacher of a pious and good life, so, too, we should misunderstand the formation of man if we were to regard it as instruction in the way in which a pious and good life is to be attained. Christ is the Incarnate, Crucified and Risen One whom the Christian faith confesses. To be transformed in His image – this is what is meant by the formation of which the Bible speaks. To be conformed with the Incarnate – that is to be a real man."

Dietrich Bonhoeffer, *Ethics*

FOREWORD

Every day of our life is our direct response to the incarnation and life and death and resurrection of Jesus. We're simply the current generation of men whose daily task is the same task given to the original apostles on the Mount of Olives: "You will be witnesses to me, not only in Jerusalem, not only throughout Judea, not only in Samaria, but to the very ends of the earth!"

The goal of these pages is a more robust understanding of the power of Jesus to transform the lives of His men. Starting in Genesis and carrying all the way to Revelation, we'll see the glory of God at work in men like you and me. Our task: Absolute Surrender to Jesus everyday. Our only hope: His Holy Spirit and Single-minded Obedience.

Along the way, I hope our hearts are drawn daily into an abiding intimacy with the Savior of the World who came for us. My prayer is that we'll actually be the branches so firmly connected to the Living Vine that we'll never cease producing fruit for the Kingdom.

One day at a time in eternity's present, my brothers! Every day has its own call for the sake of Jesus. May we give our best efforts in the direction of the One who gave His all for us. May we know that the work *and* the results are His.

For the sake of our Anchor,

Eugene
February 2014

THE DAILY PLAN

1. Read each day's listed Scripture for yourself
2. Consider the daily reflection upon it
3. Go out and Live Like Men

January 1 - Genesis 2:4-17

Commitment of your year

In many ways, the plan of God for Adam still remains the daily plan for a man after His own heart. After all, it was the not the heart of God that changed as a result of the Fall, it was the changeable heart of our forefather, Adam. God had placed him in a perfect setting: provided for; presiding over; alive in his full "fruitful" manhood. Yet, more importantly, Adam had the chance to walk in God's holy presence, totally unashamed, fully face to face. Formed from the dust of the ground, breath breathed by His God, their relationship was one of perfect harmony. God's call for Adam's life was unto full-hearted manhood in the idyllic easy toil of the Garden of Eden. He stood master over the world and its beauty and lushness, its fruit, its profuse perfection. And God had only asked for one single thing; a single-minded obedience to one simple task…

The call of God to you, this new year, revolves around a similarly simple question, O Man: Will you today – and tomorrow – and the day after tomorrow – *all year* – obey Him alone? Will you bask within the ever-present glow of His ever-available presence first thing every single morning? Will you realize His provisionary promises for those who "seek first His kingdom" are abundantly true for you? Will you *not* seek first to make yourself like Him, to hunger for the fruit of *His* knowledge of good and evil? Instead, will you "hunger and thirst for righteousness" and taste deeply of the tree and the river of Life?

In short, will you commit this New Year to being a disciple of the God you say you serve, O Man? Will you live this year within the true fullness of the manhood you were actually created for, O Man of God? Will you live the rest of *this* particular day, seeking to obey His commandments spoken to you by His Holy Spirit? Are you ready to be challenged, all year, by the life of God operating in the lives of His men?

Well then, welcome to the New Year, my friend! May it be a year of New Life together!

January 2 - Genesis 3

Leading your woman, not being led

Satan won't use extraordinary means to get you out of the game; he will deal the simplest blow that's necessary. The evil one will not employ extravagant plans of attack where he knows the easiest ploy will easily succeed. We must learn to be so present with our God, so "abiding in the Vine," that we'll grow strong and stalwart. We can't be felled by some small hatchet when the strength of God in Christ gives us strength to withstand absolutely anything...

Just as with our first forefather, Satan often uses women as a way to call our hearts away from Jesus. There's no surer way to shipwreck following Him than through our care or concern for a woman that we love. Our temptation is to please or appease her and we often miss our greatest opportunities for leading her in that action. For a woman's heart truly yearns (even if she sometimes denies it) for your complete surety, grounded in Jesus. There's nothing so dissuasive for the sin in a woman's heart than to see her man humbly following after God. His strength built upon real strength can weather any storm of discord, temptation, or earthly strife you can imagine.

Adam lost his way – and also his heavenly birthright – when he gave to Eve's way the entirety of his manly attention. Even in your loving care for your wife, you are *not* released from God's call upon your own life, O Man. You must live the life to which you have been called even if you find that way to be at odds with your personal ease. God is the God who understands our human relationships better than anyone; He will honor your obedient honoring of Him.

Will you follow Jesus today with the entirety of your life and thus set an example for your lady's heart? Will you serve her, help her, love her, honor her, and, in that way, be leading her closer unto Jesus? Will you *not* allow the journey of your day to be decided by the voice of this woman God has given you? Will you strive to follow Him alone, trusting that your hearkening to His call will, of itself, lead her life?

Will you be the man she *thinks* she wants today? Or will you be the man she actually needs? Will you stand up strong where Adam was so weak and be the man who loves and serves his wife by his own obedience?

January 3 – Genesis 4:1-12

Bringing all of yourself

The battle of Today will be decided everyday upon the battlefield of Cain and Abel. We're either masters of the sin within our hearts, accepting our "new creation" status, or we're pitifully mastered by its presence in us. We're either bringing God "fat portions" of our day and of ourselves, or we bring Him just "some of the fruit." So, as His men, the question of Today becomes the everyday question for us: Are we following Him with our everything? Are we following Him by following His precepts, His commandments, His truth, His very voice within us? Will we live the circumstances of this day within the light of His eternal plan for our whole earthly lives? Will we subjugate our waywardness of thought unto the steady-minded, clear-eyed direction of His holy Word? Will we offer up ourselves as the only actual true "living sacrifice" His heart desires?

Or, like Cain, will we give Him "some" of ourselves: *some* thoughts, *some* ideas, *some* actions, *some* glory? Will we "bring forth fruit" when it happens to occur to us; when we suddenly remember what we're supposedly "about"? Will we be a "restless wanderer," charting courses out into the shadowland between ourselves and His best for us? Will we subtly try to live today beneath the elusive banner of so-called "Christian manhood," rather than according to His Way?

We men must follow Jesus – top to bottom, head to toe, mind and soul, brain and heart – *only Jesus*. The way of Cain, the way of the flesh, will beat to death our half-hearted attempts to "try to be more like Abel was." O Men of God, we must actually be Abel. That's the only way to overcome Cain. We must rise up from our reading of His Word with hearts changed and fully ready to be wholly His, each day. We must listen through this whole day to leadings of His Holy Spirit and be acting in accordance with them. We can't hope to somehow "half-Abel" the way we live today and see its being anything less than "half-Cain-ing." May we be the men of *undivided* hearts who bring an *undivided* offering of all we are today. May we never rest until we've learned to give Him of the first – and the best – of every part of ourselves in each day.

O Man, Jesus is worth your everything. Now are you prepared to give it?

January 4 – Genesis 5:21-24

Walking intimately with your God

The little that we know about the life and times of Enoch is enough to base our lives around: Enoch was a man like we are; a father; he "walked with God"; and God chose to spare him earthly death. The one clear thing we're told about his life was how he paced his life according to the footsteps of his God. For to "walk with God" can only mean a daily step-by-step-by-step-by-step following after Him, wouldn't you think? It must surely mean that Enoch lived his days with a listening God-aware spirit and acted upon God's promptings. Enoch surely "considered everything a loss" compared to the wonder of knowing his God more intimately…

Through Jesus Christ, you have the opportunity to be a man who knows that earthly death means nothing at all anymore. You've been set free from death, its "sting," its fear; you are fully free to live with Him right now. But for what will you live, this day? And, more importantly, for whom? Will you learn to walk in step with the God who chose to create you, who came for you, who died to redeem you? Will you be a man whose eulogy contains those same simple words of praise, "He walked with God," like Enoch? Will you strive to "live by the Spirit," thus choosing to "keep in step with the Spirit" all day long?

O Men of God, don't be afraid that "walking with God" will slow the harried pace of your busy important modern life. To be honest with you, you have no idea of all the joy and adventure that He longs to show you down this wild glorious path. But, O Man, you must actually start down this path! You must turn down this wonderful "straight and narrow" path of His choosing.

So, today, let's be starting upon it together.

And let's never ever stop.

January 5 – Genesis 6:5-22

Doing the absurd for Him

Oftentimes the highest callings in the lives of God's men bear the marks of a complete absurdity. There's nothing in the story of the ark and Noah's faithful construction-project that should make you feel at all comfortable. You shouldn't jump ahead because you know the ending of the story where the covenant is eventually made between him and God. If you want to learn the lesson Noah learned, stand upon the dry plain with God's spoken promise only. Stand strong with only a chisel and saw and some lengths of cypress wood and start to build with faithful Noah. Feel the heat of rainless days beating upon your sunburned breaking back, working day-in and day-out. Listen to the laughter of the crowds and hear the silent plaintive worries of your wife, watching you work yourself to exhaustion. Wonder if the lasting legacy you're leaving to your children is a father who went raving mad…

The call of God is never of our own choosing; the man following his "own way" is actually lost already. All the sharpness of your potential calling will be blunted everyday where you're living from a self-chosen waywardness. There's nothing wrong with working mindlessly 9-to-5 if God has called you to be working mindlessly 9-to-5, O Man of God. But the peril of a life wasted comfortably is the risk we run when we turn our back upon the call…

What were you made for, O Man?

And, O Man, are you fulfilling that call?

If there's any absence of absurdity in how you live your life for Jesus, think of how you're actually living. God rarely calls His men unto an easy earthly comfort, picking up paychecks, simply surviving like everyone else. Ask the Lord for eyes to see how He might want to use your life for the purpose of glorifying His Name upon the earth. And be ready for the absurd, my friends. It runs side-by-side, hand-in-hand, with Life.

January 6 – Genesis 9:1-17

Your witness is your blessing

The Blessing given Noah and his sons was like the blessing of a new day's dawning over a fresh Garden of Eden. In essence, God regifted Noah and his progeny with the mastery over the earth once accorded to their father, Adam. "All the beasts of the earth and all the birds of the air" are now handed into their manly dominion for safe-keeping. They're given all the freedom of a life lived perfectly freely within the confines of His stated commandments. All the blessings of the ages are bestowed upon their living of their earthly lives – for Him – with Him – in Him. Will they prosper in His presence, assured of His provision, humble in their primacy over the earth?

And then God goes even a step further, making them a witness forevermore between Himself and the world He'd created. He wouldn't ever again allow such watery destruction to destroy mankind so totally; they were His witnesses…

And then they watched Him paint the sky with all the colors of the rainbow and they stood in awe of His overwhelming grace. They walked away with lives painted with the power of His story; they were the new race of rainbow-graced humanity…

O Man of God, the blessing of your new day's dawning is the blessing of His ever-available mercies: "new every morning." You're graced to bear His grace within your heart today: repent anew; be washed afresh by His cleansing blood. And then go forth for His Kingdom, strong in His covenantal love and promises, bearing witness of His steady goodness. He's chosen you to be one of the bearers of His Gospel, His love, His grace, His story, His name!

Will you count yourself equal – *by His strength* – to the challenges sure to come to you during the day ahead? Will you realize your blessing is the task of bearing witness to the world of His amazing grace? We mustn't shirk our work of telling all of Jesus, saving all from the destruction that is the lot of all the lost. There's no manlier task than witnessing to the story we've seen with our own eyes, experienced with our own souls…

Have you seen His grace for yourself, O Man? Has it forever marked your heart? Will you count yourself blessed like Noah was, covenantly living with your Savior, binding your heart to His work today?

LIVE LIKE MEN

January 7 – Genesis 11:1-9

Humility

"If hope in life is reborn," Albert Camus once philosophized, "God is powerless against human interests." (Or: If mankind somehow finds a nebulous "hope" in Camus' concept of "life," we become somehow invincible before the omnipotent God.) And, in the same vein, John F. Kennedy once opined: "No problem of human destiny is beyond human beings." (Or: If we really "apply ourselves" to the issues of this fallen world, we can work out any given problem found therein.)

The Tower of Babel never stops rising above the plains.

The heavens continue to seem within our human reach.

Truthfully, such secular humanisms are the foundation of many of the credos we're taught are today's highest truths. The rise of man in his own humble estimation certainly isn't a new thing; by no means! Yet, day to day, this steady chorus of Me-focused, humanocentric "truth" can begin to wear down our strongest beliefs and defenses. We begin caving to the sinful notion that "Perhaps I am the center of my own universe" before we even realize it. Or we think: "Maybe if we really try our best as humans, we can solve all the world's great needs on our own." Or: "Maybe the problem of evil isn't actually such a problem when we constructively apply ourselves to doing concrete good…"

But what is good anymore, O Man of God? Can a "hope in life" supply what's needed? Can we found the tower of our lofty human aspirations on the quicksand of our passing human emotionalism? Can we fight a battle against "evil" when the final word on "good" is defined by today's celebrities and politicians? Can we labor in the world with only thoughts of "good intentions" when the world actually needs Jesus Christ only?

Our God won't be mocked by words or deeds or towers or by lofty "ideals," no matter how great they sound to our modern ears. He isn't impressed by moralizing humanism "frothing pious platitudes" built upon foundations of our passing fancies. You and I are men placed in this broken world by our Savior-God for a very real purpose on this particular day. So will you "act justly, love mercy, and walk humbly with your God," regardless of the time and place you happen to inhabit? Will you be a man filled with the truth, even when God's truths are mocked and said to be lies by all around you? Will you look to Him for strength and "make a name" for yourself through His asked-for humility, regardless of the cost?

This world will go on making its Towers of Babel. We must go on "building upon the rock," O Men. Let's become His master-craftsmen. May we follow only the Good and Humble Carpenter.

January 8 – Genesis 12:1-3

View yourself as a spiritual patriarch

It would seem the greatest goal of many men's lives is hitting sixty-five with a certain amount of money in the bank. The idea of "passing on a legacy" to sons and daughters often seems to only mean a solid earthly inheritance. We plan and prepare for every eventuality, live our lives toward retirement, "sock it away" for potential "rainy days." We worry if our waning years will have "enough"; if we've succeeded in providing for "what we'll need" in some distant future. Yet God's call to Abram is a study of God's view of the legacy we're meant to leave as the men of His choosing. Abram will become the spiritual inheritee of "all peoples on earth," God assures him without a hint of hyperbole. For his faithfulness, Abram is chosen as the seed of the spiritual family tree from which our whole faith has grown up. He's called to start "a great nation" of the hearts and souls that are changed by the love of God found within them. He'll reign forever as the patriarch of faith, a progenitor of heavenly hope, a man among all men to come. His self-perception of his life would eventually come to mirror that bestowed upon him by his God: A Chosen One.

You too are a chosen one; a seed of the faith; a spiritual father that the Lord's making in His image. Will you leave behind a legacy of faith, an inheritance of hope, a godly life worth emulating, O Man of God? Will you view yourself as one within the bloodline of faithful Abram, a spiritual father to others coming after you? Or will you waffle with the "elementary truths of God's word," never choosing to delve deeper for yourself? Will you embrace your role as a man placed within the lives of the people God has purposefully put in your current life? Will you view yourself as God views you – *"Chosen"* – and today choose to pour out His spiritual inheritance unto others?

You are Abram to the people around you today. May we purpose to "be a blessing" as he once was.

January 9 – Genesis 12:10-20

Complete honesty

Invariably, the moment that we're tempted into a lie is a moment of our own personal cowardice. It's usually fear that dominates the seconds leading up to any untruth we tell; nothing less and nothing more. If someone should catch us in our fear, we fear, the whole truth of our human frailty might be exposed to the world. So we quietly wade into the waters of hazy half-truths, white lies and doublespeak to protect ourselves. In business, I've seen the finest men reduced to afterthoughts because of their lifetimefulls of lies and falsehoods and deceit. I, myself, have seen my own personal fear of God-honest straight stout truth reduce me to an outright liar…

"My brothers," I can hear James speaking straight to me, full of righteous indignation, *"this should not be."*

Abram knew three things: the beauty of his wife, the lust of the Pharaoh and his possible predicament in Egypt. And yet he also knew three other things: the voice of God, His promises for him and God's fulsome faithfulness.

So why did he sin in this way, O Men of God? What was it that caused these lies of his?

Just the very same fear that you and I feel when we're asked for an answer that we can't seem to answer straight and true. Just the very same white-lying prevarications that we hear ourselves offering when we feel backed into a corner by our circumstances…

Everyday we'll all be tested by the call to speak truth regardless of our particular circumstances, O Men. And we must simply do it, if we want to be His men, and trust Him with the reaction of our hearers. We're only called to measure out our words against the rule of His righteousness and answer truly truthfully. We must trust Him that the world is better off without our cloying, sugar-coated, "white lies" and "half-truths."

Let's be the men today who refuse to participate in any form of lying, exaggeration or untruth that might cross our mind. May our mouths be like a wellspring of life, pointing always and only to Jesus, speaking as He Himself would.

January 10 – Genesis 13

Trusting despite your setbacks or triumphs

We can't be men of God if we won't put our full and total trust in the perfect providence of the God we serve. We can't be proper heads of families, fathers of godly children, the men we're meant to be, unless we truly believe in His complete power. Abram had some valid principles in mind when offering Lot the opportunity to part their ways for the future. He desired peace in the family, a smooth-running business, wide-open fresh spaces to roam with his family and flocks. Yet notice how he let the final call fall to Lot: "If you go to the left," Abram promised, "I'll go the right." As the elder, he didn't insist on his way, his decision, his view, his first-choosing in the matter of the pasture-land. Regardless of Lot's choice, Abram believed God had the power to fulfill His promises to him, no matter what. He believed that any piece of land *with God* was far better than the perfect piece *without* Him…

O Men of God, it's been my observation that we view ourselves as the victims of cruel fate far too often. We define our life by the way "somebody screwed me over" without taking into account the powerful hand of God at work. And, on the other hand, we often idolize those pieces of the past whereby we've rocketed to our current position in life. Yet no force of man, no force of blind "Fate," has ever done a single thing to you in your earthly life, O Man. In fact, you yourself are Abram standing quietly beside God on a hillock with the plains sweeping before you into the distance. Do you hear the sound of His providential leading in your life: past, present and eventual future? Do you resist the easy impulse to lay blame upon the Lots in life who've seemingly set your path for you? Do you rest your thoughts upon the beauty of God's perfect plan for you, engineered only by Him, only for you?

Even if your life has dealt some rough blows, you're currently standing in the midst of His prefect placement for you, O Man. Or if your life's been seemingly smooth perfect sailing, you're called to use your final course for His purposeful ends. May we not be men defining daily life and how we live by the crazy "twists and turns of life" all around us. Let's be men so full of life that we define our everyday with full knowledge of the providence of God.

January 11 – Genesis 14:14-20

Financial Giving

We lose the power of tithing of the "fruits of our labors" when our labors lose the flavor of the battle we're in. If we don't understand the work entailed with being men of God, we forget we're actually called to be modern spiritual warriors. We forget the call to battle when we become apathetic in the knowledge of our assured victory in Christ. We begin attending to our own "needs" and "wants," while too often forgetting the self-denial required in the service of arms. Men in battle fight with all their power, all their knowledge, all their skill, all their tactics, all the training they've received. And only when the fighting is done do they enjoy their rest; only then do they pause for self-reflection and analysis.

At least, so it went with Father Abram…

Fresh from the rescue of his nephew and the defeat of the four kings, Abram was returning from his hard-fought victory. He'd engaged in a battle he was clearly called to fight; he'd utilized all his strength upon the bloody battlefield. But when he heard the prayer of Melchizedek and saw those communion-like elements, he was reminded of one all-important truth of his life: The strength of his human arms, the victory of the day, the spoils of war – *everything* – all of it came from the Lord. Everything he'd become was a testament to God's power, God's knowledge, God's plan, God's promises for his earthly life. And for that reason, giving the tithe to Melchizedek felt totally natural to Abram and a fitting end to his labors.

Your money and your possessions are gifts that have been given directly to you; they're arrows in the quiver of God's battleplan. Yet if you've ceased to view yourself as one who's called unto a battle, of course it's hard to give it away on any given Sunday! After all, you've got your bills, a hefty mortgage, your college savings plan, a retirement account that you can't ignore. But it's the God of the universe who's got a long-range plan of attack and he'd like to see you participate in all of it. He'd like to change your view of possessions so that you'll see that your possessions are really a weapon in His heavenly arsenal. He'd like to use you – *if you'll let Him* – by teaching you to trust Him implicitly with your earthly wealth, your holdings, your "stuff." So will you let Him use you in that way? Will you start by tithing, at the very least? A man must learn to know the true source of his wealth and also realize that it all belongs to his God, anyway. So let's give, give, give, O Men. And then let's give some more while we're at it.

LIVE LIKE MEN

January 12 – Genesis 15

Actually living from the New Covenant

The heart of God for men will always be a covenantal heart; our hearts for God seem to work more contractually. You and I live in a world of changeable contracts, contestable vows, broken promises; a man's "word" has become fickle. We're products of the shifting nature of business: addendums, amendments, due diligence, appendices etc. But God will always be the God of perfect Covenants: unchanged, unchanging, truthful, always true. God chose Father Abraham before he *was* an actual father to become the father of innumerable offspring. He called Abram even before he was a perfect follower to be the model of a simple God-honoring faith. Speaking with His true hyperbole of Lordly eternal blessing, God gives Abram every strange land around him. He then spills blood to show the unshakeable, supernatural way He'll bring Abram into the fullness of these promises…

Our *new* Covenant spilled the blood of Jesus Christ in that same supernatural, unshakeable way that God always deals with us. The Father tells us if we emulate His Son ("blessed are the meek"), we will "inherit the earth" just like Father Abram. Furthermore, and pointing back to Abraham, God calls for a daily life of faithful discipleship and humble-hearted belief. And, from discipleship, and from going out to make further disciples, we're creating generations of Christ-followers after ourselves.

O Man of God, there's nothing different in the man you are today from the man Father Abram was, back in those days. You're called to be a father, just like he was; one who's blessed in the Lord's presence, living life with faith in His promises. You're called to walk the steps of this particular day, fully aware of the future and yet focused only on Him. You're washed in the life-blood of the Lamb and sustained by His eternal promises; the Covenant is yours – *now live like it!* Live fully in the promised eternal blessing, becoming more and more detached from the things of this world. Live knowing that the call of God to you is actually the greatest gift you could ever ask for. Live life from that "mystery of the ages," that ultimate glory alive within your manly heart: "Christ in you."

There is a Covenant between you and God today. And all the work is already done!

January 13 – Genesis 17:1-14

The Mark of Obedience

It's no coincidence that God would call for a painful loss of blood in the sealing of His eternal Covenant with mankind. Abram went from being Abram ("exalted father") to Abraham ("father of many") with a marking that he'd never forget. He bore the mark on himself as an eternal and yet temporal testament to the truth of God's everlasting promises to his bloodline. In fact, he eventually would conceive a child with the Covenant of God clearly shown upon his scarred manhood...

Throughout the scriptures, hardly a man is ever called who won't eventually show the wounds and marks of his God upon his life. Very few will run the glorious risks He calls for and live as His mighty men without bearing a few scars in the end. Yet, beyond this, not a single man of God has ever lived his life without a marked change of his heart and spirit. Not one of His mighty men has ever lived the life for which God calls without visible marks of change.

With what sort of "mark" can we mark this day? How can we show that our faith is really real? What kind of "stripe" can we all show upon ourselves to prove that we've "stripped off every weight" and every earthly encumbrance?

Obedience only.

Only obedience.

As Dietrich Bonhoeffer wrote: *"only he who believes is obedient, and only he who is obedient believes."* Abram went from being sterile unto virile only through a scarred member of his earthly human body. Now God wants marked members of His heavenly body – *His Church* – to produce everlasting spiritual fruit for His Kingdom. But we can't produce His fruit without a daily true obedience unto His commands for our daily lives. We can't hope to be the men He wants us to be without laying down our lives, our plans, our everything...

Very few of you who are reading this will ever be called to bear physical scars for your following of Jesus Christ. Yet how many of us may have the chance to point to the mark of true obedience in the way we live our daily life today? Will you view your following of Him as foremost, everything, all-important, as if there's nothing else at all for you? Will your reading of the scripture, your prayer-life, your listening to His Spirit, your worship, make you obedient unto Him? Only today will tell, O Men of God. Your day today is your whole story.

January 14 – Genesis 18:16-33

Having a heart of mercy

People who'd call themselves "Christians" often say the most hateful virulent things you'll ever hear from anyone. How quickly we become poison to "the cause of Christ" when our mouths choose to depart from the teachings of Jesus! We promulgate and prove the worldly notion that religion is an evil when we follow only religion and not our Savior. We truly only follow after the way of Jesus when we're following, in truth, and only, Jesus Himself.

Abraham had a heart of God's choosing simply because his heart was one akin to that of Jesus. He didn't long for God's "justice" only; his heart bled with mercy and grace for the lives of other men around him. He couldn't stand by while these people went to their graves without a chance for a heavenly rescue-plan hatched by the Father. So, over and over, he here pleads for God's hand to withdraw from Sodom "if only…if only…if only…"

If only **we** were filled with this kind of compassion and with Jesus' sort of love, we'd be fully changed too, O Men. If only **we** had hearts so full of His mercy, we'd actually have the heart of Jesus for this world we inhabit. If only men of God would stand upon the Rock of Jesus Christ and stop all argumentation in favor of His bountiful mercies! If only one man – *How about* ***you****?* – did that very thing right now, Jesus would be glorified greatly today!

Fill your mind with thoughts of His mercy and how He's showed it so richly to you and then live from that mindset all day. Let's so fill our hearts with mercy flowing down from our gracious Lord that we can bless all others with a taste of His mercy. If we'd want to be the men of Jesus for the modern world, *let's actually live like men of Jesus today*. Let's be so mercy-minded that we actually start to look like Him in the actualities and practicalities that this day calls forth.

Such fountains of mercy have flowed unto you, O Man!

Now let's let it flow back out!

LIVE LIKE MEN

January 15 – Genesis 19:30-38

Going on the offensive against sin

The strength of a man is only just as strong as the weakest temptation that's required to destroy him. After all, mighty Achilles had a heel to deal with; gleaming suits of armor have chinks that'll be the death of the wearer. We're defecting to the Enemy's side if we offer countless opportunities for simple daily defeats in our lives. We must know the weaknesses particular to our journey if we're to live for Jesus without ceding constant ground to the enemy. Like Lot, we might have a real enjoyment of liquor and the "fun" that goes with it, even if that fun has hurt us many times before. And, of course, we would be lying to ourselves if we discounted how often sex has proved a snare to our minds. We must know and name our potential "beachheads for sin" before we let Satan use them against us in the heat of battle. We must utilize the power of Jesus Christ to know them, name them, "stand our ground," and fight to the end on those fields.

The Armor of God must be our weapon and defense against the counterpoints in the evil one's malevolent arsenal. We must put "the belt of truth" around our waist as a fortifying strength against his constant barrage of lies in our lives. We must put on "the breastplate of righteousness" to protect our hearts from his temptations into daily deadly sin and waywardness. We must fit our feet with "readiness" to lure our lazy selves away from any apathy in our day-to-day lives. We must hoist the "shield of faith" against pointlessness, lack of belief, a rudderless manhood aiming at nothing. We must wear the "helmet of salvation" because our thoughts must be of Jesus' suffering and His sacrifice for us. Lastly, we must wield "the sword of the Spirit" because the Word of God is truth, a source of life amidst the world's death. We must fill the places of weakness in ourselves with the strengths only to be found in and through Jesus Himself.

Don't start this day without a reminder to yourself of all the places where Satan has most easily attacked you in the past. And then go out and defend those places today. Manfully. And through Him.

January 16 – Genesis 22:1-19

Sacrifice *your* life

We must know our journey-life with Jesus is sure to be marked by hardship, testing and great personal sacrifice. After all, disciples of a Master shouldn't hope to live in ease when that Master's way was forged through suffering. Those men who'd daily strive to follow Jesus must also become men who know the beauty found in sharing that suffering. They "consider it pure joy…whenever [they] face trials of many kinds," because of how it tests their faith in their Lord. Like Abraham, they hope in One who's called them unto true hope, not just to the *idea* of "having hope." Abraham didn't question God about the slaying of his promised and only son; he did exactly what he was asked to by His Lord. He didn't wonder why the very answer to his prayers was laying on the pyre, looking up into his weeping eyes. Father Abraham believed in the Promiser, not just in the promise; he hoped in God, not in some nebulous hope.

We, as men of God, must follow in the way of this sort of lifestyle as we make our way through this very day. It's easy to become adept at living our lives for our ease, for our comfort, for our security, for our wealth, for our position. Yet we're only following in the way of the Way when we lay our lives down for the comforting of others. We follow in the footsteps of Jesus when we *don't* demand our own way, when we fight evil with His goodness and His grace. We mustn't hold back anything when the God we claim to serve actually gave His only Son as a sacrifice for our lives. "For the eyes of the Lord range throughout the earth to strengthen those whose hearts are *fully* committed to him." (2 Chron. 16:9)

Is your heart committed today, O Man? Is it fully committed *to Jesus*? What are the pieces of your life you need to lay upon the Lord's altar and watch go up in smoke? What items are so untouchable, held-to, absolutely clutched in your unwilling hands that they've actually mastered you?

Imagine what He'd do with our lives if He found them uncluttered with the things of this world for one single day! Now let's be the men who climb to the top of that mountain, trusting in Him, and sacrifice our lives for the sake of the Kingdom. That is where true life is actually found. That's the Way of our Savior Jesus.

LIVE LIKE MEN

January 17 – Genesis 25:27-34

Patience, not immediacy

Immediate gratification is an enemy of patience, wisdom, and tough vital manhood. It's not the man who satisfies his every "need" that's sated, it's the man who puts his trust in the Lord God alone. It's the man who waits with patience for the Lord's promised provision who knows that everything actually comes from the Lord. The man who sees no earthly obstacles between his wantings and havings will never get to learn that brand of trust. He'll never learn those subtle wisdoms gained through persistent patience, longsuffering, goings-without for periods of time. And he'll sadly see his thinking creep from Jesus unto the "satisfaction" that this world seemingly offers to him…

Esau was a mighty man and a great hunter; he was tough, rugged, desirous, impetuous, strong – *and stupid*. He's like a prefiguring saint for the world we now inhabit: immediacy seems to reign above all else. His manly hungers mattered more to him than his family's good name, his own future, his father's promised birthright. He let his momentary "needs" trump the truth of his life; he sold everything for a moment's stomach-satisfaction.

How often do "the needs of the moment" – *whatever they may be right now* – control your life, O Man? Does "Christ's love compel" your thinking more than that new car sitting on the luxury car lot on your way home? Do you find yourself selling out the "birthright" of being called by Jesus for the ease of "fitting in" to this world? Do you sell your soul for the normalcy found within the acquisition of the so-called American Dream? Would you rather be found rich in the blessings of the manifest presence of God or be rich in the world's watching eyes? How chafing is the *not* having, *not* owning, *not-*now, if He's calling you to live without some earthly things? Would you be totally satisfied to learn His patience, His wisdom, His longsuffering, instead of having all else the world offers? Would you like to live from the fullness of your birthright, unconcerned with the "red stews" that this life offers you?

We must learn to shun the ways of the world that are leading us to believe that we're actually the center of the world. Be wary of the world's immediacy, O Man. Be patient and enjoy His real present blessings.

January 18 – Genesis 28:10-22

Spiritual "vision" for Today

A man of God must give his heart, soul and mind to being a visionary for the past, present and future of the Kingdom. He must, once in a while, lay upon his back to remind himself of who it is he's serving with his life and livelihood. He must yearn within himself for the Holy Spirit's vision of the spiritual realities: the real truth of his life in the world. He must "pray…that the eyes of [his] heart may be enlightened" to "know the hope to which he has called [him]," the unshakeableness of that hope. He must then take hold of that hope, ever thankful for his past, and looking out into the Lord's promised future. He must know the One who "is the same yesterday and today and forever," and only follow Him to the end of his days…

Today, sit in perfect silence and be thankful for, contemplative of, and moved by the love of Jesus for you, O Man. Concentrate your mind and spirit, in silence, upon Jesus…and upon Jesus only. Take the time to be moved by the greatness of His glory and the perfection of this One who's called you forth. Long for a visionary picture of your Savior, invite His Holy Spirit's fire to consume all of you…

After that, take the time to thank Him for your past – good *and* bad – and how it's brought you into His present presence. Make note of the special ways His providential plan touched down in the days that have already gone by in your life. Give thanks for your calling unto His discipleship, the moment of your rebirth, the beginning of your real Life in Him. Thank the Lord for His intervening lessons and the teachers He's given and all the various ways He's shaped the man you are today…

Now stand strong, knowing that the God of Abraham and Isaac is also your God; this is the One who called you by name for His purposes. Be reminded of His strength for your life and His sacrifice for you and then go forth for Him today. Be guided toward the Future with your knowledge of the Past and the power of His Present love for you. Be the man who unifies his understanding of the ubiquitous Lord: past, present and future, *He's always the same*! Today, you must pause, O Man of God. Get "caught up to paradise" with Jesus. Take time to reflect upon Him. Then may we all get going.

January 19 – Genesis 29:14b-30

Work for your wife today

A man will go to unbelievable lengths when he's hoping to be rewarded with the love of a beautiful woman. The way Jacob worked wasn't some anomaly; many of our own stories probably bear the same sorts of "love work." We saw the "perfect" girl and knew we "needed" her, felt we "had to have her," and then went about "getting" her. And, while we worked, the long days "seemed like only a few…because of [our] great love for her," didn't they? By that beautiful blinding of love, we worked and fought and sought and struggled for her womanly fleeting attentions. We would've borne with any form of hardship for the fulfillment of our greatest desire: To make this beautiful woman "ours."

Well, do you still feel that way about her, O Man? Does your lady feel that sort of love today?

A man of God will show the sort of man he is, what he's actually made of, by the way he treats his lady *now*. We can't act as if we're servant-hearted in the world if we've forgotten how to serve our wife at home everyday. We can't claim to have the heart of Jesus when we're afraid to help our wife with the simple day-to-days of life at home. We shouldn't be proud of anything in life unless we know that our wife is feeling perfectly at peace in our marriage. The real mark of your manhood was not in the attaining or the chasing or the capturing of her heart in the yesterday. The real mark of manhood is waking in the morning – *everyday* – and seeking to serve her all day – *everyday*. Imagine where we'd be if we sought to serve our wives with just that spirit with which we first went out and caught her attention. Imagine how she'd feel if you did something for her everyday that she absolutely didn't expect from you…

Today, seek to work for your wife with the same sort of passion with which you started out, O Man of God. Try doing something simple and unasked-for, something that you know she hates doing around the house. If you find yourself coming home from work and vacuuming the living room tonight, know you're starting on the right track. A real man will lay his head upon the pillow tonight, knowing he's worked to serve his wife *all day*.

She was worth it back then, wasn't she? And she's only grown to be of greater worth.

January 20 – Genesis 32:22-32

Struggle with the Lord as He chastens you

A man is never proven in the comforts of his life; it's a real fight that tests his might. Men must never expect to grow when the only aim of their life becomes avoidance of the trials of existence. We won't see the fruit of God's real work within our lives if we'll never push ourselves to the furthest limit. If we refuse the chance to wrestle with God, we're refusing the joy of being remade into His perfect likeness. Jacob understood that grappling with God was a form of drawing closer to the actual heart of his Maker. He understood that fighting through this particular night was a test he was being put to, a gauntlet thrown down by the Creator. And so he held on to his God and he wouldn't let go and, for that reason, he was blessed with a heavenly renaming. He was changed from the one who "grasps the heel" (Jacob) to the man of God who "struggles with God" (Israel), because of his efforts. He'd proven his own mettle in the middle of the darkness of night: God was justifiably impressed with his resolve.

How far will *you* go with your God in the quest for a manhood that's redeemed, that's after His own heart? Will you be the man who grasps a hold of Him and holds to His truth unswervingly, despite the various challenges? Will you never knuckle under when He's purposefully challenging you and trying to make you personally stronger in Him? Will you trust that the trials of your life – *right now* – are actually in His complete sovereign control, O Man? Will you stop your daily worrying about your struggles and be a man and remember why it is He's testing you? "You have perhaps lost sight of that piece of advice which reminds you of your sonship in God: My son, regard not lightly the chastening of the Lord, nor faint when thou art reproved of him; for whom the Lord loveth he chasteneth, and scourgeth every son whom he receiveth." You're loved not only in your current struggle, you're clearly loved by Him *because* of this current struggle, O Man. The world may laugh at the limp He's chosen for you, but you should wear it proudly as a badge of your true sonship through His love.

Today, hold onto Jesus. And hold on mightily. Be the kind of man who wrestles mightily with his God and knows that that's the best kind of intimacy he can ever know.

January 21 – Genesis 37:1-11

Godly Tact

The kind of love that offered up the particolored robe to Joseph is the kind of love that's yours today, O Man. Yes, yours is the Father so extravagant in love that He's "chosen gladly to give you the kingdom." Your Heavenly Father wraps you up in His outrageous love: His multicolored, unconditional, omnifaceted sort of love. And, even beyond that, He's given you the eyes to see the truth of His story written all throughout human history. He's blessed you not only to know Him, but, even more importantly, to be known by Him absolutely perfectly. He's filled your life with "every good and perfect gift," showering His mercies upon you every single day of your life…

A man of God must know the blessings of the Father's love and delight himself in all their wonderful glory and multiplicity. He must realize his privileged position and not cease for a second to live his life with a son's joyous relish. However, seeing what we see in Joseph's story, he must *also* know he's called to a humble godly tactfulness about it. He's called to live out the love of the Father and not be a boasting idiotic braggart to those lost brothers around him. He's called to know his calling and not act as a judge of others, but to serve as "Christ's ambassador." He's called to use God's "dreams" for him as a reference point of love, not as a proof of being somehow personally better than others.

Today, you *are* a son of God, chosen by Him personally, divinely appointed for a wondrous life in Jesus. You've been called to all the blessings of a life as His chosen heir, a life filled with His everlasting bounty of love. Yet may we never live our lives in the manner of spiritual snobs or prima donnas of haughty predestination. May we feel His calling to a godly tact with words well-thought-out and choices chosen carefully for the sake of others. May we understand our role as sharers of His Gospel to a world that's lost and dying all around us, everyday. May we measure how we tell our own story, wrapped in His story, so that it breathes out only life and never death. May we see ourselves as sons loved like Joseph. And, yes, may we feel that love everyday. And yet, in feeling it, let us go forth with His love, filled with His tact, and tell His story to our utmost strength.

January 22 – Genesis 39

Sexual self-control

A man of God must view the entirety of his life as the forum for a testing of his heart and faith in Jesus Christ. There may be no warning signs before tests are already on their way; our faith and life will intersperse without demarcation. After being bought as a houseservant, Joseph clearly gave his life to God in this strange new land anew. He didn't think that hardships entering into his life meant the direction of his life was somehow off-course, did he? He resolutely resisted the temptation to start feeling sorry for himself: he trusted God and he actually prospered. He became a strength and support to the men he eventually came to serve, including to mighty Potiphar.

And *then* the true test came into his life…

Sexual temptation is so ready to derail the course of our lives – *all of us must know that!* It might come for you in straight overt advances like Potiphar's wife's or as subtly as by your laptop computer's browser. It might be that woman at work who's been making eyes at you or in the lingering thought of her, later on. It might even be in your trivialization of your marriage-relationship as if it's only a place for sex…

A man of God must have the self-control that Joseph showed in this text; it doesn't matter how "difficult" it might be for you. If you're one who's struggling with online pornography in your current life, *don't look at online pornography today.* If you're tempted to go sleep with another woman, *stop thinking about it; don't even look in another woman's direction.* If you're struggling with the thoughts within your head right now, *say a prayer; think about something else that He's happy to give you.*

We make the way of Jesus infinitely more challenging for ourselves when we only halfway follow Him with our life. After all, it's He who called our hearts to obedience *in every single facet of our lives who also gives the strength to do it.* So let's stop thinking about "how hard it is" to be a godly man in our "oversexualized modern culture." Instead, take your struggles to the One who lives within you, give him the hours of your day, and see how He'll clear your mind. O Man, He will do it. You need only *ask and believe.*

January 23 – Genesis 40

Always being of use

The heart of God for man is beating constantly; our God never rests; He's ever true to each of us. The heart of man for God, however, is just about as fickle as the day-to-days of life and the "busy-ness" of his schedule. If we find we're in a "season of our life" where we're feeling "pushed and pulled," we're apt to cut Him out of the equation first. Never mind the call to "harvest work," it's hard enough to find a single moment even for a "daily quiet time." Yet look at Joseph, sitting in his prison cell for a crime he didn't commit, still making himself useful to the Lord. He didn't view his circumstances, good or bad, as a means to any avoidance of the call of God upon his life. He used the very place he found himself and offered up himself for use and God actually used him, right there. He defined and fought a pitched battle in prison, rather than letting his circumstances beat him down and defeat him. He chose to make himself available to the Lord, instead of letting life's schedule choose his course for him…

Whether you'd say you're in a "fine time" or a "downtime" of your life, today's your only actual day of it, O Man. Whether you're sitting in the prison of despair or in a palace, your heart must never be dismayed or swayed in the least. You can't allow the circumstances of this morning, noon or night to dissuade you from the call of God upon your life. The world is in need of spirited men with the Spirit of God upon them: active, living, alive, ready for the work of the Kingdom. Will you be like Joseph was, doing what the day demands *with the call of God always on your mind*? Or will you put God's plan in the prison of *your* plans, *your* schedule, *your* expectations for the kind of day you have today? Will you use the voice He's given you within your sphere of influence as a means to the end of making Him known to all? Or will you sit at desks of despond today, "getting your work done," entirely neglecting His work in the world around you?

We should rather be in actual chains than to ever let the call of God go slack in our life and work for the coming Kingdom! Let's break the chains of our "work" and "busyness" today and take up the call of Christ's cross wherever we're going. Let's use our actual circumstances, regardless of what they may be, to do the work of Jesus today. There is no other work. Don't fool yourself into thinking otherwise.

January 24 – Genesis 41:1-40

Following Jesus can lead to earthly good

It's at the peril of our souls (and possibly also our future) that we ever downplay the mighty work of God in our lives. We assume that fitting in with this world, being "normal guys," means the exclusion of our faith far too often. We seem to forget our lives are glowing with the supernatural power of the risen Christ and His Holy Spirit wherever we go. We act as if we haven't got a call unto the world, as if we're not "God's workmanship" constructed "to do good works." Yet what we miss when we're remiss with the truth of Jesus living within us is the opportunity for greater good. Yes, of course, the opportunity for the good of all mankind – *but also for our own lives sometimes*! We miss the ways that Jesus' call can sometimes lead the way for temporal good in our current life-situation. We miss the holy humor of He who'd test our faith before, suddenly, bringing us out from the prison into the palace…

Yet, whether you're currently in prison or palace, will you stand the test of standing firm on your own two feet today, O Man? When called before today's version of Pharaoh, will your first thoughts be of Jesus and of His calling upon your life? Will you answer every question with the first thought that came to Joseph's mind: "I cannot do it" on my own? Will you, instead, turn the current of your life in the direction of Joseph's perfect confidence: "but God will give…"?

Only God can give our lives their real direction and actual fullness of hope, perfect Christly confidence. Only by the blood He shed do we become the men we're called to be – *fully* – in and through His life working within us. There can be no mutual exclusivity between your "life" and the living of your calling in the world today. You don't know the ways Today, and your obedience to Jesus' demands today, might effect the rest of your entire life. As Leo Tolstoy once wrote: "The work that our life accomplishes, the whole of this work, the meaning of it is not, nor can be, intelligible to me … To understand it, to understand the whole of the Master's will is not in my power. But to do His will, that is written down in my conscience, is in my power; that I know for certain. And when I am fulfilling it I have sureness and peace." And that's the way we'll live today. Now let's go do it, O Men.

January 25 – Genesis 41:41-57

Work hard, be "extraordinary"

Our first three verses tell the tale of Pharaoh's improbable delegation of Egypt's administration to a former Hebrew slave. They also paint a poignant picture of the way we've been chosen by our God and appointed to His wonderful service. Pharaoh speaks his words of affirmation over Joseph's style of leadership; Jesus gave to us the Great Commission. Then Pharaoh dresses him in the jewelry and the robe of royalty; we're called to be a "royal priesthood" for Christ. Pharaoh grants his second-in-command a fearsome burnished Egyptian chariot; we're called brothers-in-arms with our Savior. Men shout "Make way!" for the coming of Pharaoh's chosen consigliere; we shout "Make way!" for the chosen One...

The crazy call of God for the life of Joseph ended up with Joseph in this vast and powerful secular role for His purposes. In the same way, many of us are placed by God in secular situations where He'd ask us to be exerting His heavenly influence. The question is: Will you be a prudent, shrewd, and hardworking worker in the midst of that chosen place, O Man? Will you exercise the sober kind of judgment, the brilliant use of godly wisdom, that characterized the earthly rule of Joseph? Remember: "Whatever you do, work at it with all your heart, as working for the Lord, not for men." (Col. 3:23) We're judged not only by the "ministry" aspects of our earthly lives, but also by our everyday example in the world. Will you be an extraordinary workman for the Kingdom, not only in the spiritual matters, but also in your current workplace? Will you work for God and not for men, counting your earthly hard work as another call to Jesus' discipleship?

Day by day, God desires men who'd work their hardest for Him in the midst of whatever work-setting they're placed in. Whether it's some form of jobsite, a church, in a garage, in a store, in a classroom – wherever you should find yourself. Will you endeavor to work your hardest for Him today, utilizing His wisdom and strength, and be blessed in your work by Him? You and I are called to a life of excellence – *for the sake of Jesus* – whether we're at home, at play, at work; wherever He should send us.

January 26 – Genesis 45:1-15

Don't take revenge. Trust!

There's something in the hearts of men that loves a tale of vengeance, a story of incredible personal payback. We love to see a wronged man righted by violence in a movie; we love ourselves to speak a sharp retort when it comes to mind. Most times, we'd rather strike a blow with greater fury and turn a phrase with greater bite than "turn the other cheek." It's just so difficult to reconcile Christ's call unto that sort of behavior with being a real and modern man in this world…

Yet that's the Savior we want to serve, isn't it? Isn't He the one who went to the cross for us? Don't you think He might've meant it when He called us to this life of "other-cheekness," this radical personal self-denial?

Joseph was a man who truly understood the deepest feeling of betrayal and yet he didn't strike back here. Yes, he did put all his brothers through some trials and tested out their mettle, but he didn't do what they truly deserved. Instead, Joseph trusted God's will and let his brothers know their evil actions were actually used by his God. Joseph saw the betrayal of his past in the light of God's plan as being actually *part* of God's perfect plan. In fact, "it was not you who sent me here, but God," he says to his brothers; the betrayal was of great importance in his life. A trusting man of God will see the betrayals of his past selfsamely – as trusted tools that'll help him learn to trust his God. We can't use personal vengeance or biting words or any human action to avoid the hand of Almighty God, can we? So why don't we believe that the trials and betrayals within our life can't be used by Him for His greater good? Why do we plot and scheme and backtalk against the ones we think "wronged us" when the wrong is really for our good? Because, truly, anything at all that teaches us to turn the other cheek is a trial we should revel in, O Men! We should count ourselves blessed whenever we're personally struggling; here's another chance to "cast your cares" on Jesus! He's giving you another opportunity to share the burden of His suffering: Be a man and take it! That may be the highest calling on your day today. Be the kind of man who takes his licks with eyes on Jesus.

January 27 – Genesis 49:22-26

Speaking blessings into others' lives

A man must use his patriarchal positioning – be it actual or spiritual – to speak constant blessing into people's lives. We must learn to use the voice the Lord has given us for the benefit of creating vision for the "sons and daughters" around us. It's so important that the world should see godly men using their tongues for edification and encouragement, not for hurt. This world is so consumed with useless verbiage and vocabularies of death; our daily spoken words must absolutely be Life. Our words must ring out with the life of Jesus, the power of Jesus, the message of Jesus, the hope of Jesus, the truth of who Jesus is. We must look into the hearts of other men – be they sons, friends or neighbors – and ask where Jesus asks us to speak. We're called to speak with love into other people's lives, using the instruction of the Holy Spirit as our guide each day. Notice how Jacob used his knowledge of Joseph's personal spiritual journey as a guidepost for his life-blessing unto him. Note how he commends Joseph's grace under the pressures of "hostility," how "his bow remained steady." How he trusted in "the hand of the mighty One of Jacob," the "Rock of Israel," "your father's God."

Does the way you live your life and use your words make perfectly clear who your life is actually following after, O Man? Are you raising up your "sons" in the clarity of true knowledge of their Heavenly "Shepherd": *What will be your legacy?* Will you bless with your words and your actions and your love all those people God chooses to place around you? Will you raise your children under the tutelage of a man who's following after God, giving an absolutely clear example?

Jacob was a man who tried to follow the God of his father; Isaac was a man who gave a clear example to follow. Will you yourself be a man worth following after, a man with a life worth emulating, so that your children know our God, O Man? Will you use your words today as a blessing and a guide to those trying to follow after your way of life? People will follow those worth following. People will follow a leader who blesses.

January 28 – Exodus 1:6-14

Don't be enslaved by your comfort

Whether it comes through apathy, comfort or sheer boredom, a man must never allow his life's blessings to become his master. The house of Israel found in Egypt safety from their gnawing hunger, but they also walked directly into a trap. Although God had clearly told Abram of being "enslaved" in "a country not their own," here the Hebrews actually find themselves. Here they're slaving in the place they thought was their safety; here they're oppressed by their former Egyptian "friends and neighbors." Here they're living "lives bitter" in a place that once had seemed so welcoming, so totally friendly, so safe…

We ourselves will be most easily enslaved whenever we allow our earthly lives to lull us into false securities. When we start to feel "the paycheck's pretty good," the "house is nearly paid off," we aren't speaking God's kind of language. We're confusing earthly comfort for the blessing of His presence when we dictate our days by such temporal thoughts. We mustn't allow the soft security that makes modern men sissies to turn us into today's slaves; we're better than that!

Look again at the Hebrews' situation: They actually outnumbered their masters yet the masters were in complete control of their lives. The Egyptians dealt more shrewdly and went on the early offensive and the Hebrews were cowed by their cruel long-viewed cunning. Will we be the sort of men who take control of our own lives in Jesus and aren't ruled by our earthly comforts? Will we see the "blessings" in our lives as only being a blessing in proportion to their usefulness to the coming Kingdom? Will you live your day amidst His sort of adventure, listening for Jesus' eternal plan in today's moment-to-moment? Will you *not* view the day as being "just another day" – *a slave's mindset* – but as a day for the call of Jesus?

Henry David Thoreau wrote: "We now no longer camp as for a night, but have settled down on earth and forgotten heaven." The Hebrews settled down in Egypt, well-fed, and they forgot the calling to their own promised land. We mustn't allow the comforts of this broken world to wash our minds of the beauties to be found in our Heavenly Home. Be a man who fights for the blessing of His presence; do not "settle down" into any sort of slavery, O Man.

January 29 – Exodus 3

Know (and follow) your calling

If you follow Jesus and you're reading through this sentence right now, you too have a high heavenly Calling. There's something God has called you to do through the power of His Son and He'd ask you to be all about it, all the time. Perhaps by the particular gifts and talents He's given you, He's leading you down a certain life-path of work and usefulness. Maybe it's your personal proclivities and your "interests" in life that should be your first clues for what you're "for." There might've been a time you "felt" something "happening inside you," but weren't quite sure what it was all about. Perhaps you find your current life to be savorless, not "what you were made for," seeming drear and dull as you enter your day…

Moses wasn't built to be a shepherd for some sheep grazing in a field; he was made to shepherd God's people. Peter wasn't meant to be a fisherman for the rest of his earthly life; Jesus called him to "catch men." When the call of God is clear (or once was clearly given to you), you must follow after it – *no matter what*. You must never retreat from burning bushes He's placed within your life: They're the call of God to you, O Man.

Are you currently doing what you were "made for"? If not, what is it you think you're actually "made for"? Do you believe the plan of God for you – "your Calling" – is the highest available expression of who you actually might be? Do you not only believe in the story of Moses' burning bush, but also in God's meaning within Moses' burning bush? Have you ever asked God "what I'm for" and then actually listened to His answer and then lived accordingly from His response(s)? Have you lived for your necessities – "providing," "putting a roof over your head" – instead of living for His eternal necessities? "Don't you believe that God will make you what He created you to be, if you will consent to let Him do it?" (Thomas Merton)

It will never be Jesus' "life to the full" if every choice in your life has been chosen by you, O Man. Ask God today if your path is His. If not, ask Him what your path should be. This might actually be the most important day of your life. Now just be ready to be a listener.

January 30 – Exodus 4:1-17

Faith grows when used

There's a direct proportionality between the enrichment of our faith and the actual weight our faith carries, day to day. Your life will be as exciting as your investment in your faith is; the Lord's heavenly economy pays rich living dividends. Who knows how much more of Moses' life would've been utilized had he not been so chickenhearted in this particular moment? If he hadn't been such a coward in the midst of his calling at the burning bush, who knows what might've eventually been? He was given Aaron as a partner in his duty and in his work on behalf of the Israelites, but also as a crutch. God had already said he'd be fine on his own, yet Moses allowed his shaky faith to be the voice for his fears: "But what if they won't listen to me, God?" (Even though God had already promised that they would absolutely listen.) "Well, I'm not a very good speaker, God." (Yet this was the God who'd made the mouth he'd actually be speaking with.) "O Lord, please send someone else to do it." (God didn't oblige this stupid request but he was clearly displeased by it.) Unlike Father Abraham, Moses had the chance to take God at His word and simply chose not to do it. He'd heard the call of God from God's own lips, spoken straight to him, and yet he hesitated in his fearfulness…

Yesterday we wrestled with the image of the burning bush and its meaning for our lives in Christ. Hopefully, you spent some solid time praying about your Calling and then listened for God's response to your prayer. So, what's next, O Man of God? How will you react today? Will you actually do what He's calling you to do, or will you act like Moses here, quavering at His voice, questioning His clear call? Will we choose to live the life of His wise choosing, regardless of our life's current circumstances? What is it we're actually so afraid of? Growing in our faith? Being truly of use to the Kingdom?

You know the nature of the One who calls your name: His goodness, His richness, His unbridled love for you. Now we must dive into the calling upon our lives and experience the enrichment of our faith in actuality today. For today is all we have, my brothers. Tomorrow is not, and never shall be, ours.

January 31 – Exodus 6:1-11

What are you "for"?

Moses heard the call of God, the Calling for his own life and the *entire plan of God* in a very short span of time. Now, here he is, actually standing in Egypt as just another Hebrew, struggling to figure out how it'll actually work out. Coming off his first tete-â-tete with Pharaoh, Moses feels like an abject failure in his work for his imprisoned people. In actuality, he has made the Hebrews' working-life worse with his first request for their eventual exodus. Perhaps Moses began to wonder whether God's plan, his personal Calling and the call were a figment of his imagination. After all, the speaking of impossibilities from a burning bush doesn't seem so plausible in the presence of a physical Pharaoh.

Especially after some rejection…

And after some time has passed by…

And when "reality" begins to set in…

Yet God here reminds him of the plan and the Calling and the call by reminding Moses of what he's really "for." Moses is *for* Yahweh, *for* his people, *for* their rescue; he will lead them out from Egypt in the timing of God. He'll be the one through whom God will speak His perfect word to His people; the one through whom God will rescue the Hebrews. He'll be the tool to "draw out" (the actual definition of "Moses") the people of God from their slavery to these evil earthly masters.

In a similar way, pondering upon the call and your own Calling, don't lose the savor of what you've been made "for," O Man. You are *for* Jesus Christ, *for* people, *for* their rescue; you must lead them away from the "law of sin and death." You must be the one through whom God is able to speak His perfect Word; one through whom He may effect heavenly rescue. You must be a tool with which He'll draw out others from their slavery to death and sin, just like the Hebrews.

So, absolutely regardless of what you're thinking about your personal Calling, you're *not* excused from being a man "for" Christ today. You're still asked, regardless of your current thought-processes, to be a worker sent out into the Master's harvest. Will you go with Him today full-heartedly? Will you go where He sends you gladly? Will you continue listening for your personal call *without* missing that greater general call – "follow Me"? O Men, may we ponder His call while in the battle. Only weak men ride the sidelines, wondering.

February 1 – Exodus 12:21-30

Marking your home "for Him"

A man cannot be walking with our God if he refuses to "paint blood" upon the doors of his own household. If we don't claim our home for God – including our wife and children – we're forfeiting our godly manhood to the world's influences. You and I are called to stand on tallest tiptoe, reaching up with outstretched brushes, until the lintel of our home is blood-red. We must stand upon the Rock and build our lives upon the Rock; we must claim our home for His sake and purposes. We're called to know the Son "and the power of his resurrection and the fellowship of sharing in his sufferings," O Men of God. And we can actually learn the power of the Lamb's blood and share in His sufferings when we dip deeply with our hyssop-brushes.

The Hebrew men were doing nothing more than staying the avenging angel's hand with this act of painting their Egyptian doorways. They weren't doing anything beyond marking their home as a home where the Lord's own people resided and desired His coming salvation. A month from now, we'll be looking at Joshua's claiming of his family's house as a house where the Lord was "served" and honored. But, today, we must ask ourselves – *if we really want to be His men* – if we've ever marked our homes as being "for Him." Have you set aside your house and household as a place where the Lamb's blood has truly set you free? Do you view yourself as ransomed, a "Passovered" heart, a man who's "not ashamed" of the Gospel of Jesus? Have you spoken with your wife and children about acknowledging your family's true identity that's brand new because of Jesus? Do you view your home as an extension of the Kingdom, a place "set apart," a covey of "peculiar people" in this world?

In whatever way the Lord would lead today, set a mark upon your family and home as belonging to the Lord Jesus. We're called to be a people totally changed, marked forever by the blood of God's Son that was spilt for our lives. Mark your home for the Lord today, O Man. Claim His reign over your household.

February 2 – Exodus 13:21-22

Seeking and receiving guidance

If you don't believe the Lord would lead your life in such a clear daily manner, you've clearly never asked Him to do so. If you believe modernity excludes such "simple-minded" Christ-following, who are you actually following after, O Man? The God of Israel – the God of burning bushes, Joseph's slavery, Jacob's wrestling, Abram's sacrifice – is your God. He doesn't cease to show Himself to those who'd "seek His face," who'd seek to live their lives for the good of His coming Kingdom. He doesn't change the "gameplan" simply because mankind has become so wise in its own estimate, so sure of its own way. Just because Copernicus moved the earth from the center of the universe doesn't mean our God shouldn't continue to be the center of ours. A man who lives his life looking up – following the cloud by day, fire by night – is the kind of man our God wants. That's a man who studies every step and makes his life's decisions based on the Lord, not "leaning on his own understanding."

Like the Israelites, you've been set free from the bondage of a slavery; yours just happened to be to your sinful nature, not the Egyptians. You've been brought out from another land and "chosen by him"; there's a great purpose for your "journey" through your life. But will you live your journey with the same kind of trust with which you first trusted Jesus for His salvific grace? Will you look to Him – *and Him only* – for the direct leading of the daily day-to-days of your current life? Will you follow Him both day and night, listening to the voice of His Holy Spirit speaking directly to you, from within you? After all, don't you realize the God of Abraham is also the God who's living in you, right now, this very moment?

Take the time today – morning, noon and night – to seek the exact way of the Lord in the way you live out your day. Ask Him for His clear direction for the course of your journey through today – *and He will truly lead you!* But will you let Him lead you, O Man? And, more importantly, will you follow? Our God is storming through the world with fiery power and He's watching for the kind of men with eyes upturned toward Him. We're those kind of men, aren't we? Yes, my brothers, we most certainly are.

February 3 – Exodus 14:5-31

Will you "be still" in His power?

If any man will "be still" while the Lord is fighting a battle on his behalf, he'll be blessed with an eternal invulnerability. He'll be "strong in the Lord and in the strength of His might," he'll be a man with strength that's really, truly strength. He'll watch the Holy Spirit fighting rearguard actions just as surely as the Angel ranged himself against these Egyptians. He'll see his arms held up through nights of the toughest travails; he'll see his own arms used for other people's deliverance by the Lord. If a man will simply "be still and know that I am God," there's nothing in this world that can stop him. After all, because he waited for the Lord and only fought "the Lord's battles," David was prophesied to be the founder of a dynasty. (1 Sam. 25:28) Because he trusted in the Lord's view of power, Paul was actually boastful of his own human powerlessness. (2 Cor. 12:9) We're men of God most fully when we find we're at the center of His plan and then are absolutely "still" in that place.

Is your spirit "still" today, O Man? Do you "know that [He is] God," this day?

Imagine how the Lord could prove Himself if you were more willing to let him fight your battles on your behalf. Now think of how He'd prove His power to other people if, for once, you simply trusted and allowed for His deliverance. Perhaps the story would read something like this:

"But the people of God went through the sea on dry ground, with a wall of water on their right and on their left. That day the Lord saved the people of God from the hands of Satan, and the people of God saw Satan lying dead on the shore. And when the people of God saw the great power the Lord displayed against Satan, the people feared the Lord and put their trust in him and in *you* his servant."

Be the sort of man who takes God at His word today. "Be still" and know.

February 4 – Exodus 16

Daily bread vs. Tomorrow bread

If you already have today's daily bread accounted for, count yourself truly blessed among all of mankind. We must never take for granted that the Lord has given us sustenance to deliver us from any dawn to dusk of our lives. We must never forget the people all over the world who dream of ample food on their table, clean water in their cisterns. We must never downplay the fact that God has given us our daily bread – *everyday* – up to this very day we're starting. In fact, if we hearken after Jesus' view of discipleship, we might want to stop and ponder on this particular point: Do we actually have too much "tomorrow bread" clouding our thinking on the daily living of today's call? Have we grown a bit muddled amidst our present surplus, striving and striving after things we'll actually never live to enjoy? Are we neglecting Eternity's place in our lives – *only Today* – because of our living for the storing up of tomorrow's manna?

It's no coincidence that manna quickly became so maggoty; remember how Jesus described the treasures of this passing earth? He said to His disciples: "Do not store up for yourselves treasures on earth, where moth and rust destroy, and where thieves break in and steal." When the Israelites gave their hearts to hoarding manna that the Lord had rained from heaven, they were sorely disappointed. In the same way, when we cease to see all earthly blessing as coming from Him, we begin to hoard and hoard, just like them. We begin to think not only of today and of today's "follow Me," but we give tomorrow too much of our hearts. We begin to calculate how many more tomorrows we can last "if I can just get to such-and-such a dollar amount…"

My friend, that is sinful ungodly thinking. For "everything that does not come from faith is sin." If God can rain down quail and manna from the skies, *surely He can take care of you and your family in perpetuity*. We must cease all thinking of our "responsibility" for provision for our family if we want to trust Him truly. After all, isn't that what we want most? To live as if His promises are actually true? Today, let's be men whose eyes are on this day and today's manna only, remembering that tomorrow is in the Lord's hands. Let's truly trust Him for this day only. Today is simply all we have.

February 5 – Exodus 17:8-16

Uphold a spiritual giant today

Norman Maclean wrote: "One of life's quiet excitements is to stand somewhat apart from yourself and watch yourself softly becoming the author of something beautiful." I'd argue that it's even more exciting to watch the heart of God becoming manifest in another person's heart. It's one of life's most startling excitements when we see the Holy Spirit mightily authoring a work of power in someone's life. Each of us is blessed, I'm sure, with knowing a person who's standing on the brink of living a life of true substance. Many of us have friends who're mightily called to do a work of God that's just getting going or is fully underway now.

When Moses saw the advancement of the Amalekites, he knew the hand of God would give the victory to his chosen people. He didn't send out hordes of frightened fighting men – no, he told Joshua to "choose some of our men," *just some*. He didn't see the need for practiced battle plans or cutting-edge weaponry; he knew the strength of the God he and Joshua served. In fact, almost with an air of absurdity, he explained his plan of action for the day: "I will stand on top of the hill with the staff of God…"

There's a person in your life today who's climbing up the mountainside, holding to the "staff of God" alone. They might seem like a crazy person trusting in the Lord so implicitly, but isn't that what we're actually called to do? Today, commit yourself to acting just like "Aaron and Hur" did for Moses: Hold up the arms of that particular person. If they're "in ministry," write them an unexpected check; if they're a "layperson," give them your spoken or written encouragement. If we want to learn to be the men of God upon the battlefield, we must also learn to help those going out before us. We must learn to be the spiritual supply chain, sustaining soldiers way out on the front line of the Lord's war.

Will you hold up a brother's arms today? Will you be the strength he needs in the fight? Don't forget: There may come a day soon when you're the Moses to an Aaron or Hur and they're looking up to you, O Man!

February 6 – Exodus 18

Who is your elder counselor?

If you want to become a man of godly wisdom, place yourself under the tutelage of a man with clear godly wisdom. It's nearly impossible to grow within your discipleship with Jesus if you won't be another man's disciple who's farther down the road than you. If you choose to "go it alone" and become a sort of modern-day mono-monastic, your growth in Christ will surely come more slowly. You'll be hampered by your own self-conceptions and your own spiritual foibles; you need a tough trusted friend in this. Like Moses, when he looked into the grizzled visage of Jethro, you need an elder who can talk tough with you. You need a man who's seen the ups and downs of life who's also seen how the hand of God always prevails in the end. You need a man who knows the deepest dark abysses of your soul and who'll plumb the depths of those places with you. You need a man you'll actually sit and listen to; I guarantee you don't need another person to hear from you all the time!

Moses was a "friend" of God who let his life be led by God and yet even he needed a man with wise godly counsel. Jethro acted as a trusted instrument to bring the word of God to Moses regarding the need for these extra judges. Will you likewise be so humble to seek out godly men who'll counsel you in the week-by-weeks of your earthly life? Will you humble yourself to listen and let the Lord speak through those men to you and trust them with your very life?

Stop thinking that the need for wise counsel from a trusted godly man is a sign of being somehow needy. This is the circle of God's life in His men; godly men passing along their wisdom is the bedrock of Christ's Church. Just as Timothy needed Paul to train him up, so you need the training and wisdom of another man in your life, O Man. Start getting yourself poured into – *right now* – so that, when the time is right, you're ready to pour your life into another's life. That's simply how the Lord works. It's a truly tried and true method.

February 7 – Exodus 20:1-21

We must know and follow the "Big Ten"

The fear of God that fell upon these chosen people is the exact same fear we should be feeling while reading through these verses. For when we see how clear God's direct commandments actually are, can't we also see how often we forsake them entirely? Don't we see how many false gods we've lifted up to take the place of God throughout our days and our lifetimes? Can't we recall the myriad ways in which we've worshipped the creation instead of worshipping the Creator only? Do we think our mouths are truly clean from "misusing" His name; only verbal "fresh water " flowing out from our heart? Have we set aside the Sabbath-day in our families as being exclusively for the worship of our God? Have we always honored our fathers and our mothers; do we honor them by the way we're living our lives today? Have we ever murdered enemies in cold blood, just by the way we thought about them in our hidden thoughts? Have we ever gone and slept with another woman or, if we haven't, have we undressed a woman in our restive masculine minds? Have we ever stolen anything; ever lied about anything; every coveted our neighbor's garageful of things?

If we want to follow our God in actuality, we must begin by being truthful about our breakings of His perfect law. We mustn't pat ourselves on the back for keeping a couple of His laws if we're flouting all the rest with a brazen spirit. "For whoever keeps the whole law and yet stumbles at just one point is guilty of breaking all of it." (James 2:10) We must be fearful of a cavalier spirit when it comes to the keeping and breaking of God's holy Law for mankind.

Only *in* Jesus, *through* Jesus and by *following after* Jesus are we set free from our sinful nature and the pull of sin. Yet we must be men who honor God's commandments if we want to be the sort of men taking Him fully seriously. We must be the kind of men who walk throughout our day with these Ten Commandments firmly imprinted on our hearts and minds. We must never allow our freedom found in Jesus to become a laxity or "a cover-up for evil" or an excuse not to obey.

O Men of God, read over these Commandments once more. Then go out with Jesus and strive to obey them. Let's be the men who follow through on our commitment to the actual living-out of these holy Commandments given to Moses. Jesus gives us grace to live in the midst of them. Jesus also gives us strength to obey.

February 8 – Exodus 24:15-18

Yearning for His presence and glory

How is your perception of God's glory shaping the way you live your life everyday, O Man? Or, in other words, do you crave the manifest presence of our God as the most valuable thing in your whole wide world? Do you feel His presence is Life to you; the only place you long to live; the only actual way to fully live the human life? Do you ever sit and yearn that you might experience Him more and more and more and more fully with every passing day?

For the frightened nation of Israel, the "glory of the Lord looked like a consuming fire on top of the mountain." Or, in other words, the people of His choosing were actually afraid of His presence; they seemed to view it as being potentially painful. Yet, for Moses, God's glory was a "cloud" and a voice calling from the cloud and a place to personally and delightedly reside. With a joyous heart, Moses climbed up the mountain and he spent "forty days and forty nights" in the palpable glory of His Lord…

Is that the desire of your heart today, O Man? Do you want to be with Him? *In Him*?

Take the time today to seek after His presence and His glory and His power; may they be more real before you rest tonight. Don't be afraid of seeing the glowing results of His showing-up within your life – instead, *long for His coming*. Long only that you might be called to experience His measureless glory like Moses once experienced it on the mountaintop. Hope only that His Holy Spirit shines from your life with the same power as His fire and with the peace of that cloud. Will you view yourself just like a Mount Sinai; a place where His presence will be fully visible to other people? Will you ask Him to make manifest His presence in the presence of your friends and family and coworkers *through you*?

Let's all long for His glory today. Let's ask for more and be filled more, O Men. We must be the men so fiery with His presence that the world is lit alight with holy desire for our Lord. Today, let's go up into His cloud. And may we come out fully transfigured.

February 9 – Exodus 32

Spiritual impatience and its consequences

The majority of the sinfulness in our lives can be traced back to a root cause: profound spiritual impatience. We often like to say we're open to letting God take time working upon our lives, but, if we're honest, we're actually not. It's much easier, as a modern man, to "get our hands dirty" and do the work it takes to "get the deal done" for ourselves. Sitting around and waiting for God to reveal His perfect plan for us is just about as popular as watching the proverbial paint dry. But the problem with our spiritual impatience is the way it often turns our hearts to sin within its easy expedience. We start to throw the gold of our hearts into the making of forbidden idols, thinking they'll plug the spiritual hole gaping within us. Where we should've waited for God and for His divine revelation, we wind up making ourselves look like insensible idiots. (Truly, can you think of one other place throughout the scriptures where the Israelites looked and sounded stupider than in this moment?)

The spiritual patience God requires from our lives is actually for the good of our souls; He's cleaning off the dross from us. He's using patience as a tool to fire the gold within our hearts into a more beautiful burnishing for His purposes. But when we cut Him short with our spiritual impatience we aren't allowing God's fire to purify our hearts fully. Instead we're casting our hearts into the fashioning of modern Golden Calves when we don't let Him properly finish with His good work in us.

There's gold within your heart that's truly priceless unto the Lord for the accomplishing of His plan in this particular day. But will you let Him do the work of burning the dross away and allow Him ample opportunity to take His time upon your life? Will you *not* allow your heart to be swayed by your worries or the world or your busy schedule? Will you trust that the plan of God is good for you – *good as gold* – even if it seems to take "forever," O Man? Will you use your time today to grown in patience with the Lord's hand, not to take your life into your own? For your life is actually His, don't forget it! Learn to be patient; He's presently at work upon you!

February 10 – Exodus 33:12-22

You can see Him

You must say to the Lord, "You have been telling me, 'Lead these people to me,' and you have let me know that you will send your Spirit with me. You have said, 'I know you by name and you have found favor with me.' Since you were pleased to send your Son to me, teach me your ways so I may know you and continue to find favor with you. Remember that you have chosen me and that your Church is your Body to this world."

The Lord will reply, "My Presence will go with you, and I will give you rest."

Then say to him, "If your Presence does not go with me, do not send me out at all. How will anyone know that you are pleased with me and with your Church unless you go with us? What else will distinguish me and your people from all the other people on the face of the earth?"

And the Lord will say to you, "I will do the very thing you have asked, because I am pleased with you and I know you by name."

Then you *must* say, "Now show me your glory."

And the Lord will reply, "I have already caused all my goodness to pass before you, and I have proclaimed my name, Jesus, in your presence. I have had mercy on whom I wanted to have mercy, and have had compassion on whom I wanted to have compassion. And," he said, "you have seen my face, the face of my one and only Son, and now you are my face to the world."

Now the Lord says, "Yours is a place near me because you stand upon the Rock. Everyday, my glory passes by you if you abide in me. Your life is in my hand and I will uphold you. 'You will seek me and find me when you seek me with all your heart.'"

Today, seek His glory by seeking Him wholeheartedly throughout the day; you can talk to God as confidently as Moses did. He wants to hear your every thought, O Man. And He wants to be your first thought today.

February 11 – Exodus 34:29-35

Letting Jesus shine from your face

The more a man will glory in the glory of His Father's radiant face, the more the world will see the Father for itself. There's a direct correlation between your radiant (or your *not* radiant) presence and the world's perception of who God is. Do you find your times alone with Him are leading your heart and spirit into a radiant, sure, ever-glowing joy? Would the people around you ever feel blinded by the glowing of His Holy Spirit shining from your life? Does being "up on the mountaintop with Him" direct the course of your day or does your day itself direct your course? Do you shine with all the surety of knowing whom it is you serve each day or do you feel somewhat unsure?

Sadly for them, the Israelites saw Moses' radiant face as something fearful and not something to personally seek after. They preferred that he should cover up his face instead of asking how they themselves might attain to such a personal radiance. They preferred to hear the word of God through Moses and contented themselves with knowing God from a reasonable safe distance. They didn't desire that this holy glow might be their inheritance too; they were more at ease experiencing it secondhand…

In 2 Corinthians 3, the apostle Paul ties Moses' glow-veil together with the ongoing spiritual blindness of his people. He writes in verse 15: "Even to this day when Moses is read, a veil covers [the Israelites'] hearts." However, just as pointedly, Paul goes on to explain what then happens when we give our hearts to Jesus Christ in fullness: "whenever anyone turns to the Lord, the veil is taken away"; a radiant face-to-face relationship ensues between us and God.

Do you long to have a glowing face that reflects all the glory of your Savior to the world around you, O Man? Do you know your Lord so intimately that you can't help the way your face is always shining after your times together? Can people tell the difference when they look at your face; does Jesus Christ make Himself visible there to everybody you encounter? We must become the ones with "unveiled faces" and unveiled hearts, shining for Him every moment today! We must live with such awareness of His glory that our faces shine with radiance of His radiance, all the time!

Go look into His glory today, O Man. Absorb, enjoy, and, most importantly, reflect it.

February 12 – Exodus 40:36-38

Not going without leading

If we can't accept the call of God when He's calling us to stay put, we really won't be useful for His eventual sending-out. If we refuse to sit and wait for His clear spoken leadings for our lives, we show that our leading is not entirely from Him. If we believe our hearts are always called to action – to deeds and doings – we're simply thinking wrongly about the Plan, O Men. We mustn't think that we're above our very Savior who so often disappeared to rest and spend time with His Heavenly Father. We can't presume we'll be of any use to Him, going, if we treat His calls to stop as if they're of no use to us. We can't find the heart of God when we're always going, going, going without some staying, staying, staying.

Ten days ago, we saw the miraculous way the Lord led His chosen people from their bondage in Egypt. We read of how He led them out with His blazing fire by night and His glowing cloud of Presence during the daylight hours. We read of how He called them forth unto His planned movement: going, escaping, exodus and promised freedom in the Promised Land. We read of how He said to them "follow Me" through clear action and active obedience; to a faith in Him with literal feet.

Now, today, we are reading from a passage that shows how His Presence was a sign of His calling to *stop* and *stay*. How He didn't want their leaving without His leading; how He didn't want their movements to lack His proper divine motives. He desired that His people exhibited patience that depended upon their God for their every daily step forward. He knew the waiting and the wondering and the watching for His leading were immensely valuable to His chosen people.

Will you stay with Him today, O Man, waiting for His answers to the questions that are currently circling in your mind? Will you not move forward without the clear hand of God upon you, leading out into His providential directions? Will you be a patient man of God who abides in His presence until His presence clearly leads you onward? Will you be an example to your friends and your family and your colleagues by the patience to be found within you?

Our God will lead a patient man. Are you willing to be patient?

February 13 – Numbers 11:1-3

A day without complaining

Whether walking in the untamed wilderness or partying in his enormous castle, a man of God must never be a complainer. After all, how can we complain about anything when we know the depths of love and grace already bestowed upon our lives? How can we imagine there's anything else we'd ever need when we've already received everything that's actually worth having? Why do we act as if our lives are all about *us* when we know that living for self is, itself, a form of wilderness?

We're most susceptible to a complaint against the Lord when we've forgotten what we have and, also, what He's already done for us. We forget our richest blessings are actually internal when we give our hearts to things that are solely external. Like the Israelites, walking through the wilderness *because their God had already freed them*, we forget the work is done for us. We assume, seeing our "conditions" in the seemingly endless present, that our present circumstances will never change "for the better." Which goes to show we've already forgotten God's viewpoint of the "better"; His "plans to give you hope and a future…"

Whether it's something small or huge, something spiritual or temporal, don't raise a single complaint in your life today, O Man. Try to be a man who's "content in any and every situation" because of your view of the Lord's view of your life. Don't attempt to rectify some wrong done to you by spouting off human arguments or complaints or rejoinders. Simply be a man today, knowing that the Lord has got you where He wants you for the good of your heart in Him. And don't forget how God once listened unto Moses; how he'd become a man who trusted God; and how God was pleased with that. Try to trust today and be likewise pleasing. Don't complain at all *about anything*.

February 14 – Numbers 13:17-33

Having a conqueror's eye

There's something so suggestive in this passage of the way it must've felt when Jesus handed off the Great Commission. Imagine His friends back then: Standing on the banks outside the new Kingdom of God, being told to go and take the world. Yet who were they? A bunch of scared fishermen; a former tax collector; a Zealot; a world-class famous doubter! How could God expect such vast results from these two frightened groups of people, be they former slaves or scattered apostles? How can God expect that you and I will continue to be His apostles – His "sent ones" – heading out into the wilds of life? How can we continue to spread afar the Gospel and take His Promise to new lands when the job itself seems so immense?

First off, we can't be destroyed without a single battle's fighting in the way these former spies were, back then. They came back to camp with all the milk and honey in their minds' eye, but they'd also forgotten God's rich promises. When they only *saw* some possible preventers of their marching into Canaan, it was as if they'd already been beaten by them. They proclaimed their defeat without the waging of a single God-led battle because they'd forgotten this wonderful truth: "If God is for us, who can be against us?" (Romans 8:31b) And, "we are more than conquerors through him who loved us." (Romans 8:37)

O Men of God, we must become like Caleb if we want to be the men we're called to be: *Totally unafraid through Jesus.* Caleb saw the same milk and honey, saw the same "powerful" men, and yet look at his response to them: "We should go up and take possession of the land, for we can certainly do it"; he was bold and brash for the purposes of his God. We must view this world with Caleb's bold eye, knowing that, through Jesus, we'll achieve the total victory in His Name. Now let's march out upon the day together. We literally have nothing left to fear.

February 15 – Numbers 14:1-10

Quash anxiety and go!

You may have the world upon your shoulders as you enter the day today – *you must only go to God with that!* For when we take such wild potentialities to our friends or family or wife, we can absolutely destroy their hearts of faith. These spies who came to camp with their outrageous fears of dangerous foes only served to terrify the waiting, excited, chosen people of God. The Israelites then decide they'd rather be in toilsome slavery, having their sons murdered, than to trust upon the Lord their God…

Will you be the sort of man who's strong enough to take his fears, worries and anxieties to the Lord only, O Man? Will you go and do the things for which He asks and then, when the going gets tough, go to Him – *and Him alone* – with your fears? Can you resolve your manly heart to follow Jesus even in this particular commandment: "Do not be anxious about anything"? Will you not allow your fears, your concerns, your anxieties, to scuttle another's voyage with the Lord Jesus?

The Israelites would've rather had the "comfort" of their slavery in Egypt than the "battles" of the Lord's Promised Land. They'd rather return to knowns than to unknowns, simply because the new way seemed to them like a dangerous challenge. How many of us have gutted our potential for the Lord because we've fallen under the sway of the "known," seemingly safer life? How many wonderful unknown battles for the Lord have we *not* fought because we've hamstrung the Lord's personal promises for us?

The writer Antoine Saint-Exupery described this danger well in his book, *Wind, Sand and Stars*: "When the wild ducks or the wild geese migrate in their season, a strange tide rises in the territories over which they sweep. As if magnetized by the great triangular flight, the barnyard fowl leap a foot or two into the air and try to fly… But domestic security has succeeded in crushing out that part in us that is capable of heeding the call. We scarcely quiver; we beat our wings once or twice and fall back into our barnyard."

Today, what sort of man are you, O Man? Will you go or will you turn back? The Lord's strength is all the strength you actually need for this day; the question is whether you're willing to follow Him?

LIVE LIKE MEN

February 16 – Number 14:26-38

The Promised Land Mentality

It's while we're still youthful in our journey that we feel the nascent promise in the Lord's distant Promised Lands. While the truth of His Word still feels true, while the call still sounds exactly like His Call, we hearken to a single-minded obedience. Like Israel, walking across the muddy bottom of the parted Red Sea, we're happy to be following after such a Leader as Jesus. When we suddenly see Him raining down His blessings from the heavens like manna, we feel tears start to flood our eyes. But then, all of a sudden, things stop going our way; challenges challenge us; foreign fighters start to seem more formidable. All that high-flown, high-minded "talk" of old doesn't seem so "real" to us when the fight gets a little fiercer. All at once, that youthful trusting obedience seems the business of the generation following after our faith-generation...

Yet the people of God can't be the people of God when they won't trust their God, *regardless of their age or experience*. Has your life's perspective clouded your living for Him with caveats and arguments against that "past" way of living by faith? Have you seen Him work a million times before but now are struggling to find a reason to follow because of the millionth-and-*first*? Can you forget so easily your youthful vim and vigor; your rash assurances that "if all fall away on account of you, I never will"?

O Man of God, you must marry the perspective of your youthful Christ-following with your older manly wisdom. Realize that the older Israelites lost their passage to the Promised Land simply because they forsook "their first love." Don't let your world-weariness become the voice of your faith; don't miss out on His promises for that reason. Surely, we've already missed a million "Promised Land life-moments" because of our constant grumbling against Him and His goodness. Sadly, our curmudgeonly way of following Jesus has probably kept us – *and others* – from seeing Him more clearly.

Will you be a man with a Promised Land mentality in the living of your day today, O Man of God? Will you live as if His promises are true – *for you and others* – and then let others be drawn to Him and to the Promised Life?

February 17 – Numbers 16:1-35

Don't be a pointless "rebel"

The seeds of sin are sown so easily within the hearts of men who hanker after "revolution" and "revolt." It's only been in extraordinary historical cases that those sorts of leaders don't eventually descend into utter chaos. The reason? The "revolutionary," untempered by the Truth of Jesus, finds the human condition worse than expected. And where he'd sought to "set men free" by his "ideas," "plans," or "policies," he finds only the rampant results of the condition of sin.

The only answer? The only "revolutionary" who ever called the hearts of men *away*, not *unto*, themselves. Jesus Christ: The only "man of revolt" whose "revolution" meant the overturning (ie. *the turning over*) of men's hearts…

The idiocy of our culture's persistent insistence upon rebellion as human triumph is shown in our eventual warped thinking. Like Israel, suddenly seeing Egypt as the land of "milk and honey" (v. 13), we're constantly told to crave the wrong things. We seem to be told rebellion is a human virtue, yet we also see the pointless purposes random rebellion often engenders. We're told we shouldn't "trust anything or anyone," yet we know the One who made our manly hearts for a perfect trust.

O Man of God, don't buy the world's brand of revolt or rebellion or revolution for a moment of your day today. You and I were built for harmony with Jesus and with each other – *through Him* – and we only hurt ourselves by disobeying. We don't want to "run like a man running aimlessly," or "fight like a man beating the air," do we? We won't give our hearts to pointless spirits of rebellion when the true and greatest rebellion is claiming our "citizenship…in heaven."

Rebellion becomes a virtue when a mind is fully controlled by the voices it's too stupid to understand or contradict. You and I are called to be the men today who listen to a voice that is "higher than I," higher than anything or anyone. O Men of God, our rebellion subverts the human ego. Our revolt is against only Satan. And we'll rebel against the world's hollow rebellions when we seek to follow only after Jesus Christ daily. And that's the only work we need today. And we won't rest till we're done.

February 18 – Numbers 21:4-9

Lifting up Jesus is our only purpose

Oftentimes the man who can't enunciate the purpose of his life is a man who's living life without a purpose. Can you put into a sentence everything that's "of first importance" to you in the way you live your life, O Man? Would your colleagues know that the meaning of your existence is found in Jesus without a single second of doubt about it? Would your children know how best to answer the question if they were asked: "What's your father's reason for being?"

In John 3:14, Jesus told Nicodemus: "Just as Moses lifted up the snake…so the Son of Man must be lifted up…" Why? "[T]hat everyone who believes in him may have eternal life": Jesus' explanation for the purpose of His coming. Even Jesus was so compelled by this picture of Moses' lifting-up of the snake that He taught Nicodemus with it. He gives the purpose of His life so succinctly that Nicodemus must've forever remembered these words spoken to him in the darkness…

Like Moses lifting up that bronzed snake in the desert, will your life lift up your "lifted-up" Savior to the world? Will your every thought and action and decision and your words be spoken so that He's lifted high and exalted? Will you believe His call to you is totally concrete, real, true, honest, absolutely worth your everything? Will you find your life's purpose in "taking up [your] cross daily," whatever cross He's given to you? Can you picture Moses standing amidst the people with the snake upon that pole and see a whole life comprised therein? Do you realize the purpose of your life is best expressed in your lifting-up of Jesus and His Cross? "Then when anyone was [ravaged by sin, defeated by Satan, doomed for destruction] and looked at [Jesus], he lived."

That's your purpose, O Man. To lift Him up.

That must be your only purpose today.

February 19 – Numbers 22:21-35

Don't be angry. At all.

A manly anger that remains completely unchecked is often the dividing line between real men and spoiled little "boy-men." If we don't learn how to rein in our anger, we'll become the sort of men who might eventually speak to speaking donkeys. If we don't learn the godly wisdom learned by holding angry thoughts inside, we'll eventually make ourselves a laughingstock. After all, I doubt that Balaam started his day with hopes of taking a ride that would end with his talking to a donkey! He surely didn't embark upon his journey with the hope that it'd result in scripture's single funniest moment…

When you're stifled by your "circumstances" or "life," what's your first human inclination in that moment, O Man? Do you find the heart of Jesus within yourself, filled with peace, or do you find a heart filled with wild-eyed anger? Do you beat the donkeys around you, hoping to expel your rage on them, or do you turn your rage back unto your God? Do you seek His comfort in the midst of your oncoming frustrations, or do you take it out on others who happen to be nearby?

Perhaps "the angel of the Lord" is standing "in a narrow path" in your life, slowing up your progress today, like he did with Balaam. Perhaps he's needed there to keep you away from sin or to keep you from slowly wandering off from the Lord's plan for you. Perhaps you've accidentally started upon a course that's not the best for your heart or for your following after Jesus. Perhaps the Lord is cutting you off from a way that actually ends in the very destruction of your life…

Today, let's be the sort of men *not* angry, *not* growing heated, *not* taking "it" out on anyone we know. Let's remember that the Lord blesses "peacemakers" and "the gentle" and those who pursue a way that's "pure in heart." Let's be "quick to listen, slow to speak," and very most importantly, "slow to become angry" in our life today. Otherwise we run the very real risk of becoming a man like Balaam became, a jackass beating the hell out of a jackass!

Start to become a man of peace today, O Man. Simply start by controlling today's anger.

February 20 – Deuteronomy 34

Live your "legacy" today

If Moses hadn't listened to the voice at the burning bush, he'd still be standing at "the far side of the desert." If he hadn't entered into Egypt through the Lord's providential guidance, his people never would've left servitude under Pharaoh. If he hadn't trusted God's direction for the words to be spoken to Pharaoh, he never would've spoken up at all. If he hadn't believed in the power of the Lord's staff, he never would've lifted it up, never would've parted the Red Sea. If he hadn't been the patient intermediary, God might've never rained down quail and manna on His people. If he hadn't "cried out" to God for his people, they might've actually died of thirst near Horeb instead of drinking from the rock. If he didn't hunger and thirst for the Lord and for His glorious presence, the people never would've heard the Ten Commandments. If he didn't intercede for them, the Golden Calf worship might've been their final undoing for their faithlessness....

You and I are not allowed to pick our own personal Mount Nebo; we don't know when we'll be called home, O Men. We don't get to know the how or when or where – or especially *why* – of the Lord's decision for when our life is finished. It could be later on today or next year or the year after next or in ten, or in fifty, years. It might be slow and horribly painful or it might be dignified, or quick and easy– we simply don't, and won't, know.

But the call of God upon this particular day – and the way you'll respond to it – will be part of your lasting legacy, O Man. We can't expect to disobey and shirk responsibility and somehow still end up in glory on Mount Nebo's peak. We shouldn't expect to have our later years to clarify our legacy for the generations to follow after ours. We should think of Moses, long before Mount Nebo, dealing with the wily Israelites out in the endless desert years. Moses learned to trust the Lord, everyday, knowing how the days add up into our lifetimes of faithful living. Moses didn't wait until he'd seen the Promised Land to trust the Lord; he trusted daily in the Lord's promises. We must be the sort of men today who firmly cement their legacy in the living of our everyday minutiae. For there's actually no minutiae to the Lord; every day creates the Mount Nebo moments of our lives.

Let's live that way today, O Men of God. Remember Moses and his godly legacy.

February 21 – Joshua 1:1-11

Be a godly leader everywhere

This lineage of leadership given to the Israelites is the sort of leadership the modern Church needs so desperately. Our pastors and our preachers, our elders and our deacons, all of them are really wonderful – of course! But the call of God that came upon the life of Joshua should be the call of God for every man allegiant to Jesus. We must start to view our lives within the framework of this kind of call, this sort of mission, this brand of hearty manhood:

After the resurrection and ascension of Jesus, the Lord said to *you*, Jesus' disciple: "Jesus, my Son, is with me again. Now then, you and all these followers of Him, get ready to cross the River of Life. I will give you every place where you set your foot, and I will draw people unto Him – through you. Your territory is immeasurable, extending from your home to the furthest reaches of the globe. No one will be able to stand up against you all the days of your life, for 'I have overcome the world.' As I was in, and with, my Son, so I am within you; I will never leave you nor forsake you.

"Be strong and courageous, because you will lead these people to inherit the blessing of eternal life. Be strong and very courageous. Be careful to obey my Son because to 'love [Him]' is to 'keep [His] commandments.' Do not turn from this to the right or to the left, that you may be successful wherever you go. Do not let the words of the Word depart from your mouth; meditate on them day and night, so that you may be obedient. Then you will be prosperous and successful. Have I not commanded you? Be strong and courageous. Do not be terrified; do not be discouraged, for the Lord your God will be with you wherever you go."

Today, will you be a leader within the lineage of Moses, of Joshua, of Jesus Christ Himself? Will you feel the weight of the mantle of authority bestowed upon Joshua as being your own mantle of authority? For it's actually yours today, O Man. And you must live that way in every moment. We must be the leaders we're really meant to be if we'd want to turn the world to Jesus, our great Leader.

February 22 – Joshua 3

Taking steps of faith today

The steps of faith suspending fearful feet above a rushing river are the only steps of real true faith. You'll be starting upon the definition of "a man after God's own heart" when you step out without complete certainty. We can only grow our trembling heart into a heart of assurance when we're taking these sorts of steps for Him daily. We must start to read the tale of dry Jordan-crossings with an expectation of its happening in our own current lives. After all, the Lord loves to use this image of our walking and our steps as a small reminder of the greater path. As in: We are "created in Christ Jesus for good works, which God prepared beforehand, that we should walk in them." (Eph. 2:10) In other words, His perfect path is already laid and already paved; all He wants is that we'd take the steps forward. He desires that we'd really trust Him and move; that we'd listen to the call and then actually act when He says to.

"If the Lord delights in a man's way, he makes his steps firm; though he stumble, he will not fall…" And why's that? Because "the Lord upholds him with his hand" (Psalm 37:23,24); He wants you to stay the course with Him. "When you pass through the waters, I will be with you; and when you pass through the rivers, they will not sweep over you." (Isaiah 43:2a) When you delight yourself in the Lord and in His Way, He delights to take you through any trial or any danger…

Will you prove to be the sort of man who steps out in faith, knowing the Lord can create dry ground beneath you? Will you trust Him even when your foot's suspended, when the waters are rushing by unabated underneath you? Will you see Jesus going before you, like the Levites did, and simply, humbly, faithfully follow Him throughout this day? Will you *not* miss the greater path because you're looking for a bridge ahead instead of looking for His perfect Way?

"In his heart a man plans his course, but the Lord determines his steps" is a God-honest truth for us, O Men of God (Prov. 16:9). So let's be the sort of men today, following His course regardless of where it seems to be taking our present steps. After all, He'll determine those steps anyway! So you might as well get with the program!

February 23 – Joshua 4:1-9

Write down remembrances of Him

Your faith will be as deep and abiding as the measure of remembrance you store up in your heart, O Man. If you "treasure up" the things that He's done in your past life, He will certainly take you deeper, moving forward. If you look unto your past and are thankful for the work of God in you, God will work through your present heart. By remembrance, we're actually able to see the active hand of God and also its ever-present working in the course of our lives. Today, I'd challenge you to set up "Jordan stones" as a remembrance of the work of God in your life, O Man. You're "who you are" and "where you are" as a direct result of what He's done in and around you already. You're *not* "your own man" or a "self-made man" or a man doing it "my way" – you are only God's man by His design. You and I were made within "His image" and He's making us daily to be more and more like His Son…

Take the time today to grab a journal and write out all the individual circumstances of your current life. Then, from there, think backward along the ways that God engineered each of those particular circumstances for Himself. If you've got a job, think of how you "got" that job; realize how God actually placed you in it for His purposes. If you're married, think about your love's "story" and remember how He actually made you 1 + 1 = 1. Think of all the friends and enemies who've been major parts of your life's unfurling story, up to the present moment. Then see how each of those ones actually produced fruit that accounts for the character of your present heart. Map backward through your life and see how God "works for the good of those who love him" in His firm actuality. You'll see how He never wastes a moment or a circumstance in making you the man He wants you to be, O Man.

Be a man of remembrance today. Set up stones from the "Jordans" of your life. You'll find yourself astonished if you really take the time to see how today is the sum of so many of His yesterdays. But it's all only through Him. And it's only the best when it's for His purposes.

February 24 – Joshua 6

Being "used" requires obedience in action

A man who follows Jesus with a single-minded obedience sees the Lord fight and win his battles for him. Even when the call of God seems fairly strange and impractical, he chooses to follow what he hears without any question. He doesn't second-guess the Lord's decisions even when the Lord's decisions might make him an object of worldly ridicule. He's not afraid to be a "fool for Christ" or to look "weak" or be "dishonored" in the world's watching eyes. (1 Cor. 4:10) He thinks it less than nothing to walk in circles around a fortress-city when He knows the Lord has already given him that city. He carries the presence of the Lord within the "ark" of his heart and he's unafraid that any battle is too big for his God. He'll go for seven days, seven months, seven years, seventy-seven years, if he's called to do so. For he knows the shout of the Lord is of an infinite strength when it's opposed by weak and worthless human weapons. He knows "the Spirit of him who raised Jesus from the dead is living in [him]," right this very minute. He feels the immensity of the call and he's pleased beyond words to simply be called by Jesus Himself…

Does this describe you today, O Man? Would you desire that to be your description? Would you want that God would use you as absurdly, as wildly powerfully, as when Joshua circled around Jericho?

Our lives can be such a grand adventure when we give our hearts and minds and wills to the Will of the Lord only. You and I are only normal men until we give Him everything of ourselves – *every single thing* – *everyday*. Only when we listen for His voice and don't hesitate to do His asked-for deeds are we fully living as His men. Only when we get the crazy battle plan and simply go and circle cities does He conquer all the enemies for us.

Today, you're called into adventure, romance, excitement, danger and war that's all part of the Plan of God for you, O Man. Will you simply listen for His voice – through scripture and the Spirit – and then act as He asks, accordingly? Will you hesitate before your personal Jerichoes or will you shout before the Lord that today's battles are His alone? Go out and take this day for Him. Simply do what He asks when He asks.

February 25 – Joshua 7

Root out your "secret" sin

We waste our lives in judging other people's "public sin" when we will not exorcise our own secret sin. When the Church becomes a walking talking-point about the *world's* sin, we've already totally lost the battle. After all, does it really matter trying to "protect the sanctity" of anything when we're secretly the slaves of sin ourselves? Don't we understand the teaching regarding the plank and the speck of sawdust when it comes to our own personal lives? The world is not "in such bad shape" because of its current excess of sin, it's because of our dearth of Jesus' love for it. If we really want to "purify the world," we must start with the secret sin in our midst and, furthermore, in *your* midst…

Today, meditate upon the single secret sin that's quietly dominating your heart, this very minute, as you read these words. Each of us is nursing a grudge or lust or greed or pride that's currently killing us – and the other people around us too. There's nothing worse than seeing a brother suddenly getting caught at the tail-end of one of these secret sins, is there? There's nothing worse for the Church than unaccountable men doing unaccountable things in what they think is their "secret" or "private" life.

Don't be the man who speaks against homosexuality and actually has a secret savor for said sexual act. Don't be the deacon who denounces corporate greed and yet is currently quietly defrauding his clients at work. If we want to be the men of God we *say* we want to be, we mustn't follow after Achan's ancient pattern of sin. We mustn't bury the soothing secret sins of our lives under the tent of our modern churchly respectability. We mustn't be a porn addict while masquerading as the kind of man who's all about "family values." We must really live our lives "in the secret, in the quiet place" just as we do in the public's all-seeing eye…

Commit yourself to killing the secret sin in your heart that's absolutely killing your heart for Jesus, O Man of God. May we not dishonor our precious Savior by pretending we can have both Him and "it" – whatever "it" is. Understand me: Its Him or "it." There can be no thought of balancing the two.

February 26 – Joshua 8:30-35

Renew shared call with friends

If we follow Jesus, we must be men who rally other men to the "cause" of the New Covenant of Jesus Christ. We must live our lives so blatantly for Him and for His purposes that no one thinks it strange when we invite them in. We must live out our enlistment in His Army in a manner that excites the enthusiasm of other men around us. Our invitation to lost people must seem consistent with the life we're currently leading and the example we're exhibiting. No one seemed to think it strange that Joshua was chosen as their leader or that he'd recommit their living to a Covenantal lifestyle. In the same way, we must bring our brothers around a commonality of New Covenantal living in this day. We must gather for the enlivening of our common duty; a recommissioning of the Great Commission in our generation. We must use today as a day where we recommit ourselves together to our call, knowing this is actually part of the call!

Whether it's by text-message, phone call, email or lunch appointment, gather with some other brothers during the course of today. Even if it's only one friend, call him up and invite him to a time of refreshment in the presence of Jesus together. There's nothing more important in this day than using every single minute of it to enliven your joint calling. There's no meeting or "deal" or deadline that can compete with your Savior's simple "follow Me," for you and your brothers.

A great general is one who generates passion for the battles still ahead of his army, not the battles in the past. Joshua knew the way would be tough, hard-fought and certainly not easy for any of the Israelites he was leading in the Lord's way. Yet he also knew "the battle is the Lord's" and that the fighting over Canaan was a divinely holy endeavor. Which is why he used his powerful position to unite the Hebrew body in the living out of the Covenant.

In the same way, will you unite some brothers today? Will you use your voice for the Lord's words to them? Will you be like mighty Joshua, encouraging other brothers to the fullness of life only to be found in Jesus?

February 27 – Joshua 10:1-15

Remembering the "supernatural" and trusting Him

There's no limit to the power of our God because the God we serve is actually omnipotent, O Man. We can wonder at the *meaning* of the "sun stopped in the middle of the sky," but we can't debate the *results* that played out. We can see how Joshua cried out to the Lord and then the incredible supernatural way that God answered him in the battle. We can feel the fear of the five kings as they watched how their armies are destroyed by those hurling hailstones. We're awed by the idea of "the Lord was fighting for Israel" because we read of His supernatural workings on that particular day. But are we living with expectancy in our own day, just as Joshua did, for today's similar supernatural happenings?

We can only live our lives with any power when the power that's on our minds is the Lord's great power. Each of us has seen the mighty hand of God do something in our lives that was akin to the sun actually stopping. Each of us has known at least a single moment when we turned our eyes to heaven and then saw the Lord's clear hand. How can we forget Him in our trials when we've already seen so clearly how he fights for us, all the time? How's it possible to turn our thoughts to ourselves, to our own ability to fight, when we've seen what He Himself can do? Do we not remember what He did within our own personal battle at our own personal Gibeon, O Men? Can't we reconjure our own trustfulness, trust His patient lovingkindness, on the battlefield that's called Today?

A test for the mettle of your faith in His supernatural abilities is the amount of sleep you're currently getting. Do you toss and turn each night, thinking of the battles waging around you or do you simply trust and rest? Do you find your eyes scanning the clock at 1, 2, 3, 4, 5, or are you faithfully fast asleep? Do you go to bed each night, knowing He's the One who fights your battles for you, or do you lay awake pointlessly?

Today, let's absolutely trust Him, O Men. Let's trust absolutely. We must know – *or we must learn to know* – that God gives peace to those who trust in His power regardless of their circumstances.

LIVE LIKE MEN

February 28 – Joshua 14:6-15

Live expectant of eternal promises

A man who knows the promises of God and lives his life with an ever-present expectancy will remain "vigorous." He won't be a man torn apart by the vicissitudes of life; his vigor will be heavenly and eternal in its nature. He's already seen the Promised Land through his knowledge of the Savior; he's not rebuffed by any possible future enemy. He's crossed the Jordan River through his justification by the blood of Jesus Christ; he is fully alive in his Risen Lord. He's watched throughout the years just how the Lord has fought his battles for him; he's unafraid of anything anymore. He welcomes old age and his eventual death with heart wide open, knowing that his vigor will endure forever in Jesus. He's not afraid to lay claim to the stated promises because he knows, full well, that "he who promised is faithful." In short, he's a man who absolutely knows *without a doubt* the God he says he serves with his life. He's a man, through and through, who the Lord has found to have a "willing mind," a "wholehearted devotion." (1 Chron. 28:9) He's really a man – *a true man* – because he actually takes the Lord at His word whenever he hears it...

You've spied the blessings of His amazing grace, O Man, and have already "crossed over from death to life" yourself. You've seen the Lord fight battles for the good of your heart and seen Him be victorious on your behalf so many times. You've heard the promises of Life, of eternity, of His presence, spoken from His very lips to your heart. You've already a got a patch of land in heaven, proven by the Spirit's "deposit, guaranteeing what is to come."

Today, let's all be like Caleb in the vigorous expression of our ever-present expectancy, O Men of God. When we've already got everything that's actually worth having, why should we ever worry about anything? Let your spirit dwell upon the blessings of His grace which have already been given to you and truly feel their immensity. Realize the amazing implications that the God of Caleb is also the God you serve with your life today. For "God is not a man, that he should lie, nor a son of man, that he should change his mind. Does he speak and then not act? Does he promise and not fulfill?" (Numbers 23:19) He will fulfill His promises given to you. Live from that knowledge today.

March 1 – Joshua 24:14,15

Claiming your family for the Lord's service

Joshua's certainty when he's speaking of his "household" is the certainty our own families demand from our lives. It's not enough to claim to follow after Jesus just for ourselves; we must take these others along with us daily. The sort of man who'd stand before his whole nation saying these sorts of things with certainty is the sort of man we need to be. We mustn't live under the assumption that the serving of our Lord is *not* a father's once-and-for-all choice for his family. We can't presume that our children and wife will always choose rightly if we don't ever speak aloud our commitment. If we won't be bold and say the words "as for me and my household," what sort of foundation are we laying, O Men? If we won't speak out with Joshua's clear guiding voice for his family, what sort of voice will we use for them instead?

There's something so powerful and yet peaceful in the way that Joshua chose to describe his family's service unto the Lord. Firstly, a man of God who claims his family for God's Kingdom is a statement of the utmost power in our broken world. When the children of that man can look into his eyes and know what they're "about," there's unshakeable confidence to be found there. They're not left blindly searching for their way, wasting time upon the world, they can live their lives with certainty. Secondly, the man of God who speaks his family's purpose can unite their hearts with God's promised, perfect peace for them. They will not be wandering alone, tossed upon the daily tides; they will know their abiding identity found in Jesus. They will know the peace "which passeth all understanding" when their father keeps their family's way upon *the* Way. You and I must use our fatherly voice, both powerfully and peacefully, to so guide and direct our families each day.

On February 1st we considered how the painting of "the lintels of our houses" was an absolute must-do for us. Today, let's go even a step further in the claiming of our family for the real act of service for the King of Kings. May we be the sort of men who stand before our families, pure in heart, and direct the way for our joint future together. May our children grow up with surety, confident in the purpose of their lives, serving God with their father alongside them.

March 2 – Judges 3:12-30

Be daring for Him today

The relationship between smoke and fire is the exact relationship that exists between our derring-do and our *actual* power. There's never existed a man of power who exhibited anything less than a true daring-heartedness in his outward life and actions. It's possible to be called a "Christian leader," to be considered a "strong man," without actually having any personal power. But the man of God who doesn't want the *Lord's brand of power* in his life is not following after Him at all…

"The Israelites did evil in the eyes of the Lord," and so the Lord gave unto Moab "power over Israel." The whole Hebrew nation is in bondage, once again, because their hearts weren't true to the Lord their God. For eighteen years, they are languishing, slaving, back in the place of sin-caused servitude as if they'd never left from Egypt. What they need is one who follows the Lord – *with power* – *with outrageous daring* – to come deliver them from their earthly captors. What they need is simply a man, filled with the power of their God, who actually follows after their God day-by-day. What they need is some true daring – something to unite themselves around – and a fighting spirit within their hearts…

O Man of God, what was the last truly daring deed (or word or activity) that you went after for the sake of the God you serve? When was the last time you stood up, stepped out, did something almost crazy for the sake of His coming Kingdom? When was the last time you stood before the king of an enemy nation and stood your ground, completely and totally without any fear? When was the last time you felt no personal fear at all, knowing that the hand of God is truly with you and upon you?

Today, let's be the sort of men who'll simply do the things God's calling us to do for Him, O Men of God. Let's do some daring deeds that He'd request of us; actions potent with power that will thrill others' hearts for Him. May we bear believing hearts full of holy divine bravado, trusting in Him, and ready to serve all those around us. Let's be the sort of men so daring with their lives that the presence of the Lord's power can't be questioned. Let's be the men whose lives will act as rallying points for those others fighting for the Lord and let's band together. Let's be like Ehud today. Let's dare to be daring.

March 3 – Judges 6:1-16

You are called Warrior

A modern man is only weakened by the notion of his "wearing many hats"; he's a man or not; that is all. The question "What do you do?" can't be the one by which he defines himself; "What are you for?" is actually the operative question. We must source the whole of our destiny within the definition given to us by the God who created us for His own purposes. We shouldn't pigeonhole ourselves by following vocations that make following our God only an occasional avocation. We must hear the haunting whisper of our God through His Holy Spirit, in our spirits, each and every "workday." We must know the name He's given us, above our given names, our one and only work: "mighty warrior."

Gideon was hiding in a winepress while he fearfully threshed out his wheat and yet God called him a "warrior." He was confused by the conquest of his people by the mighty Midianites and yet God still called him "mighty." He was wondering why the wondrous "wonders" of God had seemed to ceased and yet God told him that he'd have the "strength" needed. He was from the weakest clan of Mannaseh, the "least in [his] family," and yet God said He'd be with him, no matter what.

O Man of God, the only name you're currently carrying that should carry any weight is the name the Lord's given to you. You're not defined by the "work" you happen to do, by your so-called "Christian name," only by Jesus Christ's name. The implications of your knowing how the Lord views you and what He wants to call you have some serious daily ramifications. Gideon only becomes a "mighty warrior" because he *believed* in the Lord's valuation of his eventual fighting value. Gideon only goes to fight the Midianites because he knows the Lord's naming of him is actually the truth…

Today, may we not be living a life of "wearing many hats" but, instead, may we be listening for the Lord's name for us. That name is always the same for the men of choosing – "mighty warrior" – and that's who you'll be today, my friend. Now let's go live that way today, modern Gideon. Your "daily grind" must cease to be your winepress.

March 4 – Judges 7

Trusting in His strength, not ours

The world's view of modern manhood is a view fraught with definitional deficiencies; something you could call "manhood *plus*." As in: Men are only really men when their lives are filled with extras, with added bonuses, with additional add-ons. And men aren't really men until they have the perfect girl, the fastest ski-boat, the biggest SUV, the right brand of beer. And they shouldn't hold their heads up unless their retirement accounts are of the suitable size to impress other striving men. They can't really be seen as victorious (whatever that means anymore!) unless their home is in the right physical location…

But the Lord's view of our manhood is the only view we should actually take into account if we want to be His sort of men. We must look into the eyes of Gideon, the "winepress warrior," if we want to see our God's triumphant results in surrendered men's lives. We must quietly creep into the enemy's camp and listen to his fear of us and be aware that this is really the Lord's battle. We must fight the battle of our lives with a "manhood *minus*" viewpoint, trusting *not* in ourselves, "leaning not on our own understanding."

If you want to enter the battle with 22,000 trained fighting men, that's pretty good *human* battle-planning, O Man of God. If you want to sharpen your sword and practice setting up your phalanx-formation, that's good shrewd *human* warcraft. If you want to live the course of your life for the purpose of your "comfort," that's normal *human* thinking nowadays. If you really believe your manhood is incumbent upon the "pluses" of the world, read again in Judges 7…

O Men of God, thinking we can trust in our "strength" is one of the enemy's greatest ploys to derail our modern Christian manhood. When we think we'll battle the modern Midianities by the strength of our own arm, we're basically already defeated. For "a man's life does not consist in the abundance of his possessions" or his strengths or the world's idea of pluses. And if "anyone loves the world," including its vapid view of modern men, "the love of the Father is not in him." Today, let's be like God's "mighty warrior" Gideon, trusting in the Lord's strength, entirely detached from our own "strength." May we see the weakness of our arms as a blessing, as an actual *strength* for Jesus, and find our strength for the day alone in Him.

March 5 – Judges 11:1-33

Your past is no excuse

If a man of God retreats before the enemy of his Past, he'll never have a future worth having. If we settle for the "cards" that we've been "dealt," we'll never stand upon the legs of the Lord's assured and final victory. When we feel our shoulders sag beneath the weight of our "upbringing" or our "family" or our "checkered past," Satan is winning. He's all too happy to have you sitting out the battles of Today because of yesterday's mere flesh-wounds, O Man of God. He becomes the victor whenever we point entirely to our past as the reasoning for where we are today. He's smiling every time your life discounts the restorative hand of God alive in your human life *right now*…

Jephthah was an actual true bastard, the son of a prostitute, the outcast son of a hateful broken family. He was actually driven from his home by brothers who couldn't care less if they ever saw his face again. He found himself living in a foreign land surrounded by wild-eyed fighting men and dangerous "adventurers." And yet what did God do with Jephthah's life, O Man? What was the Lord's perfect plan for him? Didn't the Lord our God use a bastard's strength as His own mighty strength against the evil king of Ammon? Didn't He think that Jephthah, this son of a prostitute, was the pristine soldier for His own earthly battleplan?

It's only weak men, living out of *human* weakness, who resort to blaming their whole life on their past and its pain. It's only those who don't believe the Lord's promises are truly true who can't ever seem to let the past go. Today, may we take the time for honesty about our past pain, giving it up to the Lord *once and for all*. Be prepared to actually let it go; stop lingering there; you must stop leaning upon the past, O Man of God. We must stop and redirect whenever we let the Lord's strength go slack in the ever-present excuses of our past life of pain.

Do you believe in the Lord's promises today? Do you believe in His possible restoration?

Then let the Past go, once and for all, today. For this day is your only touchstone with eternity.

LIVE LIKE MEN

March 6 – Judges 16:1-22

You can shape your wife

There doesn't exist a spiritual lathe or chisel or flame that will shape you any sharper than the woman you choose to love for your lifetime. There's not another human being who'll have the same effect on you as the woman across your breakfast table from you. Yet you'll always be defined by *her* definition of your manhood if you're the sort of man to always acquiesce to her. You'll follow paths of *her* choosing if you aren't the kind of man who'll lead her with a mighty and humble hand. Mighty Samson was a mighty man of God until it came to his choosing of an earthly female companion. He tried to listen for the voice of God to him unless he was in the mood for some good ol' fashioned sexual satiety. He was a Judge of Israel but not exactly a great judge of the characteristics needed in a human helpmate. His arms were steely and dangerously muscular; his thinking, on the other hand, was a muddied mess of mangled manhood.

Will you be the sort of man who'll act upon his calling to be the spiritual leader for the woman of his choosing, O Man of God? Will you shape your wife by godliness in your own character before God or will you let her always lead the way for your life? Will you sit upon the spiritual sidelines, letting your wife wear the spiritual pants for your whole family? Or will you be a man of God for her and help to shape your wife's character by the way you choose to live? Do you realize that Samson could've been a voice for the way of God in the life of Delilah? Do you think she would've sold him out for silver if he'd given her the gold of God's word, instead? Don't you think that God can use you in your home, just as He'd say He'd like to use you in the world around you? Don't you want to see the love of God, "the aroma of Christ," radiating from your wife's inner life to others? Don't you want to be a part of her lifelong spiritual journey with Jesus, instead of just a weak afterthought or footnote?

Let's be the sort of men who go on the offensive in the caring-for, serving-of, leading-to, of your wife's life. Let's stop thinking that our passive sorts of osmotic Jesus-discipleship will register with her womanly heart *at all*. No, be the man who takes his wife's hand, states the purpose of your union, and then lives from that purpose. You can actually shape your wife for Jesus. Now start to believe it today.

March 7 – Judges 16:23-30

Find your "pillars" and push

Each of us is placed within the "temple of this world" with our hands upon some of the pillars that support it. God places us in settings and in callings and in workplaces suited to the strengths He's purposefully chosen to given us. Now He's asking that we'd place our hands upon the pillars holding up the current lies of this world *and begin to push*. He reminds us that we're "not of this world" for a reason: so we won't succumb to it whispering succors. We've often seen how it turns out when another man has had his eyes gouged out by believing in Satan's lies. We've seen how he "performs" for the world by living out all the fallacies sown within his heart. But the call of God to us, to the men with intact eyes and hearts, is to have our hands upon those pillars today. Whether it's your job or your eldership, being a "Big Brother," you're called to push back against the evil one in all you do.

Push mightily against the world's current lies, Satan's pillars of untruth supporting the worship of self and sin. Don't be afraid that pillar-pushing might be the death of you; fear not the world's approbation or its abuse. You're standing everyday within the fearful temple of modern Dagons, "led like a sheep to the slaughter." Perhaps you've simply forgotten that we're "aliens and strangers in the world"; we're supposed to be different, O Men! We're supposed to have a strange sort of strength that has its source in the power of our Sovereign Lord. We're supposed to fight the fight that we've been given until our last and dying breath, like Samson once did.

Today, ask the Lord to show you how to place your hands upon the pillars He's already chosen for you, O Man. Seek out His perfect will for the battle He's chosen for your particular strength and then fight that battle to the end. May we never choose our own battles, swayed by predominating modern "Christian" movements and thinking. No, let us be the soldiers taking orders directly from the General, from His whispered truths for us. May we push mightily today. Nothing but our deaths can stop us.

March 8 – Ruth 2

Helping someone downtrodden today

A man of God who doesn't have a heart of justice for the downtrodden doesn't understand the heart of Jesus Christ. If we don't see a perfect portrait of godly manhood in Boaz, we need to have our eyes and hearts examined. Boaz was a "man of standing" not *because* of his earthly wealth, but because of the way he *used* that wealth for God's purposes. He was clearly a man who used his worldly means as completely diffusely as God uses His amazing grace upon us. He saw his earthly holdings as a heavenly opportunity, not just as an end already attained for himself. He used what God had given for the purpose of fulfilling God's commandments; what a wonderful example for our lives!

So let's do the same today, O Men of God. Let's live for this one commandment all day long: "Religion that God our Father accepts as pure and faultless is this: to look after orphans and widows in their distress…" (James 1:27a)

Be a Boaz today. "Look after" someone downtrodden.

March 9 – Ruth 4

Be entirely a man of his word

The world is full of many men who are happy to "give their word" until the keeping of their word proves personally difficult. If circumstances warrant a "slight change" in the "earlier understanding," they're totally sure "you'll understand, right?" They hope you see "the rub," the way the change of settings or of seasons must slightly change the original agreement made between you. Hopefully, you're a "good guy, right?" – a guy who doesn't expect integrity in other "good guys."

But we, as men of God, are called to keep our word wherever we give it, whether it's easy or difficult or, sometimes, hard work. Boaz promised to do his best to "redeem" Ruth (Ruth 3:13) and he didn't hesitate to do the challenging work involved in the process. Did you see him start to waver when he saw the work required in talking to the other redeemer at the gate? Did he quaver when he sat before the elders and let this other kinsman-redeemer stake his claim upon Ruth? Didn't he come armed with a shrewd plan-of-attack, an idea already in mind, so that he'd surely win her hand in the end? Wasn't Boaz "as good as his word," honest to a T, the perfect model of a manly uprightness? And doesn't it seem fitting, when reading through this passage, that Ruth's redeemer should be in the family line of **the** Redeemer, Jesus? Boaz was a man – *a man following God* – and it showed in his actual life and conduct toward all around him.

Today, let's focus our attentions on intentionally keeping our word with anyone to whom we've given it. Even if you're in a deal that's "gone bad," what does Jesus call you to do in that particular situation, regardless? "Simply let your 'yes' be 'yes,' and your 'no,' 'no,'; anything beyond this comes from the evil one," He tells us. (Matt. 5:37) We must be men who are above the earthly ways of getting out of keeping our word – we must simply keep it, no matter what. And if you think you're in a situation where you'll eventually have some trouble keeping it, don't give your word at all in the first place! Let's keep our word today, O Men of God. There are no halfways with Jesus.

March 10 – 1 Samuel 2:12-17

Don't "fudge" on trust and obedience

The places where we "fudge" upon the truth in our life are the places where we're allowing sin to enter in. We're like the wicked sons of Eli when we "treat with contempt" all the promises that are given directly to us by our God. If we know that God is really "for us," should we be carrying ourselves in the world like we have to fight our own battles? If we believe He really can provide for us, do we need to scrap and fight and clamor for every scrap of bread we "earn"? If we think our citizenship is really found in Heaven, do we need to be constantly embroiled with the things of this earth? Like my good friend, Randy Eims, is often heard to remind men: "You *will* live out the things you really believe in." We become the sons of Eli when we "fudge" upon the commandments and the carrying out of our calling in this world. We waste our lives and efforts whenever we start thinking it's our own arm that carries the day – or our human destiny.

Apparently, the priestly class believed that God would provide what He desired for them whenever they thrust the fork into the pot. They trusted that His ancient promise of provision would always be met by the ordinary pulling up of boiled meat. However, the wicked sons of Eli only saw what they *weren't* getting when they plunged the fork into this offered meat. They preferred to fork a solid cut; "to take what they could get," not really caring what the Lord would choose to give them.

How much of our lives are wasted in attempting to preempt God's stated promises for us, to force God's hand upon the earth? How many men have lost the "straight and narrow" simply because they "fudged" on obedience, "fudged" on trusting the Lord implicitly? Today, may we think about our personal conduct and the way we often similarly "fudge" in our following of Jesus Christ. May we be wholehearted keepers of our word and of His truth by living out His Word's truth in every moment. May we trust and obey today. For there's actually no other way.

March 11 – 1 Samuel 3

Have a childlike listening heart today

The word of God is rarified whenever men of God refuse to listen for the sound of His voice. We shouldn't aspire to become more like Samuel unless we're willing to listen for the sound of the Lord's voice like a little boy. Young Samuel was one called upon by God because He knew that Samuel was the kind of boy who'd actually listen to Him. He knew that Samuel wouldn't purposely stop his ears, wouldn't stop at *anything*, until he'd answered the call of God for his life. When he went and spoke to Eli, it was with a childlike innocence; he really thought the voice was his mentor's voice And yet, when he found the voice indeed was the Lord's, he was likewise ready to respond with the same innocent expediency…

You and I would be inestimably farther along in our journey if we listened for the voice of God speaking to us, O Men. We'd be so much more certain, so much more filled with faith, if we'd actually have faith in His available, leading voice. If we laid awake in bed and listened for the voice and the leading of our Lord, we'd sleep with a sweet restful ease. If we'd drown out all the voices shouting at us all the time, filling our hearts with truth, we'd be absolutely clear-headed. Yet modernity has certainly won the mind of the modern Church, as evidenced by the skepticism of our outlook. After all, would you even believe it if the Lord should audibly call your name in the middle of the night, one of these next nights? Would you sit up in your bed and be prepared to answer into the darkness: "Speak, for your servant is listening," like Samuel? Do you really believe that God might speak your name, might have a plan for you, might actually tell you all about it? More importantly: Do you really *want* that God might speak your name, might have a plan for you, might tell you all about it?

The Lord our God will be most manifest to the men who constantly listen for Him like boys, openhearted and true. May we sit and listen and expect that He'll actually lead us by His voice today, or by His Word and His Holy Spirit. Will you sit and listen today, O Man? Don't ever forget: Samuel's God is your God.

March 12 – 1 Samuel 4:1-3

Glorying in your defeats

A modern man becomes a man of God by trusting in his God, by believing He's in complete control of everything. But when we realize we're in the valley of a terrible personal slaughtering, where do we find our thoughts are going to, first? Do we, like these ancient elders, seek to understand the reason God has placed us in defeat, in destruction, in despondency? Do we wonder what the Lord is trying to accomplish when our "best laid schemes" come to absolutely nothing? If we really believe that God is who He says He is, we should realize that absolutely everything is His. If we practice faith that goes beyond theoretical ruminations, we'll know "the earth is the Lord's, and everything in it." A violent victory or a dastardly defeat must call the men of God's making into a deep-seated discernment in His presence. "What is God trying to teach me with _____?" should be the everyday question if we want to seek His will for us. If we hope to be the sort of storied men who live our lives by His Spirit, we must trust His Spirit everyday. We can't expect that all His plans will mean an earthly "blessing" of human comfort when our lives are meant to be eternal.

You'll see the true hope of a man's hearts whenever he's brutally defeated; when "life" seems to destroy everything in his life. If you hear his thoughts running only to the practical – how to quickly "bounce back" – that man's God is just Sunday-theoretical. But if you see him sitting perfectly still and peacefully, asking the Lord for His lesson, that man's God is actually God. That man understands the blessings best forged by defeat; that man understands the true heart of Jesus.

We serve a God who came to us in chosen weakness, who actually *won through defeat*; why do we expect anything less, O Men? May we learn to crave the Lord's divine defeats instead of the world's "victories"; may we seek a deeper discernment thereby. Let's be the ones who ever seek the face of Jesus, knowing that that face was bruised and broken for our sake's. Even if you're currently defeated, rejoice, O Man! You're following a King who triumphed by "defeat."

March 13 – 1 Samuel 7:2-13

Truly repent today

When a man begins to "mourn" for the presence of the Lord, he's starting to express the right kind of daily repentance. When men have actually turned and "sought after the Lord," the Lord has turned around and richly blessed their seeking after Him. When we clearly see the error of our ways, the first and most important step involved in the process is that step turning back to Him. But woe to us if we want to turn around *without* an "all your hearts" single-minded repentance in our hearts! We must notice here how Samuel calls the Israelites' repentance incomplete until they "rid themselves of the foreign gods." They haven't returned to right relationship with their God until they start to serve the Lord their God and "him only." Yes, He will "deliver you out of the hands of the Philistines," Samuel tells the people, but only if you're truly turning back to Him. God will know the difference between a real whole-hearted repentance and the slyly-stowing-away-of-our-gods for a rainy day.

In Chapter 4, the Israelites were defeated not just once, but also a second time, by the Philistines in fierce pitched battles. They then lost the Ark of the Covenant to those hated long-time enemies; the Lord's presence departed from their broken land. When we don't give the Lord the "ark of our heart" in compete and total surrender, we'll start to feel similarly, O Men. When we seek to follow Him with disconnection between our hearts and minds, we'll be soundly defeated by the enemy. When we don't love our "God with all [our] heart and with all [our] soul and with all [our] mind," we're clearly not following Him. When we give our hearts to Baals and Ashtoreths within our present day, our repentances are insincere and incomplete. If you want to draft your heart and soul and mind into the Lord's battles today, you must repent, O Man of God! Repent for each and every single "little" sin you can actually think of, things both "done and left undone." Ask the Lord to arm you for the day ahead with a heart made fresh and clean for His purposes, totally remade by and through Him. Then watch the way "the Lord thunder[s] with loud thunder against" the schemes of the evil one when they're launched against you. O Man, see His mighty hand for you – His truly repentant remade son – and be in awe of your Lord today. He's fighting on your behalf right now. You are His precious son.

March 14 – 1 Samuel 8:1-3

The Way is the only way

When Jesus was only hours from his death upon the cross, He took the time to remind His friends of this one all-important truth: "You did not choose me, but I chose you and appointed you to go and bear fruit – fruit that will last." (John 15:16a) This choosing and appointment are a part of that ever-echoing call of Jesus to His men throughout human history: "follow me." We ourselves did not choose Jesus; He clearly chose us; we've got an appointment just like the disciples once did. Like Samuel's sons, the Father looked upon our lives and thought us fit bearers of His name and His appointment. Like Samuel's sons, we've received an example and are called to walk only in His clear, given ways for us. Jesus wasn't joking or speaking with hyperbole when He said to His twelve friends: "I am the way and the truth and the life." In fact, early believers went so far as letting themselves be known by the name "followers of this Way." (Acts 22:4)

When we "walk in his ways" alongside of "the Way," there's only one way to actually live: The Way of Jesus. We can't presume to "turn aside" like Samuel's sons did and then find ourselves walking on the right path through our lives. When we "turn aside" for anything other than the audible call of Jesus, we're off the Way of Jesus, plain and simple. He didn't term the road "narrow" because it boasted a multiplicity of easy drive-off exits for our personal convenience. He didn't call the gate "small" because it's the easiest sort of door to jump through at any point in our earthly lives. If we want to follow God's plan for us, we must follow after Jesus, following He who is the Way of life. Jesus Himself is both the means and the end; the Alpha and the Omega; the call and destination of our human lives...

Today, let's not "turn aside" from our "walk[ing] in his ways" in *any* way; let's look to Him and to His Way only. Look to the One who calls you forth unto Himself, drawing you on by His grace, personally making "your paths straight." May we walk on, in and with the Way. Let's use Him as our only roadmap for our lives.

March 15 – 1 Samuel 8:4-22

How do we make other things king?

Many "men of God" gathered together and came to Jesus Christ at the foot of his rugged cross. They said to him, "Your commands are hard and we are not sure if we will be able to keep your challenging way. Now let us have some of the comforts and the things of this world, such as all the other nations have."

But when they said, "Give us the comforts and the things of this world," this broke the very heart of Jesus. So he prayed to the Father. And the Father said: "Listen to all that these men are saying to you; it is not just You they have rejected, but they have rejected Us entirely. As the Israelites did from the day I brought them out of Egypt until the day You were born, so these men are doing now. Now let them have their way; but warn them solemnly about the effects of the things of this world."

Jesus said, "This is what the comforts and the things of the world will do to you: they will possess your sons and make them serve the Prince of this world; they will run in front of his chariots. Some he will assign to destruction, others to an easy comfort, and still others to be weapons in his arsenal. He will take your daughters to become everything I didn't intend them to be when I lovingly created them. He will give you the best of his fields and vineyards and groves to lull you into his false sense of security. He will help you hold back a tenth from your giving unto Me, out of human practicality. Your money and houses and cars and sense of normalcy will be tools for his own use. When that day comes, you won't cry for help; you will not know you're lost; then I will weep for you."

But the "men of God" refused to listen to Jesus. "No!" they said. "We want the comforts and the things of this world. Then we will be like all the other people, with the Prince of this world to lead us, and to fight our battles."

Today, may we examine the ways our double-hearted hearts actually betray the heart of our Savior, Jesus Christ. Then may we repent of any of that spirit within us. And then go forth with, and for, Him today.

LIVE LIKE MEN

March 16 – 1 Samuel 9:15-27

Acting only from humility today

Despite what he'd eventually become, Saul started out upon his journey to the kingship with the right sort of spirit. He didn't believe that Samuel could possibly be speaking about him when Samuel said he was "the desire of Israel." His first inclination was actually humility, asking "am I not a Benjamite, from the smallest tribe of Israel[?]" And, furthermore: "is not my clan the least of all the clans of the tribe of Benjamin?" Instead of hearing the words of Samuel and immediately going to a place of personal pride, Saul starts with self-abnegation. Instead of hearing these words that pointed to a bright and glowing future for him, Saul points back to his humble roots. Where he might not have been in the wrong to dwell upon his newfound power and prestige, he refers to his own weakness. Saul presents an example of an attitude *not* common to our modern sort of manhood, one of manly modesty...

The reason we most often try to live from pride is the subconscious sense that we don't actually have what it takes for this life. Our greatest motivations for becoming a braggart are the quiet insecurities that we hide within ourselves, most of the time. When we seek to be self-serving by our speaking only about ourselves, it's generally because we're so unsure of ourselves. When we tear another man down for acting in a way that's "so bigheaded," it's usually because we wish we were the big deal!

Despite where you've been or what you might eventually become, you must arm yourself with thoroughgoing modesty in all you do. You must be the kind of man who's always surprised when he's actually noticed, not the one surprised when he's *not*. If you seek to live a life that's called "successful" and yet coupled with your Savior, be prepared to give up your pride. For "God is opposed to the proud, but gives grace to the humble"; He's actively against any form of our modern manly pride. He actually won't be on your team whenever you're standing on your own sidelines, cheering for yourself. But He will give grace when you're living your life humbly, holding up your arms in His final assured victory. Today, let's be truly humble, O Men. I promise you, the world will notice that.

March 17 – 1 Samuel 10:5-11

Having ears only for the Holy Spirit

You'd be so utterly amazed by God's power if you really, truly believed that His power is dwelling within you. If you woke up every morning with the knowledge that His Spirit is upon you, you simply wouldn't be yourself anymore. You'd start to be the man you want to be, the man *He* wants you to be, if you lived from His Holy Spirit everyday. If the "Spirit of the Lord [can] come upon you *in power*," you will actually be a man of His living-breathing power today. If even Saul can come across the path of prophets and become a "different person," you can be changed by the Spirit too. You can "do whatever your hands finds to do" when you're walking with His Holy Spirit living within your chest. You can bond together with a band of brothers who are similarly seeking after their God and you can change others' lives. You can be the ones who are "coming down from the high place" aglow, living lives filled up with His manifest Presence. You can be the one of whom the question's asked: "What is this that has happened to the son of _____?" You can be the man of God you hope to be when you're placing your every hope for your life in your God Himself.

There are very few men who live from the power that's offered to them by the Holy Spirit who lives within them. There are very many men who "have faith," who are trying to "follow God," who are trying to "live life in the right way." But if you want to "live right," try listening to the patient guiding voice that's speaking to you from within you. If you want to "follow God," He's giving you directions *all the time, everyday, right now, every minute*. If you want to "have faith," have faith in the presence of your God, the Holy Spirit, who's dwelling in you. Stop giving intellectual assent and thinking your intellectual assent is the meaning of Christ's "[life] to the full." Stop thinking that your decent understanding of the scriptures is the only means of following Jesus. If we want to be the men who change the world, we must be changed everyday by our listening to His Holy Spirit. We mustn't leave today until we've sat and listened quietly for His personal leading for us; you have to wait a little. Let today be the day you live a life of power that's lived by His Spirit: listening, trusting, obeying. If it worked for Saul, it can certainly work for you. But will you actually do it, O Man?

LIVE LIKE MEN

March 18 – 1 Samuel 10:23-26

Run risks for God; be "valiant"

Not a single man who's reading from this page wouldn't want to be known by the naming of a "valiant man," would he? There's no accountant or mechanic or attorney or doctor or teacher who wouldn't want that title attached to his name. There's hardly a man throughout all history who wouldn't want to be known by that wonderful manly adjective: "valiant." We'd be lying to ourselves if we said we didn't want a little risk in our modern-day lives…

And yet I'm *not* talking about being the "best climber," the "fastest downhill biker" or the "first in the Apple Store line." For if we must seek our adventure only in the rise of our adrenaline, we've lost all understanding of real, true valor. The man of God who lives his life most valiantly is the one who allows his human heart to be most "touched" by his God. He doesn't depend on anything – other than his God Himself – for the risks that God is asking him to run each day. He doesn't chart his life for comfort or for cravings; he's valiant by the way he follows after the Christ, Jesus. He doesn't live his life with valor for the sake of the valor itself; he lives his life for the sake of his Savior only…

If you're being totally honest with yourself, would you call yourself a modern-day "valiant man," O Man of God? Are you running great risks for God through obedience to His call or is your life more of a hum-drum daily nature? Do you believe there's actually a possibility of your being called a valiant man simply by obeying God everyday? Do you see the living of your Christ-calling as an adventure or as the antithesis of an adventurous sort of life? Do you get your "kicks" from things outside yourself or by the simple daily following of Jesus Christ?

What would your friends say about you, in these questions?

More importantly, what would your wife say?

My friend, we can be the modern "valiant men" of God *only* when our hearts are open to be "touched" by Jesus Himself. Is your heart open to Him today? Will you allow it to be "touched"? Will you live with such a valiant heart today that people can't possibly miss the presence of Jesus in you? That is the life of a modern man of valor. Let's start this day out with that sort of heart.

March 19 – 1 Samuel 12:1-5

Have a "Here I stand" mentality

Many years from now, you may have a day when you get the chance to speak some words to an assembled crowd like this one. You might have the opportunity, if you're very, very fortunate, to say where it is you personally "stand" in the Lord. You may stand before those people who are dearest to your heart and speak the truth of where you've long stood in Him. You'll stand before the fleeting beats of Time and say to the people around you where you hope they'll stand for themselves…

Can you speak like that today, O Man? Do you already know what you'll say?

Samuel was a chosen man of God because of moments like this particular one and its particular message: "Here I stand." He could rise before the people with a totally clear conscience and know full well that he'd followed his Lord obediently. He could stand before his Lord and expect to hear the same sort of answer he then received from the people standing before him: "You have not cheated or oppressed us … You have not taken anything from anyone's hand," they affirm. Samuel was the same sort of man before his people as he was within the sight of his God, all throughout his life. He was a man who knew his precise purpose and purposefully followed after it every single day of his earthly existence.

Right now, God is giving you a place where He's calling you to plant a flag for His coming Kingdom's sake. He's giving you distant horizons of new thoughts, spurs to big sorts of action, huge dreams to be dreaming for His purposes. Can you wait and contemplate the current thought or direction that He's asking you to take a stand upon, right now? Perhaps it's one single verse He's bringing to your mind time and again; an idea "you just can't seem to get rid of." Maybe it's a certain person in your family or your office who He's drawing you toward, someone who needs His attention. Maybe there's a timeliness of something that keeps finding itself in the forefront of your day-by-day thinking…

Whatever that "thing" might be, today is the day during which you must say "Here I stand" and then act upon it. If He wants you to be memorizing scripture for the good of your heart, do that with all your heart today. If He wants you to speak life into the life of someone near and dear to you, do it for His sake immediately. We must take hold of all those things to which our God is currently calling us and, in that way, *actually live for Him*. We must be like Samuel when he stood and said so strongly "Here I stand" and then

LIVE LIKE MEN

we ourselves must actually stand, O Men! Let's attack those places today. Let's let "Here I stand" become our stand.

March 20 – 1 Samuel 12:6-25

Don't let your sin define you

The most dangerous moment in the course of a man's life is the moment directly *after* he's succumbed to personal sin. When he's done with yielding to his momentary temptation, he's standing in the very worst place he can possibly be standing. He's in a place more fraught with deathly danger than the place of his actual temptation; the next moment's the key one. For it's where he turns in the *post*-sin moment that determines who he'll be the next time he's personally tempted. It's in those humble moments that a man's truest identity is forged – whether he's for Jesus or against Jesus. It's in that instant that he preaches to himself whether Jesus is actually Lord or whether He's actually not. Will he be a man defined by the sin that's found within him or a man "set free indeed" as the Lord said he is? Will he be a man with "no condemnation" or a man who condemns himself as hopelessly heedless?

"Do not be afraid," Samuel said to the people, "you have done all this evil": No question about the matter. "Yet do not turn away from the Lord," he goes on, "but serve the Lord with all your heart": You must move beyond it. It's in the moments of our sinful sulking that we most often shape the course of our future identity in Christ, O Men. When we fall into the sense that our sin is the greatest power that shapes us, Satan wins a great victory over us every time. If we let the sin that hinders how we live become a name for ourselves, we're horribly mistaken about our identity. We must remember that the One who came to save us is the One who came to save us – *from sin and self*. We must know the heart of He who says He's giving us a "new name" which will be known only to us and Him. We mustn't let our sin become an earthly badge or warrant for futures filled up with more and more sin. "We must throw off everything that hinders," including the sin that knocks us off the path of life in Jesus Christ…

Do you have a single sin that's become a pet or a problem for you; a nuisance or a false name for yourself, O Man? Have you let your life be ruled by the naming given to it by your sin or by the naming of your Savior? Will you choose to walk away from sin instead of letting sin become a new identity for your life? Can you commit to try to serve "with all your heart" despite the niggling voice of sin fighting against you, within you? Then, today, let our hope be found only in Jesus! And also our new identity!

March 21 – 1 Samuel 13:5-7

We can't go "back"

Satan would be fearful of our power if men of God would bind themselves together, fully alive and fully committed. If we went out everyday within the power of Jesus' name and calling, Satan would start shaking in his devilish boots. Yet he laughs when he instead can watch the hearts of "men of God" becoming terrified at the prospects of (fill in the blank). He's elated when a single armed foe, or a certain "rough patch," proves too much for our feeble brand of faith. He absolutely dances a dance of delight when we play funeral dirges simply because "life isn't going my way today." There's nothing fonder to the heart of Satan than our own personal recrossings of our own personal River Jordans…

The Israelites had seen the hand of God as He was fighting all their battles for the entirety of their people's long history. They'd seen the way He'd pulled off supernatural defeats against their enemies that were absolutely silly in their God-obviousness. They'd heard His audible voice from the clouds, seen His fury in the holy fire, watched His power in the Red Sea's and Jordan's crossings. Yet, here they are again, frightened in the oncoming face of a foe and crossing back to the other side! Here they are again, seeing an earthly army coming out to fight them and turning tail and running away!

There can be nothing weaker in the lives of God's men than any form of retreating back to "the other side." We can't turn tail and return to the way "it was before" if we've actually experienced His power in the first place! If we want to live within His daily presence and become a presence for His sake, we can't ever retreat, O Men. We've crossed the River Jordan once and for all – *we're absolutely His now* – it's time to stand and fight whenever He asks.

If you're feeling "disconnected" from the heart of God within you, today's the day to reconnect your heart with His. If you've come "under attack" and are feeling like the battle's "just not worth it," pick up your Sword and regain courage, O Man. If you feel as if you're down within a "valley" of your faith, climb back up to the peak of and regain perspective on Him. Your faith is the only thing in your life worth always having, your true identity: Don't give it up at any cost! You can't recross the Jordan if you've ever truly crossed it for the first time: Hold your ground today, O Man! Be a man and fight for the fervor of your faith. That is what Satan truly fears.

March 22 – 1 Samuel 13:16-22

Use your weapons and sharpen others' weapons too

A man will be most easily disarmed by the soothing voice of worldly things if he chooses to live his life unarmed. He'll be as ineffective in the fighting of today's battles as Israel was when they had no swords at all. He'll find himself naked on the battlefield; a man with no munitions; frankly, not a man at all. He'll watch the enemy riding roughshod over the "faith" he thought he "had" last Sunday morning in the comfortable pews. He'll be amazed to see how quickly his "good morals" are destroyed by "the thief" who comes to "steal, kill and destroy." He'll be surprised how his "good guy status" can evaporate under real terrifying battle-day pressures. He'll be mortified to realize the strength of his arm is really *no* strength; his spiritual arms, flaccid and weak. He'll be tempted to go "down to the Philistines" and away from his God if it seems to help his personal cause under pressure…

We can only fight the fight of God when using the weapons He's given to us, His mighty munitions for His spiritual battles. We can't dispense with arming and rearming and *re*arming ourselves with the full Armor of our God at any point in our lives (Ephesians 6:10-17). Yet, too, we must look around the Church and realize its dreadful need for some capable "blacksmiths." There are very few men so sharp with the Holy Spirit of God that they're actually sharpening others' lives in the midst of battle. And if there's not enough swords to go around, it's the fault of us men who are not sharpening anyone at all. We've been told that "as iron sharpens iron, so one man sharpens another"; don't we actually believe those words? And if we aren't sharp ourselves, or seeking out those already sharp, where will be stand on the actual day of battle?

Do you have a brother in your life who's the blacksmith for your heart, a trusted true fellow warrior in the fight? Do you have a friend whose very voice is a whetstone to your will and a reminder of the call of God upon your own life? Conversely, will you choose today to be a blacksmith for another brother, encouraging his heart in the Lord Jesus? Will you stand together when you're called to fight the fight, knowing that you're most properly prepared when you're standing together? Today, take hold of your weapons, O Man. And keep them sharp for the fight of your life ahead.

LIVE LIKE MEN

March 23 – 1 Samuel 14:1-14

Apprentice a warrior

A role that's nearly forgotten in our harried modern world is that role which used to be ubiquitous in all men's lives. In the "old days," hardly a man could ever learn *any* profession without first being an "apprentice" to another man. One would start out at the bottom of the ladder and yet he knew he was headed for much brighter future things. However, firstly, it was necessary that he learn the ropes of his work unto perfection; be observed; then set out on his own course. Once finished, he was confident of skills he'd learned "on the job," not from some dead textbook or in "theory." He'd always hearken back to the sound of his master's patient voice, showing him the proper way of doing everything…

Likewise, an "armor-bearer" was an apprentice of the battle; he lived or died depending upon his master's strength and will. He'd be as meek or mighty as the master whom he chose to serve; his toughness would reflect his teacher's battle-toughness. If his mentor happened to be as daring as Prince Jonathan was, he'd learn to fight with the power of many trained men. He'd never question whether odds were in his favor, he'd know that the battle was the Lord's and then he'd fight with courage…

First off, do you readily submit yourself to God's mastery with the spirit of this armor-bearer, O Man of God? Do you hear His plans and say, "Do all that you have in mind; I am with you heart and soul," like Jonathan's apprentice? Do you actually believe that the circumstances of your current life mean nothing against His bold battle-plans for your life? Will you go against the way the world always tells you to feel: that you're weak unless you're seen as being "strong"?

Secondly, if we truly follow Jesus, we must follow the example of the spiritual apprenticeships He gives us. If you aren't actively and currently acquainting a younger man with the battles of the Lord, *why in the world not?* Why claim to follow Jesus' way (WWJD?) if you aren't actually trying to "make disciples," as He asked you to do? How can generation follow after generation if one generation refuses to generate the teaching of the next? Today, make a point of contemplating how your armor-bearing for the Lord is teaching you to follow Him more intimately. Then seek after His wisdom, through prayer, for the armor-bearer He'd like you to start training up for the battles ahead. And then begin to do it, O Man. Just like this man said, "heart and soul."

March 24 – 1 Samuel 14:52

There is a battle; wake up!

The dearth of mighty men within the modern Church reflects upon our view of how the "war" actually is. If we knew there was a "bitter war" ongoing between the devil and our Lord, we would certainly act like men should. We wouldn't sit back and reflect upon the hardness of the pew or the Monday morning board meeting we're dreading. We wouldn't forget the Sunday sermon by the time of Sunday dinner or critique it as being "not the pastor's best." We wouldn't live lives overconcerned about our mortgage or our jobs or our bank accounts; about any worldly thing at all. We wouldn't see our best strengths utilized *only* when it's for the purpose of our own "getting ahead" in this world. No, if we truly saw how bitterly the battle rages for the heart of our fellow man, we'd be absolutely enraged. If we were aware of how pernicious is the Prince of Darkness' plan of attack, we'd go on the counterattack everyday. If we realized Jesus' word is actually Life for us in this battle of our lives, we'd really start to listen to it. We'd become His "mighty" men, His "brave" men, if we actually started believing that we're actually fighting in a battle. If we saw ourselves as warriors – *at all* – we would cease to seek our refuge in civilian status. If we felt the bullets flying, saw the swinging of the sword, would we stand our ground or would we run?

If your faith in Jesus is anything less than the entirety of your life, get down on your knees today and repent, O Man. For Jesus said that "any of you who does not *give up everything he has* cannot be my disciple." (Luke 14:33) And "anyone who does not *carry his cross* and *follow me* cannot be my disciple" either, He said. (Luke 14:27) There will always be issues with the level of your trust if your trust does not reflect a real totality. You can't be found as "fit for service in the kingdom of God" if you put your "hand to the plow and [look] back." (Luke 9:62)

How's your view of the battle today, O Man? Are you "all in" on what Jesus is doing? May we be the kind of men who are fully aware that this war is terribly bitter and go out and fight it anyway!

March 25 – 1 Samuel 16:1-7

Be the conqueror of your Inner Life

A man who wants to come to grips with his calling as God's warrior must fight the first fight *first* in his life. There's no known earthly battlefield that'll ever present the dangers that are present on the battlefield of his heart. A man who won't first fight the warring spirits of his lusts, of his thoughts, of his selfish ambitions can't win the war. We can't follow after Jesus if we won't attempt to tame the Inner Life found within ourselves. The Inner Life of another will always be inscrutable if we won't begin to know the topography of our own manly heart. If we can't rein in the wild rompings of our daily thoughts, how will we ever help another to do the same? If we want to be of any use to our brothers, to our God, to ourselves, we must fight the fight of our own hearts. We should read the Lord's qualifications, the things "he does *not* look at," and then go to war within, O Men.

Even Samuel was a prey to the world's ways of looking at a man; he liked Eliab's great physical stature best. He seemed to forget that Saul's self-consumption was probably tied to his worldly vainglorious displays of manhood. Samuel fell into the patterns of this world; he "considers his appearance [and] his height" as if foremost. But God "does not look at the things man looks at"; we're reminded that God Himself only "looks at the heart." (Which, by the way, is a rave review for David; but what does it say to you about your own heart, O Man?) Are you comfortable with the notion that the God of the universe judges you by the content of your heart today? Do you think your heart a fit dwelling place for the Spirit of the Lord: well-swept, well-kept, clean and pure? Are you daily fighting "the good fight of the faith" within the confines of your own Inner Life, my friend? Or are we letting Satan have his way with our minds by allowing him unbridled free-rein in that space? Are we surrendering everything about ourselves by allowing him a place in our minds at all?

One sure way to figure out the quality of the battle you're currently fighting for your heart is this one simple test: "out of the overflow of his heart his mouth speaks," Jesus said; what's pouring forth from you, O Man of God? Today, let's focus on our minds and our hearts. By actually focusing our minds and hearts.

March 26 – 1 Samuel 17:1-32

Hear Satan's taunts and be steeled

Now Satan gathered all his forces for a war and assembled at the door of your modern-day Church. He pitched his camp directly outside its doors, between its body of believers and the world outside. Your Church and its body were assembled and camped in the sanctuary, each and every Sunday of the year. Your pastor tried to draw up battle lines, each and every Sunday, to meet the devil's army. Satan's army occupied one hill and your Church another, with a valley stretched between them.

The world's champion, Satan, came out of their camp; he was over nine feet tall. He had a bronze helmet on his head and wore a coat of scale armor of bronze weighing five thousand shekels. On his legs he wore bronze greaves, and a bronze javelin was slung on his back. His spear shaft was like a weaver's rod, and its iron point weighed six hundred shekels. His shield bearer went ahead of him.

Satan stood and shouted to the ranks of your Church, "Why do you come and line up for battle? Am I not the ruler of this world, and are you not the servants of Jesus Christ? Choose a man, or some men, and have them come down to me. If they are able to fight me in the name of Jesus and cause me to 'flee,' we'll become your subjects. But if I overcome their supposed faith in Jesus, you will become my servants and serve me." Then Satan said, "This day I defy the ranks of Jesus, the ranks of His Body! Give me a man – a few men together – bring them out, let us fight each other..."

It was Goliath's own words that would prove his final undoing; he asked for "a man" and he certainly found one in David! May our spirit be like David's spirit today: "Let no one lose heart ... your servant will go and fight him." If we want to be the living Body of Christ to this world, we can't ignore the taunts of Satan anymore, O Men. But we must go forth fighting only in the strength of Jesus Christ and fighting with His weapons alone. Do not let Satan win the day today. Obey the Lord Jesus and fight.

March 27 – 1 Samuel 17:33-54

Yesterday's faith, today's fight

The dividends of faith can best be measured by their ever-growing strength; great faith begets greater faith. When we look upon our past and to the moments we've been faithful, we can actually see how He was faithful unto us. When we see just how our faith met with His faithfulness in the past, we're re-renewed in the strength of our present faith. Your faith in Jesus today is stronger only if you've trusted Him, time and again, and actually *paid attention* to what He then did. You can only fight today's Goliath-fights if you've been fighting bears and lions in your yesterdays, O Man. You can only grow to real godly manhood if your faith finds its courage in the Lord Jesus Himself.

It can be a boyish voice that yells aloud the words, "You come against me with sword and spear and javelin…" But it can't be a boyish sort of *faith* that shouts across the battlefield, "I come against you in the name of the Lord Almighty." It was within the proving grounds of trusting in the Lord's strength that David became a man after God's own heart. He'd seen his own arm armed with strength by the strength of the Lord too many times to doubt Him ever again. Can you look back at your life and point to ways in which the Lord has given you strength for the fights within your life? Can you speak to deadly battles with "the lions and bears" in your past days that prepared you for today's Goliaths? Are you itching in your spirit for a battle of the Spirit that befits the growth of your faith in Jesus Christ? Do you long to walk across the battlefield with only sling and stones, with nothing else but your God's strength behind you?

David and Goliath's epic battle is a perennial favorite of the "flannelgraph crowd" sitting on comfy carpet squares. But how long's it been since you thought about this battle in the context of your daily spiritual life, O Man? Where would you rather be: Walking out to fight the giant, or, like Saul, sitting back in the comfort of his kingly tent? Do you want to be the one who's known for slaying spiritual giants or yourself be slain in your lack of a godly spirit? For me, I'd actually rather be dead than off the battlefield, lounging in the "comforts" of normalcy, of "modern manhood." But that's just me, O Men of God! Now how about *you*?

March 28 – 1 Samuel 18:1-4

Take friendship(s) to next level

Our ideas of manly friendship don't really begin to capture what was happening in the relationship between David and Jonathan. Our hanging out with our buddies over football, brauts and beer doesn't really get to the core of what they seemed to be experiencing. Would you characterize any relationship you currently have in your life with the words and the meaning behind, "became one in spirit"? Do you truly think you model each and every day the kind of friendship that would "love him as himself"? Do you have any relationships for which the true foundation is the only true foundation: Jesus Christ Himself? Are there brothers in your life with whom you don't have a single common interest except growing together toward the Lord? If you couldn't play a sport, watch a game, gamble over poker, what would you do with your best male friends? Would you be content to let the Holy Spirit do what He wants with your man-to-man friendships?

The kind of love we see between David and Jonathan was the kind of love we'll need if we want to follow Jesus Christ. It's going to involve a friendship "covenant"; setting up a relationship founded on *nothing else* but Jesus' new covenant. It involves a nakedness of spirit, a heart-level kind of disrobing that will leave you with no masculine pretense at all. It includes the giving over of weapons, the *not* hiding behind our masculine defenses of speech and subterfuge…

Will you be the one who takes the step – *or the many steps* – that are needed for the deepening of your male relationships? Notice how it's Jonathan who made the first move for the covenant *and* the clothing *and* the weapons in this scenario. Be reminded that it's Jonathan who wore the signet ring of the king; who was himself set to be the next on the throne. It's a princely robe and tunic that were thrown around the shoulders of this humble shepherd boy, David. It's a prince's sword and bow; it's a royal golden belt that now girded the loins of our young hero, David. Will you, similarly, be the one who calls his other brothers to a greater depth in relationship founded only in Jesus? Will you humble yourself and be the one who "speaks his mind," who calls godly men to a godliness of depth? May this quest start today, O Man. Go out and find your own David.

LIVE LIKE MEN

March 29 – 1 Samuel 18:5

Redefine success and live it

If David were a shepherd in our day and age, he probably never would've left the cozy confines of Bethlehem. If he sought our form of modern man-achieved success, he'd probably have stayed beside his father watching the flocks grow larger and larger. He'd have watched his stock within the family business slowly rising as the shearing returns grew each and every year. He'd outstrip his brothers' understanding of the proper grazing grounds and shoot right to the top of the family's corporate ladder. Why in the world would he ever depart from Bethlehem, home of comfort and security, for the uncertainty of battle? Why would he become an indentured warrior in the service of the king, instead of saving up for his eventual retirement? What could've possessed a "ruddy" young man with his "handsome," "fine" features to go out into such hard brutal service?

The call of God upon his life, O Man of God.

That.

And nothing else.

If you didn't have to think of bills, homes, money or security, what would your daily life actually look like, O Man? If you didn't give a second thought to the world's view of "success," what would you do with every day of your life? If the Lord were calling you to do something totally different, would you be a man like David was, and simply go? Have you ever listened to the Lord's opinion of your earthly life; His view of what success is really supposed to be? Would you rather be in the heart of the Lord's war for the hearts of mankind or simply be "successful" in the world's eyes? Would you rather fight in the muck and mire of stormy spiritual battles or have a tidy rainy-day fund? Do you ever think of what "success" actually is; why the living of our manly lives is so defined by its pursuit? Have you ever tried to reconcile the aims of the modern American Dream with the commandments of Jesus Chist in their entirety? Do you want to live a memorable life in the service of your King or be an absolutely fleeting memory?

I hope you're chafed by these questions – perhaps even angered – and thinking to yourself: "Who does he think he is?" For I myself have wrestled long and hard with these sort of questions and the Lord showed up mightily in my ponderings. So take a walk today; take a long think; take a hard look at the way you personally define yourself. I guarantee it'll be worth it. He is worth the cost of any price.

March 30 – 1 Samuel 19:18-24

Thirty-minute session in the Spirit

The Holy Spirit's purposes often seem so unintelligible to us; the plan of God like a mystery we'll never solve. "You hear [the wind's] sound, but you cannot tell where it comes from or where it is going," Jesus Himself said of its movements. (John 3:8) The Holy Spirit seems to fill the slack sails in certain people and yet to leave some other ones nearly unmoved. There are a class of men possessed by a purpose that's so clear, while so many of us seem to wait around and wonder. We all rise up each morning – even today – and then must ascertain the way we're meant to live out this particular day. We all wonder how the major and mundane, the details large and small, will define our life before we rest tonight. We're lying if we say we never wonder if the "path that I'm on" is actually the "right path for me?" We all lay awake at night, many a night, and allow our mind to wonder about the worth of our human existence…

But may it *not* be so this day, O Men! Let's together take some bold action! For if the Holy Spirit was able to seize Saul, a man clearly *not* after God's heart, He can seize you right this very minute! If a man like Saul was laid out by the power of the Holy Spirit, there should be no stopping us in our pursuit of Him! If the Spirit can choose to invade a human heart, just imagine what's possible when you invite Him gladly into yours! If we'd seek to be the men we claim we want to be in Jesus, let's go after it now – right now!

To that end, give no less than thirty minutes to inviting the Holy Spirit's power into your life today, O Man. Sit in perfect silence and recognize that He's within you; ask only that He'd come and fill you more throughout the day. Close your mind to thoughts of business, of your life, of your worries, of absolutely everything else, except for Him. Pray that every single step you take would be completely led by His "still small voice" speaking to your heart and that you'd obey Him. Ask that His fire would absolutely consume you; that power like the mighty book of Acts would run right through your earthly life. And then be prepared for *something*: whatever it is the Lord desires to give you, *and only you*, for this day. Now will you seek that out, O Man? Will you give Him just these thirty minutes?

March 31 – 1 Samuel 20:35-42

Make a covenant today

The work of God is never at a stand-still in our lives; God is working upon our lives everyday. He doesn't cease to work upon His promises in lives obedient to Him: He is ever faithful unto us. He doesn't make a covenant with any man without the perfect foreknowledge of where that man's path might eventually roam. He didn't call you to Himself in vain; He doesn't mean to let your life become endangered or unfruitful…

In the same way, Jonathan, the ever-true brother of David's life, doesn't let his covenant go unheeded. He, in fact, affirms and then *re*affirms his promises to David almost to the point of personal exhaustion. He runs around in circles with his father and his quiver-carrier in order that David might survive his father's hateful wrath. He'd rather see the "house of David" prosper, to the detriment of his own, than betray his word to a friend.

Three days ago, the challenge of calling other brothers into deeper godly friendship was our stated action-step for the day. Hopefully, you prayed and considered that, then took direct action, actually did what you deemed to be necessary with those brothers…

Today, let's take time in our time with the Lord to consider how we might now go even *deeper* than that commitment. What sort of holy covenantal measure(s) might you take with that brother, or group of brothers, to go even further? What are your personal non-negotiables "in speech, in life, in love, in faith and in purity" when you look out toward your future? Can you write down all the things you'd like your lives to be, aims aimed for better through some honest accountability? Can you think of wholly holy attributes that you'll need some help to attain to, and then ask for that help from those brothers? Will you seek your brother's good, even if it means the end of your "house," because you promised him you'd do so? Will you fight your brother's fight upon the day when his arm is too weak, when he desperately needs your help in the midst of war? Will you be like Jonathan was to David, both affirming and reaffirming your covenant with your brothers constantly? Today, actually make a covenant with your brother(s). Call him/them up; decide upon its content. What will your lives be about *together*? Only you can decide that *together*.

April 1 – 1 Samuel 22:1,2

What sort of people surround you?

There will always be a tinge of defeat about our life's victory; Jesus' resurrection, after all, was preceded by death. If we relish only in the reality of His eternal hard-fought victory, we'll often forget the "defeat" that came directly before it. We must stand in awe, shaky-kneed, and watch the way our Savior went to that old rugged cross of his own volition. We must listen to the weeping and wailing of men and women who'd come to love Him, watching as He died so terribly. We must bear within our Christian certainty the *un*certainties of those long forty-eight hours as they hid out and wondered. We must feel the broken hearts of those who set out for the tomb and the shock and joy that followed directly afterward…

David was the anointed King of Israel and yet we find him running for his life from the *actual* king of Israel, Saul. Despite the wondrous victories of his recent past and those prophesied still to come, here he is, forced to turn tail and run. Yet, echoing in the knells of David's present defeat are the distant clear notes of God's future victories on his behalf. There was something humble and yet still very mighty about the timbre of David's heart that drew the distressed, the "discontented," to him. There was something of the Lamb of God – no matter what his current circumstances were – within this man living on the lam. Whether he was slaying his "tens of thousands" or was languishing in terrible defeat, only God's clear purposes mattered to David.

Whether you're hiding for your life or living life "on your own terms," what sort of people are most drawn to you? Do you keep the company of your defeats and victories separate; do you demarcate your daily relations in that sort of way, O Man? Jesus Christ came for the "sinners" and "the sick" and *they absolutely knew it*; they crowded to Him at every chance. There was something in His human heart that spoke of David, his forefather, every single day of his life.

We can be assured of how much "fruit" we're actually producing when we see how many "bad apples" are drawn to us. If you find you're deluged with distressed, indebted discontents, you can absolutely know you're on the right track, O Man. For that's the track our Savior walked all the way. Now let's continue walking down along it today…

April 2 – 1 Samuel 23:7-14

Who do you go to?

If David were a little more like me while he was living through these particular chapters, he'd probably already be dead. If it were my anxious heart with which he woke up every morning during these days, he'd have operated out of fear, not courage. If he'd had my waffling sort of modern mind, he'd probably have heard of Saul's approach and figured out how to cut his losses. If he'd had my quavering sort of faith in the Lord, he'd have internalized his fears, *not* externalized them through prayer. If it were still the age of constant mortal combat like David's day, would you and I even survive through the day, O Man? If battling meant the bloody battlefield instead of cushy corner offices, how would our hearts do, O Men of God? Is there enough of David's heart within your heart so that the day-to-days of life don't strike you dead everyday? Is there enough of David's spirit in your spirit so that you wake up every morning and can operate from faith, not fear? Is there enough of David's mind within your modern mindset to hear of Satan's latest "schemes" and not waver in the least? Is there enough of David's faith about your faith so that you "cast all your anxiety on him," never internalizing your personal worry?

The sort of God we serve will best be evidenced when our "back's against the wall," when we're out beyond the end of our tether. But if our faith depends upon the comforts of our day-to-day existence, that's some damning evidence against us, isn't it? If we're afraid of God-ordained daily divine adventures, be they "hard" or "easy", do we foreordain our faith's eventual fall? If we don't reach out for the ephod in the face of fiery trials, where will we reach our hand instead, O Men of God? Where would you go if you were penned within a gated, barred city: to the Lord or to those men living around yourself? "Where does [your] help come from" when you "lift up [your] eyes to the hills": from your "Maker" or from other men just like yourself? Will we rest today within the comfort of the Lord's abiding presence or in the presence of our earthly comforts? What is your first inclination when any sort of trial starts to arise against you: to go to Him or to go off and away?

There *will* be a trial in your day today – fiery or flickering – how will you react in that moment, O Man of God? For it's in these final moments before our daily embarkation that we have the chance to decide: Who will be our God today?

LIVE LIKE MEN

April 3 – 1 Samuel 24

Living out the command unto mercy

The beauty of our studying through the "life of God in the lives of men" is the way His truth is revealed in the midst of action. We aren't the servants of a sermonizing seldom-acting Savior; we seek the Master's actual movements in the midst of this world. We aren't called to spiritualistic subtleties or to the fleeting of a feeling, we're called to a real actual manly obedience. There's something mighty in the ministrations born from hearing His voice as it speaks softly right within our daily hearts. There's something calming about the call whenever we hear how it sounds, proceeding from His kind and loving lips. It's glorious to know the hands of victory are also those hands marked with scars; He gave Himself for the sake of these lives we're currently living.

In much the same way, David spared the life of sinful King Saul, knowing his own obedience to his God mattered more than anything. He wouldn't live out his days according to the "dictates of his own conscience"; he'd live within the path of the God who'd called him. He would live within the perfect mode prophesied to come for him; he'd personally prefigure his own perfect Offspring. He'd be a man of mighty and manly mercy, letting "the Lord judge between [him] and [Saul]."

You and I aren't called to live out lives that haven't been lived out before us; do we understand that simple fact about the Word? Do we understand that David's act of mercy was like Jesus' act of mercy, calling us to present acts of mercy? Do you know that God "causes his sun to rise on the evil *and* the good, and sends rain on the righteous *and* the unrighteous"? Do you know that mercy applied with proper care actually causes broken human hearts to look at Jesus Christ Himself?

Will you see yourself within the story of David and Saul today; will you hear the heart of Jesus' forgiving heart for others? Will you be a man so marked by His mercy that the movements of your life point to a steady, still Source of Life? Will you follow His commandment – "love your enemies and pray for those who persecute you" – *no matter what it costs you*? Will your life be patterned after David's life and after Jesus' life; will you show this teaching by direct actions? May it be so today, my brothers. May our feet fall in his merciful pre-trod footprints.

April 4 – 1 Samuel 27

Don't worry about "perceptions." Just do.

Oftentimes we act as if the shaping of men's perceptions is the same thing as actually winning their hearts for Jesus. We spend a lot of time and effort for the purpose of winning ourselves a good personal public perception, don't we? We seem to think that it matters what "they think of me" almost as much as what they think of our Lord and Savior, Jesus. We divorce our life from the works actually *required* from our life in Christ and make this strange self-marketing tantamount to obedience…

David was physically pursued by Saul to the point where he's now exiled in the dreaded "land of the Philistines." At that point, he might've either despaired of God's hand in his life or begun devising a plan for the perception-shaping of King Achish. He might've tried to spend "a year and four months" only in the sucking-up required to tame this terrible tyrant. He might've lived it up in luxury in Gath, going the easy route of perception-pushing instead of Godward obedience.

But, instead, David boldly asks for land and then begins upon his campaigns against the ancient enemies of Israel. In this place of exiled-living, he begins to serve his God where he actually is, not lolling his time away in wishful thinking. If he can't obey the Lord's commands as the king upon Israel's throne, he'll fight Joshua's unfought battles in the mean time. Even while he's on the run from Saul, David is thinking first and foremost of God's perfect will for his life. Even while he's in the wilderness of Philistia, he "fights the good fight" – the fight assigned specifically to him. Even if his life is currently "hard" or "uncertain," he'll do the only certain things he can do each and every day…

And how is Achish's "perception" of David's life? What did Achish think of David's presence? Regardless of his secret insubordination – *actually called for by his God* – David appears as a perfect "servant" to this man. Regardless of his current obedience to God that might've got him killed by Achish, he's seen "as an angel of God." (1 Sam. 29:9)

Today, may we set aside the shaping of perceptions to pursue our purpose in the doing of God's will in this world. May our guides for life today be Scripture and His Holy Spirit, not the whims and wills of the people living life around us. May we never be frightened of any human "perception"; God Himself can shape the perceptions of other people far beyond our understandings. O Men, just do His will today. O Men, simply trust our good God's goodness.

April 5 – 1 Samuel 28:3-20

Listen to His silence; don't cheat it

A man will be defined by how he listens to the silences of the Lord; the Lord's holy silence speaks rich volumes. Any time you pray or meditate upon His heavenly promises, the Lord *will* answer you – rest assured of that, O Man! Be assured that He's searching right now through your heart for the answers to some very important questions: "Does this man desire to see My will above all else in his life; has he counted the true cost of my discipleship? Will he persevere even if my chosen path for him should take him through the 'valley of the shadow of death'? Does he really want My whole plan for his life or a nice comfortable counterfeit existence in the present moment?" If you want to hear the Lord's voice, be the sort of man to whom He's able to speak *by always listening for His voice*. If you want to live the "life to the full" of which Jesus spoke, subjugate your human heart to the perfect will of God.

Saul was ready to abolish all the witchcraft in the land of Israel…until he felt he needed a witch's actual services. He was also ready to inquire of the Lord for the purposes of His perfect plan…until God wouldn't "answer" him. When you feel you're being thwarted by the silences of God, what is your next practical action-step, O Man of God? Do you hear the silence as an answer in itself, a call to wait for Him, or a reason to go another way? What sorts of "expelled" personal sins do you find you want to run toward when you start hearing silences from God? How comfortable is your heart with the waiting for His word that might last for long months, even years, of your life? How willing is your spirit to sit quietly and wait for the leading of His Holy Spirit's direction for your life? How able is your mind to rest easy in His chosen silence; to trust in His perfect plan for you?

We can't assume the word of God will come as free and easy as a text-messaged or emailed form of modern communication. We should have the kind of faith that's humbly moving forward with Him until we sense His silence asks us to stay where we are. Will you give your earnest prayers to the Lord and then wait for His actual stated responses to what you've asked of Him? Don't be put off by His weighty silence; that is actually an answer and a cause to draw closer to His heart. Let's wait upon the Lord today, O Men of God. Only His plan for us actually matters.

April 6 – 1 Samuel 30

Share the spoils of life; don't let money master you

Whether you're a brilliant entrepreneur or a normal nine-to-five workmen, *nothing that's yours is actually yours, O Man*. Whether you've invested brilliantly for quick returns or patiently socked it away for years, *nothing that's yours is actually yours, O Man*. Whether you've only got your daily bread today or you're already starting charitable trusts, *nothing that's yours is actually yours, O Man*. Whether you're living in a regular modest home or in a palatial kingly mansion, *nothing that's yours is actually yours, O Man*. Plain and simple, "No one can serve two masters. Either he will hate the one and love the other, or he will be devoted to the one and despise the other. You cannot serve both God and money." (Matt. 6:24)

If we're fighting in the spiritual battle of our lives, we must realize that nothing we have is actually ours, O Men of God. If we plan to gain the victory in this battle, we must fight "all-in"; like nothing else matters to us at all. If we won't use our earthly goods for good, we're letting Satan use them in our lives for his own brand of evil. If we start worshipping worthless purchased possessions, we're clearly not the foot-soldiers needed for this particular bloody fight. Right now, there are many brothers in your life who are actively fighting in the spiritual battles of our God. They are missionaries, pastors, youth pastors, "parachurch" leaders that the Lord has placed in your life's path. Yet if they're ill-equipped for battle – lacking even today's rations – what will be our excuse for ourselves, O Men? If we think that we're "too busy" to "get involved," will we not *at least* share a healthy share with these faithful brothers? Will we help them get the help that they need to raise the funds needed to keep fighting where they're called by the Lord? Will we see our earthly things as a way to serve the Lord, not as a distraction from our Savior and His plans for us?

If you and I started sharing like the Apostolic Church once shared, miracles would constantly happen right in our midst. If we started thinking everything we have actually belongs to our God, we'd realize the mastery money currently has over us. If we started giving it away, regardless of its tax-deductibility, we'd be blessed for our faithfulness to Jesus. If you want strength in the battle you're currently fighting, take some time today to help a fellow soldier in this spiritual war. Only slaves to money can't give it away. Let's get going on our giving.

April 7 – 2 Samuel 1:1-12

"Mourn with those who mourn"

If you'd call yourself a man who's striving to follow after Jesus, your heart must be reshaped by His life growing within you. You must bear the inner evidence of a heart that's continually coming closer to the very heart of Jesus Christ. There must be a single point of time when He took your "heart of stone" and personally replaced it with His loving "heart of flesh." There must be some striking similarities in the tenor of your daily spirit and His "new spirit in you." If you wouldn't personally mourn the losses of Jonathan and Saul, there's may still be some work to be done in your heart. The Lord is not about the blessing of those ones choosing not to mourn; He's looking kindly unto those who will. "It is better to go to a house of mourning than to go to a house of feasting," better to have Jesus' tender heart for the brokenhearted. You and I will gain the reshaped heart of Jesus very quickly when we weep and mourn with those presently weeping and mourning. We'll become men in His image when we bear a broken heart for those whose hearts are currently broken by this world.

Today, may we bear the soft-spoken, understanding, comforting presence of our Lord Himself, O Men of God. May we mourn the loss another person is feeling; mourn the sadnesses in this world; be His presence in the midst of pain. May our knowledge of His final victory create a softness in our spirits that's comforting to other people around us. May we have the eyes that look for hurt in others people's lives and then speak right to it with the love of Jesus.

If you know a person who's currently in a place of personal mourning, make the time for them today in your busy day. Don't wait to "feel" like mourning with them; mourn immediately as a testament to the heart of Jesus living within your heart. If we wait for our human hearts to set our course instead of Jesus' own heart, we'll *never* mourn for the "Sauls" of the world. David became a man of God because his heart was filled with tenderness for others and not only for his friends. "For if you love those who love you, what reward do you have? Do not even the tax collectors do the same?" (Matt. 5:46) Let's go beyond the comfort of our comfortableness to "mourn with those who mourn" today, O Men of God.

April 8 – 2 Samuel 5:17-25

Listen to His marching and go!

If you've never heard the "sound of marching in the tops of the balsam trees," it's time to open up your ears, O Man of God. If you want to fight the battle of Today, you must know the presence of the Lord going before you and trailing behind. You must realize that Jesus came for you, that He's "out in front of you," that He's with you *this very moment*. You must "move quickly," quickened by the drumbeats of His mighty warplan and the marching of His awesome army. You must never fear, knowing that the final victory is assured through the finished work of Jesus at Calvary. You must listen for His steady "sound of marching," ready to lend your own feet to His fearful heavenly phalanx. You must live like David did, going to his God alone when he drew up battle-plans for the fight of his life. You must see yourself as God sees you, as a warrior in His war, and then go after the day today....

> In the beauty of the lilies Christ was born across the sea,
>
> With a glory in His bosom that transfigures you and me:
>
> As He died to make men holy, let us die to make men free,
>
> While God is marching on.
>
> *Glory, glory, hallelujah!*
>
> *Glory, glory, hallelujah!*
>
> *Glory, glory, hallelujah!*
>
> *While God is marching on.*
>
> He is coming like the glory of the morning on the wave,
>
> He is wisdom to the mighty, He is succour to the brave,
>
> So the world shall be his footstool, and the soul of Time His slave,
>
> Our God is marching on.

Will you march with Him today, O Man? Will you "die (to yourself) to make men free"?

LIVE LIKE MEN

April 9 – 2 Samuel 6:12-19

Be filled with zeal and joy for the Lord today

Any man who won't dance "before the Lord with all his might" shouldn't be surprised by his stale, dead "Sunday faith." If you and I think we're too staid for ecstatic exclamations of our joy in Him, we're practically joyless already, O Men. If we think we're "too (whatever denomination you are)" for delighted dancing, we're damning the God-given joy of Jesus. If we don't see a correlation between our joy and faith, the world won't see Jesus in our lives at all. King David was a newly-minted king within a new capital city; this was certainly a time for power. Most of us would rise to the throne and think of how we could best capture all the hearts and minds we now were seeking to rule over. Many of us would strike a tone of terror in the hope of consolidating power for ourselves, in our rank and our position. We'd start to think of proper delegation of the ruling of our kingdom; how to shore up our borders against enemies etc.

But David was a man of God first, a king second, in the way he let the Lord rule over his earthly life. And if the Ark was bringing blessings to the house of Obed-Edom, David wanted the ark nearest of all to him. If God enjoys the public worship of His Name and wild crazed dancing, David would be crazier than anyone in His presence. If God would bless the journey of the Levites for only six steps, David would sacrifice a bull and calf to honor Him.

We mustn't assume that there are preset lines upon the pages of worship that define where we should color or not color. We can't expect to "worship God" *only* according to the tri-fold "Order of Worship" bulletins whilst sitting in Sunday pews, O Men. If we won't shout aloud the praises of our King without an ounce of shame today, who is actually our king today? If you've started thinking the worship of today's younger generations is "absurd," how do you define your version of worship? Do we think the silent meditations of our manly hearts are the only way to follow after Jesus, as modern men? Have you ever burst with zeal for the Lord like David did, here; have you ever *once* leapt with acclamation?

Today, may we take a joyful view upon the world around us, knowing how the Lord delights in our sheer delight in Him. Regardless of today's circumstances, bathe your mind in joyful worship of your risen King and worship with "all your might." "Be joyful always." That's a direct order!

April 10 – 2 Samuel 9

Elevate the status of the needy

If we can't see ourselves within David's interactions with Mephibosheth, do we actually understand the Gospel of Jesus? If we don't see our own withered crippled limbs dangling at Jesus' banqueting table, do we actually know our Savior? David's preferential treatment of this sickly son of Jonathan is the treatment we've ourselves received, O Men! David's deeding of ancestral land and livestock to a man who couldn't tend them is the same blessing we own! When we read of David's summoning of this scared disabled man to his table, we're actually reading our own story. When we see provision bordering on profligate waste, we read about the love of Jesus poured out upon our undeserving lives.

Today, may we be like King David, not only in helping others, but also in *exalting* their lives above our own lives. If we see a homeless beggar needing help, let's not buy him only lunch ; let's sit down and hear his story. If we have a friend who's going through a time of intense personal darkness, let's shine some real light upon his day. If you sense your wife is needing some encouragement, encourage her *deeply*, just as Jesus Himself would to for you.

When we undertake to elevate the status of people around us, we'll start to understand the love of Jesus Christ. When we view ourselves within the helpless state of Mephibosheth, we begin to know our true hearts before Him. If we'll exalt the lives of others in the service of our King, we're truly starting to serve that King in His own Way. If we'd live like John the Baptist, making our Lord "greater, [we] must become less," we must lift the lives of other people.

David was the man he was – a man after God's heart – because he sought to replicate the heart of God everyday. It's as if he'd actually heard the admonition of his perfect Progeny: "be perfect, as your heavenly Father is perfect." (Matt 5:48) Even though I'm sure he knew he'd never be perfect, David didn't use that knowledge as an excuse not to try for it. What he saw within God's perfect love for him became the pattern of his whole life; now will it be *yours* today? Today is actually your only chance to find out. Let's be the men who go that extra mile.

April 11 – 2 Samuel 11:1-5

Battling for God helps in our battle against sin

It's much more difficult to fall apart with sin when we're actively engaged within the work we're called to be doing, O Men. When we're fighting in the battle for our own and others' lives, we'll become more acute to the evil one's stealthy attacks. There's no doubt that Satan likes to attack those ones who are more actively battle-engaged, but we'll learn to fight him better while we're active. We'll grow in our awareness of the things he's doing in the battle when we're actually in this battle for ourselves. "At the time when kings go off to war," only coward-kings aren't gone and fighting in the war on their people's behalf. At the time when Jesus has called His men to "go," only men of weakness don't go out everyday for the world's sake. If we want to live a life of self-indulgence, we're indulging in behavior that'll eventually end with Bathshebas. If you'd rather that your battle-wounds were self-inflicted sins, Satan is happy to indulge those selfish impulses. But if you'd rather die than let the devil have his way with your life, live the life you're called to live fully today. Battle every single moment within the battle marshaled for you; don't get lazy for a single second of your day. Satan hates to see those men who rise up every single morning, clear-eyed, looking for their purpose within God's plan. Satan loves to see those men who live haphazardly within the calling upon Today, wishy-washy amidst God's will for them.

We're never farther away from sin than any next subtle Satanic attack, any temptation we've started growing personally weak to. We all live our lives upon the borderline between our strength and sin every single minute of our daily lives. But if we actively pursue the plan of God, parsing His will within our lives, "[He] will uphold [us]" with His "righteous right hand." He'll place His power in your heart within the moments when the subtleties of sin would start to seem most enticing to you. For "when you are tempted, he will also provide a way out so that you can stand up under it" – that's His promise to us. (1 Cor. 10:13)

Are you in the battle today, O Man? If not, will you re-up for the Lord? Satan may attack you all the more because you're "active duty" for your Savior, but you'll be exactly where Jesus wants you!

April 12 – 2 Samuel 11:6-13

Only rest when He gives you rest; otherwise fight

A man becomes a warrior in the battles of the Lord when he's actually fighting in the battles of the Lord. He becomes a scarred-up veteran when he's tough enough to go time and again into the ugly fray of war. Only there will he begin to understand his true identity within the identity granted to him by his God, not by the ways of the world. His only "R&R" is taken at the direct bidding of his King; the Lord "will give [him] rest" when He's good and ready.

Let's let Uriah be our model today, O Men. May we think and act as he once did:

So Satan sent this word to his general: "Send me a supposed 'man of God.'" And his general sent one to Satan. When the man of God came to him, Satan asked him how his general was, how the soldiers were and how the war was going. Then Satan said to the man of God, "Go down to your house and wash your feet." So the man of God left the palace, and a gift from the evil one was sent after him. But the man of God slept at the entrance to the Lord's palace with all the servants and did not go down to his house.

When Satan was told, "The man of God did not go home," he asked him, "Haven't you just come from a distance? Why didn't you go home?"

The man of God said to Satan, "My Lord was crucified for me, and there is still a battle going on. How could I go to my house to eat and drink and relax like every other man does? As surely as you live, I will not do such a thing!"

Then Satan tried a different tack: "Stay here one more day, and tomorrow I will send you back." So the man of God remained in that place for that day and the next. At Satan's invitation, he ate and drank with him, and Satan tried to make him drunk. But in the evening the man of God went out to sleep on his mat again…

Today, may we be the men within the pattern of Uriah, O Men, knowing that the battle is ever raging. We "will lie down and sleep in peace" only in the "safety" of the Lord, not within the comforts of this world's softness. May we fight steadily today, my brothers. May our only rest be found in Him.

April 13 – 2 Samuel 11:14-27

Don't compound sin with sin

If we don't teach our hearts a true repentance as a weapon against sin, we'll eventually go down this same road. If we aren't aware enough to realize both our follies and our faults, we'll compound sin with sin throughout our earthly life. Further sin can start to seem like safety when we're walking on our own, not walking with the Lord who actively leads us. In the ways of the former life, the fleshly life, sin becomes a way to right the wrongs that we've accumulated. Yet, clearly, when we watch the interaction between David and Uriah we see sin *and only sin*. David doesn't find an ounce of personal peace when he compounds his sin with further sin; in truth, he finds only perdition. First, his kingly heart had been so clouded by his lazy not-going-to-war-thinking that he'd initially slept with Bathsheba. His non-cognizance of sin then led him, *not* to repentance, but to further sin by plying her husband with some drinks. Then, still fully unrepentant, futile in his schemes, he commits the grievous act of this distant pathetic cold-blooded murder. At any point along this spectrum of sin, David had the opportunity to realize his folly and then repent before the Lord. At every moment, he had opportunities to throw himself upon God's mercies, knowing God's "anger lasts only a moment." All he needed to do was what he'd done so many times in his life before this episode: be cognizant of wrongdoing and repent. All he needed to do was realize that his sin with Bathsheba was a sin against his Lord and God only. And, with that in mind, he only needed to go straight to his God without schemes or prevarications or excuses – *only repentance.*

If you want to stand a fighting chance against the wiles of the devil, stop your sin directly in its tracks today, O Man. Don't try to fight the battle against sin with more sin; don't try to dam its tide with worse and worse behavior. If you know your heart is struggling with a certain sin today, seek a way with which to part your way from its way. Don't try to hide your sin beneath the cover of another and worser sin; seek the Lord in humble-hearted repentance. "In your struggle against sin, you have not yet resisted to the point of shedding blood"; be strong; be fully repentant. May we know our hearts and minds so totally completely that we realize our sin and then can stop ourselves earlier than David. Today, let's flee from our sin, O Men of God. Let's find His peace through our ongoing repentance.

April 14 – 2 Samuel 12:1-13

We're all hypocrites

The weakest condemnation that a man can give another man is that laziest of labelings: a "hypocrite." We seem to gnash our teeth against the vile hypocrisies of everyone we know except our own hypocritical selves. It's all too easy to elucidate the way some other guy is clearly "ewe-stealing" from some "poor man" we happen to know. There's no denunciation we deal out with greater ease than the calling-out of others' dirty deeds and dealings, is there? But the problem with this high-handed assigning of the label "hypocrite" is the blatant worthlessness within ourselves. The issue with our codifying others' hypocrisies is the false rift we're making between ourselves and those people. You and I are both hypocrites – *everyone's a hypocrite* – the world is full of hypocrites, O Men of God. We say and do the things we hate to see another person saying and doing every single day of our earthly lives. We hate the "sinfulness" of our "broken modern world" and yet we're all sinful broken modern people ourselves. We can't stand the world's "false agendas" and yet we often falsify the purpose of our Lord's true purpose.

O Men of God, may we hear these words of Nathan as a dagger to the heart of our own vile hypocrisy. May we realize the sinfulness created when we're quick to judge another for the selfsame sin as ours. May we understand how God is calling our sinful hearts to transformation and is making them into hearts filled with mercy for others. May we know our own worthlessness and use that knowledge as a springboard for the purposes of His grace in others' lives. May we never be the men so mentally, intellectually and spiritually lazy that we ever call another man a "hypocrite." May we never claim to see a single grain of "sawdust" in the eyes of the men around us through our own "plank"-filled eyes…

You won't become useful to the Lord until you realize the uselessness of your sinful heart before He redeemed you. You won't show a grain of mercy till you understand the vastness of the mercies that He's already showered upon you. Today, may we be the men who recognize our own hypocrisy and who refuse to judge it in another person's soul. You might actually become the spirit of refreshment that's so needed when you finally recognize your own need for Jesus. Look only inside yourself today, O Man. And be thankful that you've been forgiven.

LIVE LIKE MEN

April 15 – 2 Samuel 16:15-17:14

Divine, not human, discernment

The places where a man discovers discernment are the primary places where his life will either rise or fall. We'll either become the mighty men of God or modern willy-nilly weaklings through the providence we seek along the journey. If we seek out words of wisdom in the Word – go to Providence Himself – there's nothing in this world that can stop us. But if we choose to wax and wane upon the promptings of another changeable person, we'll often end up weakened. It's telling that the first inclination for our anti-hero Absalom was to seek the wisdom of men, not the wisdom of God. Instead of going to the Lord, as his father always had, Absalom seeks out the thoughts of Hushai and Ahithophel. Hushai was a trusted friend of David and it's obvious he was honey-tongued in the praising of this pretender-king. If Absalom hadn't been so blinded by his sudden rise to power, his near-prominence, he would've been filled with doubts about him. Yet he so obviously wasn't, was he?

The greatest problem with our seeking out the providence of man's imperfect wisdom is the "itching of our ears." We're more apt to think that mankind's plans are actionable when we hear those plans aligning with our own personal desires. Yet the issue with our trusting in the mores and modes of men is that most men are as changeable as the wind. What was clear and helpful in the speaking of a friend, just yesterday, might be totally changed by the time tomorrow comes. The one you thought to be a trusted confidante turns out to be an enemy when their "wisdom" starts to unravel…

The reason we must seek out our discernment only in the word of the Lord is that His Word never changes or fails. "God is not a man, that he should lie, nor a son of man, that he should change his mind," we are told in the book of Numbers. God is not what Oswald Chambers calls "an amateur Providence," doling out wisdom that's shifting like the sand on a sand dune. God will not mislead our listening ears; He'll never shine a light upon the wrong path for our earthly lives.

Today, take some time to analyze the way you gather wisdom and the process by which you discern the will of God for your life. Ask the Lord to clearly give you of His wisdom for the questions on your mind today and every other day too. He will do it, O Man of God. He desires only that you ask.

April 16 – 2 Samuel 18:1-18

Not building monuments to self

We controvert the truth of God's power when we live our lives as if our power is actually any power at all. We give the lie to our profound professions of faith when our actions profess other false gods' presence in our lives. If we use our earthly days to build up "monuments" to the greatness of ourselves, we'll certainly leave that legacy behind! If we spend our time on "pillars" to ourselves, we'll absolutely pass along the worship of self to our children and grandchildren. We see Absalom as the darkness to David's light, as a final expression of the ends to which selfish means lead. But when we're honest with ourselves, O Men, don't we often self-honor with professions of the same sort of worship? The path that ends with men hanging from the oaks of self-importance is certainly a well-trodden path in our modern world! If we'd seek to seek the way of Jesus – giving the truth to past professions of faith – we must instead learn to lay our lives down.

I've always been refreshed by the irony of Shelley's *Ozymandias*:

> I met a traveler from an antique land
>
> Who said: Two vast and trunkless legs of stone
>
> Stand in the desert. Near them, on the sand,
>
> Half sunk, a shattered visage lies, whose frown
>
> And wrinkled lip, and sneer of cold command
>
> Tell that its sculptor well those passions read
>
> Which yet survive, stamped on these lifeless things,
>
> The hand that mocked them and the heart that fed.
>
> And on the pedestal these words appear:
>
> "My name is Ozymandias, king of kings:
>
> Look on my works, ye Mighty, and despair!"
>
> Nothing beside remains. Round the decay
>
> Of that colossal wreck, boundless and bare

> The lone and level sands stretch far away.

We may laugh at Ozymandias' (or at Absalom's) self-perception until we realize how often we mirror it ourselves. May we be the men of God who unite lifestyles built on conscious self-abasement with a pure daily love for Jesus Christ. Those two run as rivers, parallel and confluent. May we live our life from His tributaries of love.

April 17 – 2 Samuel 19:1-8

Learning to be properly vulnerable

We must never be the men who are dishonest in the struggles and pains accompanying our walk with Jesus through this life. We must use the nearness of our dearest lifelong friends as a soundboard to our darker thoughts and worries all throughout it. We must also *be* that soundboard for the struggles and anxieties that'll surely come up in the lives of these same friends. We must offer up some hope within those times when we're feeling "up" and accept it in the times when we're feeling "down." But we mustn't be the brand of "vulnerable" men whose vulnerability causes the downfall of others' journeys in Christ. We mustn't mourn and wail for the "Absaloms" in our life when that might derail others' budding faith in the Lord and His great goodness. We can't drop our armor in the presence of a one who's not prepared to see a vulnerable heart so openly displayed. We must never "bleed over [our] own personal tragedies" (Hemingway) to the detriment of the Lord's other warriors in the spiritual war.

David certainly felt the terrible personal loss inherent when a father loses a son, be he good or bad. Yet he still remained the anointed king of Israel – *especially now* – in these days right after the royal near-coup.

Do you know the power placed within your hands, everyday, by the places God has chosen to put you, O Man? Do you know that your own life can either help or hurt your spiritual standing in the lives of others around you? If we always let our "spirit of vulnerability" set our life's course, we'll become known as just that – *only vulnerable*. If we aren't extremely careful in the choosing of our closest confidantes, we might confuse some other brothers' faith. On the other hand, we must never begin to think that shows of false strength are actually strength; we must never put up false front. Yet if we know and daily access the power of our God through Jesus Christ, there's no earthly limit to our earthly lives.

May we utilize the Lord's strength in the living of our story today, not our own brand of "strength," O Men of God. May we utilize the brothers He's given us as confidantes, certain that our mutual vulnerability is truly good for our lives in Jesus. Yet may we not become the men so vulnerable that we hurt another's faith, letting our vulnerability become pregnability. We're the chosen warriors in a vicious fight – *don't ever forget it!* – let's let the Lord rearm our arms with His strength today.

LIVE LIKE MEN

April 18 – 2 Samuel 23:9,10

Hold fast to the Sword and the fight

Our only battle is called Today; our only sword is known as the Word; may we be like Eleazar in the heat of things. Even if the mass of men may turn and run away from the battle, may we fight on with the only weapon we have! May we not see fearsome armies as any kind of earthly obstacle; any foemen as a danger to our lives or livelihood. May we be so certain of our Sword that not just our hands, *but our hearts*, get "frozen" to its steelyness and strength. May we "stand our ground" when called to hold a certain piece of turf; may we know the call upon our lives in Christ. May we bear the leoninic heart that comes with following the Lion through the storms and battles of the life He's given us.

O Man of God, you're nothing less than Eleazar back in his day if you'll stand strong in the strength of Christ for today. If you give your heart to Him, seek His face within the battle, He'll give you every ounce of power that's needed. Do you know the strength available when men of God are humbly trying to follow every command from the lips of Jesus? Do you know the way the Sword of the Spirit becomes fastened to those humble hearts who study it, love it, obey it? Will you take His Word today as a weapon and defense for your life, even if you currently feel alone in the battle? Will you fight the fight to which He's called your life, even if the other men around you all run away? Will you *not* be frightened by the "odds," or by the enemy's "strength," knowing who it is you serve, O Man of God? Will you choose this day to be like Eleazar was, fight like Eleazar did, last like mighty Eleazar?

"[But] those who hope in the Lord *will* renew their strength. They *will* soar on wings like eagles; they *will* run and not grow weary, they *will* walk and not be faint." (Isaiah 40:31) Only when we trust the Lord's perfect Will do those "wills" I italicized become the truth about our fight for His Kingdom. May you really believe in the battle and in your place within this battle and your hope within Jesus Christ's battle on your behalf. May you become so glued to the Word and to your Lord that your strength will outstrip Satan's every single day of your life. Keep fighting today, O Man. Humbly follow His Word.

April 19 – 2 Samuel 24:1-17

Don't let "taking stock" become a god

The practical beauty of a wartime view of living is that battles must be won before a soldier enjoys their plunder. He's forced by such attrition to divorce his mind from mundane daily things; he must focus only on what's happening Today. He can't attend to all his worries about tomorrow when he's still within the battle that might end his life before that comes. He can't take stock of anything, except the enemy force arrayed against him, once the battle's ready to be joined and fought.

There's something similarly day-to-day about the way a shepherd might himself view his life and his chosen lifestyle. A shepherd forced to wake up early every single morning will only do the work required of him for that particular day of grazing. He can't attend to predators or droughts or deluges that might happen on the morrow's watch – what would be the point of that? He can't take stock of anything, except the day that's dawning before him, trusting in the Lord's providence for him…

David had within himself the mind of both the shepherd and warrior; he'd tasted both those daily toils personally. He'd felt some fearsome fights-to-the-death and also the Lord's provision of "green pastures" many times in his previous life. Yet the slackness of no-battle-left-to-fight and peacetime-barns-filled-with-grain led David into this sinful censusing. When he took his eyes from the Lord, he was blinded to the pride that was welling up within himself…

Would you say that there's a link between your times of lesser faith and the frequency of your "taking stock" of your life, O Man? Do you literally start to check your stocks (or bonds (or your whole life life-insurance policies)) when you're feeling "distant from the Lord"? How much faith and trust do you divest from the Lord's sovereign plan through your passion for your "plans for investment"? Do you know how quickly our "portfolios" become our modern-day idols if we put our trust in them alone? Do you really think that "[storing] up for yourselves treasures in heaven" is of infinite value next to your current stock account? Do you study God's Word with the same sort of concentrated diligence as this very morning's *Wall Street Journal*?

Today, let's take no stock of anything that might run interference against our simple daily discipleship to Jesus. We'll only be as strong, or as "rich," as the faith we'll choose to lean upon for the activities of the day ahead…

April 20 – 1 Kings 2:1-12

Create your own four-part charge

We'll become the kind of men for our children to emulate when we know and speak our vision for their lives in Jesus. And if we spend some time enumerating upon that spiritual vision *now*, we can actually be assured of their coming to someday understand it. We can also rest assured that writing out this "charge" will encourage our hearts to a clearer Christ-like living in our present. If we write the steps-by-steps for our kids' futures, we'll actually be preaching the same to ourselves for this very day...

David spoke to Solomon of manhood (v.2), following God (vv. 3,4), his history (vv. 5,6 & 8,9) and doing acts of goodness (v. 7.) Similarly, take some time right now in composing your own "charge" in these four same areas for your sons or "spiritual sons":

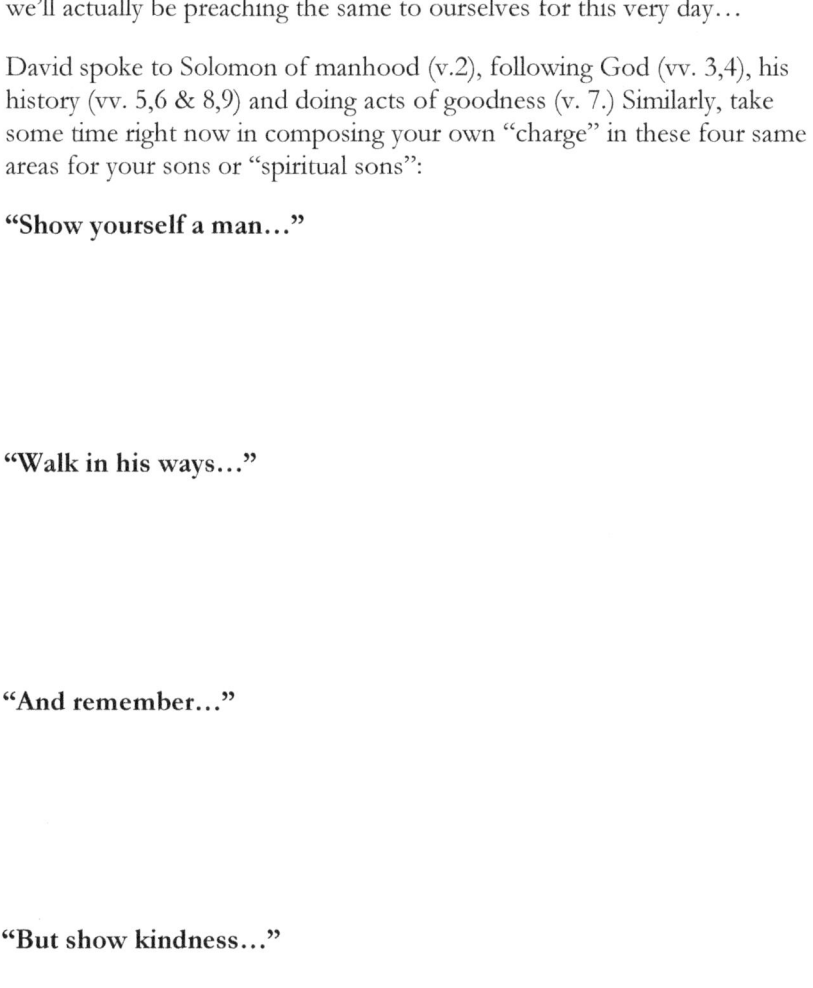

"Show yourself a man…"

"Walk in his ways…"

"And remember…"

"But show kindness…"

April 21 – 1 Kings 3:1-15

You must pursue discernment

A man who understands that discernment is a gift bestowed by the Lord is a man destined for the greatest heavenly things. Any man who thinks his "life experience" will provide him with that same spiritual discernment shows himself to be a rank fool. If we think we'll gain great wisdom "on our own," we're on the same track as thinking we can "win" our eternal salvation. If we think we should become "wise by the standards of this age," we must know how God views that wisdom – as "foolishness." We must realize that learning to live with Christly discernment is the same as following Jesus; the road is the same road. We can't divorce our thoughts of walking in discipleship from our learning true discernment; the two are inextricably connected. If we want to know the answer to any question, even those we think of as "earthly," we must seek the Lord's wisdom first. We must know that nothing good will ever come when we refuse to seek the Lord's face in *any* given situation.

Nearly every man has probably had the thought: "What would I say, if God asked me the same question as Solomon?" And nearly all of us have probably thought a similar next thought too: "Well, I suppose I might've asked the same thing..."

Today, God *is* asking you the same question; the content of your heart will reveal your mind's greatest desire to Him. He wants to know if you're a man who actually believes 1 Corinthians 2:16, that you already "have the mind of Christ." He wants to see how in the living of your day you'll display a desire for godly discernment: Do you truly want His wisdom? Do you wish that every question of your mind might be resolved by His clear guiding voice for your life? Do you long that you'd be filled up with such stores of His wisdom that your words might be hearkened to by others for direction? Would you hope that you'd be spiritually blessed in your work, in your family, in your faith, in absolutely everything you do?

Then, today, let's ask for His wisdom. May we desire His discernment only. Quite possibly, "[we] do not have because [we] do not ask God" for His wonderful wisdom for our daily life in Jesus!

April 22 – 1 Kings 4:29-34

Not going from wisdom to an "Ecclesiastes mindset"

There's every likelihood that the one who was so fabulously blessed with God's wisdom also eventually authored the book of Ecclesiastes. The one whose "breadth of understanding" was "as measureless as the sand on the seashore" probably was the same one yelling out, "Meaningless!" The king whose wisdom was an aggregate equal to the wisdom of all the East said: "The sun also ariseth..." The one to whom "men of all nations" pined to listen became the voice so vainly vowing, "I hated life..." King Solomon, the son of mighty God-honoring David, ended his life with a voice filled with despondency and despair. Where he'd clearly started out with such a desire for discernment, he ended with a voice full of depression and sorrow. Where he might've brought the wisdom of the world into beautiful accord with God's boundlessness, he obviously didn't. Where he might've followed God within the bounds of his great God-given understanding, it appears he instead "leaned" on his own. (Prov. 3:5)

As you think of how King Solomon started out and how he finished, where do you see your own path headed today? When you think of God's rich blessings upon your life – what He's done for you already – where does your mind go to, next? Do you see life as a blessing or a curse; sweet or sour upon your lips; do you see your life as His only? Do you hope that how you're living your life today might give full vent to the feelings you feel for the wonderful God you serve? Are you thankful for the trials that result in deeper maturing wisdom; do you see His path as fully purposeful for you? Will you end your days a hard-bitten worldly intellectual or as a soft-hearted servant of the King?

Today, know that how you're living your Today results in the writing of your own life's Book of Ecclesiastes, O Man. The way you choose to honor and obey Him – or to groan and gripe against Him – will determine your tomorrow's path. We define the source of wisdom we're personally following when we winnow out the voice of the evil one from our lives. Today, may we concentrate our minds upon the clear-voiced directives He's giving us, just for this day, trusting Him for tomorrow. For "tomorrow will take care of itself." Now that's some true helpful wisdom.

April 23 – 1 Kings 5

Using rest to rearm and times of peace to grow

There's nothing easier than to use our times of "peace" as the times for our own personal relaxation and personal enjoyment. There's no temptation quite as tantalizing as the subtle call to put our spiritual feet up and take a breather from the battle. Yet we'll be disarmed more quickly in the battle if we've used our times of personal peace as a chance to rest from our calling. We'll find our temples unprepared – *totally unbuilt, in fact* – if we slack off during these nice serene times in our lives. If we let our current lack of hardship be a boon to the battleplan of Satan, he'll use that opportunity shrewdly. If we don't see how the Lord might actually use our "rest," we'll resort to the lowest common denominator every single time. Solomon viewed his life within the scope of what the Lord was doing within it, not just how it seemed to him in the moment-to-moment. Thus, because "the Lord my God has given me rest on every side," Solomon knew the time for building had arrived. He wouldn't wait to lay foundation-stones until he started to "feel like it," or until the Lord might further clarify construction plans. No, he viewed his time of "rest" as being provided by the Lord for provision of a temple to be built *for* the Lord. He saw whatever time of life he was in – good or bad, war or peace – as the perfect time for the serving of his King. He'd utilize the quiet of his nation, all the wisdom of his mind, for the purpose of this great service unto the Lord.

If you're currently in a time of "rest" in your life, there's nothing changed about the Lord's call for you, O Man. If you've had the time to "tear down barns and build bigger ones," what will you do with your excess holdings – *right now*? If the Lord has called a halt upon the battle you've been fighting, will you rearm in the time that you're "off" from war? Will you concentrate your easeful times of peace upon the building up of godliness, vigor, strength for His great purposes?

A man must use whatever place he's placed as the perfect place to serve the Lord his God in the present moment. Will you even use the "rest" that you've been given as a place of sacred service, a time for holy toil for the Kingdom? Today's directive is the same as every other day – "follow Me" – whether you're in a time of war or peace, O Man. May we be the men who build our own temple for the Lord in the quiet of our God-given rest. Even downtime must be His time. Every moment of our lives is His.

LIVE LIKE MEN

April 24 – 1 Kings 6:38-7:1

Where do your best efforts lie?

A lifetime's service to the Lord will best be measured in its balance between temple-building and personal palace-building. Each of us will "all be judged according to [our] works" by Him who knows the true content of our hearts, O Men. (Rev. 20:13) How we spend our every hour of our days of our weeks of our months of our years is *actually known to Him*. The true purposes behind every action we do, the decisions we make, the words we speak, are crystal-clear to Jesus Christ. If we set out everyday within His purpose, giving our hearts to His calling, He knows and sees that everyday. But He also knows when "seven years" have passed and we continue along with construction of our own dream palaces…

Are you giving your heart most fully to the building of the temple of your life, or to palaces that can't and won't last? Do you still pay undue attention to the things of this world, or are you consumed with things that are eternal and unchanging? Can you proportionalize the balance of each day's labors reserved for the construction of His temple vs. your palace? Would you say you give the best of all your efforts to construction of those structures that are God-desired and eternal?

Listen to what God desires: "Heaven is my throne, and the earth is my footstool. Where is the house you will build for me? Where will my resting place be? Has not my hand made all these things, and so they came into being?" declares the Lord. "This is the one I esteem: he who is humble and contrite in spirit, and trembles at my word." (Isaiah 66:1,2)

Today, may our personal focus be on what our lives are actually working toward: *God's temple or our own palaces?* May we be the men whose hardest daily work is for the good of the Lord's Kingdom and for the people He puts in our path. May we so honest that we can directly repent of all the days and months and years we've already wasted working for ourselves. Today, let's give our hearts to the Great Carpenter. May we be of use to His best designs.

April 25 – 1 Kings 8:1-13

Fight for His presence

If a man will daily offer his "temple" to the Lord his God, he'll see these same results happening in his own daily life. If he daily consecrates himself so that his God might dwell therein, God will rest His presence there mightily, daily. If he won't give up in times when the Lord seems "distant," he'll be fighting in the only battle actually worth fighting. If he conducts his life in order to keep his earthly temple "magnificent," God's presence will descend to dwell upon it in power.

If we gave up anything else in our lives as quickly as we'll often quit on God, we'd all be complete abject failures, O Men. If we didn't go to work every day that "I don't feel like it," we'd all be homeless bums, begging on the street corners. If we let competitors win every secular battle the way we cede our souls, we'd be daily defeated and destroyed. If we fought our lives the way we fight the battles of eternity, we'd be vanquished before the work-week was out…

If you think the word of God is true – *that you really **are** His temple* – don't ever live your life without His manifest presence! Don't go a single day without refreshment of His Spirit within your spirit; *draw your heart to Him and really live*. If you're feeling "out of touch" with Him right now, don't proceed another step until you've gotten back in step with Him. If you're feeling like His presence is an illusion, are you sure you've ever actually experienced it, O Man? We men of God must know that only in the presence of His presence are we free, and strong enough, to actually be His men. Only when we truly give obedient hearts to Him do we begin feeling how His presence is pulsating within our hearts. Only when we fight the inner battle of our hearts and minds are we fit for His battle-plans within this fallen world. If we run away from Him because "I'm not really feeling it today," have we ever really truly felt it at all? If we want to follow Jesus, taking up our cross daily, don't we believe that following after Him requires some effort? If we'd want to become men after his own heart, don't we want to have His presence within our hearts, this very day?

Right now, let's make the preparations necessary to be ready for the fullness of His presence in our human hearts. Let's become – ***and be*** – the men who never settle for anything less than everything when it comes to the Holy Spirit of God.

LIVE LIKE MEN

April 26 – 1 Kings 10:1-13

Noticeable and recognizable wisdom

When a man begins to gain fame for "his relation to the name of the Lord," he's found the only fame worth having. When a man can rest his destiny upon the worth of God's perfect wisdom, he's within God's perfect will without a question. When his trust is in the Lord and in the Lord's plan for his life, he'll be rewarded by a life that's actually worth living. He'll find his "righteousness will shine like the dawn"; that his life's own "cause is like the noonday sun," glorious and dazzling. He'll know that God is personally blessing him, regardless of his life's "circumstances," by making Himself known to him. He'll feel the riches of the world would be a poor substitute for the riches of his growing wisdom in Jesus. He'll become like King Solomon was with Sheba: "nothing was too hard for the king to explain to her." He'll be so rewarded by the growing of his faith that he'll never look back to the "old life" or to the world's ways *ever*.

A man who gives his thoughts to delving into pools of godly wisdom will become a man deeply sought after. He'll become a man of "fame," not by our modern foolish definitions, but by the Lord's perfect definition. He'll walk in utter daily surety, knowing of, and known by, the God who gave Himself for his life's sake. He'll see the world's great "wisdom" in the light of God's Wisdom; he'll seek his only reward in the latter, not the former.

Would you say you're currently worthy – *by the Lord's definition* – to receive this sort of recognition, O Man? Can you sit in perfect silence and let the Lord's perfect wisdom be the guide for your own thoughts each day? Do you find yourself sought after as a source of godly wisdom by any modern-day Queens of Sheba? Are there any who'd sit there at your feet, asking you "hard questions," knowing they'll receive a God-given response?

Only when we line our minds with His Word and listen for His voice daily will we gain true godly wisdom. Only when we seek to serve within the callings of His Holy Spirit do we find ourselves actually growing in Him. Today, let us live a life of true godly wisdom, seeking only that we might find our life's "fame" in Jesus. May we ask that we'd become like Solomon started, being sought after for his wisdom founded only in God's wisdom.

April 27 – 1 Kings 10:14-11:13

Don't let your comfort lead to sin

It's been my observation that men are quicker to be callused by their comforts than to be hardened by their hardships. It's easier to sink into the softness of our flesh than to fight against a clear hard foe in a real pitched battle. You'll often find that when the ease of your existence becomes the hope of your existence, you'll actually become more hopeless. If you haven't got a need in all the world, you'll often find your life crippled by your many wants instead. If we give our hearts and souls to the treasures of this earth, Satan's found the chink in our armor, hasn't he? When we start to think we're "comfortable," the siege is already being laid at our rapidly weakening defenses. If he can take us from the battle by our thoughts about a minor skirmish, he knows he's already won the entire war. If we're spending time on gilding useless shields, we're giving him the chance to shoot his flaming arrows in, undeterred…

King Solomon didn't falter in his following of the Lord because of terror or some terrible undue hardship in his life. He wasn't tempted to "curse his God and die" because of coming bloodshed, personal poverty or certain painful death. No, Solomon was lured into his lurid acts of sin by the smallest steps of earthly comfort lulling him into total defenselessness. By the time he started to make silver "common as stones," he was "comfortable" enough to take a thousand wives as well…

Do you have a certain "comfort" in your current life that's calling you to callused-hearted living, O Man of God? Is there any tipping-point activity that might just take you from the kingship to the slave-ship, like Solomon? Are you allowing Satan free rein through the reign of certain comforts in your life that might actually be taking you away from your God? Are you letting comfort dictate to your heart about the meaning of your life – *and actually believing that definition*?

Today, may we be aware of all of our "comforts" and beware the ones that lead us from the Lord's holy presence. May we have the strength to cut out all the comforts that might end up with our eventually following after false gods. Let's be the men who see our challenges and comforts as being the very same: handed to us by our God for His purposes. Let's honor Him by continuing in obedience – peeling off our earthly calluses – to live for Him and His coming Kingdom.

April 28 – 1 Kings 12:1-19

Get out of God's way

Have you ever given thought to the possibility that the world might actually *want* to know more of Jesus Christ? Has it ever crossed your mind that we're following in the footsteps of the most magnetic personage in all human history? Do you ever stop to think of how the Lord might make His Way better known if we weren't always getting in His way? Can't you see the ways the natural and supernatural realities were daily mingled in the mighty book of Acts?

If Rehoboam had just listened to the elders and not spoken in this way, who knows what might've happened to his kingship? If he'd let things run their natural course (barring the plan of God, of course!) he might've ruled over all of Israel. Yet the pride that power placed within his heart became unstoppable and Rehoboam couldn't abide wise counsel. He became consumed with such a potent pride that simple wisdom seemed impossible to understand, much less follow. He only heard the voice of all his hot-headed idiotic friends, not the easygoing words of the wise elders. He wouldn't let the people have their own way; he was certain that he knew the way that was best for everybody...

Today, let's focus all our attentions on *not* doing anything that might be getting in our Lord's perfect way in the world. If He'd like to use our humble selves for the good of His coming Kingdom, let's just be humble for His sake, O Men. If he'd have you speak a simple truth to a heart that's presently hurting, go ahead and speak it without a second guess. If he'd ask that you'd avoid a certain sin that might be the cause for another's stumbling, then simply avoid it because He asked.

It would seem that there are times within our lives when we're being called into a deeper shade, or season, of thoughtfulness. There are times when subtle wisdoms are the key for others' salvation, moments when we're being personally prodded and pushed along.

Today, however, may we give our hearts to the actions that are as natural as a spring breeze blowing through the budding trees. If we can learn of anything from Rehoboam's kingly folly, may it be that we must sometimes shut our stupid mouths! If we'd have a "share" in Jesus Christ, we must learn to follow His words, His guidings, His truth to the very end of ourselves. Today, let's focus on Him entirely, O Men. And let's let Him do His wondrous work.

April 29 – 1 Kings 12:25-33

Not cutting corners in following our God

A faith that feels easy or convenient might be an indicator of a faith that's been remade in our own image. If we find that following Jesus starts to seem like "there's nothing to it," perhaps there really is nothing to our *version* of it. If it seems as if our faith does not require any personal exertion, perhaps we've already added too many expedients. If we only need occasional trips to "high places" to "restore balance," maybe we're totally off-balance in our Christ-following. Jeroboam didn't need to ask the Lord for His direction or for guidance; he simply made his own gods instead. When he saw the issues raised by covenantal worship in Jerusalem, he decided God had initially asked too much. He decided it was "too much for [the Israelites] to go up" there; he pandered to them with a plotting heart, hungry for power. He was even out-of-touch enough with his own people's history that he'd actually remake Aaron's golden calves for worship. He'd so placed his own temporal needs above the commandments of the Father that he set a new standard for evil in his people's land. For many generations, the "sins of Jeroboam" would become the tarnished high-point for all evil-doing Israelite kings…

What are ways in which you see the modern Church "making it easy," allowing expedience to trump godly exertion? What are ways in which you see your home-church doing the same, cutting corners in the way one worships in that place? And, most important, what are ways you see your own worship of the Lord clouded by a need for ease or earthly expedience? Do you find a tinge of Jeroboam's plotting in your heart; ways in which you corner-cut the Lord your God? Do you ever hear His call unto obedience as being "too much," God's voice to you as far too demanding? Do you bow to any golden calves of modern Christianity, instead of simply bowing down to Jesus Himself? Are you, unbeknownst to yourself, setting precedents for a dangerous sort of worship for your children and for their children?

Let's take the time today to ask ourselves some very hard questions about the ease of our experience with Jesus. And if we find there are any elements – *even one* – of Jeroboam's sinful "worship" in us, let's ask the Lord to rid us of them. May we listen only for His voice today, O Men. Nothing He ever asks is "too much."

LIVE LIKE MEN

April 30 – 1 Kings 13:1-10

Work up to your destiny through daily obedience

Have you ever experienced the feeling that you're doing exactly "what you were made for"; have you felt "afoot with [your] vision"? (Walt Whitman, *Leaves of Grass*) Have you ever stood upon a precipice, regardless of its certain dangers, and felt certain of your calling to that particular place? Have you ever felt the hand of God so strongly leading you down a path that the path's destination was of no concern of you? Have you ever felt so certain of His daily divine direction that you didn't think of anything but that particular day?

Most of us are living our lives as if we're searching for the "reason" for our earthly existence, O Men of God. Even if we know the Savior of the world as our own, there are many of us still looking for some great "purpose," aren't there? We regard fulfillment of our "destiny" as if we're living from the daily light of Hollywood, not His Holy Word. We act as if our vain attempts to "name" ourselves are of more value than the name actually already assigned to us by our God.

What if God's entire purpose for your life was the very same one assigned to this particular "man of God"? What if you were given one great task that was the entirety of your "destiny" – *only one single thing*, O Man? What if you were called to be the certain person who will lead a certain person to the foot of the Savior today? What if you were called to be the next Saul/Paul whose identity-shift would lead to the changing of the entire world?

We can only know and claim the mighty purposes of the Lord when we're faithful in the day-to-days of our life. Only if we listen for the voicing of His Spirit's small commandments do we learn to obey greatly in the "great" ones. If you'd like to know the purpose of His plans for your whole lifetime, give him wholly of your life for this day alone. If you'd parse the enigmatic course of human destiny, be obedient to the simple tasks assigned to you now – not tomorrow. We can only live one day in touch with eternity; our tomorrows and our yesterdays are impossibly beyond our reach. Let's be the "men of God" concerned *only* with the tasks assigned to us this day, rather than fretting about tomorrow. For, small or great, you are His today. Let's learn to be "afoot with *His* vision" for our lives!

May 1 – 1 Kings 13:11-32

Don't let sin take you from your destiny

There's a very real possibility that you're riding out today upon the donkey of your destiny's great calling, O Man. You don't know if today's particular circumstances, plus the Holy Spirit's leading, might create a perfect storm of His power. Perhaps you're the guy within your office who'll say a certain important thing that will change one of your coworkers' hearts forever. Maybe you're the motorist who stops to help a stranded driver who'll be the one to change the world entirely. When we follow Jesus Christ within the borders of the "everyday," we're offering Him the chance to really use our lives. If we'll only just obey – *just like we spoke of yesterday* – He may have a single perfect purpose for us in this day. However, just as we must listen and then do the things to which He's calling us, we must also *not* go the other direction. After all, it's only hours from the fulfillment of his calling to the moment when this "man of God" was slain. We can kill the calling upon our earthly lives whenever we're quick to sin, just as much as when we're slow to obey. We'll find we're resting under the "oak tree" of obedience for just a single moment; then, suddenly, we're slaughtered...

If we'd like to dream of great and powerful purposes for our individual lives, let's not lose the battle of sin, O Men of God. May we not fulfill and then be killed, or be killed *before* fulfilling, our God-given destiny through Jesus. We must be so fully prescient to the Prince of Darkness' schemes that we're never fooled by some false prophet's prophecy for us. We must understand the Word of God so richly that we'll never be dissuaded from our calling by any personal sinfulness. Can you focus your mind so fully on fulfillment of Christ's calling on your life that you're constantly aware of attack? Will you pray that He'd be standing beside you throughout your day today, so that you have His mighty strength? O Man of God, you're already part of something great beyond your wildest dreams: fulfillment of Jesus' Great Commission. But – *beware!* – the path is swarming with enemies, snares, false prophecies, trials, all attempting to crush the spirit found within you.

Recommit your heart to your battle against sin in this particular day; live fully in His strength for you. He's looking for the men who'll stand up in the midst of the fierce battle and fight with all His power for this fallen world.

LIVE LIKE MEN

May 2 – 1 Kings 14:1-18

See through Satan's disguises and denounce him

One of the greatest weapons in our arsenal against Satan is our ability to denounce him and his activities. If we truly know the powers ranged behind and before us in Jesus, we have every right to shut him down immediately. Right now, Satan is hoping to take you out of the game through his constant use of clever, ingenious, insidious disguises. He's thinking he'll defeat you easily within the guise of that contentious guy you're currently fighting with at your workplace. Or, if that should happen to fail, he's there behind the fleeting look of lust you'll receive from a woman at some coffee shop. Or, better yet, he'll feed a simple thought into your brain with which you'll struggle, and be blinded by, all day…

Listen now to a new version of Ahijah's answer. Imagine the voice of the Lord speaking thus: "Come in, Satan. Why this pretense? I have been sent to you with some bad news. This is what the Lord, the God of Israel, the God of the cross, says to you: 'You have tried to raise yourself up above all others and make yourself the ruler of this world. You tried to tear God's kingdom away from Jesus, but you are not worthy of it; you are evil – and evil only.

"Because of this, I am going to bring disaster on the house of Satan. I will cut off from Satan every last one of his servants – slave or free. I will burn up the house of Satan as one burns dung, until it is gone. Dogs will eat those belonging to Satan who die in the city, and the birds of the air will feed on those who die in the country. The Lord has spoken!

"The Lord has raised up for himself a King of Kings who will cut off all the family of Satan. This is the day! What? Yes, even now. And the Lord will strike down Satan, so that he will be like a reed swaying in the water. He will uproot Satan, and his allies, from this good earth and will scatter their ashes beyond the River…"

Today, may we be aware of Satan's many-faced disguises and remember whom it is we serve with our lives, O Men of God. If you feel attack at your fore or flank, simply denounce him with the very power of Jesus Christ found in you. Today, make yourself aware of that power. Use the weapons that you already hold in your hands.

May 3 - 1 Kings 14:25-28

Don't trade God's gold for anything

It was through his willful disobedience that Rehoboam lost this decisive battle to the king of Egypt; it was in his *not* approaching God that God allowed his total defeat, plus the ransacking of the royal riches. God had looked upon his "high places, sacred stones and Asherah poles" as an abomination against His holy name. He'd seen how quickly David's honoring way had turned to Solomon's way, and then, even worse, to Rehoboam's wicked ways. Now, following this terrible military defeat, God was watching and waiting for a change in the life and rule of Rehoboam. In the absence of his father's famous "gold shields," would Rehoboam call upon His Name as had his grandfather David? Would he see the symbolism in the taking of those shields that had themselves been such a useless use of a precious metal? Would he finally turn his heart to God as his own "rock of refuge," or would he harden his heart against the Lord, the God of David?

As we see, Rehoboam didn't take this opportunity to turn his disobedience over to his grandfather's God. Where he couldn't afford to re-gild brand new regimental shields, he instead made the "practical" choice for their back-up in bronze. Instead of turning to the Lord who was the "strength and shield" for his grandfather, Rehoboam goes with his own ideas. Instead of seeing his defeat as a divine sign from God Himself, Rehoboam simply tries to rebuild his human arsenal.

What are ways that we're turning the "gold" of heavenly possibilities into the "bronze" of our own human idealism? How are we not seeing divinity in our defeat, opportunities for obedience through the destruction of our *dis*obedience? How are we trying to protect our human lives through using "bronze shields," when we know the Lord is the only one who is our "shield"? How do we turn to the "pattern of this world" when we're defeated; when we feel as if there's no one "on our side" anymore?

O Man of God, may we never be like Rehoboam, using weaker means to replace our own human weaknesses. May we ask the Lord for His divine protection – against Satan, sin and disobedience – and then trust His fully capable arm. Let's cease to trust in human shield today. Gold, silver or bronze; they're nothing next to Jesus!

LIVE LIKE MEN

May 4 – 1 Kings 15:1-3

Live as you'd want your sons to live

A man will sprout up from the seeds of what his father taught with his *life*, far more than by his chosen spoken *words*. If we're striving only to speak of what we'd have our own sons do, there's every possibility they'll do the exact opposite. If we think we're clever when we play a sinful "shell game" with our lives, the ending might turn out as an absolute tragedy. The sins of fathers often carry down the lineage of their sons' sin struggles, even if the fathers never know it. Even if the father talks a "good game," there's every possibility that the son will actually know better throughout his life. Sons emulate the goodness *and* the badness of their fathers, even if they personally know what's right and wrong…

Abijah was born and raised within a palace where the worship of the Lord certainly wasn't the prevailing form of worship. One can imagine that he saw his share of strange occultic worship on the hilltops and "under every spreading tree." One can also guess that he wasn't exactly brought up on the stories of King David, or even of Solomon's early and better days. One can bet that he'd learned the ways of Rehoboam from his own personal watching of his father's actual *life*.

Do you think that how you're speaking to your sons (or your daughters) is enforced by how you're living your life, O Man? Would you say there's symbiosis in your words and your lifestyle; complete consistency in your talk and walk? If you tell your kids to not "be so impatient," are you living a life of complete, studied, personal patience yourself? If you say "don't hit your brother or your sister," do you live a life refraining from all *verbal* swipes at other people? If you don't want them out drinking during their high school years, do you ever act as if your own drinking is "pretty cool"? If you don't want them to sleep with every girl they'll ever date, have you taught them how to actually honor women?

You and I can only live our own life; we're not allowed to get a "pass" because of our own earthly father. We can't be those men who manifest a modern-day victim mentality; we must make our own way with Jesus. But, today, let's take time to clarify the message we're sending our own children through the living of our every single day. May we break the chain of sin, not only by our spoken words, but by the actual effectual living of the love of Jesus. May we bless our children's lives this day. By the way we're endeavoring to live our own.

May 5 – 1 Kings 15:9-15

Raze any sin strongholds

There must be some seasons in the battle with our sin when we're vicious in the razing of its strongholds. Asa couldn't follow in the footsteps of his great-great-grandfather David with shrine prostitutes running around the countryside. Neither could he have a heart so "fully committed" to the Lord if he was letting his grandmother speak lies into his ear. So he "cut down" and "burned" all the aspects of his kingdom that weren't in line with the keeping of God's perfect Law. He saw the fight for what it really was – *life or death* – and wouldn't go half-way with ridding Judah of its wickedness. He rehonored God with new articles of silver and gold; he served God "all his life," like David had…

You and I can only serve our God for "all our life" in how we live today; we must remember that, over and over! We can't be "fully committed" in the living of our tomorrows; we can only live that way in the present, and fleeting, moment. If we truly want to end our lives with something like the reputation of Asa, we must purge ourselves of sin *today*. We must cut down, burn and raze the sinful strongholds we've erected in our wayward hearts – *today*! We must name the name of every single sin with which we're struggling, right now – *this very day*! We must ask the Lord for strength to turn away from sin that's become its own identity in us – *right now*! We must seek out other brothers who will hold us to our word regarding our battle with sin – *before this day is out*! We must stand with strength against our sin and temptation; make the devil flee in fear; fight the battle of *today*!

Are you ready for that, modern Asa? Will you arm yourself with God's strength alone? Will you tear down every obstacle that's posing itself as a foe to your intimacy and abiding with Jesus Christ? Will you seethe with holy anger when sin is trying to stop you in your path, and fight it to the death instead? Then, today, let's do the only thing we can do – *live today* – and be ready for the onslaught brought upon us. May we have the fierceness needed to stamp out our personal sin; may we follow in the footsteps of Asa in this eternal fight!

May 6 – 1 Kings 16:29-33

Root out any "trivialized sins"

The sins a man considers to be "trivial" in his life will be the determination of how trivial that man's life is. If he starts to view a sin – *any sin* – as somehow "trivial," he commences down a road that leads to disunion from God. If he starts to think there's certain "smaller" sins with which he's willing to do business, he'll end up morally bankrupt. It's so easy to move up (or is it down?) the destructive ladder of sin once we've set our foot upon a single rung! Once we've made our peace with pride or lust or greed or hate or anger, it's really nothing at all to make peace with all of them. Once we make ourselves the slaves of any sin, we've actually already made our choice: *We are now the "slaves of sin" only*. We can't expect to base our lives on any sin and yet be close with God; remember: "God cannot be mocked." The Lord doesn't delight in willful acts of personal sin, whether or not we've trivialized them down to earthly inconsequence…

King Ahab will always reign as king of all the men in history who've cut a deal with sin and still expected to prosper. He showed "contempt" for all "the riches of [God's] kindness, tolerance and patience" by not turning his heart unto any form of "repentance." He acted as if God's patient longsuffering was a form of divine weakness, not a show of God's great gracious strength. He misconstrued the silences of God's watchfulness for a tacit form of "okay" for the "trivial" sin in his life.

Is there any part of you where you've constructed that falsest foundation, a single "trivial" sin? Have you let one sin become a "gateway drug" to any others; has a single sin led to forms of "Baal worship" in your life? Have you let your secret greed become the silent reason for a string of business-related lies, half-truths or outright falsehoods? Have you allowed the quiet lust within your mind to take you farther down the road of other lusts, O Man of God? Is there any sin that's started feeling as if "less of a sin," any evil that's been condoned by its trivializing?

Then, today, may we *fight* the urge of evil Ahab: the lessening of the weight of certain sins in our lives. May we see all sin as toxic to our intimacy with Jesus and then root out ones we've already trivialized. Today, don't "provoke the Lord" in His anger, O Man. Provoke your heart to run to Jesus and away from sin.

May 7 – 1 Kings 17:1-16

Actually trusting Him for your needs

There may be no other challenge to our faith that eclipses how we think about our daily physical needs. Even if we have enough to last this day, we're often tied in knots thinking about tomorrow, aren't we? Even if we've put enough away to last us for ten years, we're often worried lest a downturn should turn up. We'll often lay awake at night and count our many costs and perceived needs to the detriment of both sleep *and* trust in the Lord. But if we believe that God could really feed Elijah from the dirty beaks of ravens, *why do we not trust?* If we hear of how his trusting in the Lord's provision also blessed this widow, *why aren't we at peace?* Might we trust the Lord for the good of our salvation and *yet really not believe that He can take care of our daily needs?* Might we talk of Jesus' "life to the full" *but then live lives that make it look as if our only reward is in heaven?* Might we rob the very Gospel of its power if we refuse to trust the Lord in His actual teachings about our lives? Is it possible that we really don't believe that God can provide for our personal needs unless "I go to work today"?

Then reacquaint yourself with the following truth *and actually start believing in the following truth, O Man of God*: **"Therefore I tell you, do not worry about your life, what you will eat or drink; or about your body, what you will wear. Is not life more important than food, and the body more important than clothes? Look at the birds of the air; they do not sow or reap or store away in barns, and yet your heavenly Father feeds them. Are you not much more valuable than they? Who of you by worrying can add a single hour to his life?**

"And why do you worry about clothes? See how the lilies of the field grow. They do not labor or spin. Yet I tell you that not even Solomon in all his splendor was dressed like one of these. If that is how God clothes the grass of the field, which is here today and tomorrow is thrown into the fire, will he not much more clothe you, O you of little faith? So do not worry, saying, 'What shall we eat?' or 'What shall we drink?' or 'What shall we wear?' For the pagans run after all these things, and your heavenly Father knows that you need them. But seek first his kingdom and his righteousness, and all these things will be given to you as well." Give your whole life to this mindset today. Actually believe Him for your needs, every moment.

LIVE LIKE MEN

May 8 – 1 Kings 18:16-46

Being so sure of Him that you're wild for His purposes

There should be such boldness about our lives that we're always bordering on wildness, bordering upon pure mania. If we know the Lord and trust His great commandments for our lives, we should have His mighty confidence within our chest. There should be no modern prophets of Baal who stand a chance in hell before our certitude and confidence in Jesus. We should laugh with holy laughter when our faith in God is mocked as "weak" or as being somehow "make-believe." We should stand before our children and our wife with holy confidence in Him, wholly His to the end of ourselves. We should know this fire from heaven is our wont whenever we're filled with the fire of the Holy Spirit already.

O Men of God, may we strive to feel the wild spirit of the prophet Elijah coursing through our own veins today. You and I, of course, should never laugh at the follies or the sins of this world; we should be helping others to know Him. Yet if we possess a portion of Elijah-type God-confidence, we should start to exude power – *His power* – from within ourselves. We should stand betwixt the laughable schemes of Satan and the people who need Jesus and pray for them everyday. We should stand atop a mountain of His strength and see the distant forming stormclouds of His Coming coming. We should have a steely hardness to our will if we're firmly in His will and stand strong where He's placed us today. We shouldn't fear anything or anyone, except the God who's Judge of everything and everyone.

Would you say you've ever personally worn the mantle of a modern-day wild-man for God, a true "fool for Christ"? Have you ever been audacious in the service of the King who audaciously gave His life for your sake? Have you ever had such confidence in Jesus that nothing mattered but your following after Him, your discipleship? Do you realize how truly wicked is our world and yet how strong is the God we boldly choose to serve within its confines?

Today, put on boldness – wildness – craziness – in the service of your living Lord and mighty Master. Follow in the near-crazed ways of the prophet Elijah. You'll be blessed by the effort.

May 9 – 1 Kings 19:9-18

Make the space to hear His voice today

Even if a man of God should choose to go into a "cave" today, he'd probably bring his smartphone along for company. Even if the "word of the Lord" should come to him, he'd probably be completely consumed with some pressing work-email. Even if he thought of himself as being "zealous for the Lord," his zealotry would be limited by his time constraints. He'd hear a "gentle whisper" just about as often as he hears a gentle spring breeze or the sound of the birds singing. He'd be hard-pressed to find the solitude to hear the voice of the Lord even yelling, much less whispering, in his ear. He'd feel the rumble of the mighty earthquake, feel the heat of the blazing fire, and maybe just shrug his shoulders…

Have you ever heard the voice of the Lord, O Modern Man of God, or the "gentle whisper" of His lips…*ever?* Have you ever even attempted that He might have the opportunity to speak to your listening human ears…*ever?* Have you ever had the "mystical" thought that God might actually exist in the world, and in your life, not only in the scriptures? Do you actually even think that He'd like to have your ear; do you think His voice is audible in any way for you? Have you ever made an effort – as in, going into a cave – that the Lord might have the space to speak to you personally? Do you really want that sort of God-relationship in your modern life, one where He's minute-to-minute actually in it?

Then clear the air by clearing time and space and, especially, plenty of "mind-space" for some listening to the Lord's "whisper" today. If you can't hear wind or earthquake or fire or His scriptures speaking to you, then hear this word to you right now: "My sheep listen to my voice; I know them, and they follow me"; our listening to Jesus is absolutely imperative. We must know the very timbre and the tone – *the actual sound of His voice* – if we'd want to be His humble sheep. We must come to know the sound of the Shepherd's call if we'd want to actually follow Him during our lives…

So, today, let's make the space to hear Him. Ask Him that He'd speak directly to you. Then be prepared for listening, listening, listening, listening, listening, listening, listening, listening, until He actually speaks!

LIVE LIKE MEN

May 10 – 1 Kings 19:19-21

Lighten your load for a pilgrim's perspective

If you've already been chosen by Jesus as one of His disciples, you've already experienced what Elijah did for Elisha, here. You were plowing in some worldly field of life when Jesus walked right up to you and "threw his cloak" around your shoulders. You were thinking that you knew "what life's about" until you felt His calling's warmth wrapping the whole of your future life. If you thought you had some ideas about your future, He removed those and replaced them with glorious divine uncertainty. If you felt you had some knowledge about *anything at all*, He asked you to lay it down at the feet of His "follow Me." If you possessed some sort of worldly possessions, He asked you to embrace the holy perspective of a life-long pilgrimage…

Why did Elisha burn his plow, kill his oxen, give away the meat to eat, after Elijah called him to follow him? Why did Jesus' friends leave their boats, forget their nets, leave behind "security," when He called them to His ministry? Why did Jesus tell the Rich Young Ruler (who He "loved," by the way) to sell off everything and come follow Him? Because we only carry those things along that are light enough to be carried if we truly want to follow Jesus on this pilgrimage! Because the weight of worldly things is just a weight around our necks when we're only called to "carry our cross daily!" Because we must divorce our lives from anything that proves a hindrance to the "heavenward call" of Christ Jesus!

I like the sentiment of this poem that Dietrich Bonhoeffer quotes in his famous *Cost of Discipleship*:

> *We walk as pilgrims through the earth,*
>
> *With empty hands, bereft and bare;*
>
> *To gather wealth were little worth –*
>
> *'Twould only burden life the more.*
>
> *If men will go the way to death,*
>
> *With them we will party company;*
>
> *For God will give us all we need*
>
> *To cover our necessity.*

Today, may we ponder on our worst hindrances and our best helps in this pilgrimage with Jesus Christ. May we never forget that we "have clothed ourselves with Christ" already; may we wear the "cloak" of His choosing proudly. Today, strip off anything you don't need. Strip off everything that He doesn't need.

May 11 – 1 Kings 21

Protecting your name's meaning and usage

Have you ever been in social settings where only the speaking of another person's name results in praise or in mockery? Have you ever heard another person say of an acquaintance, "Tom Smith? Oh yeah, Tom's a great guy!"? And have you ever heard the exact opposite response: "Tom *Smith*?! Tom Smith is a total jerk!"? Have you ever been the one who did the praising or the mocking; been the one whose name was praise or mocked? Have you ever stopped to think of how your actions and your lifestyle result in other's delight or derision of your life? Have you ever thought, as well, of how the carriage of your name results in praise or in mockery of your Savior, Jesus?

Naboth was the kind of man who'd stand against an evil king for the sake of keeping his "good name" actually good. He wouldn't allow the fleeting whims of Ahab to control his earthly life; he wasn't afraid to stand his ground for the right reason. Naboth understood the lasting implications of his family's good name and what it meant to honor his own "fathers." He wouldn't forget the passing-on of his name's and land's great legacy; he'd never *ever* sell them out to another man.

On the other hand, King Ahab was so lax about his name and authority that he let his wife go absolutely wild with them. She thought it nothing as she "wrote [her] letters in Ahab's name," commanding murder for the sake of Naboth's vineyard. King Ahab either was so dense or so completely willing to excuse his name's abuse that he let it all happen to him. As he walked into the vineyard, and his meeting with Elijah, he was acting as if everything was in its proper kingly order…

Have you ever let your name become a mocker's subject by the way you actually let it be profaned, O Man of God? Have you sold any of your integrity by the way your name's perceived, by the way you're known in your community? Do you work for an employer where you know of actual wrongdoing, yet are quiet because "it's not actually me doing it"? Have you ever let your half-and-half behavior (half-good/half-bad) become your identity through its ongoing consistency? Do you challenge all the people within your family with the bearing and the upkeep of your family's good name? Will you leave your name on earth with meanings holy or horrific, with a legacy or a curse for the next generation?

Today, let's give thought to how we'll each protect our name's legacy and its meaning within our earthly lives. May we realize that how we'll live our lives directly affects our name's perception and the good name of Jesus. Protect your name today, O Man of God. May its meaning be found in Christ alone.

LIVE LIKE MEN

May 12 – 1 Kings 22:1-28

God's honesty, first and foremost

We would know such freedom in our lives if we all chose to live life with Michaiah's manly honesty. When the Lord moved him to go before the thrones of both these kings, he went there only armed with truth: *God's truth*. When he heard the provocation to provide a soothing answer like the other prophets, he simply smiled and replied to them: "As surely as the Lord lives" – *which is awfully sure!* – "I can tell him only what the Lord tells me…" Michaiah wasn't scared of anything, any man, because he knew the God who led him was the God of all power. He wouldn't deal with other "prophets" who'd personally profit by the spinning of good yarns, by the tickling of Ahab's fancies. He was free within the speaking of the truth – "What can man do to me?" – he was safe within God's perfect safety. Even if he ended up by sitting in the "bread and water" prison of privations, he was a man after God's own heart.

Don't we know that nothing gives us perfect freedom like unfettered God-following in the speaking of His complete truth? Can't we see how many self-inflicted trials and tribulations have come upon us by our not being honest before? After all, we all know that terrible feeling when we're caught within a lie, from our choosing of *dis*honesty. We've all been offered ample opportunities to speak only the truth and yet we've failed so very often in our lives…

Today, whether your life seems earthly or eternal, spiritual or secular, you're called to speak the honest-to-God truth only. Wherever God has placed your life around the lives of other people, He needs His men to speak completely honestly. He's not impressed by ways we alter, bend or break the truth each day; He's never wowed by our clever modern "ways around it." He doesn't transact with the temporal use of dishonesty for the good of man; He Himself is actually "the truth." (John 14:6)

Today, will you speak only the truth, O Man? Will you guard your mouth and watch what you say? Will you honor Him by speaking only what He gives you and what you know is truth; will you obey Him in this?

May 13 – 2 Kings 2:1-14

Actually believing vs. having "beliefs"

The devil has dissuaded many men from earnest Christ-following by belittling their daily belief in their "beliefs." He succeeds whenever we're reading of Elijah's passing of the Spirit to Elisha and think: "What a great story." He triumphs when we read of mountain-moving by the "faith as small as a mustard seed and say: "Hmmm, how interesting…" He's actually laughing when we act as if the living out of Acts isn't a strong potential possibility for our modern lives.

O Man of God, do you really believe that a "double portion" of His Holy Spirit might come to belong to you? Do you ever ache to realize the power of the Lord and His Holy Spirit that's living in you *right this very minute*? Do you never allow the turnings of Elijah to dissuade you from your following after him, just like Elisha? Is your eye so tuned to following after Jesus' daily leads that you'd never miss the comings of His "chariot of fire"?

In short: Do you want to be a man of power – *of the Lord's power* – or do you want to be a spiritual weakling all your life? Do you want to follow in the footsteps of Elisha – *never turning* – or be turned away by absolutely everything? Would you rather do whatever it might take to get that vaunted "double portion," or be happy with the world's portions? Would you rather be a Man or a boy about your faith; would you rather follow Jesus or simply follow men?

O Man, spend some time today in praying that our God would lead your heart to seek His heart – *only that!* Ask Him that He'd arm your heart with a full-hearted Belief, not just quavering mental assent to Christian "beliefs." If we really want to live our lives with power like Elisha once did, there's every possibility it can be so. If we really give our days to earnest searching for the "double portion" of His Holy Spirit, it will be granted.

Today, let's learn to believe in our God. Let's stop talking about having "beliefs." For there's very little distance between faiths lived apathetically and men's lives lived pathetically. And we won't be those sort of men, will we? Absolutely not!

May 14 – 2 Kings 5:1-16

A life lived powerfully in Him will change lives

Modern men will scrap and scheme and fight and foment and do *terrible* things if it gets them into positions of power. They'll mangle, maul and mutilate their fellow man in the name of centralizing power within themselves. They'll seek to unify disunited minds of populated peoples by their shows and speakings of hollow useless rhetoric. They'll terrify and terrorize their powerless populace if it means their keeping of temporal thrones for another "cycle." They'll promise things and deeds impossible *tomorrow* if it leads them into more power over people *today*. They'll offer strength behind their arms of human weakness if it makes the people feel "secure" and "safe" for the present moment. They'll offer up their personal attributes with words that ring of divine power, knowing secretly of their own powerlessness. They'll speak to futures – *good and bad* – that bring the Present to its knees in the face of their own human political presence…

Yet the shows of God's power in this world will always resound with the only power that's actually power. It's humble-mighty Elisha sitting in his little clay hut that speaks with divine power to the leprous warrior Naaman. It's "mighty" Naaman, stamping off in his idiotic childish anger, that's correspondent to all human forms of "power." And it's his washing in the River Jordan that shows God's power to be independent of all man's high-flown ideas about power…

When was the last time you truly felt God's power, O Man? What were you doing in that particular moment? When was the last time that the Lord's power working in and through your life made another person say: "there is no other God"? Do you recognize that earthly forms of power are a joke when set beside the Lord's great and almighty power? Have you sacrificed all earthly hopes for personal "power" that might have you sacrificing any of the Lord's strength in you? Would you set aside ambitions that are of an earthly nature if you realized they weren't of the Lord's nature? Would you rather be Elisha in his hut, armed with God's strength, or the "strongest" man in the modern world's eyes? Would you rather that His power was so manifest in you that it turned another's heart toward the Lord Jesus? Would you rather be seen as "weak" in the world's view of weakness than be "strong" in its foolish conceptions of strength?

Today, let's pray for His might, O Men. Let's pray for His form of strength in us. Let's become so clear-eyed in His truth that we can see the gaping difference between His power and the world's. For we can be the men of His power. We can live for Him like Elisha did.

May 15 – 2 Kings 6:8-23

Know the power of His "host" around you

If we'd actually recognize the might of God's celestial band of warriors, think of what we might accomplish, O Men of God! If we'd see upon the hills of our travails *not* the armies of the enemy, but the Lord's Army, we'd conquer quickly! If we'd wake up every morning and remind ourselves "Don't be afraid," we'd be starting out the battle with the right spirit. If we knew that "those who are with us are more than those who are with them," we'd be completely and totally unafraid everyday. O Man of God, we must start our reading of these moments in the scriptures with a heart of very real faith. We must see about Elisha's circumstances, and his cool reaction to them, the model for our own modern manhood. For if we lived as if the host of heaven were arrayed out there before us, wouldn't we fight the battle today and actually win it? Wouldn't we cease to worry for our own protection and our distant future if we only thought about His highest for Today? If we chose to give our hearts unto a lifestyle of this sort of divine detachment, would we be touched by anything? Would there be a single earthly trauma, tragedy or trouble that could touch that type of real true trust in Jesus?

"When the servant of the man of God got up and went out early the next morning, an army of (mortgage payments, marriage troubles, economic downturns, broken relationships, painful past issues, concern for the future, disobedient children etc) had surrounded the city. 'Oh, my lord, what shall we do?' the servant asked.

"'Don't be afraid,' *you* said with calm heart. 'Those who are with us are more than those who are with (all of that.)' And *you* calmly prayed, 'O Lord, open his eyes so he may see.' Then the Lord opened the servant's eyes, and he looked and saw the hills full of horses and chariots of fire all around *you*."

Today, may we go with holy confidence springing from our *knowledge* of the forces surrounding our earthly lives. May we be so sure of our assured deliverance and salvation that there's nothing in this world that can shake our hearts. Your awareness of His omnipresent power can do that. Only, O Man, will you start to believe?

May 16 – 2 Kings 10:18-28

"Assemble" sins and vanquish them

In the last few weeks, we've spoken of the daily need to battle against our sin in three specific ways: At the onset of May, we talked of how an individual's sin can lead him away from perfect union with the God he desires to serve. Then, a few days later, we talked of both the need for razing sin's "strongholds" and also not trivializing our sin. We talked of how our lives will become as big, or as little, as the sins we let define our daily lives and outlook. We talked of how we must be vicious with ourselves in robust honesty, asking ourselves the very hardest questions. We talked of not allowing sin to win the day-to-day of following after Jesus; not to let ourselves be "defined" by it. We talked of giving this battle to the Lord, asking for His strength for the fight, so that He might fight it on our behalf. We talked of never giving up, how we need to stop giving in, and never letting Satan win without a fierce fight...

So how's that going in your life now, O Man? Are you fighting in that battle, still? Are you giving of your best when Satan's giving you his worst; are you growing more aware of your own sin? Are you learning to be constantly attuned to both his plans and also your weaknesses; learning to fight this enemy more intelligently? Are you learning godly honesty when you're dealing with these struggles in yourself, sensing your frailty unto folly?

There might be nothing that's more helpful for this ongoing sin-battle than to "congregate" our knowledge of it. If we take the time to gather up the "ministers of Baal" in our lives, we can absolutely slaughter them. If you'll take the time to sit down with some paper, a pen, some prayer and *your honesty*, the Lord can call up all your sins before you. If you'll let His Spirit move within your spirit, He'll call up all your weakest places; you can write them out for further pondering...

Then, filled up with the same righteous indignation that caused Jehu's bloody actions, pray the Lord would give you strength for the fight. Ask Him that He'd walk beside you in the living of your Today; that He'd help you slaughter your sin wholly. Ask Him that He'd give you special sorts of prescience for the battle so that you'd have the upper-hand against your enemy, Satan. Don't start this day without a strong provision of His strength for you; don't try to battle your sin alone...

O Men of God, may we never give up on this battle for our lives; may we fight with His great might today. May we be the ones whose every single day is hearkening unto *His* tomorrows; let's fight within His army now!

LIVE LIKE MEN

May 17 – 2 Kings 13:14-20a

Having huge God-expectancy

A man of God is hampered only when his expectations of the Lord are equivalent to an earth-bound understanding. A man of God is weakened only when his thoughts of God's eternal power are compared with something humanly relatable. A man of God becomes distracted and downcast when the bulk of his thoughts are given to things of this earth, not to heavenly things. This man will find himself defeated only when he thinks he's fighting in his own battle, to the exclusion of the Lord's...

To the moment of his passing, there was never any moment when Elisha exhibited confusion about his life's mission. Even as he lay at death's door, there was nothing in Elisha's life *not* speaking of his God's complete power. When Jehoash came to visit him, he was only able to view him as the shell of his formerly strong prophetic self. He wept and wailed before he'd understand the mighty strength still contained within Elisha's spirit and his trust in the Lord. He underestimated God's almighty power by carrying expectations only equivalent to his own earthly understanding. He weakened Israel's arm by approaching God's almighty strength as if it was something humanly relatable. He felt himself downcast within the presence of the mighty king of Aram, not focusing on God's Army. He limited his victory over the enemy by not expressing overwhelming trust in the Lord and in the strength of His arm.

We're given strength whenever we live as if the God we claim to serve is the all-powerful God of the universe. We're utter fools when we beat the arrows "only three times," thinking that we've done "enough" for Him already. We'll be strong whenever we "open the east window" and shoot wild crazy arrows of His strength for our lives. We'll be weak whenever we limit our own vision to our human understanding, calling that brand of nonsense "trust."

Would you rather be dead upon your death-bed in the strength of the Lord than half-dead in a false useless faith? Would you like to be a mighty warrior in the cause of your King, or a "good Christian" going to church on Sundays, O Man? Can't you see how God provided a vital strength for Elisha, even in the moments leading up to his earthly death? Wouldn't you like that kind of strength to be the definition of your daily life, the defining characteristic of *you*?

Then, today, ask the Lord for expectations that are worthy of His name; strike the ground "five or six times." You and I will only become men as mighty in His strength as the measure we're currently willing to ask Him for. Let's ask Him for more today, O Man. And let's be visionaries of His power.

May 18 – 2 Kings 18:1-8

Worshipping God alone, not conceptions of Him

Sometimes the *conception* of our God we're actively worshipping is as dangerous as the worship of a false god. If we worship any *form* of God devoid of His absolute entirety, we're on the road to worshiping a manmade idol. If we worship at the altar of a *memory* of the work of God in us, we're actually bowing to a foreign god. If we don't unite our greatest understandings to the immensity of the Godhead, we sell Him terribly short of who He is. If our faith is only borne out by His workings of the distant past, we'll damn both our present and our future. If we won't embrace the awesome immeasurability of His "everything-ness," we'll start to make Him nothing at all…

Hezekiah was a faithful king in his breaking down the sacred stones, high places and evil Asherah poles. "There was no one like him among all the kings of Judah," we're told, including even David, his most famous forefather. Yet interesting among his vaunted kingly accomplishments was how he "broke into pieces the bronze snake Moses had made." Almost unbelievably fascinating is the fact that God's own people started worshiping a symbol, not their Savior. When they burned incense to Moses' bronze snake, was there any actual difference from the worship of a foreign god? Just because the Lord had used the snake to signify His awesome power in the past, was this not a terrible idolatry?

How do you portray the God you worship by the manner, mode and method of your daily personal worship? Is your faith displaying *false* worship by worshipping your God as if He's somehow stuck back in ancient history? Do you view your God as if He's only alive through the lens of your own memories, or is He real and alive for you each day? Would you canonize the creation or the Creator; cause or Causality; your version of god or *the God of the universe*? Do you ever burn unholy incense at the altar of a you-created re-creation of the God of all the world? Or, like King Hezekiah, do you "hold fast to the Lord" and "not cease to follow him" ever, O Man of God?

Today, may we pay close attention to the version of Jesus we're following; *there is actually only one Jesus to follow!* May we be of such an honest nature that we're truthful if we find we're really worshipping a "bronze snake Jesus." Ask the Lord for revelation only of Himself and then worship Him in the manner that He'd actually ask you for. May we be the men who follow after God and not some human misconception of our own personal choosing. Today, let's follow after Jesus. And Him only – *only*.

May 19 – 2 Kings 19:5-19

"Spread out" your troubles before Him

Trusting in the plan that God has laid out for your life is the same thing as a total invulnerability. Yes, you will go toe-to-toe with Satan, hardship and all kinds of worldly anxiety, but you'll be rewarded with the fruits of faith. Yes, you may have moments where a dark defeat looms before your eyes, but you know that God is with you, by your side. Yes, you may have all Assyria waiting at your gates to tear you to pieces, but you know the Lord's plan for you is perfect…

When Hezekiah read this latest missive from the evil Assyrian king, he did the only thing he could possibly do in that moment. No, he didn't redraw his battle plans or recheck his siege defenses; Hezekiah walked straight into the temple to see his God. He went to the Lord and he "spread…out" Sennacherib's letter in His presence; then he humbly prayed for the Lord's almighty help. He reminded God that he was fully aware of His immense exaltedness; he knew full well of God's awesome and perfect power. Yet he also spoke the truth of his own present earthly trouble, the horrendous facts of Sennacherib's brutal past campaigns. He was honest with the Lord in his great worry, "but in everything, by prayer and petition," he "presents [his] requests to God."

Have you lately "spread out" your anxieties before the Lord and allowed Him to reward you with His perfect, and promised, peace? Have you spoken of your worries and your battles with a spirit that's actually open to His supernatural intervention? Do you go to Him – *and only to Him* – when it seems as if Assyria's at your gates and ready to break in? Do you believe His plan is actually so perfect that it's truly worth trusting, even when your life feels terrifying?

Today, may we place our lives within the hands of the One who came to Israel's strong defense back in Hezekiah's day. May we know the strength of God who "put to death a hundred and eighty-five thousand men in the Assyrian camp" that fateful night. May we honor Him by honoring His perfect plan for our lives and by actually trusting Him within our day. May we go forth with the equanimity of King Hezekiah for this day, trusting in the Lord and in His wonderful plans for us.

LIVE LIKE MEN

May 20 – 2 Kings 20:12-19

Showing off shows your insecurity

Allowing our insecurities to belie the source of our "security" is like putting a loaded gun to our own head. When we meet another person's personal entreaties with a show of our own grandeur, we're self-inflicting wounds upon ourselves. When another seeks to "get to know you better" and you *only* speak of earthly things, that's an awfully telling statement about your life. When you can't be fully conversant with another man without a "pissing contest" forming, where's your life's security sourced? Can you safely let another boast and brag without descending to comparison or are you a "one-upper"? Can you speak about your life with words of power that are *not at all* connected to your position or to posturing? Do you think that "what you do" is as important as the honesty and power that can come from "who you are"? Would you be okay with others *not* knowing what you do, *not* knowing what a big deal you are to yourself?

It was from his own sickly insecurities that King Hezekiah did what he does for these foreign envoys. It was likely from his personal need to bolster his kingly image that he acted like he did, *like a complete and utter fool*. While these men had come to offer him a gift because of his illness, it's actually Hezekiah who gives a gift to them. He gives them a perfect knowledge of his holdings and his people's power; he whets appetites for future conquest of his kingdom. He commits his people to a life of future slavery by his overwhelming need to toot his own horn before men. He commits great sin by thinking earthly abundance is itself security and thus he shows the root and depths of his insecurities…

Do you feel the Lord is your security, O Man, that the Lord is "your shield and helper and your glorious sword"? Do you only place your trust in His provision and not in the quicksand that's your bank account, retirement account, 401(k) etc? Do you find discussions with your friends revolving around the so-called "security" to be found in money and possessions? Are you almost always tempted to receive another's interest in you by revealing what a "winner" you are? Do you think that all your "silver, gold, spices and fine oil" are displayed to others because you're *so* darn secure in yourself? Or, is it the other way around, that we're tempted to belie our false security by showing off our "things"?

Today, let's just be ourselves. *Only*. Today, let's just follow Jesus. *Only*. Let's stop showing off our earthly goods as if they're actually something, when we've got to know they're really nothing! Let's stop greeting visiting envoys with the shows of our false strength; let's simply trust the Lord today for

His estimate of us.

No more Hezekiah-style insecurity, O Men.

The Lord our God is our eternal security.

May 21 – 2 Kings 23:1-3

Renew your March 31st Covenant

Two months ago, we gave ourselves the challenge of creating a personal Covenant with some other brothers in our life. We spoke of how we might pursue a deeper friendship through our mutual calling-up toward the higher places in Jesus. We spoke of setting non-negotiables together "in speech, in life, in love, in faith and in purity." (1 Tim. 4:12) We looked at how the brotherly bond created between Jonathan and David was irrevocable and how, presumably, we'd all want that for ourselves…

Did you take that challenge back then, O Men? And, if so, how's that going in your life now? Do you need to re-remind those chosen brothers – *and yourself* – about what those special commitments to each other were? Do you need to find those vows that you created and then re-vow to each other that you're Jesus' men only?

Today, take the time for mutual renewal of your brotherly commitment to your co-created Covenant. Stand by, and before, the brothers who are pillars in your life "in the presence of the Lord," and then recommit to that lifestyle. Strive "to follow the Lord and keep his commands, regulations and decrees" with all your heart and soul. Spend time with those same friends "confirming the words of the covenant" you created back in March, and then go after them!

In Malachi 3:6, we hear of God's perfect constancy to His Covenant and His people: "I the Lord do not change." Today, let's recommit ourselves to the striving after such great constancy as the Lord has already shown to us. Let's follow that Lord today, O Men. Let's renew our brotherly covenants.

May 22 – 1 Chronicles 5:18-22

Are you in the battle?

The formula for fighting any spiritual battle to victorious conclusion is quite clearly spelled out right here: "They were helped in fighting [the Hagrites, Jetur, Naphish and Nodab]...*because they cried out to him during the battle.*" The Lord "answered their prayers" and gave them total victory over their enemies "because they trusted in him," the Lord their God. They "seized the livestock," "took one hundred thousand people captive...because the battle was God's," not theirs at all.

O "able-bodied" man, do you feel you can "handle shield and sword"; are you able to "use a bow" in the battle? Do you feel that you've acquired proper training for the war ahead, that you're ready now to fight it for Jesus' sake? Do you have the firm resolve that you're actually called to fields of God's choosing, that you're a chosen warrior of His? Do you sense within yourself the ready real trust that will "cry out" to the Lord during a fierce pitched battle? Do you know of His great mercies that are found within the fight, of the faith that grows when truly utilized? Do you desire that you'd be ranked amongst the hallowed halls of mighty men who've stormed Satan's castle for the good of the Kingdom?

Then, today, plain and simple, being honest, ask yourself this first and foremost question: "Am I actually *in* the battle?" Have you sought where the Lord would choose to place your particular skill-set for the glory of His final and assured victory? Have you ever opened your mouth to the Holy Spirit and to His leading and to His speaking of the truth through your life? Have you ever tried to see if His commandments, properly carried out, actually lead to His promised "life to the full"? Would you take up his great parlay: that a faith that's properly forged in the battle is the only kind of real faith? Would you test out all your trust within the bloody messy confines of a body-strewn modern spiritual battlefield? Will you actually put your faith where your mouth is, leaving behind the confines of the pew-bound Sabbath soldier? Will you labor dawn-to-dusk in this only labor that's actually worthy of our lives: the call to follow Jesus?

We can't refuse to venture out into the battle and then expect our faith to grow; that's simply impossible! If we're never crossing swords with the enemy's army, he'll never have to worry about us being a danger to him, will he? But if we'd seek to be like "Reubenites, Gadites and the half-tribe of Manasseh," we must join in with our whole heart. We must ask the Lord where He's wanting to use our lives so that we're of the greatest value – *to Him and to His battleplan*. And then we must simply go, O Men! We must

LIVE LIKE MEN

fight the good fight right now!

May 23 – 1 Chronicles 12:8

Is your face becoming like His?

A man who gives his undivided attention to the seeking of his Savior's face will begin to reflect that face himself. He'll find the strength of God reflecting from his visage when he starts to turn his vision only unto his God, everyday. The world will see more power, purpose, peace and a calm resolve chiseled into his face when his heart is fully the Lord's. All his friends will start to look to his lead when they can actually sense the Lord's strength in his courageous carriage. David had the sort of countenance that consistently called men to himself; he had power written on his very face. He attracted mighty men whose "faces were the faces of lions" because his own was a face reflective of *the* Lion. He drew stealthy men who were as "swift as gazelles" because his feet had been made just like "the feet of a deer." They came to join his ranks of mighty men because they sensed the Lord had "enabled [him] to stand on the heights."

Does your face reflect the calm certainty of God's calling and appointment, His holy choosing of your life? Have you spent such vast amounts of time in His presence that your own presence radiates with His sort of strength? Would you say your day-to-day demeanor is derivative of the King; do you source your strength within His strength? Do you draw your daily dose of Jesus' love every morning; do you live from His great purposes for your life? Have you gazed long at His visage to the point where your own face is beginning to look like a copy of His glorious face? Does your face look like a lion with the Lion's sort of strength or does it look like a scared boy's? Would you rather that you'd radiate His peace by the strength He gives you or confusion by your constant carewornness? Would you rather become confident in Him and in His plans, or be harried and harassed like all other men?

Reflect on this passage from II Corinthians 3 and contemplate how God might use your face today: "But we all, with unveiled face, beholding as in a mirror the glory of the Lord, *are being transformed into the same image* from glory to glory, just as from the Lord, the Spirit." May we be the sort of men whose earthly countenance bears eternal power through the strength of the Lion we serve. May we have the faces of lions, O Men. May we be as swift as gazelles with His love for this world.

May 24 – 1 Chronicles 14:1,2

Acknowledging God's blessings

I'd imagine there will be few of us who'd look upon these pages from the position of an actual earthly king. Most of the men currently reading through this sentence are just like I am; we're normal average everyday followers of Jesus. We're guys who wake up every morning with the knowledge of the present-day responsibilities that we'll work through today. We're men who know the worries of the world; we've "seen our share of things"; we've oftentimes gained our wisdom "the hard way." We've all "put childish ways behind" ourselves for the purpose of becoming real men in the way of Jesus Christ. We're men who sense the calling upon our lives, the full potential that's actually promised, when we give our hearts to our Savior alone.

David knew "the Lord had established him as king over Israel" because he'd constantly acknowledged God's blessing. It was easy from his privileged position to be humble, for he'd always been a man of humble heart…

Today, whether you're rich or poor, feeling particularly strong or weak, you have every reason to be likewise thankful, O Man. The God of the universe has actually chosen you; you're a man whose life is marked for His own eternal purposes in this world. So let's take the time, below, to write out everything He's done for us, how He's set us on our current path. Let's write down some of those blessings that He's blessed us with; let's remind ourselves of the tremendous ways He's "shown up!"

* * * * *

May 25 – 2 Chronicles 13:1-18

Drawing dividing lines for the battle

The Lord will lead the charge for the men who'll let Him lead; He'll fight for the men who put their whole hope in His eternal Fight. He delights to hear the raucous shouts of men who shout out "God is with us"; He'll fight for those who lift Him up as their "leader." He'll rout the allied armies that flock to Satan's side; He'll vanquish the "powers" that this fallen world musters against Him. If we turn our hearts away from things temporal, asking the Lord to be our General, He'll actually fight for us, O Men!

Like Abijah, take the time to write a battle cry, below, that states the clear divisions between yourself and the enemy. Re-read how Abijah starkly set his cause against the enemies' cause; replicate his "line drawn in the sand." Address your words to either Satan or the world; speak the truth of how the Lord has rallied you to His glorious cause. The devil hates when men choose to define themselves as being clearly *not* his; when a man will stand his ground, prepared to fight…

* * * *

"Satan and the world, listen to me…"

May 26 – 2 Chronicles 16:1-9

The "fully committed" will gain strength

The eyes of God *don't* range around the earth to strengthen those whose hearts are "sort of" committed to Him "when they feel like it." No, "the eyes of the Lord range throughout the earth to strengthen those whose hearts are fully committed to him" *already*. The Lord is *not* searching for the men who'd talk as if they're following Him; He's already fully aware of those who are His. He knows right now if your "commitment to His cause" is really real by the fruits your faith is actually currently bearing. He knows already if all your high-falutin' talk of following Him is fact or if it's well-wrought fiction. He knows already if we bear the hearts worthy for his "strengthening"; if our "salt" still truly tastes "salty." He knows already of every thought you might be thinking while you're reading through these words; He knows "the very hairs of your head." He knows already how all your daily/weekly/monthly/yearly conduct matches up with His perfect stated commandments…

O Man of God, can you say with total confidence that your desire is for a "fully committed" heart for your Savior? Do you even *want* to want that in your life; does it cross your mind daily; would you do what's truly necessary? Would you rather barter with a Ben-Hadad than trust in the Lord for His provision through His perfect providence? Would you rather that your confidence was founded on the Lord or upon the shrewdest use of your available resources?

Today, let's consider the words of our Savior when He said: "whoever has will be given more…he will have an abundance." If we'll purify our hearts and give full value to a "full commitment," He'll "strengthen" us fully and completely. Yet "whoever does not have, even what he has will be taken from him"; He's not impressed with men of half-measured living. Let's be the men who ask Him for a "fully committed" heart and then follow through with all the "following" that's involved. May we not give in to even starting to think that our commitment doesn't matter, that a full commitment's impossible. May we feel "the eyes of the Lord" ranging upon our manly hearts and aspire to rid our hearts of every earthly hindrance. May we be the men who "fully commit" today that we'll be "fully committed" to trying our best for a "full commitment!" Let's give our very best today, O Men. After all, He's the Lord who gave us His all.

May 27 – 2 Chronicles 26:16-21

Spiritual Pride

It would seem the pride that springs up from our spiritual life is actually far more dangerous than an "everyday sort of pride." If we start to pride ourselves upon the part of us that comes from His grace, we're taking credit where it'll never be due. If we start to raise our spiritual journey above the journey of another person, we're guilty of Uzziah's brand of sin. If we think we're worthy to approach the Lord's presence *without* Jesus, we're like Uzziah entering the temple in this moment. The Lord has rescued us from out of the "miry depths, where there is no foothold"; none of us has redeemed himself! The Lord has drawn us safely from the dangers we were facing in the "deep waters"; it was His rescue-plan, not ours! When Jesus hung upon the cross beneath the darkness of that Golgothic sky, He was doing all the work Himself. So if we start to think we're better than another in our hidden heart, we heap mockery upon our Lord and Savior. If we start to think our own spiritual qualities set us apart from others, we're setting ourselves up for eventual ruin. If Uzziah's skin broke out with leprosy that represented his insides, I'd shudder to think of what my own might look like…

O Man of God, you're nothing better than the world's vilest sinner – *you must learn to make your peace with that!* Of yourself, of your own personal labors, of your paltry attempts at service, you can do nothing about your sin. There's literally no way you can save yourself from the deadly "wages of sin" *except for your Savior's perfect way*. There's no known formula, no magic incantation, that can make you better than you are *without His death on your behalf*.

Today, let's offer on the altar-of-our-continual-need-for-purification the spiritual pride that currently resides within our hearts. May we go to Him with every little piece of ourselves that ever thinks we don't actually need Him and His Cross. May we offer up the moments of our days when we're most tempted to think, "At least I'm better than (insert someone's name)." May we learn the humble-hearted kind of spirit that goes to Him with a present knowledge of the mass of sin we've been saved *from*. O Man of God, you're a sinner. And yet the Lord chose to save you. The world is still full of lost sinners. Now live your life only from the knowledge of His grace.

May 28 – 2 Chronicles 27:1-6

Be of "steadfast" spirit

So much of the power in the scriptures is because of the particular *words* that God gave men for creating His Word. There's poetry in the Psalms as beautifully incandescent as any found in Keats, Wordsworth, Byron, Blake or Frost. There are war anthems that shout out with the hot bloodlusty anger of a thousand William Wallaces or Rob Roys. There are perfect parables hanging from the lips of Jesus that make us scratch our collective head all the time. What a perfect compilation of His wholly chosen words marks the makeup of His perfect Holy Word! What a thing it is to mold a wondrous story from the clay of human history, using men's written constructs!

Today, we ready the words: "Jotham grew powerful *because he walked steadfastly before the Lord his God.*" For that reason, walking "steadfastly" must become our aim today if we're aiming for the Lord's sort of power in our lives.

stead-fast *adj* \sted-fast\ **1. a : firmly fixed in place b : not subject to change 2 : firm in belief, determination, or adherence**

Today, I'm praying that we'll "firmly fix" ourselves in God's "place" for us, thereby looking for our best Kingdom-usefulness. I'm praying that we're "not subject to change" in our faith or our feelings, in our conduct or in practical obedience. I'm praying that you'll find you're growing "firm in your belief, determination, and adherence" to your Lord and His teaching. I'm praying that this single strong word – "steadfast" – sinks into your human psyche; may it be your definition today!

"Therefore, my dear brothers, stand firm. Let nothing move you. Always give yourselves fully to the work of the Lord, because you know that your labor in the Lord is not in vain." (1 Cor. 15:58)

O my brothers, since we know our labor in the Lord is not in vain, let's give ourselves fully to it today! Nothing at all can move you when you're in Him. Let's be steadfast, "standing firm."

May 29 – 2 Chronicles 28:22,23

Trying to have it "both ways"

Jesus is the Lord of everything or He's actually nothing; He can't be "sort of the Lord" and the Lord. He Himself couldn't have made the claims He made throughout the Gospels credibly if He'd acted as if they were "sort of" true. He can't be the Lord of life if there's any other earthly lord who'd claim dominion in the midst of His *actual* dominion. He can't be our soul's Savior if His acts of earthly sacrifice were anything less than absolutely eternal in scope…

Similarly, you and I are either following Jesus or we're not; we can't be out of His presence and within it. We can't make our righteous statements based upon His Gospels' truths credibly if we don't try to obey His Gospels' commandments. We can't be the followers of Jesus if there's any other lord who'd claim dominion in the midst of His dominion over us. We don't have a Savior of our souls if we don't accept His earthly sacrifice as being everything worth living for…

Ahaz was an earthly idiot when he tried to cut his losses by sacrificing to the gods of his earthly defeat. Thinking "since the gods of the kings of Aram have helped them" is the most embarrassing human thought possible, wouldn't you say? That he'd see in his defeat a religious hypothesis of this kind seems horrendously simplistic, doesn't it? That he'd go so far as these steps in his need for "spiritual expedience" seems the height of personal sin, right?

Yet aren't there similar ways that we've ourselves offered up sacrifices to the gods of this foolish age, O Men of God? Aren't there ways that we display Ahaz' brand of half-and-half thinking, thinking that "there must be some compromises" available? Aren't there ways that we will see another man's "victory" as the sign of a need for course-change in our own life? Aren't there ways where we will deem expedience as the goal of our existence, instead of following Jesus only?

I myself have worshipped *often* at the foot of earthly altars in the service of this foolish world's ways. I've bartered faith for fallacy when inviting worldly ways into the heart of my heart's thinking about my Savior and His love for me. I've betrayed my Lord by acting like He's not the Lord of my life in the way that I've actually chosen to live. I "abide" in vines that aren't about His Way whenever I'm tempted to test ways of worldly "victory" instead.

How about you, my friend? Do you ever try to have it both ways? The answer to that simple question will determine if we're walking in the way of Ahaz or in the way of Jesus…

May 30 – 2 Chronicles 30:6-12

Humble-hearted doing

At Christ's command, couriers went out throughout the world with a letter from the King, which read: "People of God, return to the Lord, the God who saved you, that His Spirit might flare up within you. For you have been rescued from the hands of mighty Satan. Do not be like any who will not humbly obey me, who are unfaithful to the spoken commands of Jesus. Do not be stiff-necked, as your pundits are; submit to the Lord only. Be His holy sanctuary, His blessed temple, which he has consecrated forever. Serve the Lord your God, so that his anger will be turned away from others' lives through your testimony. If you'll return your heart to the Lord, live and speak from His compassion, then others will be shown compassion. For the Lord your God is gracious and compassionate. He will not turn His face from those *you* turn His face upon."

The couriers went from town to town throughout the modern world, but the people seemed to prefer their own "lukewarmness." They ridiculed His call to action as "overly simplistic"; "smacking of 'pharisaic legalism.'" Nevertheless, some men who belonged to Him humbled themselves and went out to serve in the labors of His harvest. The hand of God was on these men to give them unity of mind to carry out what the King had ordered. Those men did what they were told. Those men followed the word of the Lord.

Will you be such a man, O Man of God? Will you be such a man today?

LIVE LIKE MEN

May 31 – 2 Chronicles 32:1-8

Undaunted Living

Even though we've already read about Assyria's march on Jerusalem (May 19, 2 Kings 19:5-19), there's something special in this particular account. There's something telling in this telling of Hezekiah's kingly workings that can tell us more about his heart for the Lord. When we read of how he chose to block all the springs and streams, we're reminded of the workings of a shrewd kingly mind. When we see how he "worked hard" in repairing all the wall's broken sections, we're reading of a clearly wise man. When we hear that Hezekiah even built a wall *outside* the wall, we're hearing of some brilliant forethought. Yet it's his words to the military men whom he'd appointed that really tell us about his truest form of power as their king. It's the way he echoes Moses, Joshua and David – "be strong and courageous" – that shows he understands his holy lineage. Even though he's standing on the brink of possible horrendous defeat, he stands strong in the power of the Lord. He says: "With him is only the arm of flesh, but with us is the Lord our God to help us and to fight our battles." He knows that no amount of dam-building, section-fixing, extra-wall-construction is sufficient to hold off mighty Assyria. He knows that no extra "supporting terraces," nor his many shields and weapons, will result in earthly victory. Yet he *also* knows that "there is a greater power with us than with him"; he knows where the Lord stands in the fight. And when a man can clearly trust in the Lord, and know the strength of the Lord's might, he can speak with words like those in verse 8.

Do you feel like there are Assyrians in your life today, pressing upon the strongest defenses of your mind? Are there earthly foes who press upon you with impunity, daring you to trust in the Lord your God alone? Would you look unto the circumstances in your present life and be ready to respond like Hezekiah did in verse 8? Do you really believe the Lord your God will "fight your battles"; do you really believe that His might is right here with you? Do you really believe that "with (your problems, enemies, struggles etc) is only the arm of flesh," weak and temporal? Will you be vanquished by your worries and human thinking, "trying to do it your own way," or be victorious through your trust in God? Then, today, may we stand before the onslaught of our enemies and respond to them with words like Hezekiah's! May we be the men undaunted before anything, any situation, any person: free and ready to fight with the Lord's assistance! The Lord your God is with you today, O Man of God. Now will you let Him fight your battle?

June 1 – Ezra 7:8-10

Do you feel God's hand upon your journey?

Sometimes it might seem as if a certain class of men are on a journey of their own personal engineering. It seems like there are particular men who'll arrive wherever they'd like to; bold thinkers and doers who chart their own course. Many times it seems like *other* men are offered up the chance to pick their path throughout the days of their life. It sometimes seems like certain "lucky" men are clearly heading off to somewhere, somewhere seemingly better than us…

Yet, oftentimes, we men of God will act if our life's journey is only clear for this current step we're taking. Oftentimes, it seems to us as if the workings of the Lord's path are like a crazy man's switchbacks up a mountainside. It seems to us as if we only know the point of our departure, not the destination of this earthly journey we're on. It seem to us as if we "began [our] journey from Babylon on the first of the month" … but who knows where we're actually going now?!

O Man of God, there's nothing in your journey that matters more than if the "gracious hand" of God is upon you *right this very minute*. There's not a single question that matters more than if you currently feel His hand; if you're currently abiding in Him, "the Vine." If we seek to divinate our life's destination but aren't feeling for His handhold, we'll miss the true joy in the journey. If we worry for the places we'll arrive instead of seeking Him today, we might stall out our own steps to Him. But if we'd like to walk as Ezra once did, we mustn't start becoming anxious about arriving at places of our choosing. We must thank God that we're on a journey of His personal choosing, one we know will have eternal ramifications *planned by Him*. We must be thankful that the Lord would make us worthy to be vessels of His glory, "ambassadors" for Christ. We must devote ourselves to "study and observance of the Law of the Lord," and simply trust His eternal/temporal path for us.

I love the way C.S. Lewis described the only clear view of our life's journey in his book, *The Pilgrim's Regress*:

"If old tales were true, if a man without putting off humanity could indeed pass the frontiers of our country, if he could be, and yet be a man, in that fabled East and fabled West, then indeed at the moment of fruition, the raising of the cup, the assumption of the crown, the kiss of the spouse – then first, to his backward glance, the long roads of desire that he had trodden would become plain in all their winding, and when he found, he would know what it was that he had sought."

May we only seek Jesus today, O Men. He knows all about our journey's eventual end. May we strive that our own eyes are fixed forever forward – *only in His direction* – until He later lets us look back.

June 2 – Ezra 9

Be "appalled" by evil. Then do something about it.

If you don't feel a measure of Ezra's feeling in this chapter, you're simply not paying attention, O Man of God. If you don't observe the current state of the world and feel "appalled" like he once did, take another look around today. You and I are living in a world where evil seems to be prevailing; where Satan seems to runs roughshod over people's lives. We live in times where children find themselves so sexually advanced and exploited; where people's "urges" become their fulfilled "needs." Ours is an era that's defined by "political correctness," yet not by definable rights and wrongs that bear any tie to any truth. We live in places marred by sin; by corruption, crime, cowardice; by "power" used to no good purpose. We people pews in many millions on each Sunday, yet we seem to sense our own latent lameduckness against all this wrongdoing. We wonder if the Lord might ever "do anything," if He really "cares" about "all this evil" that's all around our lives?

O Man of God, do you care about the "way the world's going today," just like Ezra cared about his own people? Do you see within the world's current state a place for God's redemption or a place to simply throw up defeated hands? Would you endeavor to be like Ezra for the people of this world; will you bring their present plight to your Savior, Jesus? When was the last time that you actually prayed about the corporate sins of countries and the need for God's intervention in people's lives? When was the last time that you "sat down appalled" and yet then rose up as an agent of God's holy influence? When was the last time that you saw the Church's mission to be the same as Jesus Christ's: "to seek and to save the lost"?

It's important that we notice how the sins of Israel weren't the sins marking Ezra's own personal life. No, Ezra didn't intermarry and he didn't do the things that displeased his God, as Israel had been doing. Yet Ezra saw his people's separation from their God as a "calling out" for his own labors, not a call unto judgment. He felt their degradation just as much as he might feel his own personal degradation, and then he went to work to do good.

Today, may we be "appalled" like Ezra was; may we feel the weight of sin that's crushing down upon our world. But, then, may we rouse ourselves to do the work of the Lord on other's behalf; to pray, to help, to reach out, to love the people around us. Let's not become complacent in the face of evil. May we "overcome evil with good."

June 3 – Nehemiah 1

View the Church like Nehemiah's Jerusalem

God's people were in this "trouble and disgrace" because they'd actively disobeyed and been dispersed throughout the world. "The wall of Jerusalem" lay in ruins because Israel had put its trust in strong defenses, not in the strength of the Lord their God. Nehemiah personally understood the reason for the exile and the reason for the razing of the city of Jerusalem. And he also knew the promises of his God, both the blessings and the curses, to be consistent with His perfect holiness. Yet, nevertheless, seeing just how his people and his city were destroyed, Nehemiah "sat down and wept." "For some days," mourning and fasting and praying, Nehemiah sought the Lord and His will before moving forward with any plans…

And did you notice how he then addressed God? Did you notice how he led off his prayer? Did you think of how his future expectations – for himself and for his people – were expressed in those words? "O Lord, God of heaven, the great and awesome God, *who keeps his covenant of love with those who love him and obey his commands…*" Nehemiah's expectation was success – with Artaxerxes, with the people, with the rebuilding – with everything that was to come. He knew that just as God had ravaged Jerusalem, He also had the mighty power to rebuild and restore it. He knew that if he followed after God's ways, there was every possibility for a full-scale restoration…

O Man of God, there are many ways in which the modern Church needs some modern-day Nehemiahs in it. There are many ways in which the simple commands of Jesus Christ lay in ruins through our everyday disobedience. We were simply called to follow Him, living out the day-by-day adventures of His Great Commission as one Body. And yet we look around the world and all our churchly lack of effort and we know how terribly short we're currently falling…

Today, give your heart to concentrated thought upon the place(s) God would call you to restore His Body. If we men would lead the Church as we're actually called to do, nothing would be able to slow our progress for His Kingdom. If we'd concentrate our energies and our prayers with hearts that beat like Nehemiah's, we could bind the Church to its historic mission. If we'd delight ourselves "in revering [His] name," who knows what might happen for His purposes in our current generation? Well, let's start finding out today, O Men! Pray for the heart, and with the heart, of Nehemiah.

June 4 – Nehemiah 2:1-9

Using our position for God's work

A man who won't personally manifest the presence of his God through his "position" isn't worthy of whatever position that is. If we each won't use our earthly status for the glorification of our God, we're wasting our time upon this earth. Don't we remember that we've been placed within history for the purpose of continuing to spread His name to other people? Hasn't He given us the honor of carrying His Gospel "to the very ends of the earth," O Men of God? And isn't it absolutely *incredible* how He's purposefully placed you in the exact place you are, a man chosen and called by Him? Whether you're a CEO or a cubicle-dweller, pumping gas or saving lives, you're meant to be right where you are!

Nehemiah might've stayed a lowly wine-steward if he hadn't used his placement for the Lord's great purposes. If he'd never had the boldness to speak up, he might've finished out his life in pseudo-comfort in the king's palace. Yet Nehemiah knew the only form of "success" (Neh. 1:11) that would ever actually matter was his working for the Lord's perfect will. He realized that if God would bless his boldness in this speaking to the king, he'd be the man to fix Jerusalem. So, "very much afraid," yet praying to his Lord "the God of heaven," Nehemiah steps up to the throne with his big request. He saw his life as being worthy of an earthly forfeit if he'd have the chance for doing eternal things.

You and I are placed within this era, and we're placed in our current "position," for the good of Jesus' Great Commission. Have you ever looked upon your job with eyes to see how God is asking you to do His work in that particular place? Have you ever thought of how He's engineered your life for the glory of His Word's spreading to other people around you? Do you see your weekly "grind" as being not a grind at all, but actually the chance to carry Jesus into other people's midst?

Today, may we think of all the ways we might become like Nehemiah, how we might use our own "work" for His works. May we see about the entirety of our lives the opportunity to spread Jesus' love to everyone, everywhere. Today, be bold in your position, O Man. May the work of Jesus become your work.

June 5 – Nehemiah 2:11-18

Inspecting your heart in solitude

Nehemiah slipped into the darkness amidst the ruins of Jerusalem under the light of a faint half-moon. Sitting on the only mount obtainable in his shattered city, he rode out on an inspection of its old walls. Through the shadows and the light cast by the moon through broken sections of its rubble, he rode in silence, observing all. Though he saw the desolation of the holy city of God around him, Nehemiah knew the task actually belonged to his God…

Today, as modern Nehemiahs, we must ride out into solitude for an inspection of our own lives, O Men of God. We must see the places where the walls of our defenses are in ruins; where the Lord has taught and strengthened us in other places. There's no "good work" that can begin, or be properly carried out, without the proper sort of *pre*-preparation. So, today, we must acknowledge where we're feeling strong or weak, asking for His divine rebuilding to continue in us.

Today, let's lay out our lives for His personal appraisal. And then be ready for His work to go on…

June 6 – Nehemiah 4:1-3

Encouragement, not sarcasm

We inhabit times when many men believe the highest forms of speech are mocking remarks and biting sarcasm. If you watch any TV sitcom or any comedy at the theater, all you hear is more of the same, just remixed. All you hear are people always being "witty" in a way that derides everybody else in the world except for themselves. All you hear are people airing out their own intense insecurities by the way they mock other people's personal shortcomings. All you hear are people so impressed with their own brand of perfection that they can't stand another's imperfections. They mock and jeer and laugh about the tiny items in other people's lives (that they secretly must know are present in their own too.)

O Men of God, let's take stock of our own humor if we don't want to eventually become like Tobiah or Sanballat. We as men must learn to harness any humor that's tearing down another man or be harmful to their hearing about Jesus. We must learn to use our tongues for otherworldly encouragement if we want to have the intense attractiveness of our Savior. Any fool can mock another man's life; any fool can point out stupidities; real men must learn to wield encouragement.

Here's a wonderful section from Trumbull's *Taking Men Alive*: "[There] is another kind of bait that is within the reach of us all, and that calls for no miracle to use. It is a bait that Jesus himself used freely in his soul-winning. This is the bait of *honest commendation*. It will land the most slippery human fish alive. No man can resist it. A word, heartily spoken, of sincere commendation for a fellow-being, will disarm opposition and draw him to us more effectively than any other method. It is the best human bait in the world." He continues on to say: "Perhaps one reason why honest commendation is so effective in challenging a person's interest is because it is so rare..."

And it's only still rarer today, O Men! There's so very little God-honest commendation anymore! Today, may we be a voice so free and easy with encouragement that we leave behind all our sophomoric humor. May we be the men who tame our mouths and offer up their use to Jesus Christ for the purposes of His choosing. Learn to be a man of encouragement today. In short, be a real man.

June 7 – Nehemiah 4:10-23

Nehemiah's mission is our mission

Meanwhile, the people of the Modern Church said, "The strength of the laborers is giving out, and there is so much hardship that it's difficult to build the kingdom of God." Also the Enemy said, "Before they know it or see me, I will be right there among them and will kill them and put an end to the work." The world came and told us ten times over, "Wherever you turn, they will attack you."

Therefore we must station some of the people behind the lowest points of the wall at the exposed places, posting them by families, with the Sword. We must look things over, stand up and say to the others, "Don't be afraid of them. Remember the Lord, who is great and awesome, and fight for the hearts of your friends, your family and the whole world."

When the Enemy hears that we're aware of his plot and that God has frustrated it, he will flee and we'll be back to our work.

From that day on, half of our men must do the work, while the other half are equipped with the Sword and the full armor of God. Our officers must post themselves behind the people of God who are *all* working on the building of the Kingdom. Those who carry materials must do their work with one hand and hold a weapon with the other. Each of the builders must wear his sword at his side and use it, as he does his work.

Let us say to the pastors, the officials, and all the rest of the people of the Modern Church: "The work is extensive and spread out, and we will be widely separated from each other as we fulfill our calling. But whenever you hear the sound of the trumpet, join us there. Our God will fight for us!"

So we must continue on the work with half the men holding spears, from the first light till the stars come out. At that time we must say to the people, "Have every man and his helpers stay in the Light of the New Jerusalem, so they can serve as guards by day, by night – whenever." Neither you nor your brothers nor any of us men can ever rest; each must have his weapon, even when he sleeps…

O Man of God, are you working for the coming Kingdom? O Man of God, where's your weapon right now?

June 8 – Nehemiah 6:1-13

Ask others what sort of man you are

A man who prays with earnest daily prayer that the Lord would "strengthen his hands" finds his hands actually being strengthened. A man who'd put the works of the Lord above his own life and security finds his life to be secure in the Lord. When Nehemiah heard the taunts and lies of his enemies, he wasn't tempted to argue the points with them or verify their facts. He wasn't drawn to any meeting that was set to be a trap for him; he trusted in the Lord's plan for him. Nehemiah knew the kind of man he wasn't: "Should a *man like me* run away? Or…go into the temple…?" he asked. And he knew the kind of man he was becoming; one who trusted totally in the Lord's providential protection.

Today, let's think about the meaning of the phrase "a man like me" in our own following after Jesus Christ. Are we men who'll stand up under the pressures of the world; men whose prayers are for the strengthening of our hands in the fight? Or are we playing up the role that Jesus actually plays in our lives, only acting like we're working on the Kingdom? Are the earnest honest daily prayers we're praying only for ourselves or are they for the good of God's work?

Here's today challenge: *Ask the most important people in your life what sort of "man like me" they see when they see you.* Talk to all the people in your life whose lives actually define yours; the ones you know will honestly respond to that particular question. Ask them how they would define you as a man in your following of Jesus, where they see the strengths and weaknesses in you. And be ready for the good and hard and honest truth that'll make us "men like us" who know the Lord who's strengthening our hands.

Today, let's consider who we actually are, O Men of God. And then let's dream about who we can be in Jesus.

June 9 – Nehemiah 7:1, 2

Strive for Hananiah's standing

I'd rather merit mention in the manner of Hananiah than do just about anything else in the course of my lifetime. I'd rather be known as a "man of integrity" than be the richest man in all the whole wide world. I'd rather hear I "feared God more than most men do" than hear that I was personally powerful or thought of as prestigious. I'd rather be a singly-mentioned character in the chronicles of Jesus' Kingdom than an absolute no-show. The richest men in the world are hampered often by their insecurities over their money; how they'll safeguard their stores. The most powerful men are worried about the preservation of their earthly power; how they'll keep people under their control. The most prestigious men are anxious for the garnering of more of the same accolades; how they'll keep their names in the bright lights. Yet for men like Hananiah – *fearing God, filled with integrity* – there's nothing in this world that can actually stop them. The man who knows the purpose of his life's journey as the work of eternity isn't cowed by any risk he'll have to undertake. The man who knows the final victory is already won before the battle's even begun is a man who lives fearlessly.

Is there such a vital integrity to be found within your heart that you're describable simply as a "man of integrity," O Man? Does your word mean perfectly corresponding actions; does your secret life match up with how you publicly portray yourself?

How about the level of your fearfulness of the God of the universe: Do you "fear God more than most men do"? Do you see in your salvation not a "nice idea" or a novelty, but a fearful rescue from eternal death? Do you fear to sin because you know that constantly falling away is like constantly re-crucifying your Savior? (Heb. 6:6b) Do you ever read accounts of God from the Old Testament and see how serious, and completely fearful, He actually is?

Then, right now, let's recommit our lives to a lifestyle of integrity and to serious contemplation of the fearfulness of God. May we never think that this is some sort of game when it's *absolutely everything*; may we be the men who always honor our God.

June 10 – Nehemiah 8:9-12

Is the joy of the Lord your strength?

Truth be told, many of us live our day-to-day as if we have a complete aversion to the joy of the Lord. Many solemn Christians act as if the "joy of the Lord" is *not* their strength, but instead a crutch for the weak-minded. Yet how many people might be turned off to our Savior by perceiving that the joyless lives of Christians are the result of His love? How many of us are wasting every single day of our God-given lives in the joyless drudgery of our daily grind? Do we "[understand] the words that [have] been made known to [us]"; that Jesus gave Himself that we might actually live? Do we ever "celebrate with great joy" that He's chosen us to be the people of His own personal choosing? Do you ever stop to calculate the quotient of your joy; the amount of everyday that's given to its overflow? Do we not remember Who it was who said these words to us: "no one will take your joy away from you"?

The only people taking the joy from the lives of modern Christians are the Christians who refuse to be joyous in the presence of Jesus. The one who'll best rob joy from your heart is actually the man looking at you in the mirror; *no one else can even come close!* If you won't fight for the joy that's found in Jesus, what source of "strength" do you plan to lean your life upon, O Man? If we won't live lives replete with the joy that Jesus spoke of, *why would anyone else want to follow Him for themselves?*

Do you remember exactly what you were doing the last time you felt the joy of Jesus welling up inside your heart? Do you remember where you were in that moment, who you were with, what you were doing, when you felt that joy rising?

Well, *wherever* it was, *whoever* with, *whatever* you did, *whenever* it was, *you must get back to that place today!* You must replicate the joy-inspiring elements of your life; they're placed in you for a wonderful heavenly reason. O Man of God, live your life today from the joy that's given as your inheritance because of the work of Jesus upon the cross. May we never be the ones who "mourn and weep" when every single ounce of joy-filled possibility is already living in us. Today, live with joy. It's actually a commandment! (1 Thess. 5:16)

LIVE LIKE MEN

June 11 – Nehemiah 13:23-25

Vicious Accountability

Oftentimes the purpose of a "bachelor party" is getting our buddies together to absolutely humiliate the groom. We plot and scheme a way to make our "poor friend" look completely ridiculous because of his decision "to throw his life away." We plan out how we'll force him to do some particular action, carry out some outrageous dare, that'll mark his final rite of passage. Personally, I'll never forget the things we did (or that were done to us) in my circle of friends from back in college...

Yet, more important, I'll never forget the final words from one of those friends while we waited to walk into his wedding service. We were standing in a small room off the side of the chapel; we'd just finished praying for him and his new life with his wife. He then turned around and looked at us and, speaking in all seriousness, told us why it mattered to him that we were his chosen groomsmen: "Guys," he said, "if I ever even *talk* about leaving (his wife), you have permission to beat the living $#!% outta me..."

Do you have a friend (or group of friends) who actually have permission to "beat" you if you started walking away from Jesus? Do you have some friendships intimate enough that you'd be okay if they started "pulling out your hair"? Have you ever granted other men unbridled access to the darkest recesses of your human heart? Have you ever asked another to be the strength in the midst of your weakness; to be there when you most need his help? Would you permit one of your brothers to "call curses down on [you]" if you were deserving of such treatment? Do you desire Jesus enough that you'd weather personal humiliation for the sake of staying close to His side?

Today, have some frank conversations with the men you're closest with; talk about this sort of brotherly love. Talk about the beating, bruising, black-and-blue accountability we all need if we're going to finish this race together. Take some time today for honest open-hearted airing-out of sin struggles that are plaguing your current life. Together, commit to a brotherhood that stops at nothing in the service of each other's walk with Jesus.

Would you let a brother beat you down for this? If you need it, I sure hope so.

June 12 – Esther 3:1-4

Bow to nothing but Jesus

You and I cannot be bowing down to *anyone* or *anything* if we'd claim to follow after Jesus Christ. If we'd call ourselves the men who'd like to become "men of God," we can never bend our knee elsewhere. It's simply not a possibility to follow God and follow *anything else or anyone else in the whole world*. "You adulterous people, don't you know that friendship with the world means enmity against God? Therefore, anyone who chooses to be a friend of the world becomes an enemy of God." (James 4:4) We simply can't have it both ways: "'If the Lord is God, follow him; but if Baal is God, follow him." (1 Kings 18:21) We can't "kneel down" or "pay honor" at the foot of anyone that's not our Lord and Savior, Jesus Christ. We must, like Joshua, "choose for [ourselves] this day whom [we] will serve"; nothing less and nothing more…

If the job you're doing stands before your service to the King, either quit your job or stop bowing down to it! If you can't serve God because of how your married life is going, get to work on actually fixing it! If you can't bow to God because you're bowing down to your children, get up off your knees and be a real father! If you can't give your heart to the Lord because of your personal "interests," get some new interests that align with His!

There's nothing weaker than a man who claims he's following after Jesus and yet won't stop bowing to everything else around him. It's awfully difficult to follow after Jesus when you're hobbled by your false worship of other earthly things. "Anyone who loves his father or mother more than me is not worthy of me; anyone who loves his son or daughter more than me is not worthy of me; and anyone who does not take his cross and follow me is not worthy of me. Whoever finds his life will lose it, and whoever loses his life for my sake will find it." (Matt. 10:37-39)

What others things are you bowing to, O Man? Can you name your heart's secret idols? Today, let's become ruthless in our efforts to rid our lives of bowing down to anything but Jesus. Let's become the men who read that Matthew 10 passage and can honestly say, "Only you, Lord Jesus." There was no limit to His love for us. Let's learn to be unlimited for Him in return.

June 13 – Job 1:1-12

Is your life of faith worthy of "considering"?

We would be of a crazy/prideful/stupid/idiotic disposition if we ever claimed to want the terrible challenge Job received. If we've ever thought, "Oh yeah, I'd be able to take whatever Satan gave me," we're playing a very dangerous game. If you think that you're equipped with a faith that "hedges" you from the storms and struggles of life, don't get prideful about it at all. If you think you're doing "pretty well" throughout the myriad troubles you've already faced, don't start getting any ideas. Job was a good man in the eyes of the Lord: "blameless and upright; he feared God and shunned evil." Yet I'd doubt that even Job, had he known of God's and Satan's conversation, would've wanted what happened to him next…

But the question might be raised: *Would your life be worthy of God's offering it to Satan for his evil "consideration," like Job's?* Do you think that you're so intimate with God that He'd point someone to you and say: "Check this guy's faith out"? Would the measure of your faithfulness from past situations lead the Lord to believe that you're worthy of some future trials? Has your "trust track-record" proven that you're allegiant to Him only; that nothing comes between the two of you?

We should never crave the gruesome trials that came for our friend, Job; if you do, you're absolutely crazy! We shouldn't assume our faith is any stronger than it actually is; we should learn its true measure and, from there, desire ever more. Yet, also, we must hope our faithfulness to God has been so noticeable that we put a smile of recognition on His face. We should hope that everyday will merit opportunities for the advancement and the deepening of our trust in Him. Just imagine if the men who are reading this today *really* put forth faith that marked them as their Lord's. Imagine if we all would live lives "blameless and upright," fearing God and shunning evil in our every waking moment today.

Today, let's have faiths that create wondrous certainty in the heart of Jesus: "Have you considered my servant (your name)?" Let's be the men whose faith is worthy of some testing, whose trust is independent of our earthly circumstances. Give yourself into your Savior's hands, O Man. He's truly in complete control of everything.

June 14 – Job 1:13-22

Being stripped of anything must not sway us

There's not a man whose eyes are on this page who hasn't experienced his own share of personal tragedy or heartache. There's not a man alive who doesn't carry some memory of pain within the shadows of his manly heart. There's not a one who'll read of Job's horrendous trials and not remember something personal and painful from his own past. We all read our own tribulations into the tale of Job's destruction; we feel we understand some of his distraught feelings. We can understand the pain apparent in his standing up, tearing his robe, shaving his head in his utter grief. We can understand the way the trials seem to come upon him, wave-after-wave-after-wave-after-wave. We can picture how he stood beneath the heavens, a man stripped of everything that'd once defined his earthly life. Yet it's his automatic recourse unto worship that's most baffling to our minds; it seems strange and completely unnatural. It's his saying "may the name of the Lord be praised" that separates the spiritual man from the boys in this account. It's his knowing that he started out "naked" and will also depart "naked" that can teach us how to follow God fully. It's his *not* sinning "by charging God with wrongdoing" that says that I myself have a long way to go in my life with Jesus…

We seem to go along through our lives being defined by earthly things until they're suddenly taken away from us. *And it's in the eventual absence of those things where we find the definition of our actual faith in Jesus.* If we ever think, "I'd rather be dead than live without X," God might have to take away our X to get to our hearts. And how will we respond in that day, O Men? How will Sunday-only sorts of "faith" stand up? Will we get up, tear our robes and shave our head; then fall to the ground and worship our God, like Job did? Will we see that everything we've ever had (everything we currently have) is simply God's gift to us? Will we not begrudge the processes of perfect Providence if it means the very salvation of our eternal souls? Will we re-define the matters that *actually* matter in the measurements of the Lord and simply worship Him?

Today, consider how you'd operate if your X was to be taken from you; would you whine or would you worship your Savior? We must be the men so sure of our God's great goodness that we'd let Him excise anything that currently stands in His way.

June 15 – Job 2:11-13

Comfort someone who's grieving by being present

My father died while I was halfway through my first semester of college after a heart surgery that didn't properly "take." One moment, I was sitting in a mid-morning class; the next, I was on a plane flying home to say goodbye. After a whirlwind week of gathering family, making preparations, attending the funeral, I was back on the plane again to school. Within a week, I'd possessed and then didn't possess a father; was at college, home, and then flying right back again. Suddenly, all the fun of meeting new college buddies was surpassed by the loneliness of feeling utterly alone. It's awfully hard to grieve the passing of your father when nobody around you has ever actually met your father…

A few weeks later, I was overcome with grief one afternoon; I was sitting in my dorm room, studying, alone. I'd been listening to a set of songs that suddenly made me think of him; it was simply too much to handle. So I locked the door and sat upon the edge of my bed and wept loudly in the comfort of my sad solitude… Until, hearing a quiet knock upon the door and then a "Hey, Eug," I wasn't alone in the silence anymore. At the door, and wanting to know what was going on inside, was my new friend, Taylor Ludwick. And, after considering for a moment, I decided to let him in upon the embarrassment of this explosion of grief for my dead father.

What happened next would change my life forever. I have never been the same since.

You see, Taylor walked in through the cracked door, saw exactly what was happening, and simply put his arms around me, like a brother. He didn't speak a word of hollow consolation or a stock Christian phrase; he simply held onto me in my pain. For the next few minutes, he made sure I wasn't alone in my grief; he stood there and accepted the awkwardness and heartache. And when he stood there next to me upon the day of my wedding as my best man, that was the exact reason why.

Job's friend later offered up advice that was of wayward understanding, but they did start out correctly. Have you ever been an Eliphaz, Bildad, Zophar, or a Taylor Ludwick, to anyone in terrible grief? Have you ever sat for "seven days and seven nights" of pain with another who's currently in acute pain? Today, may we think of those we know who need the comfort of our solicitude through a caring and shared silence. May we go and be the quiet sort of strength to those who really need it; may we be the Jesus of a quiet love. Today, let's just simply do this, O Men. We'll be an incredible blessing by it.

June 16 – Job 42:12-17

Consistency of Job in his trial and his "latter life"

When Job was told his oxen, donkeys, sheep and camels were gone, he'd never read the "Epilogue" to his own biblical account. When a "mighty wind" blew down the house upon his feasting children, he wasn't aware of "Job Chapter 42." As he sat upon a heap of ashes scraping off his leprous sores, he couldn't envision his future "latter life." While his friends were wont to heap upon his ears unwanted "wisdom," Job was left with nothing but his faith in God…

O Man of God, our own "latter parts of life" will be built upon foundations made of bricks called Today. We can't expect to live a "latter part of life" that's inconsistent with our actual current lifestyle. We can't expect to *not* trust God with every detail of our current day and end up faithful and true in the eventual end. We can't expect that lifetimes built upon our lack-of-trust result in "latter lives" constructed upon Jesus Christ. So, regardless if you're in a Job-like time of pain or living large, we can't allow our faithfulness to sway today. Job was able to weather any storm within the consolation of God's strength *because he actually trusted in God's strength*. He was able to endure his time of testing by the Tempter because he knew God's "love endures forever." He was faithful in his final "hundred and forty years" of life because he'd already been faithful in his earlier years.

Can we commit that how we'll live out our ***today*** will be consistent with the "latter life" where we'd like to arrive? Can you venture out with visions of the morrow, built upon this very day, fully harmonic with the Lord's eternal Now? Is it possible that you'll focus eyes upon the current moment, knowing that all these current moments add up into your lifetime? Will you live today so fulsome in your faith in Father God that your tomorrows simply won't matter to you? We don't know what our "latter life" might hold, O Men. Let's make today just how we'd hope it would be.

June 17 – Ecclesiastes 1:12-18

A detached self-appraisal of your life

A man who won't view his life with Solomon's sort of detachment will tend to attach his life to unimportant earthly matters. If we won't observe the "bird's eye view" above our daily lives, we'll become more earthbound by the day. If we want to become the men who "cease striving and know that [He is] God," we must be aware of what we're actually striving for. We must know and name the reason and direction to which our strivings strive and detachedly examine their worthiness. We must speak aloud the value and the fruit of everything we're doing and be ready to denounce any unnecessariness. We must weigh the weight of the treasures that we're currently storing up and know if they're stored "on earth" or "in heaven," as Jesus said.

Solomon was "king over Israel in Jerusalem," yet he was able to feel the meaninglessness of all his earthly power. His devotion to his studies and his explorations of human wisdom brought him nowhere in the end, he felt. His clear vision for the "things that are done under the sun" led to his knowledge of their absolute pointlessness. His great wisdom brought him terrible told (and probably untold) mental anguishes when its strivings were for his personal gain.

Have you ever tallied up the balance of the "meaningful versus meaningless" in the way you live your life, O Man? Are you man enough to ask the Lord for His divine detachment; to truly judge your "pointed versus pointless" achievements? Are you living your life for any reason contrary to the calling of Jesus Christ on your life and destiny in Him? Do you sense that you've embarked upon a journey whose direction was purely for expediency or selfish gain?

May we so remove our minds from modern understandings that we have the chance to judge our lives' purpose dispassionately. May we honor Jesus by asking if our life is pointed in His directions; *pointing to Him only*. We can't be men who wait until we're old and gray to say we've wasted almost every moment of our earthly lives. Today, be detached enough to take on Solomon's wisdom; be detached enough to attach everything to your Savior, Jesus.

June 18 – Ecclesiastes 2:1-11

The way of the world is a waste of time

A reading of this passage begs an all-important question: *Are the "finer things" truly finer?* If the king who bore a name so consistently coupled with "splendor" says these sorts of things, what are we going to say? Have we so diluted truth about possessions and earthly pleasures that we can't see the way they often ruin lives? Can we truly say the acquisition of more earthly bounty ever led us into deeper, richer, truer faith in Jesus? Are we not upon a fool's errand (with its dangerous destination) when we think that "blessing" actually means "bounty"? Have we so surrendered all-inclusive following of our Lord to the world's way that we care more for wealth than for Him? Do you spend more time upon the research of a dream car than you do upon the growth of your scriptural knowledge? Do you "hunger and thirst for righteousness" more than anything else in the world; more than for any earthly pleasure or possession?

Less some hyperbole, I love this sentiment from André Gide: "I have a horror of comfort; possessions invite comfort, and in their security a man falls asleep; I love life enough to try to live wide awake, and so, even among all my treasures, I treasure a sense of the precarious, by which I provoke or at least arouse my life. I can't say I love danger, but I love a life of risk, I want life to demand of me, at every moment, all my courage, all my happiness, and all my health."

O Men of God, may we treasure the precariousness found in following Jesus far above all earthly pleasures or possessions. May we not be lulled to sleep by any asset or experience; may we be fully awake to Jesus and His call. May we love a "life of risk" developed by our day-by-day obedience to the actual stated commands of our Savior. May we hope that He'd demand of us every ounce of our courage, every ounce of our manly hearts...

Will you strive today for more and more possessions, or for possession *by* the God who chose to come for your sake? Wrestle long and deep with that question, O Man. Wrestle with the worth of your coming day's "work."

June 19 – Isaiah 6

Seeing Him leads to fear and to grace and to action

The inclinations of Isaiah's heart led him into proper action when he actually had the chance to see the Lord his God. When he "saw the Lord seated on a throne, high and exalted," he quickly knew how terribly sinful his own life was. He despaired of life when looking at the holiness of the living God; he feared the "wages of sin" that were rightfully his. He knew that, in and of himself, nothing could be done or said or changed or fixed to result in a real authentic personal righteousness…

Yet the Lord still intervened for him, didn't He? The seraph winged his way to Isaiah, correct? His "guilt is taken away and [his] sin atoned for" – Does that sort of phrasing sound at all familiar to you?

So what's Isaiah's next step? What's the natural response to seeing our God? What should we – *the men who've been transformed by the love of Jesus Christ* – be doing right this very minute, as we read this?

"Here am I. Send me," Isaiah shouts out.

Here are you. Time to go, O Men.

O Man of God, have you ever personally seen the glory of the Lord and been transformed by that vision of Him? Have you truly felt the Lord's unbelievable righteousness and also the unbelievable weight of your own sin before Him? Have you actually let Him take away your sin by His perfect sacrifice – *"finished" for you* – on the cross? Has your love for Him consumed all other causes in your life; are you sent out everyday with abundant joy in Jesus?

If we've really seen the Lord, we'll never again be the men we were before we had that vision of Him. If we've known His sweet goodness, we'll acknowledge everyday that we're totally unworthy of His amazing love for us. If He's "set [us] free from the law of sin and death," we'll no longer act as slaves to sin and death anymore. If we know this Lord for ourselves, we'll happily say "here I am," and then we'll also shout out, "Send me!"

What a joy to know this Savior of our souls! What delight we'll find while going!

June 20 – Isaiah 7:1-13

He wants you to ask for help and protection

The very phrase that God was speaking unto Ahaz is the phrase the Lord is speaking to you right now, O Man: "Ask the Lord your God for a sign, whether in the deepest depths or in the highest heights" – *anything at all!* The Lord had seen how lack-of-trust was causing Ahaz to become like "trees of the forest" that were "shaken by the wind." "If you do not stand firm in your faith," the Lord was saying to Ahaz (and to us!), "you will not stand at all." By this logic, Ahaz wasn't actually sinning when he felt fear of the enemy facing him; his fear was perfectly natural. There's nothing wrong with feeling certain fears when life is really fearsome, when enemies begin to surround your days. No, the issue was his ongoing, thoroughgoing, complete lack-of-trust despite the Lord's promised offering. The problem lay in how God promised him protection *if he'd only ask* and in the fact that Ahaz simply wouldn't ask…

In the same way, you and I will become like "trees of the forest" if we never actually trust the Lord for His protection. If we listen to the words of the Lord to Ahaz and yet still refuse to relax, there's something wrong with our faith in Jesus! If we cannot see the parallels between the promise to Ahaz and those given to us, we're missing out on perfect peace. If we won't pay attention to the Lord's request *to hear of our requests*, are we actually walking in relationship with Him?

There's nothing in your life, your job, your marriage, your fatherhood, this whole world, that can stand up to the strength of your God. There's nothing beyond His perfect ability to protect us; there's nothing stronger than the God of the whole universe. The only barrier that stands between your life and God's perfect peace is the barrier placed there by your lack-of-trust in Him. It's only in our *not* believing in our God's perfect protection that we miss out on our God's perfect protection!

Today, when the Lord should ask you to be asking for His protection, *actually ask Him for His protection, O Man of God!* Most of the time, we're not at peace because we ground our hopes on earthly things and not in our all-powerful God. May we be the men who, unlike foolish Ahaz, actually ask the Lord for His help in our actual hour of need. We'll only withstand foes when standing with our Father in the midst of His divine protection for us. Today, let's just ask for His help! He's dwelling within you right now, just waiting!

June 21 – Isaiah 8:11

Feel His hand, hear His voice; don't follow the world

The wording of this scripture almost lends itself to a formula, something like A=B=C. "The Lord spoke to me" *because* "his strong hand" *was* "upon me," *thus* I did not "follow the way of this people." Or *I did not* "follow the way of this people" *because* "his strong hand" *was* "upon me" *while* "the Lord spoke to me." Or *I did not* "follow the way of this people" *because* "the Lord spoke to me" *with* "his strong hand upon me."

Or in the converse: It's difficult *not* going the world's way *without* the hand of God *leading* you to His voice. Or: It's difficult to ever *hear* His voice without His hand *upon* you, steering you *away* from the world. Or: If you cannot *feel* His hand, you won't *hear* His voice and will easily stray off and go in the world's way. We must listen for the voice of God, mutually inclusively with His hand, if we don't want to crumble to the world's pressures…

O Man of God, do you feel the presence of the "strong hand" of God upon your shoulder this very moment? Do you sense if you're "in" or "out of touch" with hearing His voice; have you heard today's daily directive in your ear? Are you listening for the ways in which He'll lead you into the battle and away from the ways of this fallen world? Are you wanting this equivalence between A, B and C to be the real and effective directive in your life today?

Then here's the test:

Do you feel His hand? Yes or no.

Is He speaking to you often? Yes or no.

Are you *not* following the way of the world? Yes or no.

If we'll fight to feel the hand of God upon us, we'll often hear His voice and then naturally turn away from the world. And if we'll listen for His voice, we'll start to feel His hand upon us and He'll help us turn away from the world. And if we'll turn away from the world, we're more open to His hand and His voice and His guidance throughout every day. So, today, will you listen for His voice, reaching out for His hand, while turning away from the world, O Man of God? Let's give that formula a try, shall we? It sounds like something worth our while!

June 22 – Jeremiah 1

Jeremiah's call is your call

The word of the Lord came to you, saying: "Before I formed you in the womb I knew you, before you were born I set you apart, I appointed you as a prophet to the nations."

"Ah, Sovereign Lord," you said, "I do not know how to speak; I don't know that much about 'faith.'"

But the Lord said to you, "Do not say, 'I don't know much.' You must go to everyone I send you to and say everything you know about Jesus. Do not be afraid of anyone, for 'I am with you always' and will rescue you."

Then the Lord reached out His hand to you and touched your heart and said to you, "Now, I have put my Holy Spirit in your life. See, today I appoint you over nations and kingdoms to bring about My Kingdom, to build and to plant."

The word of the Lord came to you: "What do you see, O Man of God?"

"I see a tree in the shape of a cross," you replied.

The Lord said to you, "You have seen correctly, for I am watching to see that my people only speak of the Gospel of my Son, Jesus."

The word of the Lord came to you again: "What do you see?"

"I see an empty tomb after three days," you answered.

The Lord said to you, "From that empty tomb has poured forth wellsprings of grace and joy upon this earth. I continue to use men like you who'd summon all the people of the world's kingdoms.

"Get yourself ready! Stand up and say to everyone you know whatever I command you. Do not be terrified by them, or I will see that you really don't believe in my power for your life. Today I will make you like a fortified city, an iron pillar and a bronze wall to stand strong in this age. They will fight against you but will not overcome you, for I am with you and will rescue you always…"

Are you ready for this calling, modern-day Jeremiah? Then get up and go, right now!

June 23 – Jeremiah 7:1-29

"At the gate" of the modern Church

Jesus didn't commit His followers to a religion or to brick-and-mortar monuments built for His name. He didn't require the building of elaborate cathedrals or the constructs of our ready-made modern orthodoxies. He didn't ask for all our silly talk of "Christian nations," of "Christian Coalitions," or of "Moral Majorities." He actually asked that we'd "abide in [His] love," that we'd "be one," that we'd simply "follow [Him]," being "fishers of men."

Standing at the "gate of the Lord's house," Jeremiah preached against six aspects of the tainted Jewish faith of his day. He railed against the blights that blurred the lines of faith toward the ruinous regions of a mindless religion. Today, may we be the men who'd meditate upon the ways the "modern Church" is walking down those very same roads. Let's be the men who'd understand the problems and then immediately get to work on His divine solutions:

1. **False Identity (Religion v. Faith)** – "Reform your ways and your actions, and I will let you live in this place. Do not trust in deceptive words and say, "This is the temple of the Lord, the temple of the Lord, the temple of the Lord!"

2. **Lack of Justice and Mercy** – "If you really change your ways and your actions and deal with each other justly, if you do not oppress the alien, the fatherless or the widow and do not shed innocent blood in this place…"

3. **Idolatry** – "and if you do not follow other gods to your own harm…"

4. **"Cheap grace"** – "Will you steal and murder, commit adultery and perjury, burn incense to Baal and follow other gods you have not known, and then come and stand before me in this house, which bears my Name, and say, 'We are safe' – safe to do all these detestable things?"

5. **"Observance" over obedience** – "For when I brought your forefathers out of Egypt and spoke to them, I did not just give

them commands about burnt offerings and sacrifices, but I gave them this command: Obey me, and I will be your God and you will be my people. Walk in all the ways I command you, that it may go well with you."

6. **No progress or fruit; in fact, the opposite** – "They went backward and not forward…"

June 24 – Jeremiah 13:1-11

Are we different enough?

We'd be lying if we said we'd never met a foreign missionary and thought, "Hmm, he's a bit different." If you've ever been a part of something like a church's "Missions Week," you've probably rolled your eyes during a few presentations. You've probably seen a family fresh from being far afield and thought to yourself, "Where do they find these strange sort of people?" You've probably seen their dated hand-me-down missionary clothes and thought, "Those poor folks…"

Well, go ahead and stop thinking that, O Man. Really. Truly.

We can sit today and read of Jeremiah's potent prophecies because Jeremiah was similarly "different" back in his day. In fact, think of all the times the Israelites must've rolled their collective eyes while watching all the things he did. When he'd go and do the über-strange things God was calling him to do, they thought, "Where did God find this guy?" When he wandered off to ruin belts of linen "in a crevice in the rocks," they probably thought, "This poor idiot…"

But the problem with our lives isn't the way those other people's look so different, *it's that we're not different enough, O Men of God*. When we find we're making funny faces in the face of others' personal obedience, that's our own personal problem. If we find that we're uncomfortable with Jesus' commands and being sent unto the world, we're not following after our Lord. If we'd hate to feel we're standing out for the reasons He'd actually ask us to stand out, we're the ones who should be called "poor folks…"

O Man of God, if you've never done a thing for Jesus characterizable as "strange," examine yourself and your life in Him. There aren't many men who've followed Jesus who aren't required to do some bizarre things for the purposes of His coming Kingdom. There are very few men He calls into His service who don't bear the title of being profoundly "different" in the world's eyes. Is your life *different enough* that the world would know you're actually His; are you standing out or blending in?

May we be "bound" only to Jesus today. May we be men of His "renown."

June 25 – Jeremiah 18:1-6

To be moldable is better than needing "breaking"

Personally, I've always been uncomfortable with the Church's relatively newfound desire that "God would break us" etc. It seems to me that any man who's ever actually been broken doesn't ever want to have to do it again. It seems to me that God Himself will choose to break and remake us as He sees fit for His Kingdom's purposes in this world. Yet for us to ask that we'd become like Job or like Israel in their degradations seems a bit out of our faith-league. To assume we're strong enough to personally *choose* our own spiritual-breakings seems to come more from our pride than from faith. To say we're made of stuff that's ready for destruction seems to say we think our faith's already ready, fully mature…

The beauty in the story of the Potter's House is the potter's clever usage of something already marred and utterly useless. Likewise, the beauty of our stories is best spoken when we make ourselves moldable and malleable for Jesus' sake. When we'd honor Him with hearts that truly believe in His good purposes, we become the clay that's fully useable by Him. When we soften our hearts until they're ready to be fashioned and refashioned, we become real vessels for His Holy Spirit. But this practice where we pray for our own "breaking" seems to say we're already broken to the point where we're unmoldable. Our constant prayers for "breaking" might be well met with this question from our God: "Are you sure you're actually mine?"

Today, through your silence and prayer, and your time with Him in Scripture, ask yourself this very different question: "Have I softened my heart to where it's actually usable and moldable; is my heart already in His all-capable hands?" For if we truly want the Lord to have to "break" us, there must be some sort of reason that we're stubborn enough to *need* breaking. Yet far better is the sort of heart that's soft enough for molding, humbly placed in our Good Potter's hands.

Is your heart in His hands today, O Man? Is it soft enough for His molding?

June 26 – Jeremiah 21:1-10

Conviction convinces of hard truths

Even though I've always done my outreach in the "winsome" world of Young Life, there's a bit of a hardness found in my thinking. There are times when I've felt the Holy Spirit leading me to some words that seemed "harsh" – even "scary" – to my teenage friends. There are times when I've looked straight into the eyes of certain guys and said something similar to Jeremiah in this passage: "See, I am setting before you the way of life and the way of death" – there's right, wrong; evil, good; Satan, God. When I've sensed I'm right within the exact moment of a guy or girl's salvation, I'll speak just like that sometimes. When I'm feeling Spirit-full, I'll *un*temper certain words that have a chance to cut straight to the heart of a certain kid…

Consider this anecdote from the turn of the last century:

An earnest young clergyman in New England…began his ministry in a parish where his predecessor had lacked strong conviction, and had encouraged, if not cultivated, doubts. The new clergyman's beliefs were startling to his congregation. One Sunday, after the service, a bright young man came up to the minister, and said:

"I don't believe what you are preaching, and I want to discuss your beliefs with you."

"Well, my friend, there's no use in our doing that. I am convinced, and you don't want to be. I am set here to preach the truth that I believe, whether my hearers believe it or not."

Too often, we're too soft with the toughness of the Truth because we're fearful that "we'll turn people off to God." In essence, we allow convictions foreign to the Word to creep into our modern psyche because we're not convinced of our convictions. We'd let another argue and impugn these very convictions because we're fearful to ask him about his own convictions. We're unconvincing when we act as if our God-given beliefs are a matter meant for back-and-forth disputations.

O Man of God, your convictions are as strong (or as weak) as the number of occasions where you've actually spoken them. Your understanding of the truth is only as deep and wide as how often you've actually had to live directly from its ways. If you want to "change the world," start engaging with the world in the direct speaking of the truth of Jesus. Be like Jeremiah: *Speak the hard and honest truth of Jesus into a world dulled by dim and dead faithlessness.*

Today, be convinced yourself, O Men of God! It's only from that point that you'll be convincing.

June 27 – Jeremiah 26:1-16

Have you ever been persecuted?

If you've ever felt a share of persecution for the sake of following Jesus, you'll never forget that experience. If you've felt a sense of alienation because you're standing out for Him, "well done, good and faithful servant!" If you've spoken up and then been broken down for speaking about His name, you're walking on the right and only path. If you've followed His direct commandments, you're rewarded by more closeness unto Him and *that's worth anything…*

But if you've never felt an ounce of persecution for His name, are you sure you're actually walking with Jesus? If you've never had a sense of alienation, are you certain that you're not the "worthless servant outside"? If you've never spoken aloud His name to others, are you sure you're trying to walk the straight and narrow path He spoke of? If you're never speaking about His life and grace, are you trying to follow His commands *at all*?

It's not for nothing that Jesus closed out the beatitudes with these final words on the subject of earthly persecution: "Blessed are those who are persecuted because of righteousness, for theirs is the kingdom of heaven. Blessed are you when people insult you, persecute you and falsely say all kinds of evil against you because of me. Rejoice and be glad, because great is your reward in heaven, for in the same way they persecuted the prophets who were before you."

Persecution isn't meted out to men who walk as weaklings in their faith and life and following after Jesus Christ. Satan doesn't need to poke and prod the sort of men who'll stay silent in and about their so-called salvation. May we be of such stouthearted, strong resolve in making His Name known that we're targets of a constant persecution. If "the family of believers throughout the world is undergoing" persecution, we must join in for our fair share too, O Men….

Would you rather be safe *and* sorry? Only weak men choose to live like that!

June 28 – Jeremiah 28

Beware of modern false prophecy

Any teaching that would make the path of Jesus into a path of ease or luxury is a false teaching, O Man. You and I inhabit times where many preachers preach of many paths inconsistent with the actual way of Jesus. If we'd follow after One who gave His life so we might live, we're fools to think there'll be no demand upon our own lives. Our discipleship must stand within Paul's words: "I have been crucified with Christ and *I no longer live...*"

Hananiah spoke a gospel of his own personal invention to these Israelites longing for a little good news in their day. Jeremiah's previous words were clearly superceded by these silly promises of safety, "health and wealth," weren't they? Yet the ultimate test that Jeremiah pointed to is still today's test for teaching: "only if [it] comes true." Only if the Scriptures point to a Savior in a Bentley can we glean a path of zero resistance for our lives. Only if our Lord said "Blessed are the rich" can we ascertain discipleships of softness and softening indolence. Only if His shoes were shined, instead of His actually being the footwasher, can we guess that that's the way of Jesus for us. Only if our Lord was lazy and lascivious can we start to modernize perceptions about godly manhood.

O Man of God, if you're tempted to believe there's nothing wrong with lazy discipleship, you're absolutely wrong. Any person who's letting you believe "*you* must become greater, *He* must become less" is lying to your face! Any thought within your mind that nothing matters more than "getting yours" etc, is a sinful wayward modern thought. Any grain of these ideas within our midst are grains of *un*truth, scattered there by Satan himself.

Today let's ponder on the actual mighty precepts our faith is founded upon and be wary of any late or latent additions. May we modern men examine how we've been molded into thinking earthly-worldly "blessings" are the actual blessings for us. May we think of where we've started down some wrong roads, even if we started down those roads with perfectly honorable intentions. May we be so honest with ourselves, and each other, that we'll root out everything that's *not* full of Truth, *not* consistent with His Word. May we banish Hananiahs from our hearts today. Lord, grant us clear minds for that work!

June 29 – Jeremiah 34:8-16

Reflect upon, consider and then solidify your commitments

A man must keep the commitments he's made no matter what happens; a man who won't is simply not a man at all. A man's measure is not the measure of his riches or his so-called "manliness"; it's how he keeps his word to other people. It's the way he says one thing and *doesn't* choose to do another that'll say if he's a true man or not a man. It's the way commitments echo to the depths of his very being that defines what's in the depths of his being. If we'd want to be the men who follow Jesus in every aspect of our lives, consider how you commit yourself. Consider how you entered your marriage; how you enter into your business contracts; how you "give your word" to other people. Think of how you "honor God" upon a Sunday with your "worship" and then the way you carry yourself, Monday through Saturday. Think of how you promised to "love, honor and cherish" your lovely wife and how you're doing on those same promises today. Consider how often you say "I'll make sure I get to that," and remember how often you actually don't get to "that." Remember how it personally bothers you when another does exactly the same to you; how you think "I'm glad I'm not like that…"

There's nothing weaker than our waffling on commitments in the manner of Jerusalem's slave-owners from this passage. They'd like to "honor" God by freeing all their slaves…*until they remember the effect this will have on their bottom-lines.*

O Men of God, don't we similarly sell ourselves short in the honoring of our word and commitments too often? Don't we often give a flippant vow to others and then relent when we remember what exactly that vow might entail? Don't we often strive to honor God with spiritual commitments that eventually seem to get in the way of our lifestyle? Don't we often second-guess our promises that might interfere with "how I live my life" etc?

Today, sit and ponder on the many (big *and* small) personal commitments that are *the* current commitments in your own life. How are you actually doing on these, O Man? Where do you need *re*commitment to your causes?

June 30 – Jeremiah 42:1-3

Pray for guidance today

Imagine if we modern men of God, "from the least to the greatest," spent some time on the very same prayer today. Imagine what would happen if we gave our hearts to Jesus with a selfsame spirit of single-minded obedience. Imagine what might actually happen when the Lord heard our petitions and prayers for this particular time in Church History. Imagine how it really matters when the godly men in this world truly give their hearts to Jesus Christ.

O Men of God, we must pray the prayer today with which the mighty men of Jerusalem approached Jeremiah, back then! Let's get down on our knees; clear our heads of excess noise; open our hearts; pray that prayer; then rise up ready for His action. If we want to become the men with hearts wild and untameable, we must rein in our reliance on the world around us. We must seek the only way that actually matters through this life – *Jesus' Way* – and then follow it to the death…

Give your heart to those men's prayer: "Pray that the Lord your God will tell us *where we should go* and *what we should do*."

Yes, pray this prayer with all your heart today! And be ready to follow Him wherever He leads!

July 1 – Ezekiel 1:1

Look for His vision and visions of Him

Perhaps you've never experienced "visions of God" because you don't think it's possible to experience visions of God. Maybe you're missing out on mystical opportunities because you think yourself a thoroughly "modern man," O Man of God. Maybe we'd all know more of prophetic potentialities if more of us desired to see more of our God everyday. Perhaps we'd become the kind of men God is actually looking for if we actually hoped for visions of His Glory. Ezekiel was a priest in the middle of the Jewish people's exile; we're Christ's Body to this modern world. Ezekiel was a man of only thirty years; you're just as old as you are, right now, as you're reading through these words. Ezekiel happened to be walking down along the Kebar River; you're in the middle of living the realities of your day. According to this scripture, it would seem the Lord will open up the heavens to the man who's available – *and paying attention* – for His heavenly realities. It would seem as if the role of "God's mouthpiece" is readily available to those men who'd desire that mantle. It would seem as if this highest height of humanity is acquirable, possible, to those men actively looking for it. It would seem as if we all – *you and me* – should be making our eyes available to God's ready visions. If we'd want to become prophets in an age when little of God is known, we must have our eyes upon Him personally…

Have you ever seen a vision of the splendor, or the beauty, or the grace, of the Lord you're serving, O Man? Have you ever even *wanted* to see a vision of that splendor, or that beauty, or that amazing grace? Would you open up your eyes to all the wonder that He's placed within your life and be thankful for what you see? Do you strive to see the Lord within your daily machinations or are you becoming blind to Him in their midst?

We must become the men who'll walk along the Kebar River everyday, watching hopefully for His revelation of Himself. We should wake up every morning with our eyes attuned to mystical displays of His ever-present presence in our lives. If you'd like to work your way up to the seeing of His mystical attractions, start looking for Him absolutely everywhere. If we truly think that God is omnipresent, we must start to see Him all around us, all the time. Today, let's open up your eyes to Him. He's all around us, every moment.

July 2 – Ezekiel 3:10-15

Learning to feel God's emotions

It's hard to think of something manlier than taking upon yourself the emotions of the God you serve. Have you ever wondered if your daily emotions are a mirror of God's own or if they're simply your own passing feelings? Have you ever contemplated what would happen if Jesus drove down the street and got cut off in traffic? And have you ever thought about His righteous godly forms of anger that are fitting in so many *worthy* situations? Do you feel how God must feel when He looks upon our world and sees so many awful human injustices afoot? Do you sense His holy anger at inversions of His perfect will for man; at the blighting of His holy truth? Is it possible for you to *not* fill your life with stupid angers, false excitements, any emotion that's counter to His goodness? Do you wish to feel His "bitterness" when it's fitting; feel His "anger in [your] spirit" when it's actually warranted?

O Man of God, I bet we've often learned to sense another's emotions by observing the signals coming from them. I bet you've learned the ways of wifely anger; seen a mother's quiet hurt; known a father's wrath was on its way. I'm sure you've learned the warning signs that certain bosses are about to "drop the hammer" even before all others notice it. Perhaps you've noted signals in a person that later led to greater intimacy with them; they were surprised at your emotional acuity…

If so, how did you acquire that special sense of knowing what that other person was actually feeling? Wasn't it from being around that particular person to the point that subtle changes weren't so subtle anymore?

In the same way, may we give our minds to minding how the Lord feels when He looks upon our world. Imagine what might actually happen if followers of Jesus were aware of exactly what He was feeling! Think of how all worldly perceptions of our Savior might be salvaged if we felt for *Him*, not for *ourselves*. I'd imagine there'd be "love, joy, peace, patience, kindness, goodness, faithfulness, gentleness and self-control" abounding! And isn't that what we want for our lives, O Men? Isn't that what you want for this day ahead?

July 3 – Ezekiel 8:1-4

Are you available to be "grabbed"?

Only an open-hearted man will be prepared for the hand of God to reach down and take him "by the hair." The prophet Ezekiel certainly wasn't living from a lukewarm half-baked "faith" when he saw the man of fire coming for him. He wasn't allowing his daily business, family-life or foreign exile to divorce him from his ready God-availability. He was sitting with these exiled elders and yet he kept his heart wide-open for the "hand of the Sovereign Lord" to manifest itself.

Your heart is either open to the hand of the Lord or it's not; there's no halfway in this particular equation. There can't be a single question in your mind of whether you're living with a spirit that's open or closed to Him, O Man. Each of us knows how it feels when we're aware of God's presence in the living of our daily lives, don't we? And we know the feeling, too, when we're letting earthly concerns decide whether our heart is God-open or God-closed.

How's your heart doing today, O Man? Is it open to Jesus? Do you hear Him calling out across the ages with that earnest hope of His sovereign plan for you?

"Abide in Me, and I in you. As the branch cannot bear fruit of itself unless it abides in the vine, so neither can you unless you abide in me. I am the vine, you are the branches; he who abides in Me and I in him, he bears much fruit, for apart from Me you can do nothing. If anyone does not abide in Me, he is thrown away as a branch and dries up; and they gather them, and cast them into the fire and they are burned. If you abide in Me, and My words abide in you, ask whatever you wish, and it will be done for you. My father is glorified by this, that you bear much fruit, and so prove to be My disciples…"

You'll see a direct correlation between your abiding and your fruit-bearing, between your openness and your Kingdom-usefulness. You'll become more and more the man you're meant to be whenever your spirit's open and ready for the work of His Holy Spirit. May we be the men who honor God by opening up our hearts to His presence; who have actual "eyes to see" Him. May we be so perfectly available to Jesus that we're constantly interrupted by intrusions of His Spirit. Now that should be a dream of ours, O Men! That's a life that's truly lived!

July 4 – Ezekiel 20:1

Can others inquire of God through you?

If you are available, obedient and growing in God's perfect wisdom, it'll become readily apparent to other people. You'll start to become a man who's sought after because of the wisdom pouring forth from God through your daily life. If the Word of God is active and alive in how you live your day-to-day, other men will certainly start to notice. And if they're wanting "to inquire of the Lord," they might just start to come and seat themselves in front of *you*, like Ezekiel…

Would you say the way you're living your life within the wellsprings of God's wisdom is attracting others to Jesus, O Man? Would you say it's becoming frequent that another will come to you, not to another man, for direction in his life? Do you sense that you're becoming more and more a product of God's glorious wisdom or more a product of your own brand? Do you stand up like a pillar of His truth or are you swayed by the wishy-washy "wisdoms" of this world?

In short: *Are you sought after in this way?* Next question: *Do you wish to be?* Would you wish to be the man that others think of when they need some godly counsel, or a kind listening ear? Do you want to be a man where others find repositories of God's wisdom and bountiful measures of His peace? Would you feel that you were living your dream if others sought to inquire of the Lord through your following after Him?

O Man of God, you'll only be sought after *for the right reasons* when you're walking rightly with your living Savior. Men will "praise your Father in heaven" only when you "let your light shine before [them]" brightly, all the time. If we'd want to be the men wisely approached when people want to seek the Lord, we must seek the Lord for ourselves. If we'd want to have His wisdom pouring forth from us like steady rushing rivers, we must constantly seek His wisdom.

Are you seeking His wisdom, O Man? More simply put: Are you seeking Him?

July 5 – Ezekiel 33:1-9

We're responsible for the worth of our "witness"

The word of the Lord came to us: "Sons of men, speak to your modern Church and say to them: 'When I bring judgment upon the world, and the people of the Church choose their godliest men and make them their watchmen, and they see the judgment of the Lord coming against the world and blow the trumpet to warn the people, then if anyone hears the trumpet but does not take warning and the judgment comes and he is taken unawares, his blood will be on his own head. Since he heard the sound of your trumpet but did not take warning, his blood will be on his own head. If he had taken warning, he would have been saved by the blood of Christ Jesus. But if the watchmen see the judgment coming and do not blow the trumpet to warn the world and the judgment comes and takes the life of one of them, that man will be taken away because of his sin, *but I will hold the watchmen accountable for his blood.*'

"Men of God, I have made you watchmen for the world as the Body of Christ; so hear the word I speak and listen to my warning. When I say to the wicked, 'O wicked man, you must surely turn to Jesus,' and you do not speak out to persuade him to come unto Me, that wicked man will die in his separation from Me, and I will hold you accountable for his blood…"

O Man of God, who are you currently leading to Jesus?

Who does Jesus desire you'd lead to Him today?

July 6 – Ezekiel 37:1-10

Believe that the world can change through Jesus

We're of no practical use to the Kingdom if we become men who look upon this world and say: "Good riddance!" Yet if our hearts are filled with anything less than His wondrous empathy for this world, we'll quickly become its judges. If we think we're personally above the fray of folly, fear and frailty all around us, we can't become like Jesus was. If we'd shake our heads at other people, instead of rolling up our sleeves to help, we're not the kind of disciples Jesus is looking for.

"Son of man, can this oversexed world full of perversity be brought back to life through My presence in it?"

"Son of man, can this world where a baby is a 'choice' be given new life through My holy Word?"

"Son of man, can this world full of evil, hate and violence be filled with My peace wherever I send you to spread it?"

"Son of man, if I changed your heart, is there *any* human heart I can't change absolutely entirely?"

O Man of God, you'll become bone-dry in your faith if you don't really believe in the Lord's power to change people's lives. If you can't agree that Jesus' hand is capable of any kind of miracle, your "faith" will not sustain you through this life. If we're looking at our world, thinking it's far beyond God's reach, we're blaspheming against the God we want to serve. If we don't sense the Lord's sadness at its fallen state – *and then get busy about it* – we're not His sort of men for the fight.

Hear Him say: "Prophesy to the bones of this broken sinful world and say, 'Dry bones, hear the word of the Lord! This is what the Sovereign Lord says to you: I can enter into your life, and you will come to life. I can attach purpose to your living and make My life your life; I will put My breath within you. You can truly come to life; then you will know that Jesus is the Lord of everything…"

O Men of God, we must be moved by the brokenness of this world so full of dry bones, death and daily despair. We must become like Jesus in thinking, "What can I do?" instead of thinking, "Look at what they've done to themselves!" May your heart be filled with empathy whenever you're present with another who's floundering in their sinful folly. May you become a beacon of the love of Jesus, and His wondrous eternal purposes, in the lives of all the people you meet.

Son of man, you're in the valley of the dry bones now. So what will be your next step?

LIVE LIKE MEN

July 7 – Daniel 1:1-5

Striving for excellence in His name

There should be a part of us that wants to be men found excellent in everything we choose to undertake. We should want to bear an "aptitude for every kind of learning," to become men like Nebuchadnezzar wanted in his kingly court. We should hold ourselves to higher sorts of standards than the standards every other man is holding himself to. We should demand of both our lives and daily lifestyle, both our work and play, a real excellence of quality. If we'd want to represent the Lord Jesus to the best of our ability, why not try to be the very best we can personally be? If we'd want to "become all things to all men" that we might "save some," shouldn't we push ourselves to the very limit? Shouldn't we become fully conversant in a broad range of ideas so we might converse with all sorts of people in this world? Shouldn't we become the kind of men who enter a room and are readily able to relate to all present there?

In your own life, how are you excelling towards excellence; how are you pushing yourself ever further, O Man of God? What are ways you spend your time and thoughts and efforts so that you might be better spent for the Lord's purposes? Are you seeking deeper knowledge on a myriad of subjects; do you want to learn more – *for His sake*? Do you see your personal knowledge as a tool in the hand of the Lord Jesus; are you learning still to learn for His Kingdom?

In many ways, Daniel becomes the Daniel we know and admire in the scriptures because Daniel was the sort of man striving for excellence. He was in top physical shape, apt to learn, well informed, because he saw His life as God's alone.

If you want to be a man who "presents your [body] as a living sacrifice," *absolutely go for it, O Man*! Try to live your life with excellence for Jesus – at work, at play, at home – absolutely everywhere you find yourself. Where you sense He's leading you to deeper understandings of a certain subject, go there fully willingly. Where you'd see Him pushing you to push yourself to higher levels in your life, attack those places with manly vigor.

Today, let's be men of excellence in all we do. Let's become a little more like Daniel.

July 8 – Daniel 1:8-15

Taking proper care of your Temple

Daniel was the man he was because he trusted in God's eternal promises regardless of his personal circumstances. He didn't regard his current placement in the Babylonian palace as a reason to relent on his obedience to his God. He wouldn't "defile himself" with food that was unclean in God's sight simply because it would be easier to eat it. No, he stood firm and he trusted that the Lord would honor obedience just as He'd always promised his people...

On a lesser level, does the health and preservation of your earthly body matter much to you, O Man of God? Do you take care of the body you've been given, not from pride, but because it is the Lord's holy "temple"? Do you refuse to become another modern glutton, simply because you know the Lord's work will take energy and vigor? Are you taking care of what the Lord Himself has purposely given you; are you a steward of yourself?

When people think of "Christian men" today, do they think of men "healthier and better nourished" than other men? Are we representing Jesus in all we do; are we even striving for excellence in our bodily care-taking? Do you think Jesus would've stuffed His face and allowed Himself slovenliness if He knew it meant His temple would be degraded? Do you think He'd let Himself kill His energy for doing good work, simply because it's "cultural" to live like this?

O Men of God, I don't believe this topic merits more than a single day out of our whole year together. I don't want to discourage those who struggle with their weight; those for whom food is a difficult subject to address. But may we honor God by honoring the temple of our bodies, by being men who look out for our own physical health. If the Lord should need the utmost of our energies, I'd pray we're men with great personal endurance for the long race ahead.

Today, let's take care (or begin to take care) of our bodily temples for the sake of Jesus' call on our life. He needs men who are both willing and able. May we be fit for all sorts of challenges.

July 9 – Daniel 3

Would you actually die for this?

If you knew your death would bring glory and honor to the name of Jesus, would you die for His sake today? Would you trust His holy purposes for you, even if they didn't lead to any sort of earthly "blessing"? Even if you knew deliverance wasn't part of God's plan for your life, would you trust Him right up till the end? Would you stand upon the edge of fiery furnaces and be happy that you'd stood your ground for His Kingdom? Would you leap into the flames if you'd both heard and believed His words to you: "Behold, I am with you always"? Would you trust His "showing up" abilities, as did Shadrach, Meshach and Abednego, back in mighty Babylon?

O Men of God, if He's actually who He says He is, we can actually trust our God to the death; *He's worth it!* If He'd ask you to feel pain for His sake, He's asking as One who's felt pain ; *He understands what you're feeling.* If He'd ask us to experience persecution, He knows exactly how we feel when we're experiencing that persecution. If He'd ask us to lay our life down for other people, He's asking only what He did Himself for our sake...

There aren't many passages in Scripture that ring with the manliness on display in the one we just read: "O Nebuchadnezzar, we do not need to defend ourselves before you in this matter. If we are thrown into the blazing furnace, *the God we serve is able to save us from it*, and he will rescue us from your hand, O king. *But even if he does not,* we want you to know, O king, that we will not serve your gods or worship the image of gold you have set up."

Today, let's bear the sort of constancy, strength and vital manhood that rang out from these mighty words of theirs. We will not bow down to other sorts of gods; we'd rather die than deny our perfect Lord and Savior, Jesus. You and I will stand strong, knowing our lives are in His hands; that He has a plan that's perfect for our earthly lives. We'll follow through, living from the promises He's personally given us *even if it means our earthly death...*

Are you that kind of man today, O Man? Then you must trust, no matter what.

July 10 – Daniel 6:1-23

Love prayer like Daniel did; pray for brothers who can't pray

If you don't cherish prayer with every ounce of yourself, you aren't a man who understands its inherent power. If you don't love the times you get to share with the living God, are you sure you've really come to love Him? Are you sure you haven't become so accustomed to this land's "religious freedom" that your first love's actually forgotten? Do you wonder what you'd do within the time of Darius' edict; do you love to pray enough that you'd be willing to die for it? If you found yourself an outlaw for your faith, would you persist within your prayers no matter what might happen to you? If you heard the snapping jaws and guttural roars of lions in the night, would you give up your faith instead of your life? If you'd be safer with a faith that blended in against its background, would you choose to let yourself blend in? Or would you rather die than give an inch to earthly powers that deny, or seek to staunch, the power of our God in heaven?

Today, there are actual places in our world where men and women aren't safe because of their faith in Jesus. Every night, as they go to bed, they thank their God that He's kept them through the day; their fear sharpens their faith.

Right now, living wherever you live, being comfortable in your comfort, are you thankful for the gift of prayer, O Man? Do you relish opportunities to quiet your harried mind and talk to the God of the whole universe at our leisure? Do you recognize that God is listening – *and He really truly cares* – about the trials and the tribulations of your current life? Do you know that He rejoices in the prayers of a righteous man; that they're actually called "powerful and effective"?

Then let's give thanks to God that we can pray "three times a day," or however much we want to, every single day of our lives! Spend time today in praying for those individuals all throughout the "modern" world who find they simply can't. If we want to uphold our brothers in the faith whose faith is truly moving mountains, pray for those who can't pray today. And if you'd like to be a man whose faith has power to move mountains for itself, start utilizing your available prayer-life all the time!

Let's be "powerful and effective" today. O Men of God, let's start praying.

July 11 – Hosea 3

Acknowledge your faithlessness and turn to Jesus

If I were to compare my faithlessness against the world's faithlessness, I'd imagine they'd look somewhat similar. Granted, my personal faithlessness is covered by the blood of Jesus Christ but it's still faithlessness, regardless. Granted, the world's misbehaviors may look a bit more unrestrained than my life's, but I also know my heart's hidden failings. I have no room to judge another man when I know my life is filled with so much that's absolutely faithless. In the same way, the Church should claim no right to judge the world when we're all just a bunch of lost sinners before God. The grace of Jesus should be a spur to our *activity*, not a justifying force behind our self-righteous human *judgment*.

Listen to a Hosea 3 revision:

The Father said to Jesus, "Go, show our love to the chosen again, though they have given their hearts to the world and become adulterous. Love them as We love each other, though they often turn to other gods and love the tastes of the world."

So Jesus bought us by the price of His body and His blood; He gave His life that we may live. He told us, "You are to live with me for eternity; you must not prostitute yourselves or be intimate with the world, and I will live in you."

For the Church must live many days without Jesus' physical presence, without His face before our face. Afterward the Church will seek His face and seek the Lord their God and Jesus Christ their King. We must come trembling to the Lord and to His eternal blessings throughout these last days…

O Men of God, we've been unfaithful to Jesus like a faithless wife; we've prostituted ourselves just like Gomer did. We've sold ourselves too long for the comforts and the riches of this world, yet our gracious Savior loves us still!

Today, may we recognize the awful price that was paid for our lives and cease actions that proceed to further faithlessness. Like Hosea, may we become more merciful in our dealings with the dearth of worth in this modern broken world. For we are Jesus Christ's Body in it. Today, let's become more like Him ourselves.

July 12 – Amos 1:1

Use your profession to profess Him

There's no profession that excludes a man of God from professing Jesus to "all nations" of the modern world. There's no profession that excuses a man from usefulness when and where the Lord might need his life for His purposes. There isn't a place that's *not* a place for speaking the name of Jesus or living like we're truly His men only. There's no such thing as compartmentalizing Jesus into the corners of our earthly lives; He wants all of us, plain and simple. Walt Whitman wrote: "There is no trade or employment but the young man following it may become a hero." Personally, I'd say: "There is no trade or employment but the man following it can become a closer disciple of Jesus…"

If the Lord has placed you in the seat of CEO-ship, you're a CEO for the good of His coming Kingdom. If the Lord has placed you in a current state of unemployment, you've never ceased employment as His chosen man. If the Lord has placed you in a cubicle replete with braindead brutal toil, inhabit it with Jesus' Spirit working in you. If the Lord has placed you in your place (which He actually has!) stake His claim upon the way you live your life there.

Do you think the shepherd Amos was excited everyday that the Lord would use His life for the spreading of His word? Do you think he was ever uncomfortable with acting as the Lord's chosen mouthpiece, even though he was a shepherd? Do you think his life was always smooth sailing after having been so chosen; do you think he had some doubts in his heart? Do you think there might've been some quiet moments when he questioned how his calling actually aligned with his daily work?

O Man of God, will you strive in your profession to profess your Lord's name, no matter what the cost to you? Will you cease to see dividing lines demarcating your "work" from your "faith" during the course of this particular day? Will you stand within the place that God has placed you for the purposes of His heart and be ready there for action? Can we become like the shepherd Amos was, living like he saw no earthly difference between "life" and "Life"?

May nothing hinder our obedience today, O Men. Especially not the place God has placed us.

July 13 – Amos 7

Genuine hearts of genuine mercy and genuine justice

The justice we deserve for living outside of God's plan isn't what we're currently receiving, is it? The mercy we're instead receiving is entirely from Jesus' hands and it's doled out to our undeserving hearts through His shed blood. The heart of Jesus always hinges between juxtaposing hemispheres: justice and mercy; judgment and grace; wrath and rescue. If we truly want to ascertain "What would Jesus Do?" each day, we must understand the balance of these opposing pairs.

When Amos saw the Lord's prospective plans for ruining Israel's crops, the prophet yelled out: "Sovereign Lord, forgive!" When Amos saw the Lord was planning to drop fire on the land and the deep, he said, "Sovereign Lord...stop!" But when Amos saw the Lord was plumbing a line amongst his people, it was as if his mercy moved into the realm of justice. Coming into Amaziah's false prophetic presence, it was as if Amos was a new man entirely...

Is your life a life of justice only, one where you find your heart always looking for the faults in other people? Do you think it seems more manly to appear to be more "justice-minded"; is your first recourse unto judgment?

Or will you *never* judge another, or the world, or your church, because "that's not what Jesus would do"? Do you think there's *no* place for God's justice anymore; have you softened Jesus into being simply a "good teacher"?

Jesus Christ was **ALL** mercy and **ALL** justice at exactly the same time, just as He was both man and God. Anyone who tells you "Jesus was only about mercy" doesn't understand a thing about the life-work of Jesus. If Jesus was "only about mercy," why did He choose to go to the cross to meet the terrible needs of divine justice? And yet if Jesus was "only about justice," why would He choose to set free the hearts of sinful people like you and me?

O Men of God, may we learn to navigate the subtle ways of God when it comes to both His mercy and His justice. May we learn the heart of Jesus by being filled with both His mercy and His justice for the world of today.

July 14 – Jonah 1:1-3

Stop fleeing from the life of God in you

It's to our own detriment to say we have no Jonah in our hearts; *we all have some Jonah in our hearts!* We all have the gene that says to itself, "I think I might actually know better"; we all try to run away from our God sometimes. Each of us who's heard the Word of God, especially Jesus' Great Commission, hasn't done everything possible he can do about it. Each of us who claims to follow after Jesus actually spends a lot of days actively trying not to follow Him…

Jesus said: "The kingdom of heaven is like treasure hidden in a field. When a man found it, he hid it again, and then in his joy went and sold all he had and bought that field."

Just because you've never physically run away from God, like Jonah did, doesn't mean you're not a modern-day Jonah. Just because you've never heard the audible voice of God and then done the opposite doesn't mean you're in the middle of His best.

Would you say your life and lifestyle points to the Kingdom of Heaven like a treasure hidden in a field, O Man? If you'd say you've personally "found it," did you "in [your] joy" go away and sell off everything that didn't matter in order to obtain it? Have you so embraced your calling within Jesus that nothing else will ever matter like the matters of His coming Kingdom? Have you so committed to personal obedience to His commandments that there's nothing in your day that competes?

If we give Him less than everything about the way we live our lives, we're actually already on the way of Jonah. If we fault Him for commanding kinds of behavior that won't help us "get ahead," we're on the ship to Tarshish. If we live as if the death and resurrection of our Savior isn't everything, what do we have to offer other people? Instead, may we be the men who've sold off everything and who've "bought that field"; may we be filled with that kind of goofy joy! May we offer life to all who are around us by the passion flowing from us, flowing directly from Jesus! May we head straight out to Ninevah today, overwhelmed that He's chosen to make use of our lives!

Jonah is currently in you, O Man. But you can actually win that battle.

July 15 – Jonah 3

Repent anew

The presence of God's truth is a light within the darkness of the world, a flame set against sheer blackness. When the truth of God is spoken in a manner that's led by the Holy Spirit, people's hearts are always changed. There's no escaping from the ever-present question "Am I right or wrong?" when one hears the very truth of God spoken. We may deny His truth as truth until we're blue in the face, but His truth remains true *always*…

If we're steady in our study of His Word, our lives will exhibit much of the starkness seen in ancient Ninevah. If we measure out our living by the measure of His holiness, we'll be consistently drawn to a wholehearted repentance. But if we choose to *not* be steady in our study of His Word, there's a vast ocean of murkiness and foggy grays ahead. If we *don't* measure our lives against the measure of His holiness, we'll often think we're "doing just fine" the way we are…

O Man of God, you're not fine without Jesus. O Men of God, we all sin against the Lord. And if we'd want to *not* heap shame upon His death upon the cross, we must constantly *re*-turn our hearts to Him. We must examine all the starkness of the Scriptures and be cut to the quick by the darkness in our own earthly lives. We must see how often we've known the truth of God, how He's spoken it to us, and how often we've chosen not to listen. If we want to be the men who are of great use to His Kingdom, we must constantly repent of our personal ways. We must "overturn" the parts of us that lead unto destruction by denouncing our sin before Him.

Today, let's lay our sin before Him, O Men. Let's cover ourselves with sackcloth, sit in the dust.

And then let's rise and feel His grace washing over us. And, pure and new, let's go live for Him all day!

July 16 – Jonah 4:1-4

His grace must beget our grace

Listen to the words of Jesus: "Therefore, the kingdom of heaven is like a king who wanted to settle accounts with his servants. As he began the settlement, a man who owed him ten thousand talents was brought to him. Since he was not able to pay, the master ordered that he and his wife and his children and all that he had be sold to repay the debt.

"The servant fell on his knees before him. 'Be patient with me,' he begged, 'and I will pay back everything.' The servant's master took pity on him, canceled the debt and let him go.

"But when that servant went out, he found one of his fellow servants who owed him a hundred denarii. He grabbed him and began to choke him. 'Pay back what you owe me!' he demanded.

"His fellow servant fell to his knees and begged him, 'Be patient with me, and I will pay you back.'

"But he refused. Instead, he went off and had the man thrown into prison until he could pay the debt. When the other servants saw what had happened, they were greatly distressed and went and told their master everything that had happened.

"Then the master called the servant in. 'You wicked servant,' he said, 'I canceled all that debt of yours because you begged me to. *Shouldn't you have had mercy on your fellow servant just as I had on you?* In anger the master turned him over to the jailers to be tortured, until he should pay back all he owed.

"This is how my heavenly Father will treat each of you unless you forgive your brother from your heart."

Today, may we be so enraptured with the beauty of His grace that we're filled with that grace ourselves, O Men of God. Let's live out of His forgiveness all day. Let's be the vessels of His mercy to this world!

July 17 – Jonah 4:5-11

Learning the large-heartedness of God

The deeper a man will enter into other people's lives, the more he'll feel the mighty call upon his own life. The more you pour yourself into the minutiae of another person's life, the more deeply you'll start to feel the Lord's heart for them. The more you search for ways to lay your life down for another man or woman, the more you'll understand your Savior. The more you choose to view your life with the eyes of Jesus Christ Himself, the more you'll become just like Him.

It seems to me as if the measure of our caring for this world can best be measured by the way we watch the evening news. If you watch the daily stories filled with suffering and pain, and yet feel nothing, you're not investing enough of yourself. If you hear of some terrible disaster without any qualms for the thousands impacted, it might mean you've lost touch with the one-by-one. If we've become so jaded to the fate of many millions, will we do the work of Jesus Christ, person by person? If we feel detached enough to think "one million is a statistic," we must reinvest our hearts for Jesus' sake. We must be living out our lives for others' lives so that we're broken in the face of others' daily suffering.

Jonah placed himself on the altar of self-worship when he said he'd rather die than see the Lord plan unfold. He became a fool by thinking that a stupid vine bore any actual importance on the level with his life.

Can you personally name the ways you've put your lifestyle above the plans and purposes of your God for this world? Do you worship at the foot of your experiences, of your comfort, of your life, of your work etc? Do you feel the way the world has jaded your sensitivities to people, making you a hard-hearted man far too often? Is your desire that you'd be a man who bears the soft-hearted, life-changing spirit of Jesus Christ for others?

Then, today, give your heart to knowing the large-heartedness of God; seek to know His sensitivity for all people. May we be the men who'd never shed a tear for a stupid vine; may we seek the real Vine by abiding in Him daily.

July 18 – Haggai 1:1-11

His work is the only work

In this year of our Lord, on the eighteenth day of the seventh month, the word of the Lord came to us, O Men of God:

This is what the Lord Almighty says: "These people say, 'The time has not yet come for the planting of seeds, the watering or the great harvest.'"

Then the word of the Lord came to us: "Is it a time for you yourselves to be going about your 'work,' your 'careers,' while the harvest remains unharvested?"

Now this is what the Lord Almighty says: "Give careful thought to your ways. You have not planted much, and have harvested little. You eat, but never have enough. You drink, but never have your fill. You put on clothes, but are not warm. You earn wages, only to wish you earned more so you could buy more X, Y or Z."

"This is what the Lord Almighty says: "Give careful thought to your ways. Go up into the mountains and reunite your spirit with Mine, so that I may take pleasure in your use and be honored," says the Lord. "Your expectations are high, but see, they turned out to be nothing. Your 'work' for My Kingdom seems paltry. Why?" declares the Lord Almighty. "Because of My great harvest, which remains unharvested, while each of you is busy with his own 'work.' Therefore, because of your unwillingness to get involved, you are not experiencing the true fullness of life in Me. You experience 'dry seasons' in your life because you do not seek Me with all your heart."

"Come join the harvest. Come experience real life."

July 19 – Haggai 2:1-9

Re-recommit to the March 31st Covenant

Sometimes it's easy for our "modern minds" to scoff at the perpetual waywardness of Israel's behavior toward God. When we read of their unfaithfulness to the God who'd so often delivered them, it seems almost laughable to our sensibilities. When we think of all the mighty manifestations they'd seen from God's hand, it seems crazy they should ever forget Him. Yet, time and again, it seems as if we read His constant reminders to them, the "this is what I covenanted" comments…

Yet let us pause for a second here, O Men, and ask ourselves: *How faithful have we been to this same God?*

Back on March 31st, our day's challenge was to make a personal Covenant with some brothers in our lives. Then, on May 21st, we posed the question "How's that going?" and I'm hopeful we were tough with ourselves…

Today, just as Israel constantly strayed and then was reminded of its previous commitments, take stock of your personal Covenant. How are you doing in both upholding and in spurring on your brothers in their usefulness to Jesus Christ? How's your group of friends been doing in its joint following of the commandments of our Lord: *Are you making them your everything?* Do you need to recommit your hearts to full-commitment living; will you be the men whose word is good and true?

Today, let's simply recommit ourselves. And let's not stray for a single moment.

July 20 – Haggai 2:20-23

End of the Old Testament; preparing for the New

Today will mark our final day of studying the "life of God in the lives of men" in the books we call the Old Testament. Tomorrow, we'll turn unto the pages of the New; we'll celebrate the coming of our Lord and Savior, Jesus! We'll see just how our God made good upon the promises and prophecies of the old in the *new* way He personally created for us. "See, I am doing a new thing! Now it springs up; do not you not perceive it? I am making a way in the desert and streams in the wasteland." (Isaiah 43:19)

There could almost be no better segue between the Old and New Testaments than our passage for today's reading. For will not Jesus Himself "shake the heavens and the earth"; won't He "overturn royal thrones and shatter the power" of the world? Won't His Kingdom "overthrow chariots and their drivers"; won't He Himself be the stone that "became the chief cornerstone"? "Do not think that I have come to abolish the Law or the Prophets," He once said, "I have not come to abolish them but to fulfill them…"

Hear the words of Haggai spoken to Zerubbabel as a preparation for tomorrow's testamental transition, O Men. You and I are ones for whom Jesus came; you are one for whom He was prepared to lay His human life down.

"On that day," declares the Lord Almighty, "I will take you, my servant, and I will make you like my signet ring, *for I have chosen you*," declares the Lord Almighty.

O Men of God, we are chosen men; we are men who God Almighty thought fit for His holy purposes! We are men who have been armed with usefulness by His perfect power; we are men whose battle is totally real.

Today, give some time to contemplation on the ways that God has used the Old Testament in your life this year. Then prepare your heart with joy and great thanksgiving for tomorrow; be prepared for something wonderfully New!

July 21 – Matthew 1:1-17

Why are you who you are?

You might've been placed within your family and its genealogical tree for a million different heavenly reasons, O Man. You may be one who starts a line of godly men who radically change the world for the purposes of Jesus' Kingdom. You may be one who's like a Zerubbabel – God's "signet ring" – ten generations away from eternal glory. You may be the man who'll act as final culmination to a line that God is ready to use right now.

The question is: Have you ever pondered on the Lord's placement of your life in the midst of your own human family? Do you know the history of your family's line; of your family's course of faith; of the placement you now inhabit? Have you ever pondered on the Lord's possible reasons for the timing and the place and the people in your personal life? Do you realize the power held by each and every single man who's found in a family's tree?

If Abram hadn't trusted his God and hadn't his name changed to Abraham, he wouldn't be this particular tree's seed. If Boaz hadn't been a man of mighty mercy and hadn't ever noticed Ruth, he wouldn't be part of its root system. If David hadn't left his flock and father, and been faithful to his call, there wouldn't *be* the possibility of a "Son of David." If Josiah hadn't had passion for the Lord and for the temple, there wouldn't be a Christ incarnate.

What matters is your placement in the tree of your own family; what matters is the call of Jesus for you, O Man. Will you be a man who upholds godly honor, strength and integrity in the midst of our broken sinful world today? Will you be a man who lives his life with the passion and great purpose such as were shown by Jesus' earthly forefathers? Will you be the man where generation after generation points back to you as one who led the way to the Way?

Today, live the life you're called to live, O Man. Be the seed (or root (or fruit)) of your own family tree.

July 22 – Matthew 1:18-25

Your gracefulness proves your righteousness

There was every reason for this man to question whether his fiancée had been unfaithful to him. There was every worldly and cultural (and even religious) justification for this carpenter to make his lady a spectacle for mockery. There would've been nothing "wrong" if Joseph chose to call her out for cheating on him, prior to their nuptials. No one would've argued with a man who'd apparently been cuckolded for trying to get his share of personal vengeance…

But not this particular man. No, not this Nazarene carpenter. For Joseph "was a righteous man and did not want to expose her to public disgrace," regardless of his own personal feelings. Joseph didn't feel that wrongs done to him were a gateway justification for his doing wrong to other people. Joseph didn't burn with feelings of a self-righteous vengeance; Joseph was a righteous man filled with God's grace. Joseph actually gives us prefiguring visions of the Son he'd soon be raising by the gracefulness inherent in him…

O Men of God, you and I will show the measure of our righteousness by the measure of grace we pour forth unto others. You and I will be the men we're called to be when we *don't* do unto others what they might even possibly "deserve." You and I will become men within the pattern of Jesus' earthly surrogate father when we hold back from all earthly harm. You and I will become pillars in the earthly Body of Christ when we exhibit the grace of Jesus in all we do.

Today, may we grow in righteousness by reaching out to someone who needs a show of our God's gracefulness. May we email, call or talk to a person we truly need to forgive or encourage or give grace to before we do anything else. It doesn't matter if the reasons for your anger or frustration are warranted by the actions they've previously done to you. It doesn't matter if you think you've already taken some sort of self-righteous high road by your choice to previously ignore them.

May we become men as "righteous" in our actions as we are in our own "humble" self-estimations! May we set aside our *feelings* for the *doing* of His grace in the practical pattern of Jesus' earthly father, Joseph. Today, let's reach out, O Men of God. May we manifest righteousness by graceful action.

July 23 – Matthew 2:1,2

Sensitivity to the Spirit's leadings is a necessity

If the Magi hadn't been chasing after the star, they wouldn't have come to worship the Christ-child in David's Bethlehem. If the Magi hadn't been studying the skies, they never would've seen the star that led them straight to His manger. Yet the Magi *were* studying the skies and they *did* see the star that led them across the world to this Savior. The Magi *did* follow astral indicators and they *did* come to worship Jesus on this particular night…

If we want to worship Jesus for ourselves, it follows that we need to follow signs that point directly to Him now. If we want to be the "wise men" who'd give our hearts to Him today, we must have a measure of this same heavenly wonder. If God should choose to place a star within the heavens that was noticed by these few, we must expect more of the same today. We must assume that there are Holy Spirit-signs within the world – *and our lives* – that are meant only for us.

How attentive is your heart to subtle signs of the Holy Spirit placed within your day-to-day existence, O Man? Do you go about your day with eyes that look for God's leading or are you of the "more practical sort" of modern man? Do you realize that without their searching-eyes and following-hearts, there wouldn't be a marvelous story of the Magi? There would be a lesser story of the Christmas celebration if the Magi didn't lead lives filled with holy wonder…

Are you a man filled with holy wonder, O Man? Are you a man seeking after our wondrous God? Are you a man who puts the workings of the Lord in a modern box or is He absolutely limitless to you? Will you live today as if the Spirit of the Lord is at work within you: leading you; guiding you; directing you?

Because the Spirit of the Lord is in you! The question is: Will you be led today?

Don't forget: "the Lord was not in" Elijah's wind or the earthquake or the fire up on that ancient mountainside. The Lord revealed Himself in the "gentle whisper." (1 Kings 19:11-13) May we learn to become His Spirit's whisper-whisperers.

July 24 – Matthew 2:7-12

Do extravagant things for Him today

Joseph had been picked up by a local general contractor and was working dawn-to-dusk in his new job. Mary was accustoming herself to married life and to motherhood, to management of a recently grown household. After working hard all day and then coming home, Joseph sits across the table from his wife, eating their meager dinner. She looks at him and then she looks at Jesus, who's lying on the floor on a blanket, snoring softly, fast asleep. For a moment, Joseph and his young bride share a look before returning to their peaceful evening meal. They will finish up their dinner, take a walk, then settle into bed for a night of quiet sleep...

Someone knocks on their streetside door. Joseph looks across the table at Mary, questioningly. Mary rises from the table and she opens up the door to a group of tired, but rich-looking, men...

There was such a bold extravagance of worship in the worship that the Magi brought to humble little Bethlehem. I imagine there was such a sense of being "overjoyed" upon their faces that Mary felt she had to open the door!

Have you ever been so swept up with your love of Jesus Christ that you've done anything worthy of the adjective "extravagant"? Have you ever been aswoon with the Holy Spirit within you; have you been afire with Jesus' love for you?

Today, your task is living life from a place of personal extravagance in the way you conduct yourself for your Savior's call. Either worship Him with excitement on your face or be zealous in the giving of good gifts to others. Be crazy in the way you'll give your time to one who's needy of your time for the service of your King. Do something utterly outrageous – like the giving of such precious gifts to a quietly sleeping baby in a sleepy town. You and I will only grow in our belief as much as we're willing to act wildly for the callings of our Savior. We'll only become like the wise Magi when we bow our hearts and knees to the God of distant stars in the infinite night sky.

Today, pick your personal extravagance, O Man. Let's dole our day from the pool of our overjoyedness.

July 25 – Matthew 3:1-6

Will you be the Second Coming's John the Baptist?

If John the Baptist was the one preparing the way for Jesus' *first* coming, who'll be the one(s) doing the same for His *second*? Who will be the "voice of one calling in the desert" to this world as we feel that wondrous day drawing nearer? Who will be the men who stand alone amidst this world's wildernesses and proclaim Jesus' life and truth to all men? Who will be the ones who'll lay their lives upon His altar in the service of the only Kingdom that actually matters? Which of us will speak with boldness of His simple hard truths that are true, hard and so beautifully simple? Which of you will be a man so totally possessed with this purpose that he'd shun the shifting comforts of the days we inhabit?

Perhaps it might read this way:

*In these days **you** came, preaching in the desert of the modern world and saying, "Repent, for the return of Jesus is near." You are he of whom Jesus thought when he said: "Therefore go and make disciples of all nations…"*

Your clothes did not matter to you much, for you knew "your Father knows what you need before you ask him." Your food was the fare of men who care not for the world, nor for luxury, nor for softness, nor for anything but Jesus. People came out to you from home and work and the whole circle of influence God chose to give to you. Acknowledging their sins, you fully acquainted them with He who is the "way and the truth and life."

Do you use your life to "prepare the way for the Lord"; do you work to "make straight paths for him," O Man of God? Do you know that you're a kindred spirit to this wild-eyed baptist named John; that the same blood is in your veins? Will you use today to help the people in your life to see their terrible need for Jesus Christ in *their* life? Will your own example point to sweet humble-hearted repentance, to a daily hungry searching for His coming Kingdom?

"So you, too, must keep watch! For you don't know what day your Lord is coming…You also must be ready all the time, for the Son of Man will come when least expected." (Matt 24:42 & 43) Keep watch and be ready, O Men. Get to work upon your own "John the Baptist calling."

July 26 – Matthew 3:13-17

Consider your baptism and Spirit-baptism

It's no coincidence that Jesus' first public appearance as a grown man was by the waters of the Jordan River. It's no mistake that Jesus' first public act as the Messiah was to subjugate himself to his earthly cousin, John. Even though John felt that he wasn't fit to carry Jesus' sandals (v. 11), Jesus humbly asks him for his baptism. Even though this represents a turning point in the history of the world, Jesus goes down into the water in full humility. Even though He had the power to "baptize…with the Holy Spirit and with fire," Jesus knew the plan before Him was crystal clear. Even though He was *without* sin Himself, Jesus knew the Father planned to "fulfill all righteousness" through Him…

First and foremost, have you ever actually been baptized in a manner where you *knew* the meaning of your actions? Were you sprinkled as a baby; doused as a child; dunked within your church's confirmation waters at a later age? What did it mean to you on that day (assuming you actually remember how it felt when the water came upon you)? Did it represent a starting-point of full-commitment living or was it just a stairstep on the churchly way of life? Did it start to change the fabric of your being – did it "fulfill all righteousness" – or was it "just something you did"? When you think about that moment, does it give you chills of passion or just shivers "because the water was so cold"?

Secondly, have you ever been fully blanketed with the Holy Spirit and had a taste of this particular moment? Have you ever burned with the Spirit's holy passion; felt the cool of His peace; sensed the power pulsing within you? Have you ever felt that Holy seal upon your spirit that marked you as His son with whom He's also "well pleased"? Has the Spirit made His home within your heart; do you know right now that's He's really living in you?

O Man, there's something to be said for *re*-baptism if you can't even remember when it first happened for you. We should be the men who fully voice their faith and belief, not the babies who were sprinkled as spiritual insurance by their parents. Yet may we, too, be the men who've been baptized by the Holy Spirit's peace and power and indwelling presence for eternity. If you can't point to points of time when He's made that manifest in you, go searching for Him today. Experience both baptisms, O Man. Be a man of the water and the Spirit.

July 27 – Matthew 4:1-11

Memorize some scripture

Perhaps you've been a part of Bible studies where you've studied through the Gospels "trying to better understand Jesus." Maybe some of you have even sat through studies where you've studied this particular moment of Jesus' temptation in the wilderness…

If so, I'd wager that your leader (or some guy with all the answers) said something just like this: "Did you notice how He always quotes scripture; how He wasn't even fazed when Satan did the same, back?" Or: "Wouldn't it be great if we all had that kind of scriptural knowledge where you'd always have it ready to help you?" Or: "We should all aspire to have the scriptures on the tips of our tongues, like Jesus did here…"

Personally, I'd say: Wrong. I'd set the bar much higher.

We'll never be the kind of men Jesus actually needs until we actually *do* the sorts of things Jesus did. We'll never combat Satan and his temptations unto sin until we do more than "aspire" to know scripture. If you want to have the kind of "scripture knowledge" that would arm you with Jesus' readiness, commit more than "some" to your memory. If you'd like to be unfazed by such temptation and have that scripture on your lips, *put that scripture on your lips!*

Over the last ten years, every single group of guys I've led has had one thing in common. Before anything else, they've had to memorize the verse that bears the title of this book you're now holding in your hands: *"Be on your guard, stand firm in the faith,* **live like men***, be strong! Let everything that you do be done in love."* (1 Corinthians 16:13,14 – Phillips)

Today, memorize this verse, O Man. And then continue on with (many, many!) others.

It's literally the least you can do. So go ahead – *let's do it!*

July 28 – Matthew 4:12-17

Know this two-point message and speak it

Jesus didn't speak a message identical to John's because he was a thief, but because it was *the* message. And "Repent, for the kingdom of heaven is near" is still the message today for those messengers of His personal choosing. If you'd like to be a man of God who speaks His real truth to the world, measure your message against this original message: If repentance from one's sin and the nearness of His coming aren't mentioned, *you're actually doing it wrong*. If you talk a lot without a lot of talking about Jesus, *you need to reframe your message's intent and direction*. If you think you're being clever for the purpose of attracting "seekers" to the Body, *seek to seek His face again only*. Jesus is the "great light" shining on "the people living in darkness" – He doesn't need our clever tricks to get His work done. Jesus is the dawning light of heaven upon the "land of the shadow of death" in this world – don't ever forget it!

If you want to rob your life and personal ministry of all their meaning, rob the message of your Lord of all its weight and purpose. If you want to have a tree filled with no good fruit, don't speak like He actually does in this particular passage. If you'd like to add in extra thoughts and "meaning" by additions from this world, don't expect very much from your efforts. If you think you have ideas that are better than Jesus' simple solid teachings, good luck to you, my friend…

But if you'd want to bless the lives of other people, speak the message of our Lord with its full weighty purpose. If you'd want to have a tree filled up with fruit, speak the message of repentance and His nearness nearly constantly. If you expect to see Him changing lives all around you – *and your own too* – don't add a single thing to Jesus and His words. If you speak His name with clarity, winsomeness, true and earnest love, He will always be present in your delivery.

O Men, may we have the courage needed to be speakers of Jesus' unadulterated truth to this modern world. And may we never become modern-day pied pipers piping drivel that's not coming directly from His lips to us. May we be the men whose lives are so transformed that His "great light" oozes and seeps from our pores to everybody we meet. May we simply speak the truth that we've been given with the knowledge that its power is absolutely extraordinary.

Now you must know that message for yourself, O Man. And then, when prompted, speak it out with joy and clarity!

July 29 – Matthew 4:18-22

Know what you're called to; then go call!

A man who gives his heart and soul to Jesus will begin exuding the same personal magnetism as his Savior did. A man assured of his personal placement as one of Jesus' disciple will begin to draw in other men to a life of real discipleship. A man who's convinced of Jesus' power will become a man of personal power; he'll become more like Jesus in his daily dealings. A man who's heard the "Come, follow me" and then actually followed after Jesus is the only sort of man whose life will really matter…

We must know this Lord to whom we're calling others so totally intimately that they'd see the attractiveness of His lifestyle. We must know what He really means by the word "discipleship" so we have some clear honest answers for others if they ask. We must learn to know the "when" of the Lord's divine perfect timing so that we'd make effective calls into the lives of other men. We must know the places where His Spirit softly leads us so that we're always on His path and steadily moving forward. We should know why this means everything for us; we must've been transformed already by His calling into our lives. We can only know how He'd daily lead our lives when we actually *want* to be led; we must make ourselves available to Him always.

Have you ever called another person into fellowship with Jesus: Have you ever been a "witness" to the Light? Have you ever opened your mouth to what He'd ask you to speak aloud; is the "light" within you actually shining to others? If so, have you followed further on His path with that particular person: Have you led them out into His sort of discipleship? Do you think you're on His path unto discipleship personally; have you heard the "follow Me" *and actually followed*?

The entirety of Jesus' most important ministry is actually contained within this short direct passage of scripture. Jesus came to set us free – *yes, of course!* – but His day-to-day ministry was raising up His disciples for His work. And when He called out from the shore amidst the workaday workings of these fishermen, Jesus set the gold standard for our lives. He taught that there's no such thing as boundaries, whether of time, space or context, for this work of calling men unto Himself.

Who are you calling unto Him, O Man? With whom will you delve deep today?

July 30 – Matthew 4:23-25

Reach out to the sick and diseased in your life

Jesus had no buffers in His dealings with the sick, diseased, demon-possessed and bed-ridden of His day. He didn't have our modern faculty for shrugging off anothers' pain, for putting problems "in their proper context." He almost never ceased His work of loving others through the taking up of their infirmities, their hurts, their personal issues. He probably lay awake at night, looking forward to the healings and helpings that tomorrow would certainly bring to Him…

O Men, we will *all* be judged for the content our heart's actual love for the hurting, sick and diseased. Jesus didn't set His daily course *un*purposefully; He wants that we would want to help others like He did. He wants disciples who will take up their own cross daily for the sake of others; He desires men of His own ilk. He doesn't believe in thoughts of separating earthly from eternal when it comes to meeting people's true and daily needs.

Do you think the crowds crowded around Him only for the sake of hearing His teachings about the Kingdom of God? Or do you think His works lent power to the value of His words; that hearts were opened by His light caring touch? Do you think that Jesus' words would've meant anything to anyone if He'd sat upon the grass, *not* helping anybody? Or do you think the power of His eyes to see, heart to feel, hands to touch were the powers that changed everything?

O Man of God, there are many people today in your life who are actually sick, diseased, paralyzed or dying. There are people Jesus has placed within your life so that *you* might be His eyes and heart and hands to them.

Today, think about the ways that you might reach out to another with the actions, not just the words, of Jesus. May we become His men of action for the daily honest hurts in the lives of the people all around us.

Today, reach out to the sick and hurting. You are actually the hands and heart of Jesus to them.

July 31 – Matthew 7:24-29

Take hold of Christ's authority and use it

The difference between problematic "Christians" and the men who'll actually change lives is their use of Jesus' authority. When you hear a wheedling scolding sort of tone attached to any talk of Jesus, there's absolutely something wrong there. When you hear a "Christian leader" speaking words stamped with the "pattern of this world," he's always on the wrong track. If Jesus is talked about as if He's physically weak, or somehow emasculated, you can be assured the talker doesn't personally know Him.

Jesus is the One who said that He Himself is the only sure foundation for the building of one's earthly life. He's also the One who said the building of one's life upon any other foundation is absolute foolishness. He could speak with such authority because He *is* the final authority, the fullness of God in human form. And we ourselves can speak with such godly authority because He's given it to us – *but will you choose to do so?*

Kahlil Gibran wrote: "I am sickened and the bowels within me stir and rise when I hear the faint-hearted call Jesus humble and meek, that they may justify their own faint-heartedness; and when the downtrodden, for comfort and companionship, speak of Jesus as a worm shining by their side. Yea, my heart is sickened by such men. It is the mighty hunter I would preach, and the mountainous spirit unconquerable."

Will you be a man and take the reins of Jesus' authority in your hands; will you be the sort of man He's calling for? Will you found each day upon the truth of His words spoken to you; are you a "wise" sort of builder in your own personal life? Will you live and speak and work and raise your family with authority; will you be a man among this world's boys? Will you open up your heart to the amazing possibilities that are realized in the lives of men who truly follow Him?

Today, feel Jesus' authority, O Man. It's coursing through your blood and spirit. Be the sort of man the world desperately needs, not the weakened sort of weakling that it oftentimes holds up. "The crowds [will be] amazed" – I promise you that!

August 1 – Matthew 8:1-3

Be Jesus to the Church-marginalized

The essence of the message of the Sermon on the Mount is encapsulated in this action that directly follows it: Jesus comes off the mountain and He immediately reaches out to touch the diseased skin of an "unclean" leper. All at once, His disciples see the radical extents to which their own lives will be pushed by His discipleship-call. All of a sudden, "do to others what you would have them do to you" doesn't seem so simple anymore. His disciples surely looked around at each other and wondered if their own lives would be called to contain something similar. And, over time, they'd come to realize the immense power of Jesus' touch upon the skin of the ultra-marginalized…

Who are the modern Church's lepers, O Men? And what will you do about that today? Will you follow Jesus unto places of His utmost call to others; will you touch the skin of today's lepers?

Today, think about the group of people (or the type of person) most shunned by the world or by the modern Church. Your challenge is to think of how Jesus' touch might impact them; how your own Christ-touch will actually impact them. Will you reach unto the places and the people that are terribly uncomfortable for you if it's for His holy purposes? Will you make yourself available to the type of people marginalized by the sinfulness of the modern Church?

Today, be Jesus to those very people. Reach out and touch a modern-day leper for His sake.

August 2 – Matthew 8:5-13

Give over the "one thing" and believe

I'd guess that every man who's currently reading from this page has a "sick servant situation" in his own life. Right now, every single one of us is bearing a quiet worry in his heart that'll send us in one of two directions: First off, we can let the trouble, worry, fear or potentiality eat away at our daily thoughts and behavior. We can lay awake at night and hope the problem "will resolve itself"; we can pray it'll "run its course" before it ruins us.

Or we can have a faith that actually says to God "I believe" and let Him do all the worrying about our earthly lives. We can take our trouble to the foot of He who came for our sakes; we can say "Lord, just say the word" to Him. We can be the men so *without* any worry that we carry out our days according to His great plans for us. We can be the men so undeterred by any trial, fire, fear or trouble that our faith is really real and totally true.

Today, you already have an issue on your mind that I'm actually asking you to bring to Jesus for His supernatural help. Each of us is like the centurion coming to Him with our dilemma; what matters is the first word after we first pray to Him. Will you say, "I do not deserve to have you come under my roof" – "just say the word, and my servant will be healed"? Do you believe that anything that ails us is actually nothing when compared to His unlimited power to work? Will you give up any thought of your self-sufficiency in the face of any worry that's haunting your mind, right now? Will you trust just like the centurion once trusted Jesus, knowing that the ways of God are for your unquestionable best?

Just think of all the things we actually might accomplish if we didn't weight our ways with the waywardness of daily worry. Think of how the word of Jesus might further spread if we'd give our hearts and minds to the comfort of real Belief. Don't we waste away a million moments of our earthly lives in the toiling after pointless potentialities? Haven't we given away enough Todays to *not* believing Jesus is aware of, and working upon, our daily needs? Imagine what would happen in this particular day if every one of us gave that One Thing over *and then simply obeyed.* Imagine how our vast united energies might be used if we all spoke our One Things to the King *and then trusted Him.*

Today, know the power ranged within you, O Man. Then give that need – *and your heart* – back to Jesus.

August 3 – Matthew 8:18-22

What's His calling costing you?

If you feel like any part of your own following after Jesus comes with caveats, you're not fully following Him. If you've ever set your own set of terms for your discipleship, you're not the kind of disciple He's actually after. If you've ever tried to pigeonhole the providential plans of Jesus, you don't understand Jesus. If you really want to understand the heart and soul of God, you must know that you've been called unto precariousness. You're now a man who doesn't know what whims of the Father's perfect will might preclude your best-laid plans for your life. You're now a man who's called to living like the whole of human life is His Life; like nothing else matters. You're now a man who has been called to Him for His good purposes, His glory, His ever-unfurling sovereign plans. You're now a man who knows the utter joy of *not* knowing what the future holds because you've given yours to Him.

There's entirely too much self-chosen self-determined "discipleship" at work today in the modern Church, O Men. There's far too much of "This is what it looks like to be a Christian," not enough actual daily following after Jesus. The error of this teacher of the law, and also this other disciple who came to Him, was their making their demands *of* Jesus. The reason He answered them with these enigmatic brush-offs is because of one simple truth about the Way of Jesus: He doesn't respond to faiths of chosen self-trajectory; Jesus Christ Himself is the only worthy trajectory. If you want to choose your path through life for yourself, you'll never be the kind of man He's after. If you've ever heard His Call – *even once* – that's actually all that really matters for your journey with Him, ever after. He must call and you must obey Him. It's really and truly that simple.

What is your faith costing you today, O Man? If it costs you nothing, it's too cheap. May we seek to be the men whose faith and following is so costly that it costs us everything for His sake. May we lay down everything about ourselves, and then be spent, so that the world may know Him more fully. That'll be a life worth living. Only His call really matters.

August 4 – Matthew 8:23-27

Nothing is outside of His power

There's nothing in your life or current circumstances that's outside of God's knowledge or His providential planning. There's not a single storm of anxiety, hardship or terror that's outside of His "all-knowingness" about you. If you believe He actually rose up from His stern-side sleep and calmed the clamor of the Galilee sea, believe this fact also: Jesus can calm *any* storm, *any* trouble, *any* issue in your life if it's in His will to do so. There's really nothing that He can't do; nothing that prevents Him from preventing every hardship in the modern world. But what He wants from you is Belief, "you of little faith"; what He truly wants is your unswerving daily trust in Him. What He hopes is that you'd see the blackening thunderheads approaching your boat, yet be calm in the safety of His personal care. What He needs is men who pitch and trough on stormy seas of life, yet are rock-like in their faith in His absolute power. What the world has seldom seen are true Believers who actually believe in the power of this Lord of their life. If you want to change the world, start believing that the Lord who calmed the sea is at work in your day today.

If the Lord would plan out four years of hardship for the good of your next forty, would you trust Him in those four years? If He wants you in a different job, will you trust Him in the many months while you're unemployed? If His plan requires a time of tough shaping for your children, will you trust Him in their time of chastising? If He'd need you broken down to eventually build you up, will you not resist the tools of His perfect plan for you?

Simpler put: Do you believe "that in all things God works for the good of those who love him, who have been called"? Even if the storm is raging in your life today, do you trust He's able to rebuke the wind and waves around you? Will you be the kind of man who sees His life as actually being the Lord's; sees its workings as the Working of His Will? Even if it means some hardship at some points, will you count yourself as blessed that you've been personally called to Him?

Our faith must move toward a fearlessness, O Men. How can we, as His men, fear anything at all?

August 5 – Matthew 9:1-8

Becoming perceptive of others' needs

If we want to grow in learning the complementary roles of justice and mercy, we must learn to read other men's thoughts. Yes, of course, we may never *actually* read other men's thoughts; we may never acquire this faculty Jesus personally possessed. Yet I think that Jesus bore the eyes and heart to notice how one's eyes and heart were attuned – *or not attuned* – to Him. I don't think He always utilized His supernatural gifts when it came to His man-to-man perception of other men...

Are you attentive to the "language" of the face and eyes and body of your fellow man, O Man of God? Do you try to read another's frame of mind just by the way they carry themselves in their day-to-day life? Do you use God-given sensitivity as a tool to the helping of the men and women all around you? Can you "read their minds" by reading what is written in their eyes, in their words, in their everyday commonplace actions?

Jesus used this particular moment for the practice of a merciful deliverance, both from physical paralysis and sin. Yet when He noticed how the minds of men around Him were so doubtful, He also went the way of justice in this episode. Jesus didn't view His life within compartments where some portions were His "ministry" and some other parts "for Himself." He would walk into a crowded room of people and be present to those people, whether they were considered "good" or "bad."

Since the Lord saw fit to call you to His side, won't you tune your manly heart to His assignments for you today? Won't you use your every ounce of human strength upon His proddings in your heart, for His needs in others' lives? Can't we see how we ourselves were once the paralytic, lying upon the floor, stuck in sin and a dead life? Can't we conjure how it felt when He then looked upon our lives with those eyes filled with love and acted to set us free?

May we use today to study how the people all around us are in desperate need of Jesus' loving heart. May we become so perceptive of their hopes and needs and hurts that it's as if we're reading their very thoughts when we speak to them. If you ask the Lord to give you His abilities to be present in the lives of people, He'll certainly give those abilities to you. He'll give you His own gift of perfect perception if He sees that you desire to be like Him in others' lives. Let's be men of keen perception today. Let's learn to read other's thoughts *for Him*.

August 6 – Matthew 9:9

Remembering who you were when He called you

The life of Matthew was a life forever marked by how the Lord saw value in such a tax-collecting life as his. And, in the same way, I'd hope that yours is a life forever marked by how the Lord would value such a life as yours *used to be*. If the Lord could pick a cheating, stabbing-in-the-back sort of guy as His disciple, He can pick anyone, right? And if the Lord can value men of no account to anyone, like Matthew was, we must learn to value *everyone* ourselves…

Below, write the adjectives, adverbs, descriptors and all the words that once defined you when He called you to Himself. Reacquaint yourself with how truly lost you once were; how He came up to your tax-booth and said "follow Me." If the Lord can pick a man like the "old you" used to be, can He not use the "new you" to reach out to many more? If He'd pick a man like Matthew, He can certainly remake any heart to be ready for the harvest work ahead…

When Jesus called me, I was:

August 7 – Matthew 9:9-13

Is your Jesus the Jesus of Matthew's feast?

Only when we stack our chips on seemingly "bad bets" on people do we replicate the way of Jesus in the world. Only when our lives are laid down for the sake of bad investments do we get a sense of His own life's work. Only when we spend our time with harlots, "tax collectors and 'sinners'" are we working in the mold of our Savior, Jesus. Only when we give up preconceptions that we're in any way above other people do we rise to His level and stature. Do you think the tax collectors and these "sinners" found themselves drawn to Jesus because He judged their personal lifestyles? Do you think that whores and bastards flocked to His side because they got a sense that He was hateful to their sort of people? Don't you think that all these lost ones experienced a sense that Jesus was their heart's true and perfect resting place? Don't you think that He exuded everything that was a draw to men and women; a place like "home"?

When we choose to enter lives that look like every kind of lost, we're carrying on Jesus' personal mission. When we set aside the places of respect and of "clean living" for the worth of souls, we're truly starting to do His good. When we start to make Jesus so attractive that the world can't seem to resist Him, we're starting to paint Him correctly. If we make our home in Him, if we make Him look like home to others, people will respond with hearts of joy and gladness.

What image does your life portray of Jesus: Does He come off as the Lord of love or as the Scourge of sinners? Does He look like One who'd show up at a feast of unrepentant lost lives or a church-mousy sort of judge? Have you ever communed with this particular version of Jesus, sitting around a table with the worst people in the whole town? Do you recognize that *you* are one on whom He's lavished love; that *you* are a "tax collector and 'sinner'" whom He loves?

I should think the Lord is less upset when He's painted "too mercifully," as opposed to being shown "too judgmentally." I should think the Lord would rather that we'd err upon the side of mercy than upon the side of judgment, O Men. Today, may we be the sort of men portraying Jesus as this particular Jesus, sitting at Matthew's feast, utterly happy there. May we make our Lord look like the smiling loving Jesus, sitting at their table, feeling at home, *acting as home…*

August 8 – Matthew 9:18,19

Let Jesus interrupt your day

You don't have a single meeting, conference call or business deal whose importance trumps the interruptions of Jesus today. There's nothing in your day that'll matter like the way He'd like to use you in the lives of other people in your life. I'd be interested to know how many heavenly opportunities I've personally missed because of my self-important busyness, my "schedule." Wouldn't we be horrified to think we're missing daily chances for His Kingdom work because of "the way my day's going"?

Jesus was amidst the speaking of the spiritual "wineskins" when this particular ruler came and knelt down before Him. A crowd of people were hanging upon His every word; He was teaching; He was doing exactly what the Father wanted. Yet He turned His eyes upon the weeping eyes of this sad ruler and he listened to his tragic tale of loss. And when he'd finished, there was absolutely no hesitation: "Jesus got up and went with him, and so did his disciples."

Since we ourselves want to be the modern-day disciples of Jesus, won't we follow in the interruptable footsteps of our Master? Won't we look upon the day with eyes to see His interruptions as a blessing; His whispers as the Call for us? When a person at your office – or your wife – or a stranger – needs your ear, won't you lend it to them this day? If a homeless man should ask you for a fiver, can't you give him thirty minutes for a meal and your friendly presence? If you see a car broken down on the side of the road, is your day so terribly busy that you can't stop and help that person? If you get a spiritual sense that someone near you is in spiritual need, can't you ask some gentle leading questions?

We can only become more like Jesus when we're willing to become like Him in every aspect of our lives, O Men. And we'll only let the Lord into this everything about ourselves when we open ourselves to His daily interruptions. Nothing in your day today is outside of His perfect providential knowledge; nothing happens to you "just by chance." Yet nothing *will* occur if you won't at least take the time to help another, to be a listener; you won't grow without some practice.

The Lord will interrupt your day today. But will you allow your day to be interrupted?

August 9 – Matthew 9:18-26

You could be "the one" for someone today

You can't be certain who might be pushing through a crowd in desperation for a moment of your time today, O Man. It would seem that no one ever knows they're in a "once-in-a-lifetime" moment till it's already happening to them. What matters, as we studied yesterday, is how we live our lives aware of how God wants to use our every moment. What matters, as you hopefully discovered through some application, is how we orientate our spirit unto people. If Jesus hadn't quit His teaching to help the ruler's dying daughter, He would've never been available to help this particular lady. If this lady hadn't been so desperate for a miraculous healing of her ailment, we'd never have seen this momentous moment happening. When the Lord ordains that people in their desperation embark on desperate gambits, I'd hope we'd likewise be available to them. I pray I'll be the kind of man who's so available, aware, sensitive and strong, that I'll become like Jesus in my everyday life.

This day may hold the key for someone else's being set free from their sin…but will you be paying close attention? Someone may be starting out this day with thoughts of asking you a certain question…but will you be listening for that question? There's a person who's currently watching how you live in order to know more of Jesus…but how are you currently living? There's a man or woman pushing through the crowd with hopes of being close to you…but will you be of use to them?

I'd rather have a moment of this woman's sort of faith than a lifetime paying lip service to Jesus. After all, she understood that He was powerful enough to change her life with a momentary touch of His common cloak.

O Man of God, will you *be* the cloak of Jesus to another in the way you choose to live the details of your day today? Will you carry within yourself the mighty power of the "Master interrupted"; will you be His healing self for others? Will you walk throughout the crowded ways of life with Jesus' eyes for the broken, hurting, needy and desperate in this world? Will you stop a moment, have a conversation, say a prayer – *be present* – for the sake of other people's lives?

Every moment counts, O Man. Will you live the moment-to-moment life of Jesus today?

August 10 – Matthew 9:27-31

How big is your faith?

Ask yourself: If it was "according to *your* faith" that all was given you, what would you deservedly receive? Is your faith of such deep measure that the Lord would be amazed by it; that He'd hold you up as a perfect model for manhood? If it *wasn't* by the grace of Jesus alone that you were healed, do you think your faith would be the healing sort of faith? Do you think He'd look into your heart and see the fiber of your faith as indestructible, fully alive?

"Abraham believed God, and it was credited to him as righteousness" – *what do you believe about your God, O Man?* Do you truly think the Lord is in control of every aspect of your life; do you trust Him completely? In whatever trial or tribulation where you need some heavenly help, "do you believe that I am able to do this?" Can your faith look directly into the eyes of Jesus Himself, and say lionheartedly, "Yes, Lord" in complete belief?

The "shield of faith" is meant for fending off the "flaming arrows of the evil one," including apathy and doubt. Every single missile, whether passive or aggressive, that Satan shoots ast us is no match for Jesus' perfect defenses for you. Yet I remember being asked by one of my friends once: "How big is your shield? Would you be safe behind that shield?" Are we holding up our faith as a sure and strong daily defense…or as a crutch we sometimes lean upon when it's convenient?

I believe the Lord Jesus has totally set us free from "sin and death" by the work that He accomplished on the cross. There's nothing we can add or take away from what He's done; there's nothing else to say but, "Yes, Lord." Yet I also believe we rob our lives of tough vital manhood when we don't believe in that "according to your faith" statement. I believe my own life would be a much bigger one if only my faith was how I gauged "success," and not by anything else.

Let's live today as if "according to your faith will it be done to you"; may we live lives of huge faith, O Men of God. Let's be the men whose faith can actually move mountains, not the men who think that's "metaphorical talk from Bible times." In short, let's be men today. Let's be men for Jesus without reservation.

August 11 – Matthew 9:35-38

Are you a shepherd and a harvester?

If we want to become more like the Good Shepherd, we need to turn our eyes to the sheep He's personally called us to. We must hear the bleating cries of those around us who need shepherding; we must be the "shepherds of God's flock." We must exhibit the selfless hearts of men attuned to the needs of each individual number in our heavenly keeping. We must be the men who'd scale any mountain, ford any stream, if we see a lost one needing His help. We must know the voice of Him who is the shepherd of our hearts and be ready to respond to His daily leadings. And we must hear His whispered words to Peter on the beach in Galilee as a call to our own calling: "Feed my sheep."

Similarly, we must be the men of God's good earth whose hearts are constantly drawn to His earthly, and eternal, harvest. We must be the farmers who so totally understand the nature of His heavenly crop that we know precisely when to haul it in. We must each be studying our own given field for precise moments when the Holy Spirit leads us to be harvesting bountifully. We must be the men of hard work, blood, sweat and tears when it comes to doing exactly what He asks of us…

O Man, who are you shepherding right now?

And are you in the harvest field today, O Man?

Only when a farmer stands up shoulder-high amidst the ripened grains does he know the nature of the coming harvest. Only when a shepherd spends his night amidst the slumbering flock does he know the call and cry of each and every sheep.

Today, may your heart be spurred to be the shepherd you've been called to be ***and*** to go out into the harvest fields. May we be the men who don't discount any word of Jesus; who give no excuse for any sort of earthly apathy. May we use today to grow our shepherd's outlook on our lives, to learn to view the world as Jesus once did. May we use our finest energies for harvest-working in those fields of God's specific choosing for our lives.

Have the shepherd's view of life. And then get out in the rows of the harvest fields.

August 12 – Matthew 12:1-8

Learning what real freedom means

Jesus had a light of freedom shining from His daily life that was terrifying for these closely-following Pharisees. When they saw His friends start picking from the heads of grain upon this Sabbath walk, they assumed that He'd be angry Himself. They assumed that Jesus would recognize their manmade Pharisaical laws to be as fully weighty as the fullness of the Law. They assumed that He would look over His shoulder, see them Sabbath-picking their lunch, and be absolutely horrified...

But "the Lord is the Spirit," we are told in 2 Corinthians, "and where the Spirit of the Lord is, there is freedom." Jesus told us that His true followers would be led to the truth in Him, "and [that] the truth will set you free." "It is for freedom that Christ has set us free"; we're the men whose lives are already set free to live our days in and through Him. We should be longing that we all "become men of mature character with the right sort of independence." (James 1:4, Phillips)

At the same time, we all know the difficult tightrope that we're walking while we live out our "freedom" in a broken world. There's not a man of God who hasn't sometimes fallen when he's gone too far out into freedom by his own strength. We're told by Paul we shouldn't "use [our] freedom to indulge the sinful nature; rather serve one another in love." We must be careful "that the exercise of [our] freedom does not become a stumbling block to the weak."

Today, give some time to contemplating how the freedom of Jesus is at work (or how it isn't) in your own life. Would you say you're living from His perfect hard-earned freedom daily, or a guilt-ridden slavery to the Law? Do you think you understand the open heart of our Lord as He walked with His disciples through those particular grainfields? Or do you sense that there's more legalism latent in your spiritual life than His life-giving liberty and freedom?

How are you using your freedom in Jesus, O Man? For His ends or for your own comfort? Do you sense the power present when we yoke our manly freedom to His servantly calling upon our lives?

Give your heart to His freedom today. You will find Jesus there.

August 13 – Matthew 12:46-50

Do you do His will?

"See, the Sovereign Lord comes with power, and his arm rules for him. See, his reward is with him, and his recompense accompanies him. He tends his flock like a shepherd: He gathers the lambs in his arms and carries them close to his heart; he gently leads those that have young.

"Who has measured the waters in the hollow of his hand, or with the breadth of his hand marked off the heavens? Who has held the dust of the earth in a basket, or weighed the mountains on the scales and the hills in the balance?" (Isaiah 40:10-12)

Jesus was the Sovereign Lord who came in perfect power; Jesus was the great Good Shepherd from Isaiah's prophecy. He who'd measured all the waters in the hollow of His hand was the same One who used His hands to touch a leper. He who longs to take us lovingly into His arms was the very same One who spread His arms upon the cross at Calvary. He who'd held all of the dust of the earth as in a basket chose to become one "formed from the dust," just like you and me…

If we want to be the brother of our Lord, we must realize the immensity of Matthew 12, verse 50. O Man of God, do you think you're daily striving after doing the "Will of [the] Father in heaven"…or not? Do you think that Jesus was speaking hyperbolically when He asked that we should actually follow after Him with our lives? Do we think the "Sovereign Lord" is simply smiling when we don't assign His will our fullest efforts, our whole hearts?

O Men of God, fight today to be the brother and sister and mother of the God who came to save your from your sin! Desire that your life might be a life lived wholly for His sake; that your day's purpose might align with His great purposes. The Sovereign Lord will do whatever it might take to create in you the man He planned for you to be from the beginning. Yet the truest joy is found in *giving yourself* to His will, not in waiting till He has to "force" it upon you.

Will you be the brother of Jesus? Will you actively seek to do His will today?

August 14 – Matthew 13:1-9

You must be speaking of Him

You'll rarely have the chance to "share your beliefs" if you never put yourself in the right sort of place, O Man. If you aren't at all active about participating in people's lives, you'll rarely have the chance to share your "faith" with them. If you'll never rest aside the shore of life's "still waters," you'll rarely gather a crowd ready to listen to Jesus' word. If you've never placed yourself within a place where God might use your spoken words, maybe you have nothing to say at all…

You'll never have a faith that's actually worth speaking of if you don't ever open up your mouth to speak about it. It won't be really real until you have to "break it down," until you have to explain it for another's beginner understanding. If you've never seen a crowd around your faith, seen a flock that needs your care, perhaps you need some personal self-examination. The Lord will give a flock unto His chosen shepherds, He will give words to His speakers – *so whose are you?*

The world of Church and para-church ministries need a million helping hearts for the harvest going on all around us. There are thousands of opportunities to be trained in the work, to go out, to give life unto other people. Most of us are called to keep the jobs in which we're currently working, yet the need is always there for godly volunteers. The dearth of "harvest workers" hinges on the heart of every man who chooses *not* to go out into the harvest fields.

My point? There's every chance for you to speak, for you to share, for you to tell others about the Lord Jesus – *right now!* There's so much great Young Life, Navigators, Campus Crusade work that's currently being left undone because it's missing *you*. There are so many good laypeople *not* doing anything in the Church that could be doing absolutely amazing things. We have no excuse for never verbalizing about our faith when the opportunities so abound, all the time, all around us.

Jesus drew a crowd of people, curious about the power and authority that exuded from His life and words and presence. So where's your own crowd today, O Man? And what would your message be, if they showed up?

August 15 – Matthew 13:24-52

See and feel the natural beauty of His words

Jesus' spoken words were like the blowing of a warm autumn wind through the branches of a red-leafed maple. Jesus' teachings were as gentle as the silent fall of snow; they were scorching as an August midday's sunshine. They were smoother than a pebble in the eddies of a spring-fed creek; they were rough as a father's bearded stubble. Jesus gave His teachings from the heart of One who'd been divine Creator of all we see; He crafted tales from the earth He'd made.

From Kahlil Gibran: "He seemed to spin [His stories] out of the seasons, even as time spins the years and the generations…And such words would carry His listeners into their simpler selves, and into the ancient of their days…He knew the source of our older self, and the persistent thread of which we are woven…"

Today, may we take the time to notice how the divine mysteries of Jesus are elucidated in the natural world around us. Pause throughout your day to notice how the wonders of His creation show the infinite heart of our wondrous Creator. Think of all the ways in which the metaphors of nature and life lend themselves to robust godly teaching about the Kingdom of Heaven. See the way divine similes seem to rise around your life when you're paying close attention for them.

If we want to become filled with Jesus' spirit, we must learn to spin His story from the fabric of the seasons. If we want to become teachers of His cloth, we must find the "persistent thread" of which His words of life were woven. May we hunger that our minds are so attuned to His creation and His whispers that we become the truest storytellers. May we be so filled with the Holy Spirit that there's nothing *not* of Him in the way we see the world we move in…

Let creation speak to you today, O Man. It never ceases telling His story.

August 16 – Matthew 13:53-57

Something is wrong with a completely inoffensive faith

If you've never made the darkness angry with your life's light, your light is simply not bright enough, O Man of God! Of course, Jesus hasn't called us to be purposely offensive for His sake, yet the truth remains: *Jesus is offensive*. In a world where wrong is often seen as right and right is often cast as wrong, Jesus can't not offend some. In a day when many values have been stripped of their former value, worthlessness cannot stand to be exposed. In the way that Jesus walked into His hometown and spoke simple truth, we're called to live our daily lives for Him. We're called to live in places we call our home; we're called to speak of Him right there; we're meant to be witnesses to friends and to neighbors. Yet if you've never been considered at all offensive by your pointing to Him, you need to question where it is you're actually pointing. We must question whether we're pointing to the Christ if we aren't ever feeling a grain of antagonism in our daily lives.

Ask yourself: Has another person ever been "amazed" at your life, as in, "Where did this man get this wisdom?" Has a hearer ever wondered about your life or your message: "Where then did this man get all these things?"

There should be such a difference in the latter and former versions of your life that all men wonder what's happened to you. There should be such strong evidence of a wholesale swap of your spirit that men are somewhat confused by your current life.

Have you ever been offensive in Jesus' style, O Man? Have you been totally changed by Him? Do you seek to speak the direct honest Christ-filled truth from your heart, or do you hedge where you're afraid He'll offend others?

August 17 – Matthew 14:1-12

Vicious daily trust to the death

There was nothing that was shameful about the death of John the Baptist, even though the surrounding circumstances were absurd. Even though his head was served up on a platter for the amusement of some drunken guests, John didn't die in vain. John the Baptist trusted every single day of his short manly life that God's sovereignty was absolutely everything. John the Baptist surely didn't quaver in the seconds leading up to his earthly death, for he knew that the Kingdom had come…

Do you know that for yourself today, O Man? Do you trust the Lord like John did? Do you not believe that any odd absurdity, any earthly kingly whim, is a match for the King of Kings? Do you have a wild-eyed, far-seeing trust that enables you to live your life with gusto and great determination for Him? Could you go unto a death that brought Him glory with a smile upon your face, trusting viciously in your Sovereign?

In his introduction to the anthologous *Men at War*, Ernest Hemingway wrote this: "A good soldier does not worry. He knows that nothing happens until it actually happens and you live your life up to then."

For a man who later blew his brains out, there's a certain tautological "wisdom" in these words of his! A man should never be a prey of the "what ifs," a quarry of the "what might happen tomorrows," if he wants to really live. If he wants to live a life like John the Baptist, he must limit his thoughts to how God's actually using him in the present moment. If he wants to be a "good soldier" in the service of the King, he must live his life in the divine "moment-to-moment."

Death has no sting for us, O Men. Our life is in Jesus' fully capable hands. If you want to view your life with John the Baptist's godly unconcern, consider Shakespeare's words in *Henry IV*: "By my troth, I care not; a man can die but once: we owe God a death…and let it go which way it will, he that dies this year is quit for the next."

John the Baptist's life and death were in the hands of his God: *Where do you place your life and death today, O Man?* "A man can die but once." We owe Jesus our whole life.

August 18 – Matthew 14:13-21

The 5000 proves "Seek first…"

You'll never learn to "trust the Lord" until you *actually* trust the Lord for His provision for your earthly daily life. Until you realize that you've never been the one "providing for your family," your faith will be of no practical use to your family. You'll always struggle with the Lord until you finally and fully realize that He's in complete and constant control of your life. Until you see Him sitting out upon the grass, making basketfuls of bread, you'll continue to think you've got some sort of control…

O Men of God, we've ceased to honor Jesus with our hearts whenever we act as if our daily bread is somehow ours. When we think we've had success in being a "good provider" for our family, we're actually out of touch with the Good Provider. If we can't see the clear connection between His "do not worry" and His feeding of these five thousand, look again at this passage. For if our faith is not enough to think He can actually provide for our lives, we're not following Jesus Christ at all.

Jesus didn't come to bring Dostoevsky's "carts bringing bread" for the sake of simply bringing bread to humanity. He didn't choose to make a meal for five thousand (or for fifty million) for the sake of a cheap fleeting belly-deep celebrity. He made this bread so His disciples wouldn't ever again wonder if the Lord was actually able to provide for their lives. He made this bread so that they (*and us!*) might know that seeking first His kingdom will truly result in His practical daily provision.

Let's stop thinking that we've ever been the providers for our families: The Lord has showered gracious blessings upon us. Let's cease striving for the parts of life that rob us of His Life: The Lord's view of living must be our everything. Let's quit so much hoping for the comforts that would give us the kind of earthly comfort that tends to draw men's hearts away from Jesus. Let's hope only that our faiths would be the kind that knows this Lord, this passage's Jesus, from the feeding of the 5,000.

Do you want to be a man, O Man? Then trust quietly; He will provide for you.

Do you want to be His disciple today? Worry not; "Seek first his kingdom…"

August 19 – Matthew 14:22-23

Get totally alone with Him today

We can only learn the heart and mind of Jesus when we're giving ourselves ample time alone in His presence. We can only be alone with Him when we've totally disconnected ourselves from everything in the world, except Him. If you want to lapse into a life of great ongoing inconsequence, never "dismiss the crowds" from your own life. Never take the time to slow the pace of life if you're aiming for a heart that's of no practical use to the Kingdom of Heaven…

When was your last time of solitude, O Man? When were you last totally alone with Jesus? How long has it been since you full-heartedly gave your heart to Jesus; since you carved out space entirely for His purposes?

We'll never "feel close" to this Savior until we're distant to the noise and people and distractions of this world around us. We'll never be on "mountaintops of faith" until we go to mountaintops, or valley-places, or meadows, or creeksides, with Jesus.

Today, give yourself a long untimed open-ended space of solitude with the God of the universe. Go out and find a pleasant place where you can sit, unbothered, and give your heart to Jesus Christ alone. Pray that He'd give a spirit of non-distraction; let Him do what He wants with the time you're choosing to give to Him. Open up your heart and mind to the Holy Spirit's "groans that words cannot express"; *He will absolutely speak to you!*

Today, let's get away from everything, O Men. May the evening come and find men who've been with Jesus.

August 20 – Matthew 14:22-29

Adventuresome faith takes action

Peter is in the act of becoming the "Peter of the Book of Acts" because of moments like this particular one. There are shades of all that Peter will become in his every single action in the Gospels of Jesus. Every time that Peter opens up his mouth with words of passion, Jesus sees a man who's ready to be further used. Every time that Peter acts out of his wild adventurous spirit, Jesus sees the raw stuff ready for an apostle. When they saw the Lord come walking out upon the water toward their boat, twelve grown men cowered from Him in fear. When they heard the Lord's voice speaking, "It is I," the twelve sat back against the gunwales in sheer relief at His well-known voice. Yet only Peter saw this moment as an actual opportunity to bend the rules of human physical existence. Only one of twelve was ready to get out upon the water and release the sides of the rocking boat and go…

You'll always be an ineffectual follower of Jesus until you realize that these stories aren't just stories, O Man of God. You'll have a "faith" that won't move anthills till you recognize the actual need for some adventure in your faith in Jesus. I'd wager that the modern church has eleven-*thousand* "sitters-in-the-boat" for every modern-day Peter in our midst. In a world of such convenient "manly" adventures of the fleeting variety, very few men adventure in their faith.

Do you want to end your days with comfort in the boat of life or take steps upon the water with your Lord Jesus? Do you want to be the eleven bored men sitting in the boat – or the pew – who'll never taste divine adventure? Would you be willing to ask the Lord to give you opportunities – water-walking moments – so that your life comes alive in Him? Will you then be ready to actively respond to the Lord's wild ways and be obedient to the call to come out of the boat?

Are you one of the dry eleven, O Man? Or will you be like Peter on that night?

Are you in the bored eleven-thousand? Or will you chase down His holy adventures?

August 21 – Matthew 14:28-33

Total Focus

Jesus wasn't frightened of anything that life or the world or the evil one could throw in His direction. He didn't encounter any obstacle impeding His complete trust in the perfect will of His Heavenly Father. In fact, He was so sure of the perfect plan provided for His life that He never wasted a moment on anxiety. For instance, even though He was "in anguish" in the garden of Gethsemane on Passover night, He kept His eyes on the eyes of the Father alone…

Now we watch Peter walking on the water looking into the eyes of the One who was Creator of these very waters. Jesus holds the gaze of a man who was so ready to test his growing faith that he'd actually stepped out from the safety of the boat. For a moment, they were locked in perfect harmony; Peter is sustained and upheld by the Lord's perfect power. For that moment, Peter lived in perfect faith; he is certain that he's safe with the Lord's eyes fastened upon him…

"But when he saw the wind, he was afraid and, beginning to sink, cried out, 'Lord, save me!'" When Peter focused his mind upon the outward fearful circumstances, he was *unable* to keep the Lord's eye…

Similarly, we can only walk this path of perfect faith when our eyes and hearts are fastened on the Lord Jesus. Even if we've stepped both feet upon the water, we're still nothing if we won't steady our gaze only upon Him. If we think we're fit to walk a single day without His presence around us, we can go ahead and live our day without Him. For, yes, we can actually "make it" day-to-day without our eyes on Jesus, but our lives will amount to absolutely nothing…

Today, live by faith that's strong enough to tempt you from the boat; live life fully in His present presence. May no "wind" of fear or hardship or anxiety best your efforts to live locked within His sustaining gaze. If you start to feel the nagging of worry or the world's tempting voice, reconnect your eyes with His immediately. There's nothing at all that we need fear when we're looking into the eyes of the fearless One, the Author of our lives.

Keep your eyes fully on His eyes today, O Man. And "Let nothing move you."

August 22 – Matthew 16:13-20

Who do you say He is?

If Jesus really is "the Christ, the Son of the living God," do you think you're personally giving Him enough of your life? Do you think He merits more than Sunday mentions; do you think He's utterly amazed when we *occasionally* say a quick prayer? Do you think He was exalted by these pussyfooting answers offered up by the other eleven disciples: "Some say John the Baptist; others say Elijah; and still others, Jeremiah or one of the prophets"? And do you think the way we affirm, and constantly have to *re*affirm, our strong belief in Him will bear actual fruit in our lives? Do you think that how we measure our Lord's worth will be supported by the power shown by our daily lifestyle? If we'd quaver about His all-importance, won't we live quivery-quavery lives of unimportance in the matters of the Kingdom? If we build our faith on sandy understandings of His Everythingness, won't we be like absolutely everybody else?

O Man of God, who is your Lord today? "Who do people say [the God of your life] is?" How is the way you're charting and planning your day ***today*** speaking aloud the measure of the Lordship of this "Lord of your life"? If the world was changed by seeing Peter's vision of the Christ, what vision of the Christ are ***you*** daily showing? How completely is He Lord of your whole life; how immensely is He shown by how you see Him for yourself?

"But what about you?" Jesus asks of you today. "Who do you say I am?"

Today, may we give some time to quiet contemplation of the Lordship of the Lord in our very own lives. For it will show by your life today, O Man. And He's so much bigger than we can ever think or imagine…

August 23 – Matthew 17:1-9

Fixate on His glory

While lingering on his deathbed in Ephesus, what final images were running through the apostle John's mind? While he felt the first cutting of the sword through his flesh, do you think James thought of seeing Jesus transfigured? As he asked to have his crucifixion turned wrong-side-up, do you think Peter remembered the glory of the Lord? Do you think this image of the God-made-flesh-made-fully-glorified made it "worth it" for these favored three of His? Would you ever doubt the earthly cost of following Jesus was worth it after you'd actually seen the truth of His power? Wouldn't you walk through every day with head held high if you knew the Lord in His full and revealed glory?

Do *you* know the Lord in His full glory, O Man?

O Men, have we seen the truth of His power?

O Men of God, I believe the eyes of those three men forever glowed with the afterimage of their transfigured Lord. Nothing they ever later encountered, nothing they'd ever see again in their lives, compared with His all-surpassing glory on that mountain. If we want to be the kind of men who'd follow Jesus triumphantly, we must know the Jesus who was once transfigured. We must meditate our thoughts upon the God who "emptied Himself" of His glory in order that you and I might have His full life…

Today, may we give our minds to looking for the glory of our Lord in His word, in creation, in other people. May we be like Peter, James and John; men whose visions burned forever with the radiance of the Christ transfigured. May we recognize that we ourselves are called to know the risen Jesus; we're the men whose vision must be fully His vision. We must know the Lord in all His heavenly glory, see the truth of His power, and then give this whole day to Him.

"His life on earth is not finished yet," Dietrich Bonhoeffer wrote, "for he continues to live in the lives of his followers." Is His transfigured glory shining from you today? Well, are you willing to be shone *from*?

August 24 – Matthew 17:14-21

Where *isn't* your faith?

A man who can dispassionately gauge where his faith is actually "little" will be blessed with a greater, more abiding faith. A man who sees the places where his faith is *not* producing fruit must then ask for a deeper depth from the Lord. If we're strong enough to offer up the weakness of our faith, Jesus always show Himself to be all-sufficient. If we point to signs and miracles we're *not* doing in the world today, Jesus will arm us with the faith to do them.

There was something in the case of this boy stricken with epilepsy that was problematic for the disciples' growing faith. When they conjured up the power of Jesus to heal his broken body, there was something there that seemed to get in their way…

Similarly, there are daily obvious obstacles in our lives that dissuade our faith from moving mountains around for His sake. Whether it be our work or family or a situation from our broken past, something seems to get in the way of the works of Jesus.

O Man, where is Satan subtly silencing the mustard-seed-faith in your life and, also, its resulting fruit? Where are you *not* seeing results from your daily faith in Jesus; where are you feeling blunted where you'd like to be sharper? Do you feel that you're victorious at work, yet a weakling in your faith whenever you're talking with your wife? Or do you feel potentialities abundant while you're sitting in the pew, yet feel useless on the actual battlefield?

The places where our faith is shown as "little" are the places we must capture if we'd really want to follow Jesus. He won't make use of men who choose to be segmented about their faith; men whose faiths are sometimes "on," sometimes "off." Today, give Him time to speak to you of those places where He'd ask you to be stronger in your faith and its resulting fruit. Can you be so filled with passion for your Lord that you're *dis*passionate in analysis of where your faith is currently lacking?

You can have the "faith as small as a mustard seed," O Man. But the question is: *Do you want it?*

August 25 – Matthew 18:1-3

Consider little children's ways

The reason Jesus brought a little child before His disciples was to give them pause regarding their question for Him. For as they looked into the innocent eyes of this little one standing before them, they must have all felt stupid for asking, "Who is the greatest…?" They most likely pondered what the Lord might mean by His saying that they must "change and become like little children." They most likely thought of all the things a "little child" *is*, and of all the things that they themselves were crurrently *not*…

For yourself, make a list of how a little child *is*, what a little child *does*, how a little child *acts*. Then, for each of those definitions, think of how you might become more child-like (analogously) in your life for Jesus. If He said this, we must take it seriously. So let's consider the children we personally know, O Men.

* * * * *

August 26 – Matthew 18:21,22

Forgive "that person" today

It's been my observation that most men will have a person in their life that they're absolutely refusing to forgive. There's something we seem to think that's powerful about holding something over someone that's actually absolutely sinful. If we want to follow Jesus, we must give up anything and everything that would hinder our allegiance to His grace. And if we can't personally hold out grace to everyone – *all the time* – *no matter what* – we simply aren't following Him.

In most evangelical churches, the "Lord's Prayer" is spoken from the reading of the King James Version of the Bible. (Thus, from the King James Version of Matthew 6:12 – "And forgive us our debts, as we forgive our debtors...") Yet many other modern translations take the aorist-tensed verb as a sign of "recent past" action in our lives. Thus it reads, in the NIV, ESV, NASB, ASV and ERV: "as we *also have* forgiven..." In these words, there's a sense that we're coming to God for His forgiveness with a heart that's already been active in forgiveness. For how can we presume to ask so much of His forgiveness, so very often, if we're not readily engaged with a steady forgiveness?

O Men, we are spitting right into His face when we're holding onto a "grudge," when we hold something against someone. When we think we're perfectly righteous in our manly indignation, we're often being completely disobedient to Jesus. If Jesus said to Peter that we're meant to forgive men in an infinite way, why don't we actually forgive men infinitely? How can we so shirk His strong clearly spoken commandment and then lean upon His grace when there's no grace to be found in us?

If there's currently a person in your life who's needing forgiveness, forgive them during the day today – *no argument!* May we be the sort of men who'll forgive seventy-seven times, thinking only of Jesus' clear direct command here.

These are the sort of obediences that change the world, O Man. One forgiveness at a time.

August 27 – Matthew 20:29-34

Living today with eyes of compassion

You and I can't be blind unto the hurts and needs of others if we'd want to be disciples of the Son of David. This crowd of people around the blind men was actually blinder than those ones that they rebuked; they didn't know the heart of Jesus at all. They didn't know the heart of Him who longs for hearts of believing passion; the One who "stopped and called" these men to Himself. They didn't understand that anything less than everything is deficient when it comes to getting closer to Jesus. If they'd ever heard a sermon spoken from this Savior's lips, they'd have known His love and care for these particular blind men. If they'd ever paid attention to His prodigal use of energy on the poor and disenfranchised, they'd have known better...

Are you actively looking for people deserving of compassion with the eyes of your Savior, the Son of David? Do you hear the cries for help and healing that are echoing all around you, or are you like this irritated crowd, O Man? Do you think that Jesus chose to leave the people's plight to the Roman government's safety nets, or did He personally react to their need? Do you think we can divorce our "faith" from actual acts of mercy and compassion and still claim to have a faith at all?

We must be the men whose lives are given definition by compassion; whose eyes are fully open to others around us. We mustn't blind ourselves or try to quiet the cries of people's hearts that scream for Jesus amidst their present painful circumstances. We must be the men who turn a constant attention upon the poor and disenfranchised; who ask, "What do you want me to do for you?" We must be the open eyes and hearing ears and healing hands of Jesus to the world we encounter everyday.

Today, look for opportunities to help the "blind men" in your life, thereby following the clear example of Jesus. May we end this day with knowledge that we *did* what we profess to *believe*; may we be so filled with His compassion for others.

Look for those people today, O Man. They are literally all around you.

LIVE LIKE MEN

August 28 – Matthew 21:12,13

Some men must clear the modern Church's temple

The history of every cheapening of any "faith-system" starts out with a single step towards unnoticed laxness. The perception of what's right or wrong is loosened over time by a thousand tiny questions or personal discomforts. Any time invalid vagaries are slipped into a canon's distant peripheries, the great change is already on its way. Any time the flanks of truth are undefended, there's every possibility of a future head-on assault. However long it took for money-changing, dove-selling, crass buying and selling to enter the temple, it obviously happened. Even if it crept its way into the temple over many hundreds of years, it was still totally unacceptable to Jesus. When He walked into the temple courts and did violence to these people and their trade, He was acting from a truly righteous anger. He was acting on a hatred that had rankled the Trinity's heart for a long time when He yelled out these mighty words…

Would you say that there are similar encroachments into the temple of the Church that are going on today, O Men? Would you say that you've brushed off certain things about your *own* church that seem to be "the way its headed anyway"? Are you strong enough to raise a holy ruckus where you see the Church's flanks being attacked by half-truths? Are you man enough to enter into the fray like Jesus did or do you prefer to keep your indignant thoughts to yourself?

O Men of God, everywhere around us men of God are falling prey to the latest "wisdoms" of the current age. Will we be so weak about the truth that we'll allow the evil one to triumph in the midst of our modern temples of worship? Will we *not* take up the fight when we see Satan feeding lies into the heart of our canon, our holy beliefs in Jesus? Will we *not* do anything while churches tear themselves away from our Savior, striving to be more accommodating to passing fancies?

From Ernest Hemingway's *For Whom the Bell Tolls*: "if you extend along a flank, any flank, it eventually becomes one man." Are you man enough to be that one man, standing out upon the flank of the modern Church today? Are you tough enough to take the rife abuses you'll undoubtedly receive when you stand and say, "sola scriptura"? Can you reckon what it's worth to Jesus to see His modern disciples cleaning up His modern temple on His behalf?

Will you be the one man, O Man? Will you be the final defense, if it's necessary?

August 29 – Matthew 22:15-22

Nothing is yours; everything is His

We all know the feeling when our day starts out with a great "quiet time," when we make the time to give the Lord our first part of the day. We all know how good it feels to unite our spirit with His Spirit; how refreshing is His sweet refreshment for us. We all know how it can feel when He leads us to a certain needed scripture, seemingly so perfect for the day ahead. We all know how right it feels whenever we're walking out the door to work, feeling we've "started the day right…"

But don't we also know the feeling when we're driving home from work and can't remember *anything at all* we read that morning? Don't we also know the feeling when we're "distant" from the Lord, halfway through the long challenging workday? Haven't you had a day where nothing of His Word has ever entered your mind; where nothing of Him seems readily tangible? Haven't we sensed that there was something probably different in the faith of Peter or Paul, when compared with ours?

In the same way that these Herodians and Pharisees tried not to give what was due, we're oftentimes following Jesus, O Men. We're living in an age where faith feels relegated to our personal morning quiet times…and mostly left there. We're living lives where we don't give unto "God what is God's" because it's simply easier to give Him less than our all. If He's worth just twenty minutes of your morning, He's not worth enough – *He wants your absolutely everything!*

O Man of God, I'm not a legalist or a taskmaster; I don't despise your personal faith in Jesus. I believe we each are striving everyday to learn more of His perfect way; the desire is certainly within all of us. Yet we must unite the passion we *first* felt for our Savior with the knowledge that our Lord demands all parts of our lives *now*. We must give our hearts and minds and souls and spirits and lives and *everything* to Him if we'd actually want to be His.

So don't just "try" to give Him "more of your day" today. He is this day in its entirety already. How will you give Him more and more and more and more of who you are until there's nothing left of you *but* Him? That's the question for your heart, this moment. Now give "to God what is God's."

August 30 – Matthew 26:14-16

Do you have a price?

Oftentimes the strivings of our days betray the price it might cost to buy our hearts away from Jesus. How we spend our days and weeks and months and years tells the story of what really matters to our earthly existence, O Men. If we've settled on some all-consuming figure to reach before retirement, isn't it possible for that to become our god? If we've focused all our attention on promotion to a certain position, isn't that our life's clearest price? If there's something that would kill you if you lost it, hasn't it attained ascendancy above your Lord already? If there's any bag of silver that consumes your waking thoughts more than Jesus, do you actually follow Him?

Judas walked into the presence of the chief priests and asked, "What are you willing to give me if I hand him over…?" Presumably, Judas had a dollar-figure in mind as he walked across the town to this little "religious" gathering. Presumably, Judas weighed the worth of his betrayal against the purchasing power of the money he'd assuredly receive. Presumably, he thought thirty pieces of silver was sufficient for the price of his human soul…and the life of his rabbi, Jesus.

Do you yourself have a price, O Man? Do you have a bottom-line betrayal number? Is there any earthly item or position or possession that attracts you more than Jesus attracts you? Is there something in your life that woos attention from your Lord unto the worthlessnesses of this lost world? Is there anything you need to offer up to Him as competition that's competing with His affections?

O Man, what's your price? Where is your heart being bought today?

We must learn to have no price, O Men of God. We must be the unbuyable ones.

August 31 – Matthew 26:26-30

Feeling the power of the bread and wine

When I think of how I shrink from the trials that might result from speaking of Jesus, I'm utterly sickened with myself. When I think of how I live for my own comfort in the face of His great trials, I am mindful of my sinfulness. After all, seeing such a man now poised before the hour of His coming death, how can I think I'd ever deserve better? How can I think that there's something manly in my human heart when I see Jesus' words to His friends, spoken here? Jesus lived His thirty-something years with crucifixion always out in front of Him: He knew what was coming at the end for Him. Sitting down to dinner with His friends in celebration of the Passover feast, He knew full well that this was to be His last meal…

O Men of God, it's important that we picture Jesus taking up the bread and wine that represented His flesh and blood. If you want to know the full extents demanded by your discipleship, see your Lord extolling His own coming death! Watch Him lift the loaf of bread to the Father, giving thanks for it, breaking the bread that prefigured His terrible murder. See Him take the cup and give thanks for what was to greet Him on the morrow; see Him ushering in this New Covenant for us…

In *War and Peace*, Leo Tolstoy wrote: "Man can be master of nothing while he is afraid of death. But he who does not fear death is lord of all. If it were not for suffering, man would not know his limitations, would not know himself. The hardest thing is to know how to unite in your soul the significance of the whole."

You and I must unify the significance of the suffering of our Lord with the direction of our daily lives, O Men. We, too, cannot become anything when we're fearful of the suffering and death our lives will demand for Jesus' sake. If we want to follow Him, we must know that we're also called to lose our lives for Him – willingly, happily, readily. We must become the men who know that earthly death and suffering are nothing at all when compared with knowing Him. If our Lord would smile in the facing of coming death, you and I must smile upon giving our lives away everyday. We mustn't accept a life that's lived without a sense of Jesus' death in the midst of our own passing days…

Today, live with thoughts of Jesus' Passover words. These are meant to be the pictures of our life.

September 1 – Matthew 26:36-46

Can we "keep watch" even an hour today?

Imagine what would happen if all the men reading these words would "keep watch with [Him] for one hour" today. For just an hour, what if every single one of us was armed with His perspective: "not as I will, but as you will"? What if we listened *only* to the Holy Spirit and then acted on His leadings without holding back an ounce of ourselves? What if we focused every thought upon obeying His commandments and lived life as His united Body of men today? Just imagine how the jaded world would view the Body of Christ if the Body of Christ was fully awake and alive. Think of how we'd show the world the love of Jesus if His love was always our first thought, always our only thought. Can you picture how the mockery of our faith's great hypocrisies would cease in the face of our simply following Him? Suddenly, we'd start to see such clear results as in the Book of Acts; the broken world finally finding its home…

The problem is: Most of us won't do it. The reality is: Most of us are asleep. The truth is: Jesus sets us in our own Gethsemanes everyday to "keep watch," yet most of us are currently dozing off…

The heart of He who said "not as I will, but as you will" is the heart of He who lives within our hearts today, O Men! That iron will that saw the "cup" of death and yet was undeterred from God's plan is the will that works within us!

The question is: Do you want to be a man who lives that kind of life; whose life is in the Lord's hands constantly? My wonder is: Will there be enough who stay awake, who "keep watch" with Jesus, whose spirit *and* body are willing?

All our talk is only talk if we can't wander into the Garden with our Lord and stay awake in His Kingdom's service. All life is utterly inconsequential that'd sleep upon the watch we're asked to keep within His providential physical absence.

"Stay here and keep watch with me," He cries out to us. O Man, will you keep watch today?

September 2 – Matthew 26:47-56

Will you turn the other cheek?

The beginning of Jesus' Passion further proves that His words always aligned with His actions; that His "walk" always proved His "talk." If you want to tackle single-minded obedience to commandments fit for real men, there are none mightier than these ones: "You have heard that it was said, 'An eye for an eye, and a tooth for a tooth.' But I say to you, do not resist him who is evil; but whoever slaps you on your right cheek, turn to him the other also. And if anyone wants to sue you, and take your shirt, let him have your coat also. And whoever shall force you to go one mile, go with him two. Give to him who asks of you, and do not turn away from him who wants to borrow from you." (Matt. 5:38-42) Or, as Dietrich Bonhoeffer wrote about this passage: "By exercising the right kind of retribution evil is to be overcome and thus the true disciple will prove himself. The right way to requite evil, according to Jesus, is not to resist it."

Today, as a preparation for Jesus' trial and crucifixion, give your heart fully to these tough commandments. Where someone does you wrong, *don't do wrong back*. Where someone hits you first, *don't hit back at all*. Where someone wants to sue you, *give them more than they ask*. Where someone wants to take from you, *give instead*.

Only true men follow Jesus' example. Only true men learn to truly turn the other cheek.

September 3 – Matthew 26:57-75

Our inaction is a betrayal

Active disavowals are no worse than silent passivities; the sitting Peter doesn't trump the cursing Peter. He wasn't "better" when he sat in silence watching Jesus from the courtyard; his quiet presence spoke out loudly enough. While he watched the court pass judgment on his Lord with false and faulty evidence, he didn't raise his voice in righteous indignation. While he watched them strike and spit upon his Savior's beloved face, he wasn't doing a single thing about it. When confronted by two girls and this mob about his possibly knowing Jesus, he crescendos up to a mighty anger. Yet, all in all, everything he does within the courtyard was an active betrayal; inaction akin to actual action…

Do you think you're worthy of the Passion of the Christ just because you've never personally "betrayed" Him in the "active" sense? Have you ever sat in judgment of the words of Peter's cowardice, unmindful of the speech of his *in*action? Do you think that our inaction on behalf of One who'd give His life for us is somehow an excusable offence? Do you think that we'll be judged upon our active works only; that nothing matters that we *don't* do?

I'd guess the bulk of my own personal sin is in those moments when I'm passive in the midst of His clear calling for my action. I'd wager that He's seen a *million* times where I've sat out in the courtyard, betraying Him by my personal inaction. It's easy for us to pass judgment on Peter for his rash ridiculous words to this rabble in the courtyard, isn't it? It's far harder when I remember that my betrayals can also be numbered by the silences and secret thoughts of my own life.

Where are you most fraught with inaction, O Man? Where do you betray your Lord in that particular way?

September 4 – Matthew 27:11-54

The Passion

O Love that will not let me go,

I rest my weary soul in thee;

I give thee back the life I owe

That in thine ocean depths its flow

May richer, fuller be…

O Light that follow'st all my way,

I yield my flick'ring torch to thee;

My heart restores its borrowed ray,

That in thy sunshine's blaze its day

May brighter, fairer be…

O Joy that seekest me through pain,

I cannot close my heart to thee;

I trace the rainbow through the rain,

And feel the promise is not vain,

That morn' shall tearless be…

O Cross that liftest up my head,

I dare not ask to fly from thee;

I lay in dust, life's glory dead,

And from the ground there blossoms red

Life that shall endless be.

September 5 – Matthew 28:1-10

Experiencing the power of the resurrection

The power that's residing within your heart is of the same engineering as the power of His Resurrection. You're not confronting the world today as just a man among all mankind; you're actually cut from an entirely different cloth now, O Man. You're a man who's been redeemed by the perfect sacrificial love of the Savior of the world who went to the cross – *for you*. You're a man that He's allowed to know the truth first spoken by a nameless centurion: "Surely he was the Son of God!" You're a man who's blessed to have been called into a full understanding of the power of His death and resurrection. You're like these first eyewitnesses, knowing that He's conquered sin and death and Satan and the world forever and ever…

O Men, do you "want to know Christ and the power of his resurrection and the fellowship of sharing in his sufferings"? Do you really realize "the Spirit of him who raised Jesus from the dead is living in you," giving "life to your mortal bodies"? Do you ever sit in rapt amazement that you're blessed enough to live for One who actually lived and died and rose for you? Do you sense the coursing of the Resurrection's power through your life; do you grasp the enormity of the Holy Spirit's indwelling of you?

In short, have you ever *felt* the Resurrection; ever *known* its complete power; ever *lived* from its constant joy? Do you walk into today with surety written upon your face, knowing all your enemies have already been conquered? Do you relish in the knowledge that this power is within you, giving strength to stand strong in Him today? And will you take the time to give your heart to living from that power; to fully live your life as He intended you to live?

Nothing in the world can stand against the power of the mighty Kingdom of Heaven: Jesus has conquered death and the grave. There's nothing in your life that actually has the power to daunt you anymore; there's no one greater than "the one who is in you." Today, will you live with power and with joy, with His surety in your heart, as you go out into the world for Him? Will you be such an oasis of His peace and His ready grace that there's constant questions as to "your secret"?

And may it be a secret to no one, O Man! May it be stamped upon our faces!

September 6 – Matthew 28:16-19a

Having the right kind of "inertia"

Your life will preach a sermon on the "authority" of Jesus by the measure of your life that's marked by "going." For that reason, you'll never be an example of apostleship until you learn to go out boldly with His complete authority. If He stood before His friends and claimed that "all authority" was given to Him, do we think that's somehow changed today? Does our lack of current "going" say we're calling His authority into question; is our lack of motion more like a blasphemy? Are we worried that our starting into "going" might result in crazy calls to do some other crazy things? Do we feel that only "certain people" have a call to "go" where Jesus calls; that "that's not who I really am"?

in-er-tia : 1a : a property of matter by which it remains at rest or in uniform motion in the same straight line unless acted upon by some external force

"Spiritual inertia" is as real a test of our belief in Jesus as any other I can personally conceive of. If we remain "at rest" after "claiming Him as our Savior," are we sure we understand that particular statement of belief? Do we understand that His "love language" hinges on fulfillment of His commandments that would signify our love for Him? Do we not see His commandment to "go" as being of first importance: a sign that we believe in His actual sending-authority?

O Man, if you give your heart to "uniform motion" in the Lord's directions, He will keep you moving and fill you with joy. He'll place you on a path of rugged manly toil that leads to abundant life and deeper pools of faith in Him. He'll use your life in amazing ways you never could've imagined at the outset of your relationship with Him. You'll become more and more a reflection of the face of Jesus Himself when you simply go *wherever He calls*.

"All authority…has been given" unto our Savior, Jesus. And today He still commands: "go…"

September 7 – Matthew 28:16-19b

What is 'discipling?'

It's possible that no other section in the Great Commission is as widely ignored as these two particular words. Herein Jesus says to His disciples – and to us who'd later follow them – that He'd like us to replicate His own chosen methods. Does He say "go gather crowds" or "do miracles" or "go be the greatest speaker the world has ever heard of"? Does He say that nothing matters more than programmatic brilliance or the latest wave in mega-church planting techniques? Doesn't He seem instead to offer up the slowest, hardest, most infuriating method for the spreading of His Heavenly Kingdom? Doesn't He seem to say, "What I have done for you, do for others; take time with each and every single person you encounter"?

Jesus' making of disciples is a piece of every Gospel narrative; a thread woven through His ministry years. From that fateful day when he first called those fishermen to be His followers, He taught them by His words *and* His lifestyle. Every single day was filled with opportunities where they'd glean the Lord's perspective simply by watching Him live His day. They went to bed at night with thoughts of all the day's doing, of all the things they'd seen and heard and truly learned from their Master…

To understand the day-by-day directives that are needed to disciple another, let's complete a little challenge together: Starting in Luke 5, let's read until the end of chapter 7, paying attention to *everything* the disciples saw. Notice how they would've learned the vital lessons that would make them into the apostles who'd one day change the entire world. Try to gain a fresh perspective on how watching Jesus "do life" would've taught them how to make disciples as He did.

We've got to *start* to start desiring to make disciples, O Men. Pray the Lord would start to show you exactly how. Don't be afraid to ask your pastor or a godly disciple-maker, and start to learn the craft from them directly. It will be the greatest adventure of your life. And in the life of another person too.

September 8 – Matthew 28:16-19c

Start to bear witness today

Whenever Jesus or His apostles spoke about the practice of baptism, it usually accompanied both acceptance and repentance. Baptism was to be a visual sign that pointed to the death and resurrection of the Savior, the whole entirety of the Gospel. "We were therefore buried with him through baptism into death in order that….we too may live a new life," Paul wrote (Romans 6:4, abridged) "Brothers, what shall we do?" the Pentecost crowd asked. "Repent and be baptized," Peter responded to them…

My brothers, if our Lord commanded baptism as a part of our work, it follows that He'd want us to bring others to *belief*. It would follow that He wants us speaking clear cogent truth about the cross and our human need for salvation. It would seem that this commandment to be "baptizing" hinges on the need to teach both acceptance and repentance. Essentially, calling us to become "(your name) the Baptist" means He's calling you to lead more and more people unto Him…

My question for you: Is the Lord putting someone in your life for the purpose of their receiving the story of His Gospel from you? Have you noticed how he's placed a certain person in your life where the situation seems completely God-ordained? Or do you find that your thoughts often linger on a person who you know is really curious about who Jesus is to you? Is there someone you can't seem to stop remembering; someone often on your mind; someone who clearly needs to hear of Him?

O Men of God, imagine what might happen if we all spoke of Him today to that person who came to our minds! What if all of us, at the very least, struck up conversations that might lead to our faith; what if we even slightly broached the subject? Granted, we may not get all the way to true belief or total repentance; we might not get to be baptists on this particular day! Yet if we want to be committed to each part of Jesus' Great Commission, we must start to think this way all the time.

Today, simply speak to that one person. Move toward your call for "baptizing," O Man.

September 9 - Matthew 28:16-20

Exhibit obedience today

After we have risen up, gone out and striven to make disciples and baptized them, it's now time to teach obedience. We must teach all those we've gone to, helped to the point of repentance, and made disciples, that Jesus' Life is found in His commandments. Only in our understanding and obedience of His simple direct commandments do we find the actual path of life. Only in our subjugation of the self beneath the weight of the Word's words do we show our real love for Him. In the way that His disciples followed Jesus with the onus on observing Him, we must learn to observe Him for ourselves. We must read His gospels with our eyes trained upon the path we're walking; He's walking upon that road with us, all the time. We must see how each disciple saw commandments not as some legalistic checklist, but as the way of life itself. And, each of us learning how to obey in everything He'd call us to do, we'll learn to teach the same to others who'd come after us...

O Man of God, do you love your Lord; would you seek to know Him better; do you think He's truly worth your everything? Have you given total observance to His gospels with the focus of His twelve friends, walking with Him everyday? When somebody asks you for "your wisdom," can you answer with the words of Jesus because you happen to know them so well? Are you learning by your study, by obedience, by the Holy Spirit's leading, what the life of Jesus looks like in the lives of His men?

Surely He is with us always, to the very end of the age; *but are we walking with Him everyday ourselves?* Do we understand that nothing separates us from the power of His presence like our unwillingness to obey Him? Understand me: "neither death nor life...nor anything else in all creation, will be able to separate us from the love of God..." Yet we must recognize that we rob ourselves of His power and His peace whenever we refuse to be obedient to His commandments.

How will we become Jesus' sort of teachers, O Men? By knowing the subject in word *and* in deed.

September 10 – Mark 1:1-8

Go after John's humble focused view

There's not a man who's looking at this page whose life or legacy will be greater than the life and legacy of John the Baptist. I'd guarantee that nothing we'll ever do will rate comparison with being the prophesied preparer-of-the-way for the Messiah. And I'd venture, too, that John would find our times a tad bit soft in the way that "holy men" succeed and temporally prosper. Would the story of the Baptist read the same if John was tempted into softness by our fleeting modern "spiritual success"?

"And so John came, baptizing in the church's brand new wing and preaching a baptism of 'trying to give yourself' to following Jesus. A whole crowd of the people and some others curious about the latest Christian celebrity went out to him. Saying they'd 'try their best' to leave behind their sin, they were baptized by him in the church's new $100,000 baptismal font. John wore a Hugo Boss double-vent made of camel's hair, with a Gucci leather belt around his trim organic-eating waist. And this was his message: 'After me will come one who I'd like to try to follow; One who I'll let wash my feet and hopefully do 'my best' for. I baptize you with water, but he will baptize you with the Holy Spirit – if that's the branch of Christianity you're into…'"

O Men of God, are we rugged, tough and humble enough to be modern disciples and followers in the way of John the Baptist? Would you renounce *everything* – every personal status, strength or symbol – that would point to yourself, not to Jesus? Would you go into the wildernesses of the modern world if it meant that Jesus Christ was truly magnified for others? Would you be content to live a small and somewhat strange sort of life if it meant that others had the chance to know Him?

The "greater" we become should give us ample opportunities for making ourselves lesser for His Kingdom's sake. The higher up the "ladder" He might call you should give rise to greater chances for the lessening of yourself in the world's eyes. The man who'd follow after Jesus must understand his life is actually nothing; he's unworthy to untie the Savior's sandals. We must seek inviolable invisibility in the way we live our lives; not "celebrity for Jesus' sake."

O Man, fade into the background of our Savior. Arm yourself with John's kind of humility.

September 11 – Mark 2:1-5

Your "friend-group" must reach out together

Every group of men I've ever encountered possessed one trait in common: the presence of some looser-fitting outliers. For every clique of strong manly friendship, it seems there's always a few satellites not quite within the closest orbit. If the group is focused on a certain type of sporting event, these others are not *quite* as proficient in that particular activity. If the group is focused on a certain manly undertaking, the outliers aren't quite as competitive as the alpha males. However, where this subtle similarity becomes a real problem is where *faith* becomes the difference between those insiders and outsiders. We're not pushing brothers further along in their journey if we don't – *together* – reach out to the lost ones around us...

These men who brought their friend unto the foot of Jesus are the perfect pattern for the lives we must strive to lead, O Men. They wouldn't accept defeat when it pertained to their paralyzed friend's life; we must do the same for our friends' *hearts*. They weren't frightened of appearing to be lunatics on the thatched roof of this house; we mustn't fear anything when it comes to our friends. They expressed their faith by sharing in the burden of their friend's immediate need; we must share the work of reaching out to our friends.

Today, gather together with your best friends and start being strategic in the reaching of your "faith outliers." Make a list of the names of men who've been strategically placed near your circle for the purposes of the Lord in their life. Then talk about some actual actions steps: *How will each of you take a corner of your friends' pallets in the direction of Jesus?* Don't let this challenge be a challenge that you simply let pass by; be amazed that you're of actual use to the Lord!

Who will be your paralytic on the pallet? And how far will you go to get them to Jesus?

September 12 – Mark 3:7-12

Be the leader for the crowd around you

Have you ever had a day where crowds of people were pushing and shoving in order to be the closest ones to *your* side? Have you ever had a day where people traveled many, many miles because they'd heard the tales of all that you'd been doing? Have you ever had to push out in a boat because the seaside crowd was swarming to the point you were uncomfortable? Have you ever been so desired that your day filled up with the same list of things that filled up everyday of Jesus' life?

No? Well, me neither.

O Men of God, the important thing is living as you'd live if there were actually crowds around, no matter your current "crowd-size." The Lord will place the people in your presence that He wants there; the question is: *Will you actually lead those people?* Will you shepherd those the Lord puts in your path; will you be a man whose eyes are open to the ones around him? Will you be a man found worthy to lead others or are you stuck in ruts of feeling that others need to be leading you? Is the writer of Hebrews speaking unto you (like he often speaks to me!) when he writes these particular words: "At a time when you should be teaching others, you need teachers yourselves to repeat to you the ABC of God's revelation to men. You have become people who need a milk diet and cannot face solid food! For anyone who continues to live on 'milk' is obviously immature – he simply has not grown up. 'Solid food' is only for the adult, that is, for the man who has developed by experience his power to discriminate between what is good and what is bad for him. Let us leave behind the elementary teaching about Christ and go forward to adult understanding." (Hebrews 5:11-6:1, Phillips)

Jesus drew a crowd because He was the Messiah, yet also because He led the people like a leader has to lead. Jesus opened up His day to all the needs and hurts of regular sinful people and *that must also be the pattern for our own lives*. Can we grow up past the "milk" of modern manhood to the "solid food" of knowing that this Jesus now dwells in us? Can we be leaders of other people so that their hearts are always led to Him; that their lives are changed because of His presence in us?

Be the kind of leader drawing a crowd to Jesus today. His magnetism already lives within your heart!

September 13 – Mark 3:13-19

Discipleship to Apostleship

Have you ever personally gone up on the mountainside with Jesus and accepted your position as His chosen apostle? Have you ever really felt the eyes of Jesus searching the earth and then coming to rest upon your own face? Do you sense the sort of calling that was given to the Twelve; do you know the binding nature of apostleship? Have you ever felt the hand of Jesus resting upon your shoulder and accepted the honor of being known as *His*?

O Men of God, we've been "sent out" just like the Twelve were once sent out; the call of Jesus still is sending us out today. We're men He's taken up the mountainside and personally set apart; we've been made holy by His work within us. But we're only able to accept His high call when we accept that we're nothing without Him and His magnificent grace. Only when we tell ourselves that we have absolutely nothing else to offer – *except Him* – do we understand our apostleship.

The original apostles had no understanding of what He planned to do later; they couldn't foresee the cross looming ahead of Him. Perhaps they thought that they were on a track destined to rule the Messiah's kingdom, to become His earthly chosen governors. Perhaps they would've second-guessed this mountaintop moment if they'd known where it would take them – *away* from all earthly power. Perhaps they didn't fully grasp the greatness of their mountaintop-call to a life like His, full of death-to-the-self.

Do you fully grasp this life that is bound with death? Would you ever second-guess it?

Do you know what you've been called to, O Man? Do you see the cross before you?

You and I are men now blessed with both hindsight *and* foresight; men who know the opening and the narrative and the ending. We apostles to the modern world are sent into the midst of people still starving for the truth of Jesus today. You're being sent today to people who need knowledge of our Savior and His cross; the sending story is just the same. Will you be like these apostles on the mountainside, ready for whatever their sending might eventually mean?

Are you ready for absolutely anything today? And are you ready to go out *right now*?

September 14 – Mark 6:6b-13

Shedding any weight that hinders your apostleship

After reading of the simplicity with which the Lord sent out His men, consider the facts of your own life in Jesus: *Are you making your apostleship more complicated by complicating it with the ways of the world He wants to reach?* Are you going out with fetters you've personally clasped around your own ankles because of the worries of each passing workday? Do you need to rid your life of certain "tunics" that are turning your eyes from Him and unto the things of this world?

Some poetic verses for reflection:

> *Nerve us with patience, Lord, to toil or rest,*
>
> *Toiling at rest on our allotted level;*
>
> *Unsnared, unscared by world or flesh or devil,*
>
> *Fulfilling the good Will of Thy behest:*
>
> *Not careful here to hoard, not here to revel;*
>
> *But waiting for our treasure and our zest*
>
> *Beyond the fading splendour of the west,*
>
> *Beyond this deathstruck life and deathlier evil.*
>
> *Not with the sparrow building here a house:*
>
> *But with the swallow tabernacling so*
>
> *As still to poise alert to rise and go*
>
> *On eager wings with wing-outspeeding wills*
>
> *Beyond earth's gourds and past her almond boughs,*
>
> *Past utmost bound of the everlasting hills.*

Christina Georgina Rossetti

LIVE LIKE MEN

Apostleship requires every ounce of "nerve" and "patience" so that we're "unsnared" and "unscared" by our calling. May we be like swallows "tabernacling" with the "eager wings" and "wing-outspeeding wills" to go out today, O Men. May we aim "beyond the fading splendour of the west" today; may our eyes be on the "good Will of [His] behest." May we seek our "treasure and our zest" wherever He may choose to lead ; may we return with wondrous stories of His goodness…

O Apostle, are you ready for this particular day? Are you aiming for those "everlasting hills"? Will you shed all bread, bag, money, belt or tunic that competes with the "upward call of God" to you?

September 15 – Mark 6:30-32

Proclaiming the victories of the year

You can feel the fiery fervor and joy that lit the twelve apostles' faces when they "gathered around Jesus" here. You can almost hear the stories of adventure they "reported" to Him in this moment: "all they had done and taught" for His Kingdom. You can picture how the face of Jesus showed His own excitement as His friends were finally in the battle too. And, like a victorious general should, He now invited His men to R&R; He entreats a rest from all these mighty labors. He'd have them find a quiet place for recollection of each victory; a rejoicing for what God had done through them. I imagine He planned some teaching in the midst of this escape; humble reminders of the long war still to come…

O Man of God, I don't doubt you've seen your share of godly victories over the course of this year we've spent together. Small or great, I'm sure He's used your life in many ways to be a blessing in the lives of others around you. I'm sure the world has seen the face of Jesus Himself because of the way that He's been shaping you into His wondrous image. So now's the time to take your rest, give thanks and "report" *to Him* all the things you've seen, done and been taught this year.

* * * * *

This year, I've…

September 16 – Mark 6:53-56

Praying for the "even greater things" through us

If we think the promises of Jesus are meant for us, we must hold them with a vise-like, never-letting-go grip. We must read the scriptures, not as some dead academic exercise, but as the very words of life for our lives. We must see within these promises once promised to the *original* disciples the promises now meant for us. We mustn't think that on that day of His Ascension to the Father there was any sort of ending to His earthly life. We must listen to these words and hear their echoing throughout the centuries, taking hold of their full worth for our day. We must ask the Lord that *we'd* become the men so fully capable of belief that we really, truly, finally believe…

"I tell you the truth, anyone who has faith in me will do what I have been doing," Jesus said to His disciples. And furthermore: "He will do *even greater things* than these, because I am going to the Father." (John 14:12)

Two months from now, we'll be reading of an instance when Simon Peter put these words into practical daily practice. You'll be reading how he interpreted these promises as truth; how he brought these "even greater things" to life. When he saw the "sick on mats" and "in the marketplaces," Peter saw the power of the Lord to actually heal them. When he saw them begging Jesus "to let them touch even the edge of his cloak," he saw a glimpse of his own future…

Today, take the time to ask the Lord to start revealing His perfect power in the way you live your day's details. May we honor Him by *starting* to believe He has the power to give *us* power for His signs and wonders. If we'd want to do the "even greater things" His calling demands of us, let's pray that we'd be *ready* for that kind of power. He's willing to make use of men who'd firmly believe – *and always ask* – for more of His power to pour forth from their lives.

Start to make this your prayer today, O Man. We'll revisit it in two months.

September 17 – Mark 8:22-26

Taking our time in others' lives

Jesus wasn't blind to the physical need of this blind man; He also wasn't blind to his most gaping need. He didn't want him brought to His feet for a simple one-touch healing like He'd done so many times before. There was something special needed in this particular case in Bethsaida; something different about this man and their interaction. Jesus had that perfect honed ability to know when and where His special presence was especially needed by people. Did you notice that, unlike the other times with other blind men, Jesus "took the blind man by the hand and led him *outside the village*"? Did you feel the power of the God-made-flesh making the choice to bestow extra time on this particular blind man? We don't know the reason, but the healing even took some extra time; the man first saw his "tree people." Jesus spent a significant share of one long Bethsaidan day in order to make sure that *this one man saw*. Perhaps there was something in his visage that reported to the Lord that this man deserved some extra minutes of His time. Jesus didn't ever see His day and its full schedule as a reason for evading eternal happenings in His midst. (And aren't you glad that He would do so for *this* blind man? After all, you too were once "blind, but now I see!")

Today, all of us are tasked with taking extra time with people in the service of the Savior who did likewise. You won't give money to a homeless man and think you're "done" with him; you'll then take him out to coffee also. You won't sense a buried problem in the heart of your coworker without letting him talk it out in one hearing. You won't go home to your tired-out wife and let a moment pass until you've let her decompress her crazy day.

If the God of the universe made time so that others could have time with Him, we must learn to do the same each day. We must never assume that our day's filled-up schedule *is* the schedule for our day; the Lord might have entirely different plans. May we linger in the service of our Lord; may we learn to be the men whose time is truly not theirs. May we see the blind man's *doubly*-opened eyes as a reminder that the Lord would call our eyes to be His.

Today, "waste" your time on other people's lives. It'll probably be your only time *not* wasted!

September 18 – Mark 9:17-27

Is there any "unbelief" in you?

I'm oftentimes "possessed by a spirit" that robs me of something worse than "speech": the spirit of "unbelief" in this father. "Whenever it seizes" me, it throw me into pits of sinful deeds, sinful thoughts, sinful anxieties about my life. I'll "gnash my teeth" and "become rigid" in the ways of this fallen world when I don't ascribe my life unto complete belief in Jesus. It throws me "into fire or water to kill" me, yet I'm frozen in the fear and weakness of simply not believing Him…

O Men of God, we must be possessed by how the Spirit dwells in us and truly learn to believe in our Living Savior. We must be seized with His holy power and live lives filled with holy deeds, holy thoughts, holy comfort. We must learn to live our lives within the world with Jesus' perspective on this world, a life of holy disconnect from this age. We must trust the One who's with us when we "pass through the waters," promising "the flames will not set you ablaze."

O Man, do you believe in that One? O Man, where is your unbelief starting to show itself?

The world is full of many men who say that they believe in Jesus – but do *you* actually believe in Jesus? The world is full of "followers of Jesus" claiming to have His holy perspective – but do *you* actually believe in His holy perspective? The world is full of feeble-hearted children masquerading as manly men – but do *you* actually believe in His power in your life? After all, the world is full of unbelief – *the proof is in the state of the world* – but the question remains: Do *you* believe?

Let's ask the Lord for more belief today. May we beg His help wherever there's unbelief. May we be the men who fully trust Him when He first asks us anything, never saying "if you can…"

September 19 – Mark 10:13-16

How will you draw the little ones to Him?

A prayer from Jim Rayburn, founder of Young Life:

"Dear Lord, Give us the teenagers that we may lead them to Thee. Our hearts ache for the millions of young people who remain untouched by the Gospel and for the tragically large proportion of those who have dropped by the wayside and find themselves without spiritual guidance. Help us to give them a chance, oh Father, a chance to become aware of thy Son's beauty and healing power in the might of the Holy Spirit. Oh, Lord Jesus, give us the teenagers, each one at least long enough for a meaningful confrontation with Thee. We are at best unprofitable servants, but thy grace is sufficient. Oh, thou Holy Spirit, give us the teenagers. For we love them and know them to be awfully lonely. Dear Lord, give us the teenagers."

Today, I pray that you experience this same heartbroken spirit for the lost children of our modern world, O Man. Can you personally feel the "lostness" that's lurking in your local high school; do you see Satan's awful designs on those kids? Do you know the ways that kids today are forced into earlier adulthood by the wicked ways of this world and its passing "pleasures?" Do you know that unreached kids become less likely to ever be reached with every single day of their lives that goes by?

Whether it be by financial giving or by the giving of your time, lost children need your presence in their lives, O Men of God. The children of this world – whether in grade-school, middle or high school – need the truth of Jesus lived out in the lives of godly men. Will you start this day by praying for the unreached kids in your town, that they might somehow be reached with the truth of the Gospel? Will you think of how your life might best be used to be the presence of Jesus to them; how you might be the "reacher-out" yourself?

In short: "Let the little children come to me." How might Jesus use your life in their lives?

LIVE LIKE MEN

September 20 – Mark 10:17-22

A life of love today

Even though the story of the "The Rich Young Man" is found in three of the Gospels, this telling of the encounter differs from the others slightly. There's a phrase within Mark's version that marks its tone with something special for us, a different shading of the heart of Jesus. It's as if Mark were a painter shedding extra light on one of his painting's subjects by using different opposing shadows. For a moment, it's as if we see the face of Jesus, looking directly into the eyes of this particular young man…

"Teacher," the Rich Young Man says to Jesus, "all these [commandments] I have kept since I was a boy." And here's the beauty of Mark's telling of this one moment in from His life: "*Jesus looked at him and loved him.*"

Jesus loved this pompous rich young man because He saw within his heart all the earnestness of this theological question. Perhaps Jesus loved the passion with which he defended his faith; the observance of the Law that his life seemed to point to. Yet Jesus, even though he knew this man would *never* sell his things, *never* follow Him, *never* be His disciple, still loved him dearly. Jesus spent His earthly days the way He'd spent all eternity before He came to us – *being the Love of God incarnate*…

From Dostoevsky's *The Brothers Karamazov*: "Brothers, have no fear of men's sin. Love a man even in his sin, for that is the semblance of divine love and is the highest love on earth. Love all God's creation, the whole and every grain of sand in it. Love every leaf, every ray of God's light. Love the animals, love the plants, love everything. If you love everything, you will perceive the divine mystery in things. Once you perceive it, you will begin to comprehend it better every day. And you will come at last to love the whole world with an all-embracing love…"

Today I'm asking us to give our hearts to that all-embracing love, a love that doesn't ask for returned favor from anyone. May we concentrate our attentions upon acting from the love of Jesus; may we live only from its emanations. May we love the ones who seem to be utterly unlovable, even those ones with self-righteous viewpoints like this wealthy young man. May we not distinguish any difference in the targets of our love today; may we perceive the "divine mystery" all around us…

"Let everything that you do be done with love" today. Love like Jesus loved that young man.

September 21 – Mark 10:32-34

"Resolutely" set out with Him today

Every man who wants to follow Jesus must go along on this Jerusalem journey and hear these words of His acknowledged destiny. Every man who'd seek to know the heart and mind of Jesus must be wrapped up in His knowledge of His coming death. We can't read through the Gospels without fully understanding how He knew the outcome of the days of His earthly life. We can't be followers of this Savior if we don't bear a similar understanding of the trials that are meant for us too…

In Luke 9:51, on an earlier trip to Jerusalem, we hear of Jesus' perspective, His undaunted outlook. Was He afraid of the hardships and the opposition He knew would accompany His journey to the capital city? Was He being surreptitious in His entry itinerary; was He slinking softly into the city by nightfall? No. "As the time approached for him to be taken up to heaven, Jesus *resolutely set out for Jerusalem*."

O Man of God, Jesus has you on a journey meant for the enrichment of your faith and understanding of His love for the world. He'd ask that each of us would bear a "resolute" sort of spirit in the conduct of this particular day – *for Him*. He'd ask that each of us would "share in his sufferings by becoming like him in death," that we would learn to die to our self. He'd ask that each of us not become "astonished" or "afraid," like those followers who could not equate His glory with His suffering.

O Men of God, will we be the men who "resolutely" started our journey **and** the men who'll resolutely finish strong? Will you live the tiny step of this day's part of your journey with the gusto that accompanies a real passion? Will you "fight the good fight," will you "finish the race," will you truly "keep the faith" during this particular day of your life? Will you look into the eyes of One who foreknew His own suffering – *for you* – and then went unto it anyway, willingly?

O Man, will you "resolutely" go today? Will you go with Jesus?

LIVE LIKE MEN

September 22 – Mark 10:46-52

Passion, passion, passion

The differences in the versions of this story told in Mark and Matthew are deserving of today's full and direct attention. Did you notice that in Mark's recounting (probably based on Peter's recollections), we're actually rewarded with the beggar's name? Did you notice Bartimaeus caused Jesus to fully stop and then call out to the crowd to send him over? Did you notice how the crowd, sarcastically smiling, then instructed Bartimaeus that the Lord wanted to see him? Did you notice his completely indecent conduct – "throwing his cloak aside" – and his wild-eyed excitement – "he jumped up"? Did you see him utilizing language meant for ingratiation, calling Jesus by the holy name of "Rabbi"? Did you notice Jesus setting him free from blindness with the command "go," and that Bartimaeus chose to follow Him instead? There can be only one explanation for Mark adding all these extra elements to the narrative: *Bartimaeus had memorable passion.*

Do you feel a sense of passion in the way you're viewing this day today, in its possibilities and its promises? Do you feel a rush of passion in the way you're called to live for Jesus in the midst of your world, all throughout it? Do you notice any passion welling up in your heart when you're reading about the story of the blind man set free? Does your heart flood full of passion when you read the name of Jesus; when you know that He has called you to Himself?

A great passage from E.M. Forster: "Passion should believe itself irresistible. It should forget civility and consideration and all the other curses of a refined nature. Above all, it should never ask for leave where there is a right of way…"

O Men of God, we've got a "right of way" whenever we're living from Jesus' passion for the sake of His coming Kingdom. Our nature is "refined" only insofar as it's Jesus' nature now, lived within the passion of our lives for Him. We must be like blind Bartimaeus, leaving "civility and consideration" behind for the sake of knowing Jesus better. We must know that all our passion is personified by One who is *Himself* the "irresistible" One, our wonderful Savior.

Today, live your life with some passion, O Man. Yell and jump and run to get nearer to Jesus!

September 23 – Mark 12:41-44

Giving out of your poverty, not your riches

The difference Jesus saw between the giving of the "rich" and this poor widow's was the place from which their giving came. The difference between simply giving and actual *sacrificial* giving is as different as the difference between night and day. When we give from modern livelihoods arranged around our own human comfort, it's good to give; but not the highest. When we give from our overflowing bank accounts whatever we'd deem "sufficient," it's great; but not an adventure. The real blessing comes when we ascribe to Jesus the ownership of everything we've ever had or ever will have, O Men. The real value comes when we *de*value anything that stands between us and an undivided heart for Him. The real challenge is to give of both our time and our money in the pattern of the One who gave *Himself* for us. The real excitement comes when we evaluate how we give as "How much more can I give?," not as "How much is enough?"

Today, give of either time or money *absolutely sacrificially* in the same way that this poor widow once gave. Try writing a check that you can barely afford to churches or ministries that are bearing fruit for the sake of Jesus and His Kingdom. Try giving your time – *a great expanse of time* – in the service of another or in the service of a ministry you love. May we learn to give from "all we have to live on," *not* the monthly leftovers of our carefully managed modern lives.

Give in a prodigal manner today, O Man. Give "out of your poverty," not out of your riches.

September 24 – Mark 14:27-31

What (broken) oaths have you made to God?

Jesus knew exactly what would happen with Peter's oaths before Peter even actually uttered them. He knew just how he would say them; how he'd later go into the courtyard; how he'd deny Him over the course of this very night. He'd even known all this would happen when He'd sat upon a certain patch of grass upon a certain famous mountainside. He'd known everything so deadly about broken oaths and vows when He was looking over the Sea and then taught with these words: "Again, you have heard that the ancients were told, 'You shall not make false vows, but shall fulfill your vows to the Lord.' But I say to you, make no oath at all, either by heaven, for it is the throne of God, or by the earth, for it is the footstool of His feet, or by Jerusalem, for it is the city of the Great King. Nor shall you make an oath by your head, for you cannot make one hair white or black. But let your statement be, 'Yes, yes' or 'No, no'; and anything beyond these is of evil…" (Matthew 5:33-37)

O Men of God, where are you and I like Peter in our hurry to make oaths and vows and promises to God? Where are we even *more* like passionate-hearted Peter in betraying God by breaking those oaths and vows and promises? Where are we tempted to equate our high-flown *promises* of obedience with the actual actions *required* for obedience? Where are we thinking we're getting away with hollow talk when our God requires that our talk be backed by actual walk?

What is your word to God worth, O Man? Are there vows you've left undone?

Today, let's repent of those broken vows. Let's pay heed to how we follow through. May we move away from ready rash expressions of our feeble faith commitment and get to Jesus' "Yes, yes," and "No, no."

September 25 – Mark 14:53-62

Learning proper silence

Our faculty of speech is our most dangerous possession if we don't also practice studied silence. When we hurry to respond without a single moment of reflection, we give Satan vast opportunities for attacking us. When we don't give a moment's pause before speaking, we're rarely contemplating what the Lord would want to say through us. When we're not the men who let a little silence lead our speech, we become the men who mostly speak from out of themselves.

Jesus stood before this kangaroo court and practiced perfect silence for the good of God's perfect plan. He could've rained down heavenly fire or fiery words upon the heads of these chief priests, but He made the choice to not do so. He could've torn their ridiculous prosecution to pieces with His knowledge of the scriptures, His complete knowledge of His own Word. He could've given vent to righteous (*actually* righteous!) indignation, but He knew to hold His tongue until the proper moment...

The power of a manly use of silence is the power it portends for the moment when we finally speak. The strength we gain from muzzling our mouth is best reflected when we eventually open up our lips to His given words. If we learn to use our silence for the power of the Holy Spirit, we'll become the men whose words actually speak loudly. We'll become the sort of men who finally speak up and then notice the eyes of all are locked upon us, waiting expectantly...

"Likewise, the tongue is a small part of the body, but it makes great boasts. Consider what a great forest is set on fire by a small spark. The tongue also is a fire, a world of evil among the parts of the body. It corrupts the whole body, sets the whole course of one's life on fire, and is itself set on fire by hell." (James 3:5,6)

Let's mark our day instead with *these* words: "Everyone should be quick to listen, slow to speak, and slow to become angry..." Today, use your silence, O Men of God. Pre-measure your words; give due consideration. Let's learn to delegate the power of our lives unto our silences, not unto our many *many* words.

September 26 – Luke 1:1-4

Your life must write your Gospel

For all we know, Dr. Luke was the most important physician of his day, the first century's version of Hippocrates. For all our knowledge of his practice, he might've actually been the greatest scientific mind of his era. He might've been the doctor who created certain measures for a certain illness that are now thought to be practically ageless. He might've made a fortune hawking some great remedy for the "modern Roman's complaints"…or been an absolute nobody. All in all, all the knowledge that we have about Luke's profession and his life are completely insignificant. All we know is what we're told within this Gospel and the Book of Acts, *ie. almost nothing at all*. Yet do you think that what you're currently doing with your personal "career" will resound through the coming centuries? Let's be honest: The weight of "work" we're each doing to put bread on our family's table is usually pretty small in scope…

So here's the question: Is your life reporting your own personal Gospel to the world, like Luke's life gave us the Book of Luke? Have you "investigated everything" about Jesus that you personally can and then given it out to the world for its consideration? Does your life and livelihood point to an "orderly account" of how the life of Jesus is manifesting itself in you? Have you "undertaken to draw up an account" of the Good News that's the reason for the hope in your life?

Just imagine if the good Doctor Luke had instead decided to be focused only on his "work"! Just consider how his legacy of medicine would've died with him; how he'd be a nothing to us now…

O Man of God, will you relegate the real point of your life – *Jesus Christ* – to the background of your life's story's arc? Will you "focus your attentions" on the happenstance of work today or be building up your personal Gospel? Do you understand that how you're living your life today determines your tomorrow and also determines your eventual ending? Do you know that only three things are eternal: God, His Word and the souls of people?

What's your life writing for future generations, O Man? A Gospel or absolutely nothing?

September 27 – Luke 1:5-22

Immediate belief is what's required

You and I can become "upright in the sight of God" by keeping "all the Lord's commandments" absolutely "blamelessly." We can arise from exalted genealogical trees like Zechariah's, so that our personal faith seems somehow destined for us. We can draw the lot and be sent into the temple of the Lord with His oft' required ceremonial incense-burning. We can even have a sighting of the "angel of the Lord," but the question still remains for us, O Men: *Whether He speaks to you through scripture, vision or the Holy Spirit's voice, will you take the Lord's word or will you doubt Him?* If He says you'll have a child during your declining years, will you take Him at His word, spoken to you? Will you read a verse, or sense His Spirit's whisper, and debate upon your action step: Believing or not believing? Will you hear the voice of God and simply do, simply because He's God and you know you're actually not?

O Men of God, Zechariah was an "upright" man because of his verifiable doings of the passed-down Jewish Law. He was ever mindful of the life that God had commanded for him and his people, yet he wasn't prepared for God's actual voice to him…

On the other hand, did you notice how his future son is here described: "filled with the Holy Spirit"? Did you also notice the *timing* for God's choice to bless John the Baptist with the Spirit: "even from birth"?

Today, you and I have both been blessed with the presence of the Holy Spirit; we're chosen like John the Baptist once was. You and I both bear the mark of a holy chosen sonship proven by the Spirit within our hearts. Yet we must learn how to unite within ourselves the Spirit's presence *and* the willing heart to take the Lord at His word. We won't be overtaken by the Holy Spirit until we learn to trust the Lord like Zechariah *didn't* here…

Where is the Lord speaking to you today, O Man? Will you trust, believe, and be blessed?

September 28 – Luke 2:8-20

Expect to see His glory today

I doubt the shepherds ever expected that the "glory of the Lord" would be revealed unto them on a random starry night. They probably hadn't picked this particular pasture with the thought in mind: "*Here's* the field where some angels will surely show up." They hadn't waited with expectance through the first half of the night, hoping God would send His greetings to them. They hadn't chosen their profession for its spiritual similarities to the interplay of God (Shepherd) with His people (the sheep).

But you and I must *everyday* expect that the Lord's glory is as close as His presence in our hearts, O Men of God. We must set our life's schedule with the thought: "*Here's* a day where the Lord will surely show Himself to me." We must wait with great expectancy, knowing Immanuel actually means what it actually means: "God with us." We must anchor our professions to the worthiness, the "worthwhileness," of Jesus' charge to Peter: "Feed my sheep."

Did you wake up to this morning with an expectation of the Lord's revealing Himself to you today, O Man? Do you ever think He'll show Himself to men like you and me; men who'll long for His revelation of Himself, of His glory? Is your desire that you'd be the kind of man to whom the "glory of the Lord" is a constant and continual revelation? For if He'd show Himself to lowly lolling shepherds in the blackness of the night, why not to us, O Men of God!

Today, spend your time in scripture, prayer and worship with a spirit that's actually *seeking* for the "glory of the Lord." Ask that He'd show you more of Himself; ask His blessing on your day by His clear guiding presence within it. Look for signs and wonders woven through your day that are pointing to His Spirit's working in your life and circumstances. Be ready for His glory and not surprised like the shepherds were; He's truly near to those with expectant hearts.

"When they had seen him, they spread the word…" Let's spread the word today by seeing Him for ourselves.

September 29 – Luke 2:22-35

The one purpose and the one goal

Jesus' parents set out for the capital with their baby for the purpose of a ritual Jewish consecration. They didn't expect their visitation would result in such a radical confirmation of an old man's whole life. They didn't walk into the temple courts with thoughts of Holy Spirit-leadings in the life of a complete and total stranger. They didn't have any expectation that the day would result in the wonders of the Lord being marvelously manifest…

But Simeon surely had, hadn't he? In fact, Simeon's whole life led to this very moment! Simeon had been waiting every day of his adult life for this personal revelation of the Lord's "salvation." Simeon "considered his life worth nothing to him, if only he might…complete the task" allotted to him by the Lord his God. Simeon woke up to this morning with a heart turned only Godward and fell asleep that night with his entire life confirmed…

Imagine how it must've felt to live his life with only one set purpose, a single-minded all-focused goal. Imagine how it then would feel to feel the Holy Spirit's leading to the temple courts and know that **this** was "the day." Imagine how his eyes were ranging around the temple courts, knowing that his purpose stood within those very walls. Imagine all the joyful tear-filled wild-eyed emotion he must've felt as he sprang toward the infant Christ-child…

Is that your heart today, O Man of God? Do you have that kind of hopeful focus? Do you realize that the Spirit who led Simeon to this life and these words is the same Spirit living in you? Would you have the inner fortitude to live your life with only one such goal; a single all-consuming purpose? Do you think you're called to live a life today that's *any different at all* from the life that old Simeon was called to live?

Well, you're not, O Man of God! Today, Simeon's call is your call. You're called to be a patient waiting witness to the glory of the Lord and a herald for His second-coming Son. You're called to listen for His Spirit's voice as director of your day and your life and your whole earthly purpose. You're called to be so sensitive to the movements of His Spirit that there's nothing that competes with the sound of His voice.

Are you like a Simeon today? If not, what needs to change?

September 30 – Luke 2:41-49

Going after knowledge the hard way

Truth be told, we don't have the faintest idea of exactly how Jesus came to know and understand all the scriptures. We might think He knew the breadth of the word by simply *being* the Word; that His knowledge of it was a sine qua non. In fact, I'd bet there's many men reading this who've thought the thought before: "Sure, all that stuff's easy for the Son of God." But we might hamstring our strivings to emulate His spiritual formation with this sort of modern cynical flippancy. For to read of His undivided passion for the learning of these teachers' teachings seems to say that Jesus *actually learned something*. When we hear Him quoting scripture throughout His teachings, those might actually be the fruits of studied concentrations. Do we think that Jesus took up "our infirmities and [carried] our sorrows" without trying out our other human burdens too? Do we think He'd simply snap His fingers and rule out all the challenges of being formed to love *and* know the Father?

O Men of God, where are you pursuing knowledge of your Heavenly Father through a hard-fought learning of His ways? How are you following the lead of boyish Jesus here, sitting at the feet of great spiritual teachers, soaking it all in? Do you give unto your knowledge of the scriptures even a *tenth* of the work you're giving to your daily "work"? Are you hard-pressed to bestow an hour-a-week to such important spiritual formation or are you pressing hard to become more like Him?

Today's challenge: Pick a Christocentric writer who seems so daunting in their depth that you've always been avoidant of them. Whether it's a Lewis, Murray, Augustine, Scougall or Bonhoeffer, pick up one of their books to start reading today. Give yourself the challenge to read from it every single day until you've finished this particular book of theirs. And if you don't know which to start with, ask a trusted friend who's further along in their spiritual journey.

Don't go to bed tonight without your book picked out. Get it – *and open it* – today, O Man!

October 1 – Luke 2:51,52

Commit to the four parts of Jesus' growth

These verses give our only glimpse into the life of Jesus between the ages of twelve and thirty years old. In the course of these less than forty words, eighteen years fly by; nothing more can be known of their full detail. We don't exactly know what an education might've been like for Jesus; we can only try to give our best guess. We assume that at some early age He entered Joseph's shop as an apprentice and worked His way up to a journeyman status...

But, frankly, we can't know too much more, O Men. Nor does it really matter in the end. What matters is the simple sort of summation that we read in this wording of Luke 2:52. What matters is the way we might commit ourselves to growing in this same fourfold manner as Jesus...

So let's take time to challenge ourselves, O Men. Let's write down some commitments in these four specific areas:

"And Jesus grew *in wisdom*..."

"...and *stature*..."

"...and in *favor with God*..."

"...and [*in favor with*] *men*..."

October 2 – Luke 3:7-14

The truth requires immediate action

What if we were so completely determined in our pursuit of Jesus' call that we always met it with expectant immediacy? What if we dismantled all our theorizing about "what Jesus meant" by our pursuit of "what Jesus actually did"? What if we were like the crowds surrounding John the Baptist here, ready to be *doing something* about our "faith in God"? What if we re-read the ending of Jesus' cousin's sermon and then affirmed its truth in our daily lives today?

Put yourself in his crowd, hearing these words: "'The ax is already at the root of the trees, and every tree that does not produce good fruit will be cut down and thrown into the fire.'

"'What should we do then?' the crowd asked.

"John answered, 'The man with two tunics should *share with him who has none*, and the one who has food should *do the same*.

"Tax collectors also came to be baptized. 'Teacher,' they asked, 'what should we do?'

"'*Don't collect any more than you are required to*,' he told them.

"Then some soldiers asked him, 'And what should we do?'

"He replied, '*Don't extort money* and *don't accuse people falsely – be content with your pay*.'"

If you'd been there, what would you have asked John the Baptist, next?

And, more importantly, what do you think he'd have *answered* you?

And, even more importantly, what would you have *done* about it, O Man?

October 3 – Luke 3:23a

The pure focus of Jesus' ministry years

Being that I was thirty when I first worked on *Live Like Men* makes the age of Jesus seem doubly significant to me. It seems to me that there's something at that particular age that gives a man a certain confidence; a sense of being altogether ready. After thirty years a man should know the things he'll give his life to; what it is that's really truly important to him. If he only had the next three years to give away – *as Jesus did at that point* – what should a thirty-year-old man do with his life?

When you think of all the men who are equated with the worldly term of "greatness," what do you immediately think of? Do you think of men absorbed with petty things and petty worries, or of men who are "above" those class of things? Do you think of men whose focus is as straying as the day-to-days of life or of men who live with one mind? Do you think they're thinking of their age, or anything else at all, as if it could possibly compete with that "one thing" they're currently chasing?

O Men of God, whether you're thirteen, thirty, forty-three or ninety, all that matters is the focus of your heart today. All that mattered in the following three years of Jesus' life was the every single day He was living in, moment-to-moment. All that mattered was His single-minded focus on the Kingdom of Heaven; the building blocks of which were His chosen disciples. All that mattered were the things divine, eternal, everlasting, never-changing that He was after; the heart and mind of the Father…

A great word from Albert Camus: "At the age of thirty a man ought to have control over himself, know the exact reckoning of his faults and virtues, recognize his limits, foresee his weakness – be what he is!"

We serve a Master who had *complete* control, *was* all virtue, had *no* limits, took *our* weakness upon His perfect heavenly shoulders. You and I are men who must be giving *Him* control, *having* His virtues, accepting *no* limits in our service of His Heavenly Kingdom. Today, will you give your sole focus to the things that are actually eternal and of everlasting value? Will you have a heart that actually is His heart in the conduct of your day, or be distracted and of little value?

Jesus did it all in about three years, O Men. Where will we be in the next three?

October 4 – Luke 7:18-23

Bring out your doubts and deal with them

We'll eventually fall prey to whatever doubts we personally allow to linger in the corners of our minds, O Men. If you're toying with doubt, you might have a "faith" in Jesus that seems powerful today, only to find you're faithless on the morrow. You may stand before a crowded room of people, speaking of how "we all need Jesus ," only to give Him up yourself next week. You might raise your children in a perfectly godly sort of church-going household, only to leave your wife when you're personally struggling…

In this moment, John the Baptist sat upon the dank floor of his prison cell, waiting for his oncoming execution. In his hopes, the coming of the "one more powerful than I" was a little more powerful than his present personal experience! In his mind, he had pictures of the Messiah that included "winnowing forks" and the dreaded "unquenchable fire." But did he let these human doubts become the hiding place of the evil one or did John the Baptist decide to test them out? Did he languish in the prison with a sense of his own victimhood or did John send out these certain disciples to ask Jesus? Would he let himself be conquered by the seeds of secret doubt or was John the Baptist more man than that?

This passage answers all those questions, O Man. John the Baptist was our model in this.

O Men of God, may we use that fabled phrase of Ronald Reagan in the conduct of our faith: "Trust but verify." If there's any doubt that's creeping into your heart or mind today, you must use today to talk it out with your Savior. You must sit down with a tried and true friend and verify the value of our trust; be reminded of the truth of Jesus. And then, in going forth, you must put that doubt to death and be well reassured of He who is our certainty and hope. You and I must call each other out of places filled with gray half-truths and into the light and life of our Lord Jesus. We must verify our belief and then simply trust, trust, trust, trust, trust until we're dead and in His glory.

You'll only be as strong as your secret doubts allow you to be. May we exorcise those doubts today.

October 5 – Luke 7:36-50

A day without judgment

We oftentimes allow ourselves to judge another person when we notice how their sin is also in us. We hate the sin in other people when it matches what's in us, when we know we're just as guilty as they are. We heap curses on the world because we don't attach importance to our calling to be going out into the world. We blaspheme Jesus and His sacrifice for us whenever we're quick to judge another but *not* quick to judge ourselves…

From Henry Fielding's *The History of Tom Jones*: "The good or evil we confer on others, very often, I believe, recoils on ourselves." What we daily dole to the world "in the name of Jesus," good or evil, is the very strongest judgment upon our own lives (Matt. 7:1,2).

O Men of God, here's today's challenge for us: *A day without an ounce of judging other people's lives or lifestyle*. If you feel the need to pass a single judgment in the next twenty-four hours, here's the next challenge: *Judge yourself*.

October 6 – Luke 9:7-9

We must "try to see him," if Herod did

Jesus had such power, such appeal, such an irresistible presence, that even a man like King Herod noticed. The rippling waters that fanned out from every action in the life of Jesus went even as far as to this jaded tetrarch's palace. The doings of this simple wandering carpenter had such a vital potency that they made a powerful ruler feel "perplexed." The teachings of this humble Rabbi became the tossing-and-turning nightmares of this ersatz joke of a king…

And yet the King of Kings attracted him, didn't He? King Herod, in spite of himself, still "tried to see him." Even this one who stood to lose his everything, Herod Antipas, wanted to get nearer to the life of Jesus Christ. Even one who'd killed His cousin was so mystified by our Lord that He'd seek to see the Savior for himself…

So how about you, O Man of God? Will you seek to see Him with your *everything*? Will you give Him your attentions even to the tune of a Herod; will your personal interest intersect with Him today? Will you want to feel His presence in the midst of everything defining your day; will you fight for a heightened nearness to Jesus? Will you give Him of your time and energies; of your efforts and perspective; of your heart and your mind?

O Men of God, if a desperate despot sought to get to Jesus, we must only want to get to Jesus *all the more*. If a man whose life was conducted only for his own ends still wanted to see Him, we must want to see Him more ever more clearly. If a murderous tyrant was giving more than a second thought to Jesus, we must give more than a second thought to Jesus. We must know that absolutely nothing in this world can ever compete with the dearness of our nearness to the living Savior. We must live today like only His perspective on Today is what matters; that, in fact, nothing else matters to us. We must "try to see him" every single moment of our day by aligning our hearts with His immanent and glorious presence.

Will your interest vie with Herod's interest today? Will you seek, O Man, or simply settle?

October 7 – Luke 13:22

Keeping Jesus' schedule today

Jesus knew the calling upon the whole of His life would be fulfilled over the course of one long brutal weekend. However, as He went about the three years leading up to that particular weekend, He never wasted a moment of His life's journey. For instance, even when He "made his way to Jerusalem," He used each place through which He passed as a place to impart the Father's truth. Every single day of His life was given its proper merit by His sometimes seeming *purposelessness*. Even as He seemed to lead a wayward roaming sort of lifestyle, Jesus always had His one great Plan in mind. Every day when He'd rise up within another stranger's house, yard or barn, He knew exactly what He was "about."

Do we understand we're following after One who lived His life outside the confines of a "personal schedule?" Do you understand how Jesus lived His days; how He'd "teach as he made his way"; *un*scheduled, *un*harried, *un*bothered? Do you sometimes live your life as if the King of Kings, the Lord of Lords, personally resides within your busy complex schedule? Do you pigeonhole the Prince of Peace's plan into those parts of your lifestyle where you've made a little room for Him?

O Men of God, the life of Jesus can't be achieved in the same way we're making our way through our own earthly life. We can't expect to toil only when it seems convenient to us; to tarry only when it fits our daily schedule. Jesus made His way from town to town and village to village, teaching as He went of only the things that eternally mattered. There were times He'd stop and rest a while; sometimes He'd hurry quickly along; nothing moved Him but the Father's will for Him…

Judging from the outlook of your day and your week, where would you say your current life's actually heading to? Are you filling up your time with things that have eternal value or do you spend your time only on your personal ends? Do you fill your schedule with self-important self-serving items, or are you driven by the Lord Jesus' Way alone? Do you have the time to actually follow Jesus in this manner He meandered through His every passing day?

Who are you following today, O Man of God? The wandering One or a Christ of your own creation?

October 8 – Luke 17:11-19

Thank those who've blessed you

The less we offer thanks to people who bless our lives, the more we'll start to think we're somehow "self-made men." The less we bless the people who've blessed the formation of the men we've become, the less we'll learn to pass the blessing along to others…

The more we learn to thank the ones who've made us everything we are, the less we'll eventually think about ourselves. The more we bless the people who've poured themselves into our spiritual growth, the more we'll learn to be "poured out" for the sake of others.

Today, you and I are tasked with thanking people who've given life to us, who've been big parts of our life- and spiritual-journey. Take the time to call or write a letter or note – *not a text or email* – and bless the heart of those who've changed who you are. When we learn to put these feelings into words, we're learning to pass along that all-important love that Jesus said *must* mark us. When we men admit that we're *not* self-made, we're starting to give honor to the Lord whose plan is actually ***the*** Plan.

Make a list of those names today, O Man. Then take the time to thank each and every one.

October 9 – Luke 19:1-10

Action is the beginning and the goal of faith

Imagine if this moment instead transpired more like this: "Jesus entered Jericho and was passing through. A man was there by the name of Zacchaeus; he was a chief tax collector and was very wealthy. He was somewhat interested in seeing Jesus, but being a short man he could not, because of the crowd. So he stood right in their midst and he didn't see a thing; Jesus passed through Jericho and went along on His way…"

The difference? Zacchaeus had to act; his action was a necessary component for seeing Jesus in the flesh. His action actually proved his intent that "he wanted to see who Jesus was"; his tree-climbing was the fruit of that commitment.

Now imagine if the ending of the story were different too: "When Jesus reached the spot, he looked up and said to him, 'Zacchaeus, come down immediately. I must stay at your house today.' So he came down at once and welcomed him gladly.

"All the people saw this and began to mutter, 'He has gone to be the guest of a "sinner."'

"But Zacchaeus stood up and said to the Lord, 'Look, Lord! Here and now I'll hold onto my possessions just as before, and if I've cheated anybody out of anything, that's just the way business works…'"

The difference? Zacchaeus had to act; his action was a necessary component for learning to follow after Jesus. His action actually proved the Lord's words: "salvation has come to this house"; his profligate giving was the fruit of his new commitment.

Today, let's think of how the Lord Jesus once looked up into *our* tree; how He called "sinners" like you and me to Himself. Let's think of all the lengths He went to for the good of our salvation and the way that we've responded to His love for us. Are there actions that He's currently asking of you if you'd really want to become His modern-day disciple, O Man? Are there certain things you're reluctant to part ways with; ways you're *not* being like Zacchaeus when he met Jesus? Is there any particular thing, as was the case with the Rich Young Ruler, where you're being held back from wholehearted commitment? Are you man enough to let go of your pride – climb a tree – *do absolutely anything* – if it brought you nearer to your Lord?

Let's embrace that Zacchaeus-spirit today, O Men. Let's do outrageous things to see and follow Jesus.

October 10 – Luke 24:1-12

Death is defeated, so live!

In the parting pages of Thomas Wolfe's *Of Time and the River*, there's a haunting soliloquy on the common lot of mankind. In these phrases speak the yearning-dying-hurting hearts of men who don't know the "one hope" we've been called to, O Men. When you think of Jesus' disciples thinking He was dead and gone from them, think about the import of these kind of words. Read aloud these sad phrases to yourself, knowing their vain and desperate hue is no longer any part of your life:

"Where shall the weary find peace? Upon what shore will the wanderer come home at last? When shall it cease – the blind groping, the false desires, the fruitless ambitions that grow despicable as soon as they are reached, the vain contest with phantoms, the maddening and agony of the brain and spirit in all the rush and glare of living, the dusty tumult, the grinding, the shouting, the idiot repetitions of the streets, the sterile abundance, the sick gluttony, and the thirst which goes on drinking?"

O Men of God, there's no thirst that leaves us thirsty, there's no hunger making us hungry if we know that Jesus is actually risen! There's nothing found in the tumults, grindings, shoutings and the idiot repetitions that can touch a heart that belongs to Him! We're *not* the men who'll fool around with false desires and fruitless ambitions; our lives have been ransomed by Jesus and His risen life! The weary already have their peace in Him; the wanderers have come home to the only Home meant for our hearts!

Today, let's live a life that's grounded in the certainty of one who's personally observed the "strips of linen lying by themselves." Let's go into the tomb of Jesus, just like these women did, and we'll "not find the body of the Lord Jesus" in there either! Then let's go out into the world with full knowledge that there's nothing fruitless when we've given our hearts to the Risen and Living One. Let's let the joy of He who said, "Take heart! I have overcome the world" be the center of our whole day today…

Death has actually been defeated, O Man. Now will you live today as if it's really so?

LIVE LIKE MEN

October 11 – Luke 24:13-35

What one brother do you share life with?

Oftentimes the richest "realest" moments in our spiritual formation come when we're in concert with another person. When we'll open up our journey and our thoughts about that journey to another, we allow for greater personal learning. When we learn to actually listen to another's thoughts about following Jesus, we accord to that person's journey vast importance. When we share aloud these back-and-forths of faith in humble friendly conversation, we're actually beginning to "sharpen" each other. We're representing the "two or more" and proving by our shared growth that the Lord is truly in our shared presence. We're two separate parts of the Body of Christ and yet we're showing by our brotherhood the power of two kindred spirits…

O Man of God, who is walking with you while you're walking with Jesus to Emmaus; who is sharpening your faith this day? What brother is your brother in this battle we're waging for Kingdom supremacy in our hearts and minds? Do you have an instant answer as to whom it is you're walking with; who's the one who constantly pushes you to Jesus? Can you say you're really a brother such as that to someone else; are you in "Emmaus conversations" constantly?

The Lord will make His presence felt in ever greater measure when we're walking through this life with another brother. You'll find Him popping up on your journey when you're constantly engaged and "discuss these things with each other" all the time. He'll walk right up between the two of you and engage your burning hearts with challenging questions and with Holy Spirit promptings. He'll guide your thoughts and words and actions as He makes His life come alive in your friendship; He'll use you back and forth.

Who is that brother in your life today, O Man? Who is that comrade-in-arms for you? Who is he with whom you "call on the name of the Lord, to serve him shoulder to shoulder"; your brother for the long haul of life? (Zeph. 3:9b)

October 12 – John 1:1-9

Are you testifying to the Light?

Before the dawn of time, God had purposed that He'd one day make a man who'd be given the name (*your name.*) He'd be born in (*your hometown*) to (*your parents' names*) and be brought up (*in the particular way you were personally brought up.*) He'd go to (*your schools' names*) where he'd experience (*your experiences*); his closest friend would be (*your best friend's name.*) But, most importantly, he'd hear the call of Jesus to follow Him when he was (*however old you were when you were called by Him.*)

Now let's frame the story another way:

"There came a man who was sent from God; his name was (*your name.*) He came as a witness to testify concerning that light, so that through him all men might believe. He himself was not the light; he came only as a witness to the light. The true light that gives light to every man was coming into the world."

O Men of God, the purpose of our lives must be aligned with the predetermined purposes of John the Baptist's short life: he was "sent from God" to "testify concerning that light, so that through him all men might believe." John was born to live a life that pointed only to the "true light"; you and I were born for no other earthly purpose. Our lives must be so filled with emanations of the Light that our lives are used to "witness" to His "coming," all the time.

Or, in Jesus' words: "No one lights a lamp and puts it in a place where it will be hidden, or under a bowl. Instead he puts it on its stand, so that those who come in may see the light. Your eye is the lamp of your body. When your eyes are good, your whole body also is full of light. But when they are bad, your body also is full of darkness. See to it, then, that the light within you is not darkness. Therefore, if your whole body is full of light, and no part of it dark, it will be completely lighted, as when the light of a lamp shines on you." (Luke 11:33-36)

Concentrate your mind on the Light today. Banish from your midst all darkness. May we "testify concerning that light" – *both by words and by actions* – all throughout this day we've been given by our Lord.

LIVE LIKE MEN

October 13 – John 1:14

Having the spirit *required* by the Incarnation

The (*immeasurable, perfect, holy, righteous, immutable, eternal, beautiful, magnificent, omniscient, omnipresent, omnipotent, gracious, all-loving, I AM, everlasting, faithful, jealous, triune, only, most high, mighty, peaceful, creative, redeeming, ancient, wise, fearful, understanding, kingly*) **Word became** (*weak, unlovely, human, feeble, sickly, sorrowful, mutable, finite, singularly present, lowly, aged, aging*) **flesh and made his dwelling among us** (*sinners, saints, perverts, priests, ingrates, cretans, bastards, backstabbers, self-righteous, lovers, haters, warmongers, conquerors, conquered ones, religious, faithless, drunkards, deviants, suicides, sages, prostitutes, tax collectors, kings, princes, governors, commoners, false, true, trusting, distrustful, unloveable, and those-desirous-of-love.*) **We** (the *sinners, saints, perverts, priests, ingrates, cretans, bastards, backstabbers, self-righteous, lovers, haters, warmongers, conquerors, conquered ones, religious, faithless, drunkards, deviants, suicides, sages, prostitutes, tax collectors, kings, princes, governors, commoners, false, true, trusting, distrustful, unloveable, and those-desirous-of-love*) **have seen his** (*immeasurable, perfect, holy, righteous, immutable, eternal, beautiful, magnificent, omniscient, omnipresent, omnipotent, gracious, all-loving, I AM, everlasting, faithful, jealous, triune, only, most high, mighty, peaceful, creative, redeeming, ancient, wise, fearful, understanding, kingly*) **glory, the glory of the One and Only, who came from the Father, full of grace and truth.**

O Men of God, do we understand the unfathomability of the One who'd so dethrone Himself for the sake of our hearts? Do we understand how worthless are our profanations of love until we're similarly ready to lower ourselves for His Kingdom? Don't we comprehend that we can't ever expect a life of easy "comfort" when we're saved by the God who stooped so very low to save us? Can't we read the story of the Incarnation only as a model for our *own* incarnations for the sake of His Kingdom? Or as Paul explained: "To the weak I became weak, to win the weak. I have become all things to all men so that by all possible means I might save some."

Today, will you use your day in order to serve the "all possible means" Savior by absolutely "all possible means," O Man? Will you relegate your comforts to the place where Jesus left His own so that He might come down and save you? Will you give away your "glory" in return for His good pleasure; your "plans" for His everlasting heavenly Plan? Will you personally "become weak" in order that you might better understand the heart of Jesus Christ, the self-weakened One?

Who will you follow with your day today? How will you lay your life down for Him?

October 14 – John 2:1-10

Do we follow a "jovial" Christ?

If Jesus were a joy-killing, fun-hating, boring stick-in-the-mud, it seems doubtful we would know about this particular story. If He was a shrewish, mean, frowning, sad, church-mousy teetotaler type, it seems really unlikely that John would have witnessed it...

But if Jesus was joyful, fun, exciting, the life-of-any-party-He-got-invited-to, it makes sense that we'd read this particular story. If He was relaxed, friendly, smiling, happy, and enjoying some fine wine, it seems likely He was a valued guest...

Years ago, one of my Young Life kids, when prompted to write down discussion questions about Jesus, raised this interesting one: *"We often talk about maturity in our faith, but shouldn't we be searching for and taking on a jovial spirit through Christ?"*

Do you ever personally think of Jesus as being "jovial" in spirit, a man quick to enjoy His earthly human life? Do you ever picture how the Savior's face would light up with laughter at the joking of one of His twelve goofy disciples? Have you ever considered that making water into wine portrayed the sort of heart that was quick to enjoy life and friendship? Have you ever contemplated what it means that Jesus so relished His life that He did this sort of miracle for His friends' wedding?

Naturally, I'd never want to propagate any portrait of our Savior that's lush-like or "drunken and disorderly." I don't think Jesus made this wine because His mind was hazy and wine-clouded or because of Mary's motherly pressure...

But I ***do*** think that followers of Jesus must have relish for this life we've been given for His Kingdom's wondrous purposes. Or, in the words of the writer Sheldon Vanauken, "The best argument for Christianity is Christians: their joy, their certainty, their completeness."

Can a watcher sense your life's passion, O Man? Can a looker-on note your sheer joy in living for Jesus? Or, in Vanauken's words that follow those last ones, is "the strongest argument against Christianity...also Christians"? Are we "sombre and joyless...self-righteous and smug in complacent consecration...narrow and repressive." I certainly hope not, O Men of God! Because this One we follow is all joy, all the time!

October 15 – John 3:22

Go out and experience His creation today

When we're outside in the beauties of Creation, our soul should be arrested by the power of our wondrous Creator-God. When we're standing in the presence of His wilds, we should always be reminded that a man's heart has wilds in it too. Basking in the glories of the sounds and smells and sights of His creative process should excite our humble following of Jesus. For when we give ourselves to One who so exerted His artist's hand upon Creation, don't we come to love His perfect power? Don't we sense the mighty calling on our lives whenever we acquaint ourselves with all the things He's capable of? Aren't we thrilled to walk our lives in narrowing lockstep, an ever-closer harmony, with the One who personally did all *this*? Isn't it glorious to know a little more about the Heart that holds our heart; to feel His power and beauty all around us?

I'm struck by this passage from Somerset Maugham: "[They] felt in themselves the wide distances, the tawny wastes, the snow-capped mountains of Castile, the sunshine and the blue sky, and the flowering plains of Andalusia. Life was passionate and manifold, and because it offered so much they felt a restless yearning for something more; because they were human they were unsatisfied; and they threw this eager vitality of theirs into a vehement striving after the ineffable."

O Men of God, we must acquaint ourselves with the "flowering plains," the "sunshine and the blue sky," the "snow-capped mountains." Our life will become ever more "passionate and manifold," especially when we know the heart of the One who's so truly "ineffable." Let's go into the "countryside" with our Messiah today and devote our "restless yearning" to its true Home, found in Him. May we find that we're "unsatisfied" *only* when we're not within His presence, *only* when our hearts crave more closeness.

Today, it's your job to go out into His wondrous Creation. Go and seek His heart out there, O Man. Find that wilderness-music that's hiding in your heart and always serving as the octave to His wild and magnificent Heart.

October 16 – John 4:1-26

Bridge divides with the living water

Wouldn't it be interesting to know how much we *don't* follow Jesus because of the ways we try to insulate our earthly lives? Don't you think we stupidly hem in much of His power by the way we isolate ourselves from others' selves? I don't think we comprehend how much we've bought into the social stratums forced upon us by the societies we live in. I don't think we want to know how far we fall away from the Kingdom-view in "grading" our, and other's, lives. Do we think that "living water" will impart itself if we aren't active in its distribution to other people? Have we bought into the lie that we're only called to our own "set," that we can personally dictate the groups we're called to? Didn't Jesus purposely sit down next to Jacob's well and wait upon the coming of this woman of a "lesser" race and gender? Didn't Jesus decide to grant amazing teaching to a Samaritan (*what?!*) woman (*No!*) who "happened" to come along His path? Didn't He then go on to teach her things of which He'd only formerly spoken to others in the confines of confusing pictures and parables? Doesn't Jesus show how we must be His living conduits *to everyone* concerning His life and living water?

In the foreword to his *Taking Men Alive*, Charles Trumbull tells a story that perfectly illustrates Jesus' heart for all sorts of people. He paints the picture of a prosperous white man in the early 1900's who was walking down a crowded street in Philadelphia. When confronted by a black street vendor who was speaking about Jesus, this white man stopped to talk to him further and to hear his story. He inquired about the man's apparent faith and the man pulled out the Gospel-tract that had changed his life eternally. Trumbull writes what happened in this way: "[He] saw on a flyleaf the words: 'Presented to _____ by J. Harvey Borton.' The railroad man's heart leaped within him, for he knew Mr. Borton intimately as one of the leading business men of Philadelphia who, only a few months before, had been taken Home to be with the Lord. Mr. Borton is known to a host of business leaders as well as earnest Christian people throughout America, having been one of the leading Christian laymen of this country. But he thought it worth while, in his busy life of large responsibilities, to lead an old black man and street vendor to Christ…"

O Men of God, there are no "large responsibilities" pending upon your life like the call to follow Jesus in this given day. There can be no earthly "boundaries," no such thing as personal "divides," if we actually want to make His name fully known. Will you bridge across the places such as "race," "class," even different "faiths," if it means that Jesus' life is preached to all kinds of people? Will you sit down on the edge of wells with lost people thirsting for the living water to be found within your heart?

Hear Trumbull's final words in his foreword: "We can all do this work *if we will.*"

October 17 – John 4:46-53

"Take His word" when hearing from the Word

If each of us would only take Jesus "at his word," we'd actually be the generation who finally sees "[His] kingdom come." We could cease to be the men who speak those words as if they're theory and become the men who trust them as a fact. We could wake up every morning with such certainty about the power of His hand that we'd fully *live* our human lives. We could go to bed without a single regret because we'd lived within the power of His Holy Spirit's leadings, all day, everyday.

O Men of God, are we man enough to take the Lord at His word and then "depart" for this day today? Do we trust that His word holds all earthly power *because of its heavenly power* and nothing on this earth can possibly stop it? Do you want to live your life without anxiety; without regret; fully certain of the certainties of Jesus? Are you up to trying a challenge for this day that'll give clear testimony to the strength of faith to be found in your heart?

Well, here it is: Open up the Word of God and start to read within the passage you've been reading lately on your own. Ask His Holy Spirit to illuminate *exactly* what He'd want you to "take away" from its words for this particular day. Then go ahead and "take it away." As in: Actually live it out. As in: Take that holy commandment, wholesome comfort, harsh correction, and "take Jesus at his word" all throughout the day. As in: Do not go halfway in actually doing what you read; actually do it with your whole heart and whole will. As in: Walk into your day with the exact same mindset as this Canan royal official, walking home to his formerly sick boy. As in: Trust the Lord's perspective and His promises and His power like there's nothing else in the world that matters to you.

Because there isn't anything else that actually matters, O Man. Jesus' word is all we need.

LIVE LIKE MEN

October 18 – John 6:53-66

Too late for desertion!

The problem when we live within a so-called "Christian country" is that desertions of our Lord mostly go unnoticed. When there's not a sense that living life for Jesus requires our whole lives, it's simply simpler to "blend in with other people." It's easier to keep up appearance of a "faith" when we're living in a place of largely nominal Sunday-morning faiths. When the call of Jesus to "follow" is taught only as intellectual assent to a "cause," deserting Him is as simple as a changed mind...

O Men of God, what are you following today: *The "Word of God made flesh" or a lukewarm religion-of-the-modern-mind?* Do you understand that One who'd speak of eaten flesh and drunken blood is demanding of your absolutely everything? Do you think that our ascriptions of a passing thought or word are terribly different from a bodily bold desertion of Him? Don't you think that it was grasping how Christ-following called for *all their life* that made these early disciples run away?

Consider how your "faith" would actually operate if it meant walking with Jesus during His three intense ministry-years. Would the way you live your life look any different if He stood right next to you, trying to make you His disciple? Would the power of your words be backed by dynamic action if He'd sent you out to minister like He did with the Twelve? Does His calling so consume you, like it did when He ascended, when the Twelve were all that were left of the original "inner circle"?

You and I are all that is left of it today, O Man! Along with the "brothers and sisters and mothers" He speaks of. (Matt. 12:50) We're the remnant who might bring the world to Him as long as we're daily *not* deserting, *not* posing, *not* pretending. We're the men, just like those original Twelve, tasked today with spreading wide the Gospel, "the words I have spoken to you." Yet we must so clearly define our lives by *His* life that our days are marked by devotion, not an instant of desertion. We must give Him everything today, not the scraps of busy schedules filled with earthly passing things of "importance." We must steel ourselves with truth from His Word so that we'll *know* whenever we're tempted to desert Him and His Gospel.

We cannot desert anymore, O Men. We've simply come too far for that now!

October 19 – John 8:2-11

Knowing the depths of our depravity

When we make ourselves aware of all the sin still entangling us, we draw ourselves closer to the Way of Jesus. It's in those moments of naked self-assessment concerning our present transgressions that we're blessed to be consciously bathed in His grace. Yet it's those moments when we find we're *dis*avowing our personal sin when the evil one laughs at our weak defenses. If we'd rather deflect our self-appraisals for the chance to judge another, we're genuflecting in Satan's direction…

The perspective of the Pharisees and teachers of the law was not changed by the call of Jesus to stop their needless judgment. They didn't slink away because of brutal words that were reminders of the Torah or the Nevi'im or the Ketuvim…

No, these men slowly peeled away because they became suddenly mindful of the sin within their own human hearts. These men couldn't continue to look with judgment on the naked crying woman once they'd nakedly looked at their own sinful lives. The "older ones" surely understood that they'd been equally guilty of past betrayals and past sins that were equally ruinous. The younger ones watched them walking away with rapt amazement until they understood why stoning her wouldn't help them…

O Men of God, it's been two weeks since we collectively challenged ourselves with the idea of a "day without judgment." How did that day go for you, back then? Where did you find your mind start going? Did you find that when you gave your mind to *not* expressing judgment that you became more mindful of how often you do judge others? Did you notice how your "judging reflex" seems to be as natural as the coming of your next breath? Did you contemplate how Jesus asks that our most natural reflex should actually be of expressing His love to others? Were you draw into His presence by the absence of your judgment: What sort of day was that for you?

Today, may we give some time to knowing how fraught we are with sin; be honest with yourself about your fallenness. Only when we learn how sinful our lives are can we fully embrace the grace of Jesus that's fully set us free. Only when we've embraced His perfect pools of grace can we then go out with His Good News and the forgiveness of our sins. Only when we strive to emulate the perfectly forgiving heart of Jesus do we really "get it" at all.

Do you think you "get it" yet, O Man? I hope we're starting to, at least, get there!

October 20 – John 9:1-39

Do we "perceive" and then worship?

The constant parade of Jesus-healing-a-blind-man interactions in the Gospels is no mere human coincidence. Jesus often healed all kinds of people with all kinds of terrible infirmities, yet we don't hear as much of them, do we? However, every time we turn around it seems like Jesus is spending time healing a blind man or a group of blind men! It might seem like He was partial to those in this particular predicament; that His coming occurred for ones such as this…

And that's just what He says here! Aren't those His exact words to this blind man? (v. 39) Doesn't He speak of giving sight unto the blind and also exposing all the blindness of the spiritually sighted? Doesn't He seem to set up allegorical situations with a healing like this, purposefully done in front of the faithless Pharisees? Don't we see this blind man "seeing" Him for the first time, while these other supposed "seers" are so blind that they're hateful?

O Men of God, if the Lord has given sight to your eyes, *you must be changed by this change within your life!* We can't claim "to see" if we're still ones so tied to human understandings that we don't fully see Jesus everyday. We haven't "changed," or been given sight, if our first inclination isn't like this healed man's – to constantly "worship" Him. If our lives don't look a shade different from back before we first "met Him," *I don't think we've really met Him yet, O Men!*

Jesus didn't deal in shadowy images or in less-than-stark reminders when it came to healing the blind men around Him. He didn't leave us with some double-speaking half-truths about what He "meant" in these constant references to vision and sight. In fact, more than once He's quoted quoting from Isaiah's prophecy: "they may be ever seeing but never perceiving." In fact, it sounds as if it's possible to "see" Him and yet walk along through life without perceiving Him at all…

O Men of God, has He changed us? Has He made us able to see?

O Men of God, has that *change* changed our lives? Do we now truly perceive Him?

October 21 – John 11:17-35

Open up your day to His emotions

Stoicism will never make us men of God's personal stamp; our actions must emanate from the living heart of Jesus. It's in our choosing to ally our feelings with the Lord's own feelings where we learn to better know His heart for others. It's when we read of He who "wept" that any picture of a stoic Jesus is left by the false-manhood wayside. It's when we read of One who knew He'd soon be raising His friend Lazarus – *and yet wept* – that we read of Jesus' soft heart.

Today, you will certainly read a tragic story in your local newspaper: *Be affected by that story you're reading!* Today, you'll see a person who's dealing with a terrible personal sorrow: *Be affected by their personal sorrow with them!* Today, you'll sense a private hurt that's quietly gnawing on somebody's soul: *Be affected with them in its midst!* Today, you'll live your life within a broken hurting world that needs Jesus: *Be affected as Jesus was affected!*

Let's learn the heart of "Jesus wept" today, O Men. Give Him your emotions and let Him show you more of His love.

October 22 – John 13:1-5

If Jesus did this, we must also

Did you notice this: "Jesus knew that the Father had put all things under his power, and that he had come from God and was returning to God; <u>**so**</u> he got up from the meal, took off his outer clothing…and began to wash his disciples' feet…"? It doesn't read: "Jesus knew that the Father had put all things under his power, and that he had come from God and was returning to God; ***but, in spite of this*** he got up from the meal, took off his outer clothing…and began to wash the disciples' feet…"

If you ever need a picture of the One you desire to serve, look no further than this picture of the servant-Christ. See Him rise up from the table, stripping Himself of His personal dignity; then stooping down at His embarrassed disciples' dirty feet. Watch Him take their nasty smelly sandals off with His weathered hands and the way He lavished love by this tender footwashing. Feel the way He took His time on each foot, how He gently washed and dried them, how He set them softly on the floor. Think of how the awkward quiet slowly spread across the room as these men sat silent, waiting for their coming turn. Imagine how they must've glanced from side to side to catch each other's eye, wondering why the Lord was doing this for them…

O Men of God, if you're carrying any thoughts of self-importance, it's time to rid yourself of such useless thoughts. It's time we recognize that nothing short of self-abasing service is an actual following after *this* Jesus. It's time we shed all mantels of self-thinking, self-promoting, self-serving; any vestige of the former sinful self. It's time – *if we truly want to follow after* One *who washed feet* – that we learn to love and serve the world likewise.

Listen to these words from Henry Scougal: "Perfect love is a kind of self-dereliction, a wandering out of ourselves; it is a kind of voluntary death…" O Man of God, may you use today to serve your Savior through the self-dereliction of His perfect love for His friends. Wander out of yourself; give yourself to His death; strip and stoop down to be a footwasher for other people. May we learn to make ourselves less than nothing. Otherwise, who do we purport to serve?

October 23 – John 18:1-8

Christly power is yours

Modern man has ripped down age-old battlements and built defenses in the guise of rabid packs of lawyers. Modern man has shunned the "backwardness" of watery castle moats in favor of buffers of his ready liquid holdings. Modern man has lost his touch upon those weapons with which ancient man provided and, instead, become a "good provider." Modern man has cast off strength for his security; his power for possessions; manly might for measurable returns…

And what's our reward for this behavior, O Modern Men? Unto what have we striven with our modern strength? Have we come this far to find ourselves the weakest, flabbiest, softest men the world may have ever known? Have we traded on our birthright for the chance to die as rich men; do we "hold [our] manhoods cheap"? Do we honor God by making ourselves less than He intended, simply because it's the pattern of our modern age?

May it not be so for us, O Men of God! May it not be so for men such as you and I! May we know the strength of He whose words were like a swinging axe in the presence of these oncoming soldiers! May we feel the power of our High Priest who'd stand before armored detachments and speak mightily to them, "I am he"! May we speak His name with selfsame shows of Holy Spirit-might that can topple every sort of human might and power! May we be the men whose power isn't meted out by modern "manly" measures such as fleeting wealth or possessions!

You and I are greater than those measures, O Men. For we're the men of Jesus, aren't we? We're the "few," the "happy few," the holy "band of brothers" who comprise today's Disciples of Jesus Christ!

Is that the kind of man you are today? Only Today will give the full answer.

October 24 – John 20:24-29

Knowing the sources where your doubt starts

There's no denying that we each have been infected with the faulty sorts of thinking that prevail in our modern world. We can't ignore that we've become the products of our current place and time; that the things we see and read have actually shaped us. We don't know how much the world's skepticisms and its so-called "reason" have been meshed with our minds' own thinking. We don't know how far the plotting plans of Satan have encroached upon our faith until it's truly tested…

Thomas didn't start out his journey alongside Jesus hoping to become the only one who eventually doubted in the end. In fact, back in John 11, when Jesus started off for Bethany, Thomas said: "Let us also go, that we may die with him." So how did this one disciple transit from that earlier statement of faith to the statement in our passage: "Unless I see the nail marks…"? And, more importantly, how will we unite our private profanations of love with a true faith when it's really required?

The answer: *We must come to know the places where the evil one has already sown his doubts in our minds' thinking.* We must sit in contemplation of our own personal world-view and set it against the truth of Jesus. We can't let the silent creep of worldly doubts and "rationalism" destroy the only thing that's actually rational. We must seek out the places in our minds where we've already let the world's ways dictate our way through this life with Jesus.

O Man of God, what do you believe? Have you "not seen and yet have believed"? Have you wed your life's thinking with the thinking of the Christ so that nothing ever can come between you? Have you pored over the scriptures so that you can "demolish arguments and every pretension that sets itself up against [His] knowledge"? Do you know Jesus in such a way that real conviction has replaced initial commitment; that certainty has displaced questioning? Do you feel the humble comfort of great knowledge of His words so that the world's words sound like nonsense? Can you quickly sense the presence of *un*truth in what you read and see and hear; are you quick to remove it?

O Men of God, let's run from doubt today. That's the stuff of much weaker men. You and I are men who've seen what He can do; what He's already done for us; we're men purchased with those gruesome nail marks.

LIVE LIKE MEN

October 25 – John 21:1-19

From the Gospels to Acts

Simon Peter is my hero *not* because he walked on water or because he was the first to speak of Jesus as Christ. He isn't my hero because he was filled with such a "passion" or because he was a member of the most inner-circle "favored three." I don't admire his cutting off of Malchus' ear; that he apparently had a knack for being a Galilean commercial fisherman. I'm also not impressed that he drew Jesus' strongest rebuke or was present for the Lord's best personal teachings…

No, Peter is my hero because *Jesus* allowed his walking on the water and his speaking to His Christhood. He's my hero because *Jesus* made use of his burning passion and showed Peter how to draw in other disciples. He's my hero because *Jesus* taught him how to "turn the other cheek" in order to be a proper "fisher of men." He's my hero because he learned to speak with *Jesus'* own words whenever he sensed the Lord was calling for it…

Have you realized that Peter on this Galilee shore becomes the Peter found on Pentecost *only* because of Jesus and the Spirit? Do you know that what was separating "Gospel Peter" from "Acts Peter" was a total submission to the Way? In this passage, when the Lord is reinstating Peter three times, He's also giving Peter His (as in Jesus') life's work. He's saying to him, "Soon I will be absent from you in the bodily sense but, Peter, you're finally ready now to 'follow Me.'"

O Men of God, these calls to "feed my lambs," "take care of my sheep," and "feed my sheep" are our calls for this particular day. No one else will feed the sheep unless you and I feed the sheep; the book of Acts is written by actual actions. If we let ourselves grow apathetic when we're given Jesus' Great Commission, we're making ourselves faithless in the process. If we let our lives go past without pursuing others for Him, we're not pursuing Jesus for ourselves. After all, Peter might've let his own three-part betrayal be the ending of his following Jesus, mightn't he? He also might've let this three-part reinstatement go slack through a chasing after worldly things, right?

But, no, Peter gave the rest of his earthly life to the One whose love was so amazing that He'd draw Him back into this communion. Peter wouldn't rest until he'd made the Lord's name known to every man who didn't know Him; He committed to the Commision.

May we be the men who never rest a moment once the charge is given; men who give our all that men might live. May we be the men who "feed His sheep" with both our lives and lifestyle, our actions and our words in this world. May we stand upon this beach with Jesus and Peter, seeing the way the power of Jesus washed over *old* Peter. May we enter Acts with eyes to see how Jesus will use the men who are fully committed to His calling and listening for His Spirit daily.

Are you ready for the book of Acts, O Men? Are you ready for some real action?

October 26 – Acts 1:4-14

Our action must begin with prayer

There's been no change in the plan since Jesus' ascension into heaven; His earthly disciples must actually *do something*. They must know they're called to be His "witnesses in Jerusalem, and in all Judea and Samaria, and to the ends of the earth." They must know the Gospel only goes as far as His disciples are willing to go; so-called "witnesses" must bear witness. They must know that "asking Jesus into my heart" is only where this thing starts; "being saved" is not the journey's end. They must know that standing wonderingly upon a hillside looking into the sky is *not* the calling we've been called to. They must know that faith in Jesus requires faith in Jesus' Plan; that we're actually called to be about His personal work. They must know they're not sufficient for the task that's set before them; they personally don't have what it's going to take. They must throw their lot, and all their sin, and all their personal weakness, unto Jesus and then take up His "yoke" daily.

O Men of God, how can we begin upon a task when we already know its end-goals are absolutely impossible? How can we go from our own standing out upon the place of His ascension to the very "ends of the earth" today? How can we do the sorts of things He'll certainly ask for; how will we become "those sort of men" for Jesus' sake? How do daunted disciples become the mighty men of God today; how will we become like the original Disciples?

Well, we'll start right where they started! We'll "join together constantly in prayer." We'll bathe this day in supplication; we won't take a step until we've brought our hearts before Him….

O Man of God, be acquainted with the fact that Jesus will use your life if you'll let your life be used by Him. Be reminded that the Gospel only goes where each man takes it; that there are still "ends of the earth" to be reached for Him. Are you ready to go out and spread the Good News of the Savior; do you want to be so utilized for the Kingdom? Would you have yourself become a modern Peter, James or John in the spreading of Jesus' Gospel?

Then pray about it all throughout the day today. Begin to begin your Book of Acts, O Man.

October 27 – Acts 1:15-26

Men in this "lineage of truth" must know the truth

The lineage of Jesus extends through history because these men were joined together as the "witness…of his resurrection." After they'd joined "together constantly in prayer," it was Peter that was led to speak of this particular vocation. It was Peter who explained how subtle scriptures were foreshadowings of things that had – *and were yet to* – come to pass. It was Peter who arose, not with passion, but with Jesus' perfect poise, to speak of the need for an apostle-replacement. It was Peter who elucidated how important it'd be that they'd all seen everything Jesus had done and spoken. It's amazing how they all so trusted in God's perfect planning that they'd simply cast lots and trust Him…

You and I are brothers in this lineage of Jesus' men; we are, in today's era, bearers of the Gospel of Jesus. We're the ones entrusted with the "witness" just like the ones who drew lots in that "upstairs" room, back then. We're not called to be "good Christians," but to be the Body of Christ, for the benefit of this world we've inherited. We're meant to further everything that we've been handed; we're meant to carry on the propagation of the Great Plan. We're graced to bear the knowledge of His amazing grace and asked to spread that grace by our daily manly conduct in this world. We're meant to live as if our Savior and His words are the only meaning of our absolutely everything…

O Men of God, where do we begin once we've "joined together constantly in prayer" for our personal direction? How do we learn to discern what steps to take; how will we become like Peter in his bold first directive?

First and foremost, Peter deeply knew the scriptures to the point where he could point to such a subtlety as this one. Over time spent with the Word Himself, Peter had accustomed how he spoke to the way that Jesus Himself spoke the word. Jesus always used the primacy of God's Holy Word as the starting point for daily godly discernment. And thus Peter, if he'd follow after Jesus – "feed his sheep" – knew he'd need fulsome knowledge of the Word.

So let's give extended time to the scriptures this day. Let's pore over the word so we can be outpoured.

October 28 – Acts 2:1-4

Desiring the Holy Spirit's fire

The Holy Spirit's power is the power with which Jesus was raised to life on the original Easter morning. The Holy Spirit was the undergirding power that spoke and loved and touched and healed through the person of Jesus. The Holy Spirit was the reason John the Baptist was a man so full of courage that he was able to prepare the Lord's way. The Holy Spirit was the one to "come upon" the virgin Mary and create salvation's seed within her virgin womb. The Holy Spirit was the One that "lifted" the prophet Ezekiel to and fro, taking him to places of His own choosing. The Holy Spirit came in "double portion" upon Elisha's life because of his watchful presence at the taking-up of Elijah. The Holy Spirit "came upon David in power" and provided him with succor, strength and manly steel for his life's battles. The Holy Spirit even flooded moments of the life of Saul for the purposes of God's greater Purpose in his life.

O Men of God, Holy Spirit-power is actually impossible without the Holy Spirit's presence in our daily lives. The Holy Spirit's presence is impossible without repentance and obedience; He's "given to those who obey him." (Acts 5:32) If we cannot point to readily apparent "spiritual gifts" in our lives, do we really have the Holy Spirit within us? (1 Cor. 12:1-11) If we cannot see a marked growth in Spiritual fruit within us, do we bear the Holy Spirit in our hearts? (Gal. 5:22,23),

O Man of God, you must ever yearn for greater stores of Holy Spirit-power in your life and faith in Jesus. There's no limit to the things that we'll accomplish in His name if we're filled up with His righteous guiding power for us.

Today, let's ask the Lord to fill our spirits with more of the Holy Spirit so that we'll be the men unconquerable for His Kingdom-work. Let's sit in perfect silence, asking for His manifest presence, knowing He's faithful to provide ever more of Himself. We can't live this life for Him as it's intended to be lived if we're not pursuing more and more and more of the Spirit. Your life will be one marked as great or nothing – used or useless – full or empty – directly in proportion to the Holy Spirit.

O Man of God, do you want Him today? Then ask and desire for ever more of Him!

October 29 – Acts 2:14-39

Can you explain the "whole story"?

All our talk of "faith" and "following Jesus" and of "knowing Him" are *nothing* if we can't quickly explain what we mean. If we can't get rid of words and speech that sound like secret brotherhoods, how will we attract outsiders to Jesus? If we can't succinctly speak of everything the Gospel actually means, how will we explain it if/when we're asked? If we can't explain it to ourselves, we're deluding ourselves in saying that we're ready to "share Christ" with other people!

Below, I'd ask us each to write out your own version of Peter's Gospel sermon *without copying from Peter's Gospel sermon*. Or, in other words, if a person walked up to you today and said, "Explain your faith," *what would you actually say*? Can you paint the picture from Jesus' first Coming to His Ascension; from the Cross – to the Grave – unto Eternal Life? Can you make it sound intelligible without using any Christian-speak; are you a ready bearer of the Word of Life?

You have this page and the next one to write it out. Let's hear your witness to the Good News, O Man:

LIVE LIKE MEN

October 30 – Acts 2:41-47

Modern vs. Apostolic Church

Have you ever wondered how the Modern Church is different from the way the Apostolic Church was, "back in the day"? Have you ever wondered how we might "get back" to acting like the Church of Acts acted in its own time and place?

Well, let's ask ourselves some important questions, first: Is the Modern Church devoting all its energies to the "apostles' teaching," both in knowledge and by direct action? Is the Modern Church consumed with "fellowship, the breaking of bread, and prayer" as being absolutely foundational? Is the Modern Church so filled with "wonders and miraculous signs" that all its many members are "filled with awe" constantly? Is the Modern Church a place where men and woman are "together and [have] everything in common," materialistically? Would the members of the Modern Church be ready to be "selling their possessions," and to give "to anyone" who was in need? Would the Modern Church believe our Christly calling is a worthwhile reason for meeting together "every day"? Is the Modern Church a place that's populated by "glad and sincere hearts, praising God" constantly, all the time? Is the Modern Church "enjoying the favor of all the people," adding daily "those who [are] being saved"?

Well, ask yourself some important questions also, O Man: Are *you* devoting all your fullest energies and thoughts to the "apostles' teaching" through knowledge and direct action? Are *you* a man consumed with "fellowship, the breaking of bread, and prayer" as being absolutely foundational? Are *you* so amazed by the "wonders and miraculous signs" in your life that you're constantly "filled with awe" about Jesus? Are *you* a man who so believes in your convictions that your faith is lived "together," and sharing "everything in common"? Would *you* ever be the sort of man who's "selling [his] possessions," ready to give "to anyone" who's personally in need? Are *you* one who sees his calling as a worthy reason for an "every day," every minute, sort of Jesus-following? Is *your* heart a heart that's "glad and sincere," a heart that's "praising God" constantly for the love that's been shown to you? Are *you* "enjoying the favor of all the people" and are *you* the sort of man reaching out to "those who [are] being saved"?

May we never forget: "you are the body of Christ, and each one of you is a part of it" – *you are the Modern Church, O Man!*

So how are you doing as you start this day?

LIVE LIKE MEN

How's the Modern Church doing, because of your place in it?

October 31 – Acts 3:1-10

God only wants the whole of you

This man was carried to the temple-gate for another day of begging for some money that would hopefully feed his hungry belly. He probably didn't have any expectation that the power of God might be lurking in the fabric of this particular day. He didn't expect to go to bed that night with legs that actually worked; to be "walking and jumping" in the temple courts. He simply wanted enough money to buy a chunk of bread, maybe even some wine, that would keep him till tomorrow's begging…

Peter and John walked to the temple with a plan to pray to their Savior, their Lord, their best friend, Jesus, the Christ. They had every expectation that the power of God was *always* lurking in the fabric of their day and their "normal" lives. They expected to go to bed that night absolutely spent from all the labors to which Jesus Himself would call their lives. They didn't care about some "silver or gold" or bread or drink or dress or anything else; they were focused only on Today…

O Man of God, whether you've got a lot of "silver or gold" or not, what Jesus really wants from your life today is **you**. He's asking everyday that you and I would focus everyday – *every Today* – on the tasks and plans He has for us. Whether we're off to work or prayer time, He's asking you and I that everything should focus on Him and His coming Kingdom. Everything, whether silver, gold, bread, drink or dress, should be given into the keeping of His all-capable hand.

Today, you and I will have a day as large or as small as the way we view our Lord's view of this particular day. Since the "Kingdom of God" indwells your inner man, don't you think this day could even hold great miracles for His purposes? Don't we realize that the power living in Peter and John, back then, is exactly the same power that's in us right now? Shouldn't we allow the Holy Spirit to do His thing through each of us, just as He did through our spiritual forefathers? May we look upon this day with eyes of sheer giddy excitement, knowing the ways the Lord would like to use us fully. May we become the men of great Kingdom-utility because we're yearning that His power might flow straight out of us.

God doesn't care about "silver or gold." What He wants is you. Today.

November 1 – Acts 4:1-13

A Courageous Heart

This passage gives a pattern for the way the Lord will use the lives of men who are actually obedient to His commandments. When a man will give his life unto the *doing* of God's will, God will always arm that man with strength and a firm resolve. John and Peter used their trip to the temple for the healing of that disabled man we read about yesterday (Acts 3:1-10). Then, when a crowd of people gathered around them in utter amazement at the healing, they used that opportunity to speak of Jesus (Acts 3:11-26). And then, when they were confronted and arrested and put on trial for their actions, Peter used that chance to extol Jesus further (Acts 4:8-12). Wherever they were personally placed, whatever sort of crowd they had, Jesus' disciples made use of their circumstances for God's purposes.

Peter and John had both been present on that mountainside above the Sea of Galilee and heard Jesus' clear teaching: "Let your light shine before men in such a way that they may see your good works, and glorify your Father who is in heaven." So, when they encountered that handicapped beggar outside the temple, they shed Jesus' light upon the life of that particular man. And now, ever true to His word to them, Jesus fills them with such Holy Spirit-power that these "rulers" are "astonished."

Is anyone "astonished" by your "courage" about Jesus? Are men amazed by "Christ in you," O Man? When a person looks at your life, do they see Jesus' light shining in your every action, your every spoken word? Do they see an "unschooled, ordinary" man whose life is overpowered by the complete power of the Holy Spirit? Would they be able to "take note" that a man who lives like you must've been a man who's actually "been with Jesus"?

Have you actually "been with Jesus," O Man? Is it His light that's shining from your life? Do you give men opportunities to "glorify your Father who is in heaven" by the way you live your day-to-day? Do you make use of your circumstances, placement, and perspective to bring glory to the Lord by your lifestyle? Do you stand before the "rulers" of this world with an inviolable spirit through the power of your Savior's Spirit?

Peter and John were undaunted by anything. May nothing daunt us in our day today.

November 2 – Acts 4:23-31

Gather to pray for boldness

Imagine being seized or imprisoned or on trial or "on warning" for your speaking of the name of Jesus. Imagine yourself standing in the presence of earthly "rulers," being told "not to speak or teach in the name of Jesus" ever again. Imagine your feelings as you'd walk back outside those prison walls and take some deep breaths of the free fresh air. Imagine how you'd finish out that day; how you'd rise the following day; what your next day's prayers might actually be. Would you pray that God remove every obstacle standing in your path; that He might cushion you from future similar trouble? Would you pray that He'd give total protection from antagonism; that He'd grant you safety for your life?

Or, like these men did, would you be rejoicing that your activity for the Gospel had been rewarded with some punishment? Would you lift the rulers' threats before the Lord – not for their removal – but for greater stores of "boldness," moving forward?

Today, you and I must gather with our dearest disciple-brethren for some times of prayer for greater boldness. We must ask the Lord to "stretch out [His] hand to heal and perform miraculous signs and wonders through the name of" Jesus. We must gather to unite our minds and spirits with the power of the Holy Spirit, asking to be likewise "shaken." We must pray that we'd be "filled with the Holy Spirit" to speak "the word of God boldly" to whomever we should meet today.

O Men of God, pray for greater boldness. Pray for God to shake the room you're currently sitting in. Pray that you might be *so* filled with the Holy Spirit that you're actually dangerous to the darkness in the world. Pray that you might unite your brotherly hearts in the mission and message of our Lord and Savior, Jesus Christ. May we be the modern brothers who rejoice that we're of some use to Him today, like our brothers in the Book of Acts. May we be the kind of men who are unhindered by the trials and tribulations of our daily troubles. May we shake off anything that tries to stop us from greater shows of boldness for the sake of Jesus' coming Kingdom.

Join your brothers for this task today. You and I are men who'll stop at nothing for our Lord.

November 3 – Acts 4:36-37

Giving so it hurts

Only when we hold all earthly possessions with open hands do we make ourselves ready for a truer trust in Jesus. Only when we fully divorce our worth from any material consideration can we be considered ready for the work ahead. Only when we learn to claim nothing as our own do we understand the "emptying" Jesus did for our sake (Phil. 2:7). Only when we don't weigh our pilgrim's way with idiot encumbrances are we simply ready to "follow Me," wherever He leads.

O Man of God, put your life and "worth" and assets and retirement plans against the Early Church's view of such things. Do we not betray our "treasure" destination when we're such comfort-seekers on the temporal plane? Are we "[laying] up for ourselves treasures upon earth, where moth and rust destroy, and where thieves break in and steal"? Or are we "[laying] up for ourselves treasures in heaven, where neither moth nor rust destroys, and where thieves do not break in and steal"?

Well, which is it, O Man of God? Be honest: *Where's your treasure?* Would you share the portion you've been given so that "no needy persons" could be found among the Body of Christ today? Would you sell a field and readily bring the money to the Lord's feet, uncaring for any earthly acknowledgement? Would you sell off all you have if He'd actually ask you to do that; would you give it all for the One who gave His all for you?

Here's today challenge: Give. And, O Men of God, give mightily. Only you can know to whom or to where He'd ask you to give it; only you can know if you'll really do it. Will you give – *for Him* – today? Will you give – *for Him* – sacrificially? The answer to these questions might actually point to the place in which your treasures are laid up: on earth or in heaven?

O Man, will you do this one thing?

You have the rest of this day to choose.

November 4 – Acts 5:12-15

Revisiting our September 16th prayer

Seven weeks ago, we read of people bringing their sickly friends before Jesus for His miracles of healing. We read of how they'd beg "to let them touch even the edge of his cloak, and all who touched him were healed" immediately. Then we talked of how the Lord actually promised His disciples that they'd do "even greater things, because I am going to the Father." On that day, you were tasked with praying for the Lord to make this promise true in your life; to truly trust that promise given to you.

Did you pray that prayer on that day? And have you given it further thought since? Have you noticed any progress in the pattern of your life, any change in your perspective on His Holy Spirit? Have you paid attention to the burgeoning power found in Simon Peter's life; how the Lord made good on His promises to him? Did you notice how the people in our passage didn't ask for his cloak; they were fully content with only his "shadow"? Don't you think that Peter's resolute belief in the promise of Jesus' words was the beginning of that changing process? Don't you think that he was ready to be given more when he started believing that the promises were really real? Don't you think that his reliance on the Lord then led to greater acts of obedience that then led to more faith? Wouldn't you and I be bolstered if our faith meant actual action that then led to faith/action that led to even more of each?

O Men of God, every ounce of everything happening in this passage is a real possibility for you in this day today. There's nothing removing you from the power of Peter's "shadow" except the absence of your faith in Jesus Christ. If we made our prayer on September 16th for greater stores of power, have we found those greater stores of power? Did we pray with eager expectation to become like Peter was, armed with faith and with the Holy Spirit? Have we followed through with actions that would match our prayers' request; belief carried out in true practical obedience? Have we truly trusted the Lord will use a "man such as I" for the spreading of His truth throughout this world?

O Man of God, where's your power? Is His power flowing through your life? If the answer is yes, pray for more and more and more and more; if it's not, let's repeat the September 16th prayer. May we be the men who read the Book of Acts with every part of ourselves believing it could be so within us. For it is so already, O Men. Let's let it be so now today.

November 5 – Acts 5:27-42

Letting nothing stop us because nothing can stop us

If we don't experience similar fruitbearing to what the Early Church experienced, there might be two possible explanations. Firstly, perhaps we don't believe Gamaliel's words; perhaps we've lost our "Holy Spirit swagger" in following Jesus. Perhaps we don't believe that since our efforts come from God Himself, "you will not be able to stop these men." Perhaps our lives are thwarted by nagging doubts about the actual potency of power that's at work in us…

Or, secondly, our efforts might be hampered by an active undercutting by the evil one's minions. I believe that every time our faith feels "taken out of the game," that's an instance of his subtly conniving presence. And I believe that we ascribe too much of the challenges in our life to "that's just life" and not enough to Satan's work against us. I believe when we allow ourselves to be taken out of Jesus' presence, we're letting Satan take the day.

O Men of God, look at how the apostles were arrested and berated and then beaten for the sake of the Gospel. And what did they do about their "suffering"? Didn't they begin actively "rejoicing" in it? Didn't they "rejoice and [were] glad, for [their] reward in heaven is great," just like Jesus promised them up upon the mountainside? Didn't they jump up and down because they'd been allowed to suffer for the Savior who Himself was made "perfect through suffering"?

And did you notice the results, directly after? Did you see Gamaliel's words ringing true? Did you see how these men "never stopped teaching and proclaiming the good news that Jesus is the Christ"? Can't you feel how we are progeny of the persecuted apostles who weren't able to be stopped by anyone at all? Do you know that you're the offspring of disciples who let nothing ever stop them in pursuing Jesus?

So how will we live today, O Men of God? Will we live with stalwart spirits, unafraid? Will we know that there's nothing in all the world, nothing in Satan's arsenal, that's equal to our living Savior? Will we rejoice when we're troubled and in "suffering," for we know that He's in us, winning the day on our behalf? "You will not be able to stop these men." Let's live from those words today.

November 6 – Acts 6:1-6

Are you meant to head in a new direction?

One of you that's reading from this page today is meant to take a challenge that'll change his life enormously, eternally. I don't mean to say I know exactly what that direction might entail, but I firmly believe *that* man knows what I'm talking about. I believe he has been hearing from the Scriptures and his ponderings and the Spirit of a profound new idea for him. I believe that God is stirring some direction in his mind that'll cause a new direction in his whole life. When the Grecian Jews complained about the distribution of their daily bread, the apostles sat up and took notice. No, they didn't redirect their own ministries; they felt the clear leading to appoint others to this needed task. They took the time to let the course of current events, and also the way the Lord led them, decide the direction of the whole Church's future. They began a new ministry with men called to do something fresh and utterly different (which also happened to be highly important.)

Today's challenge isn't meant to be a challenge met by every man reading this; we're all called to follow Jesus differently. Some of us are meant to do the very thing we're currently doing; some of us are meant to be pushed in brand new directions.

But for those of you reading from these words and knowing there's something new for you, it's actually time now to do it! It's time to cease with thinking about things "inside the box"; it's time to follow Jesus' leading in this brand new direction for you. It's time to be the man "full of faith and of the Holy Spirit" who'll do amazing new things for the Kingdom of God. It's time to take the steps that only He can supernaturally orchestrate; to listen to the quiet sound of His perfect leading.

Are you that man today, O Man? Where do you know He's leading you somewhere new?

November 7 – Acts 6:8-15

What does your face look like?

A man consumed with living life from the power of the Holy Spirit will be a man *changed* by the power of the Holy Spirit. He'll find himself transfigured by His proximity to the Transfigured Christ; his whole appearance utterly changed by Jesus. He'll forever be marked by his tranquility and trust in the perfect providence of God within the conduct of his daily life. He'll be absolutely unafraid when another might find there's no recourse but terror; he'll be a bulwark within the midst of other men. He'll be like an anchor to the souls of people tossed and thrown around by the stormy seas of life, swirling around them. He'll command the winds and seas of life, "Peace, be still!"; his face will be "the face of an angel," like Stephen's.

O Man of God, have the power and peace of Jesus *so* changed your inner life that your outer life looks absolutely tranquil? Would another look to your calming presence as a place of Jesus' presence and feel the peace of Jesus through you? Do you think that His remaking of your person has extended to the way you physically appear to other people? Do you feel your face could readily be described like Stephen's was; that your visage glows with Jesus alone?

Today, take the time to ask a friend for an answer to this question: "What do you think other people see when they see me?" If we want to represent our Lord in everything we're doing, we must know what image of Him we're daily giving off. You and I must know if we're spreading pictures of a holy angelic One or an angry spiteful taskmaster. We must align our spirits with the Spirit of the Living God so that we personally have the "face of an angel" for the people we meet.

What does your face look like to other people? Well, you'll find out today, O Man.

November 8 – Acts 7:37-60

Loving our enemies

Even as he died, Stephen practiced true obedience to the commandments and the spirit of his Savior. He didn't let his "feelings" or "personal hardships" dictate how he'd personally behave; he was faithful to the very end. Even as the hurled stones were smashing against his flesh and bone, Stephen heard the distant words of His Savior speaking forth. Even as he gasped from lungs that were collapsing, Stephen heard the words from He who'd hung upon a Roman cross…

The command from the Sermon on the Mount: "You have heard that it was said, 'You shall love your neighbor, and hate your enemy.' But I say to you, *love your enemies, and pray for those who persecute you* in order that you may be sons of your Father who is in heaven; for He causes His sun to rise on the evil and the good, and sends rain on the righteous and the unrighteous. For if you love those who love you, what reward have you? Do not even the tax-gatherers do the same? And if you greet your brothers only, what do you do more than others?" (Matthew 5:43-47) And, of course, the words of Jesus on the cross: "Father, forgive them, for they do not know what they are doing." (Luke 23:34) Now look at Stephen's final cry on the day of being stoned: "Lord, do not hold this sin against them…"

O Men of God, if we want to follow Jesus, we must learn obedience to this impossibly challenging "love/pray" commandment. We must learn not only to "turn the other cheek," we must *also* take this extra step directly afterward. We must act out of our avowed love for Jesus in the way that we're available to do crazy deeds for His purposes. Even if it means we're down upon our knees for an enemy's sake, that's the call and the commandment of Jesus for us…

Today, in whatever situation you find you're facing, start to learn to love and pray for your enemies in all you do. You'll never personally scratch the surface of the Savior's heart for others until you've learned to love the truly unlovable ones around you. You and I can never draw closer to this Savior when we're harboring untold hatreds for another person. We must never claim to follow after Jesus if we're not willing to reach out with His love to those our heart actually wants to hate.

Today, pray for those ones in your life. His heart will teach you how to love them.

November 9 – Acts 8:1-8

Wherever He takes you, be His there

Jesus' final words to His disciples were a promise that they'd serve as His "witnesses" all over the world, including "to the ends of the earth." (Acts 1:8) Yet He didn't give them a "strategy," other than when asking that they "not leave Jerusalem" until "the Holy Spirit comes." Perhaps the disciples thought the Holy Spirit's coming would acquaint them with the forward-moving "game plan" for world-change. Perhaps they thought the Spirit's power might so arm their arms with strength that they'd finally throw off mighty Rome's yoke. Perhaps they hoped that speaking "in Jerusalem, and in all Judea and Samaria, and to the ends of the earth" would be an easy task for them to perform. Perhaps they thought they'd have the chance to choose just how the Gospel went forth; that His Plan would actually match up with their plan…

Instead, the Gospel started going to those aforementioned places through the proddings of their brutal persecutions. (Did you notice how the "persecution broke out…at *Jerusalem*," causing the believers to be "scattered through *Judea* and *Samaria*"?) Since they were men who'd followed the One who'd Himself been sent to the cross, it was now time to "take up [their] cross" for His sake. Since they were men who'd seen Him "teaching as he made his way" (Luke 13:22), they also "preached the word wherever they went."

O Man of God, every day of your life you have the opportunity to use your life for the purposes of Jesus. Whether you're living in earthly comfort, or are "scattered" and "destroyed," you're still a man who's called an Apostle of the Kingdom. Whether you're one who's been sent out at his leisure, or are forced by outside forces, you're still called to go out. Whether you're in Jerusalem, Judea, Samaria, or the ends of the earth, you're not exempt from the call of Jesus to GO.

Where are you going today, O Man of God? Where are you personally called to be "preaching"? What is the message that your life and faith are speaking about; what "word" are you sharing "wherever you go"? Are you feeling your apostleship (your title as one "sent out") every moment of your every day? Are you using each and every earthly opportunity so that you might be truly useful for the spreading of the Gospel?

Do you want to be used today? Then preach the word wherever you're going!

November 10 – Acts 8:26-35

A life of the Spirit and our action

Reading through this narrative gives a picture of the direct interrelationship between Jesus' voice and our physical action. If you didn't notice the way the plot was interwoven with His "call" and then the "go," here's the bulletpoints to reflect upon:

1. The "angel of the Lord" commands movement (8:26)
2. Philip "started out" and "met an Ethiopian eunuch" (8:27)
3. "The Spirit told Philip, 'Go…'" (8:29)
4. "Philip ran up to the chariot" (8:30a)
5. Clearly, God had led the man to be "reading Isaiah the prophet." (8:30b)
6. Philip asks, "Do you understand what you are reading?" (8:30c)
7. "Philip began with that very passage of scripture and told him the good news…" (8:35)
8. "Philip baptized him." (8:38)
9. The "Spirit of the Lord suddenly took Philip away…" (8:39)

O Men of God, even if we're personally preaching, discipling and baptizing, we're absolutely nothing without the living Jesus in our midst. All the brilliance of our strategies and programs for doing "outreach" are utterly worthless without leadings from the Holy Spirit. Even if you have charisma and "the words all come out right," these are pointless if they're not met with His power. It's the perfect interweaving of the Spirit *with* our plans and actions that results in Holy-Spirit-fruit for the Kingdom.

Do you think you're currently living with the mindful Holy-Spirit-listening heart exhibited by Philip in this episode? Are you so in touch with what the Holy Spirit's doing that His doings are the doings of your day, everyday? Do you listen for His Plan whenever you're making your day's plans; do you "run up" to the places where He'd want to send you? Do you use the subtle openings ("Do you understand what you are reading?") when God makes them clear for your personal use? Do you long to share the "good news" when you're clearly led to do so; do you give your time and energy to this, first?

Well, let's make that our whole plan today. May we listen/do, listen/do, listen/do…

LIVE LIKE MEN

November 11 – Acts 9:1-20

What has your "conversion" accomplished?

Plain and simple, have you ever spoken the Gospel of Jesus from start to finish…with *anyone*…*ever*? Have you ever used your spoken words to tell a person that He "is the Son of God"; that He's changed your life entirely? Have you ever been "Christ's ambassador"; do you know that He's personally given you "the ministry of reconciliation"? Do you think your "Christian lifestyle" will suffice to spread the Gospel when Jesus clearly says to use your mouth? Do you think you're living from His complete plan for you when your faith feels so completely comfortable, most of the time, or *all of the time*? Do you think that there are "others" who are "called to that sort of thing," that you're "more the 'silent example' type of Christian"?

Well, the time has come for that thinking to go. The days of silence must cease now, O Men. If we'd claim to know Him (like we say we do), we must *say we do* by our actions **and** our actual words. We can't content ourselves with talk of "being a quiet witness" when we see how the Apostles gave their lives for the sake of this Gospel. We must stop with all this silly business – this Saint Francis "when necessary"-ness – if we want to see His Kingdom come. After all, if the murderous-hearted Saul could so quickly become the preaching Paul, what's our modernday excuse for our silence?

If you've never done it, do you actually believe it?

If you've never tried to explain it, can you actually explain it?

If you've never "led a person unto Jesus," why not?

If you've never been a "witness," are you one at all?

November 12 – Acts 10:1-8

A man with humble heart is the hinging point

Because this moment marks a turning-point in how the Gospel spreads across the world, it's important that we understand its import. It's important that we focus on the way this Gentile humbled himself so we understand how men can best be used by God. It's important that we take to heart how God can use a man whose heart is His, not in theory, but in actuality. We must note this place where the Gospel changes course if we ourselves hope to change the course of our world today…

Consider this modern telling of the same moment: "In New York City, there was a man named Mr. Cornelius, a CEO in what was known as a Fortune-500 company. He and all his family were devout and God-fearing; he gave generously to those in need and prayed to God regularly. One day at about three in the afternoon he had a vision. He distinctly saw an angel of God, who came to him and said, 'Cornelius!'

"Cornelius stared at him in fear. 'What is it, Lord?' he asked.

"The angel answered, 'Your prayers and gifts to the poor have come up as a memorial offering before God. Now send men to Port-au-Prince, Haiti to bring back a man named Simon who is called Peter. He is staying with Simon the TV repairmen, whose house is by the sea.'

"When the angel who spoke to him had gone, Cornelius called two of his associates and a devout brother in Christ who was one of his assistants. He told them everything that had happened and sent them off to Port-au-Prince…"

O Men of God, may no power, wealth or earthly position we hold ever compete with the call of Jesus for our lives. We must learn to be so humble in our circumstances, regardless of what they are, that we're always ready to obey His voice. We must learn to live with *prideless* hearts, whether we're the CEO or the low-man-on-the-totem-pole in our current occupation. We must know that nothing matters but those matters He's calling our lives to; that His plans trump absolutely everything else.

Where is pride winning your heart today, O Man? Do you want to become more humble? Do you want that, like Cornelius, the spread of Jesus' Gospel might actually hinge upon your own personal humility? Now *that's* a worthy goal for the day ahead! Let's make ourselves less for His sake.

November 13 – Acts 10:9-48

Living on the Spirit's spur-of-the-moment

The reason you and I have heard about the name and life of Jesus is because of Peter's actions in these verses. Follow the logic: If he hadn't gone up to the roof for a little prayer-time, he might never have seen this vision with the sheet and animals…*and* if he hadn't been aware enough to journey into this vision from the Lord, he might never have welcomed these oncoming visitors…*and* if he hadn't been a gracious welcoming host to these Gentiles, he certainly never would've gone with them to Caesarea…*and* if he hadn't gone to Caesarea, no one in the household of Cornelius would've ever heard about the Gospel of Jesus…*and* if he hadn't preached the Gospel there, not a single Gentile might've ever received the precious gift of the Holy Spirit…*and* if they'd never received the Holy Spirit, they wouldn't have been baptized into the life and death of Jesus Christ…*and* there'd be no modern Church of Christ (excepting, of course, the Messianic Jews) if not for Holy Spirit-filled, Jesus-following Gentiles.

O Men of God, genuine movements of the Holy Spirit can be as subtle and quick-moving as the movements of this story. But if we've settled for only Sunday church-attendance and Wednesday evening Bible studies, we simply won't be sensitive enough to hear from Him. If we think we'll "grow in Christ" while excluding the ever-moving Holy Spirit, we're absolutely and fatally wrong. If you think that it was *humans* who caused the changes in the Church throughout the centuries, learn some "Holy Spirit history."

You and I must learn to have a spirit that harmonizes with the Holy Spirit and be ready for these sorts of moments everyday. We must let the "on the fly" teachings of the Holy Spirit give us hearts that are truly teachable, malleable, humble…

When was your last personal Holy Spirit interaction, O Man? Were you suitably responsive in that moment? Did you simply do whatever He commanded you to do, or did you discount how the Spirit speaks to us? O Men of God, may we take the time to listen for the Holy Spirit in our *every single moment*. Simon Peter happened to be listening one day. And that's the reason you're reading these words right now…

November 14 – Acts 11:19-26

What is your title?

Imagine if the modern term "Christian" held a *thousandth* of the meaning it held in Antioch back then. Imagine if "belonging to Christ" actually cost something; if it weren't a status quo statement in modernday America. Imagine how your "personal faith" would personally feel if being "faithful" meant a daily chance of pain and persecution for Jesus' sake. Imagine how you'd feel if being slaughtered was a very real potential outcome of being called a "Christian."

Well, welcome to 1st Century Antioch, O Man. And welcome to 21st Century Iran or North Korea. Welcome to the days of faith meaning faithfulness to the *meaning* of that watered-down word we invoke: "Christian." Welcome to a life where claiming membership within the Body actually means you've got some real "skin in the game." Welcome to the life we're actually meant to lead; welcome to the place where "following Jesus" isn't at all theoretical. Welcome to the faith where men "live like men"; where our words and deeds require every ounce of ourselves.

O Men of God, a "Christian" is the title for a person who "belongs to Christ" – heart, mind, body and soul. A "Christian" is a person who considers "everything a loss compared to the surpassing greatness of knowing Christ." A "Christian" is a person who won't ever blink about the presence of some hardship, toil and suffering along the way. A "Christian" is a person who'd go to any lengths in order to draw closer to Jesus and also draw others to Him.

So are you really a "Christian," O Man of God? Or are you just a title without meaning? Does it mean *everything – anything – something – nothing –* to you to belong to Jesus today? If it wasn't just a box to check on censuses, surveys, and websites, what would it actually mean to you? Do you even think the word is worth the paper it's written on these days: *Do we need a new name?*

If so, what would you call yourself? What's this you're doing with your life?

LIVE LIKE MEN

November 15 – Acts 12:1-11

There are no impossibilities; just believe

O Man of God, have you ever spent a night in prison and been "guarded by four squads of four soldiers each"? Have you ever been indicted for a crime for which another friend was indicted and then "put to death with the sword"? Have you ever been in trouble to the tune of Peter's trouble: *Have you ever had absolutely no way out?* Have you ever been in such a spot that nothing – and I truly mean nothing – seemed possible for your earthly deliverance?

Well, how did you sleep that night, my friend? Did you wake refreshed the next morning? Did you pass a restful night, "sleeping between two soldiers," even though you were "bound with two chains"? Did you think of Jesus' words – "Do not worry about your life" – and actually not worry about your life at all? Did you truly believe that Jesus is in control of everything; that there's nothing that He can't do where you're concerned? Did you close your eyes, assured of His deliverance, and then open them, assured of His ongoing presence with you?

O Men of God, you will never really "believe" until you believe there's nothing Jesus *can't* do for your life. You will never have "faith" until your faith allows you to be restful in His certain safety and sure salvation. Simon Peter went to sleep assured that God was in complete control of the prison and then he "came to" outside its walls. Simon Peter chose to put his trust in One who'd said to him: "But when they arrest you, do not worry about what to say…"

O Man of God, what is your trouble today? Do you truly believe the Lord can deal with it? Do you believe that all your life is in His hands; that He knows of every situation you're currently dealing with? Will you today "Come to me, all you who are weary and burdened, and I will give you rest," as Jesus invites you? Will you: "Take my yoke upon you and learn from me," "for my yoke is easy and my burden is light"?

O Man of God, our God knows no limits. After all, He broke Peter out of prison by night. Will you trust that He is able to protect you and release you from all trouble – *no matter what* – during your day today?

November 16 – Acts 13:13-44

Clean clear proclamation

A man who'll speak the Spirit-led, unapologetic truth will see similar results unfold in his personal ministry. He'll stand before a friend – or a crowd of friends – speaking the Gospel with candor, grace and godly tact and see exciting things happening. He'll open his mouth to wisdom founded in the person of Jesus Himself and reflect that very Person in all he says and does. He'll speak these points of Paul's sermon (recontextualized) and be *un*surprised when people come home to Jesus:

"Brothers, children of the world, and you God-*un*-fearing Gentiles, it is to me and to you that this message of salvation has been sent. The people of Jesus' day did not recognize Jesus, yet in condemning him they fulfilled the words of the Jewish prophets and also our desperate need. Though they found no proper ground for a death sentence, they asked Pilate to have him executed. When they had carried out all that was written about him, and all that our sin demanded, they took him down from the tree and laid him in a tomb. But God raised him from the dead, and for many days he was seen by those who'd traveled with him from Galilee to Jerusalem. They were then witnesses to others who then passed along his truth throughout the passing of generations...

"Therefore, my brothers, I want you to know that through Jesus the forgiveness of sins is proclaimed to you. Through him everyone who believes is set free from sin, a justification you were not able to obtain anywhere else. But take care that you don't hear these words, give them careful thought, and then go on as if nothing ever happened. Jesus died and Jesus rose – *for you*. His life and death and return to life require action. Now what do you say to that?"

O Men of God, may we be so nimble and well-versed in the Word that Jesus' Good News gushes from us all the time. May we stand before a man, or many men, and always be prepared with His truth whenever the opportunity unfolds itself. May the Book of Acts rewrite itself today by how we're giving Him our Today, both in thought and by action. May a man who's reading these simple thoughts be one who someday sees a "whole city" gather to hear Jesus Christ's story.

Let's be those kind of men today, O Men. Let's run wild with His story.

November 17 – Acts 14:1-7

Have you been attacked this year?

A faith that doesn't stir an ounce of personal trouble or persecution might be lacking in the "stirringness" of the Holy Spirit. If the darkness is the enemy of the light and yet you're never under attack, exactly how bright is the light in you? Is it bright enough that you speak "so effectively that a great number" of people are attracted to Jesus? Is it bright enough that the enemy is afraid of "Christ in you" and must resort to "poisoning" people's minds against you? Is it bright enough that the Lord confirms "the message of his grace by enabling [you] to do miraculous signs"? Is it bright enough that the "people of the city [are] divided" on your account: *Are you causing trouble with your light?*

Given where we've been this year and how we've tried to spur ourselves to action, I *hope* you've been a little persecuted! I pray that every man who's reading from this page is so effective that he's actually under some form of attack. I pray that our single-minded obedience to the One who gave His life for our lives is making our lives a little uncomfortable. I pray that we become so fruitful that the evil one actually sees the power of Jesus – living and active – in our daily lives.

O Man of God, have you felt a measure of Satan's personal attacks during the course of this passing year? Have you felt how he attacks you through your circumstances – big and little – in order to dissuade you from direct godly action? Have you felt how he'll use any kind of method that's convenient for derailing you from each day's Christ-following? Have you seen how truly crafty, cunning, cold and calculating he is in the way he'll attack from any and all angles?

Or have you *not* experienced even a mite of how the evil one attacks during the course of this passing year? Have you *not* felt any attacks throughout this year – big or little – because you're *not* pursuing direct godly action? Have you *not* felt how the evil one will use myriad methods because, frankly, the evil one's not worried about you? Are you *seeing* just how crafty, cunning, cold and calculating he's actually been by his subtly keeping you from the work of the Kingdom?

O Man, have you been attacked at all, this year? Have you felt your personal share of persecution? If effective work is oftentimes rewarded by the evil one's attacks, are you currently under attack? Only you can know the answer to that question…

November 18 – Acts 14:8-18

Disdaining glory, unless it's given to Him

We must be aggrieved whenever glory is given to us out of proportion to its being given to Jesus. We must never see "success" as being a means of bringing Him praise without noting how it also messes with our own minds. We must know that how we're lauded and applauded can do spiritual damage if we don't ascribe all glory to Jesus. We must know how many men have been destroyed by their "success," by their finding their all-sufficiency in it and not in Him…

When these people went down on their knees, Paul didn't appeal to them with any sort of false humility. He didn't speak to them with words that said, "Don't," and yet a heart that cried out, "Now this is what I'm talking about!" No, Paul was so distraught that any worship might be misdirected to him that he actually tore his own clothes. He'd rather die than have a grain of glory properly owed to Jesus being directed in his own improper direction. He'd rather his life not be thought newsworthy if it meant the slowing of the Good News' spreading across the world. He'd rather run away from praise and personal glory if he knew it'd bring more glory unto Jesus' name.

Let us be stung by the words of Christ:

"But how miserable for you who are rich, for you have had all your comforts! How miserable for you who have all you want, for you are going to be hungry! How miserable for you who are laughing now, for you will know sorrow and tears! How miserable for you when everybody says nice things about you, for that is exactly how [the Jewish forefathers] treated the false prophets!" (Luke 6:24-26)

O Men of God, our personal success can be terribly detrimental to our own love and pursuit of Jesus Christ. The newsworthiness of our life can do damage to the spreading of the Gospel if we're not terribly careful about it. Our sense of importance might attest to how very *un*important we've made the life and death and call of our Savior. Our exaltation lends *no credence* to the tale of One who debased Himself, "emptied Himself," for our sinful sake.

Do we need to tear our own clothes today, O Men? Are we taking too much glory?

November 19 – Acts 14:19-20

Re-up your heart for war

O Man of God, can you feel the power jumping off the page when Paul arises and returns to the city? Can you see him lying bloodied and half-dead; then arising from the ground to go back inside its walls? Do you know that nothing less than this behavior is required from our lives; that you're called to the same kind of strength? Are you man enough to take a vicious beating, feel the stones against your flesh, and go directly back to the battle? Are you tough enough to walk back through the city gates of townships where your name, and Jesus Christ's, are anathema? Are you so consumed with living for the Gospel's going-forth that you'd actually struggle, fight and die to see it go forth?

A great section from von Clausewitz' *On War*. "The fact that slaughter is a horrifying spectacle must make us take war more seriously, but not provide an excuse for gradually blunting our swords in the name of humanity. Sooner or later someone will come along with a sharp sword and hack off our arms."

The spiritual warfare with which you and I are engaged is no less horrifying than the spectacle of bloody modern warfare; we'll find our hearts becoming easily daunted if we're not aware of the high stakes that are called for in this war. Yet may we never be so daunted that we'll walk away from the battle or from beatings or from stonings for the sake of Jesus. Otherwise, the evil one has a proper "in" with which he'll come along and hack apart our faith in the One who died for us…

O Man, are you man enough for this? Are you man enough for this brand of war? Do you know that nothing else is worth your life except the calling of this Savior who gave His life *for* your life?

O Men, Paul was all in. Are you all in, today?

November 20 – Acts 14:21-28

The hardships that are oh-so-good

"Hardships" cannot sanctify our journey into the Kingdom; only Jesus Himself can sanctify by His shed blood. We're not medieval monks who load our shoulders with self-chosen burdens in the hopes of being made somehow self-righteous. We don't attain our standing in the family of God by any works of our own hands – or our mouths – or our minds – or our backs. We aren't more faithful because of sacred self-flagellations that we think might make us holier before the Judgment Seat…

O Men of God, we are justified and sanctified and made the men we are *only by the work of Jesus*. You and I are modern pilgrims who've been lightened of our load by Him who took a cross upon His shoulders. We attain our standing only by the judgment of the same "God who justifies. Who is he that condemns?" We are made more faithful as we unite ourselves with He who bore the stripes for us; who made us holy by His blood…

Today, let's spend some time on the thought that we're actually united with the One who was actually crucified for our sake. Let's lend our minds to deeper contemplation of this truth and, also, the accompanying calling found in Galatians 2:20.

Here's a possible method for our meditations:

I (think about your "story," your salvation, your calling, your identity ie. Who am I?) *have been crucified with Christ and I no longer live, but Christ lives in me.*

I have been (think of how everything has been done for you already!) *crucified with Christ and I no longer live, but Christ lives in me.*

I have been crucified (go to the cross; see His hands, His feet, His side pierced for you) *with Christ and I no longer live, but Christ lives in me.*

I have been crucified with (What does this "with" mean to you? Have you gone up to Golgotha with your Lord? Are you dead to sin through Him?) *Christ and I no longer live, but Christ lives in me.*

I have been crucified with Christ (the magnificent One, my Savior, my Brother, the Creator of the sky, the mountains, the sea – Let your heart go wild in praising Him!) *and I no longer live, but Christ lives in me.*

I have been crucified with Christ and I no longer (your life is "no longer" about your life, "he must become greater; I must become less") *live, but Christ lives in me.*

I have been crucified with Christ and I no longer live (What does it mean that "you" – everything you know of yourself – is no longer living?), *but Christ lives in me.*

I have been crucified with Christ and I no longer live, but (there's more to your "no longer living" than a simple death!) *Christ lives in me.*

I have been crucified with Christ and I no longer live, but Christ (the Risen One – dead, but no longer dead! Go to the glorious empty tomb!) *lives in me.*

I have been crucified with Christ and I no longer live, but Christ lives (He is alive and carrying out the renewing work of resurrection – feel that!) *in me.*

I have been crucified with Christ and I no longer live, but Christ lives in (Where are you feeling His presence in you?) *me.*

I have been crucified with Christ and I no longer live, but Christ lives in me (the new "me," the "new wineskins" with "new wine," the "new creation" from whom the "old has gone!")

O Man of God, have you been "crucified with Christ"? Is it truly "no longer" you who lives today?

November 21 – Acts 16:6-10

Actually seeking His direction

You'll never live a life of crystal clarity until your vision is aligned with the Lord's vision of your life. You'll never feel the peace "which passeth all understanding" if you're always barging forward, always moving ahead with all you're doing. If you never cease your striving in order to see His plans for you, you'll always be about your own plans, first off. If you never look for supernatural visions of our God's vision, you'll rob your life's direction of His perfect and eternal direction…

Paul was personally doing things and saying things that'll rival anything you'll ever read in the whole of the scriptures. He was on a path that started in Antioch and then continued to the Gospel's spreading out into brand new lands.

Yet when "Paul and his companions" tried to preach the word in Asia, or enter Mysia, they were stopped short of success. Even though they might've gone into those places, preaching mighty wonderful sermons, God's word to them was simply "No."

And Paul knew he had to listen, O Men. In fact, Paul moved along; then he stopped. Paul's nature was so sensitive to the Spirit that he understood God's "No's," just as well as His "Yes's." Paul understood that "life" is not a life unless it's lived right in the middle of God's plan for that life. Paul understood that nothing he was doing needed him; it was all the fruit of the Holy Spirit's perfect doing.

And so he went to sleep in Troas….and thus came the man of Macedonia in his dreams…and then Paul woke up the very next morning with the Father's clarity for his life, and His direction, and his next missional move…

O Man of God, have you ever had this sort of patience about the Lord's direction for the steps in your own life? Have you ever been so "in touch" with His Spirit that you've felt His subtle leadings as to where you're actually *not* to go? Have you settled down and waited till He's made the next step clear for you; have you spent your own quiet night in Troas? Or do you always forge ahead with an expectation that "the Lord will bless my efforts," even if you're not listening to Him?

O Men of God, let's listen today. Let's let the Lord lead our lives in actuality. Let's let Him make us men whose lives are led at every single turn, whose every turn is led by Jesus directly. Movement isn't always the right move. Waiting and listening always are.

November 22 – Acts 16:16-25

Let's shout our praises today

Until 2009, I'd always found the Church's more recent excitement about worship to be somewhat annoying, even frustrating. Frankly, I was sick to death of what I thought was all contrived emotion, clever stagecraft, Christian celebrity etc. I'd been brought up by a father who was of a highly manly stock and I thought that such emotionalism was womanly. I'd begun to think that aspects of our modern forms of "worship" were the stuff of weaker "experience-seekers" only, not for "real men."

But then I met a man named Matt Toth. On a Young Life houseboat trip on Lake Powell. And, all of a sudden, all the floodgates of my worship-inhibitions were thrown open and the Holy Spirit entered in. All at once, all the music and the words and the rhythms and the beats were a part of my own journey with Jesus. The Holy Spirit showed me that nothing had been removing me from His complete joyous presence *except me* – **and only me**…

O Man of God, seeing Paul and Silas arrested, imprisoned and "severely flogged," what do you think of these questions for us: Do you think these men were truly men; that they had the stuff that separates strong men from the weak? Do you think you have even *half* the personal resolve they exhibited for the sake of seeing the Gospel spread throughout the world? Do you think you'd personally have the fortitude to be locked up in stocks in prison, still "praying and singing hymns to God"?

O Men of God, real joyful honest worship – *regardless of our setting* – is actually the stuff that makes us men in the Lord Jesus. To praise this One who gives us every breath of every day is the perfect use of every breath of every day we have. To lift up earnest manly voices for the worship of the Son of Man is to honor His Living Spirit within us. To shed a tear of thankful joy and humble-hearted expectation in song doesn't make you any personally weaker…

In fact, it will actually make you stronger. It will draw your heart to the heart of Jesus. Today, may we take the time to lift our voice in joy and adulation of the King who came to save us from death. May we raise aloft our arms to Him who raised the Cross upon His shoulders to set us free from sin. Today, O Man, you must worship that One. Give your heart – and your voice – to Him alone.

LIVE LIKE MEN

November 23 – Acts 16:26-36

Would you spend your whole life for His purposes?

If the Lord wanted you to quit your job, sell your house, give your possessions to the poor, move away, would you do these things, O Man? Would you pull up roots and go to a foreign field of ministry where the Lord would ask you to go – ***today*** – ***right now***? Would you go out to that place, even if you knew you'd never ever return – ***you and your whole family***? Would you go out to that place if it meant the certainties of hardship for His sake; if it meant persecution – ***everyday***? Would you go if God revealed that He'd use the rest of your life for the reaching of a hundred lost people? Would you go if God revealed that He'd use the rest of your life for the reaching of just a dozen, instead? Would you go if God revealed that He'd use your painful *death* for the reaching of that same dozen people? Would you go if God revealed that He'd use your painful death for the reaching of just one lost sheep of His?

O Men of God, Paul and Silas went out upon their journey so that the name of Jesus might spread to the whole world. They went out that people just like you and me should one day hear the word, accept its truth and be truly set free from sin and death. They chose to go out even if their lives were forfeit for the good of Christ's Gospel; it was absolutely worth it to them. They went to prison – took the floggings and the stocks – in order that Jesus might reach into the life of this one cruel broken jailer…

What is your life worth to you, O Man? What is your life worth for Him? Do you know your every day is the only form of currency you can actually spend for His name's sake? Do you know that only how you live today determines the worth of your life: So what is it truly worth? O Man, truly, what is your "faith" worth? O Men, what is our Lord worth to us?

November 24 – Acts 17:13-17

Being restless for the work

The more a man inhabits places of the Holy Spirit's habitation, the more dangerous he'll become for the Kingdom. He'll become a man who's whisked from one place to another because he's causing Christly trouble all the time, everywhere. He'll become a man whose refuge is the Lord and who's a refugee from the forces of the evil one's minions. He'll become a man who's restless and "distressed" whenever he's *not* in the middle of doing God's doings in the world. He'll become a man like Paul was, unable to rest until he's spoken of, pointed to, made Jesus known to everyone. He'll become almost unhinged when he's personally out of touch with Holy Spirit matters, feeling cut off from his truest calling. He'll become so overwhelmed with others being brought to the place where he's been brought that he'll work to bring them there himself. He won't content himself with sitting around the city of Athens and being silent with this truth that's changed his life entirely…

Do these words describe you, O Man? Can you not *not* preach the Word of God? Are you restless and "distressed" whenever you see a city full of idols, knowing what you know of the goodness of the Lord Jesus? Are you able to speak up whenever you see the chance for a Christ-conversation "with those who happened to be there"? Are you itching for His opportunities to make themselves ever clearer for the speaking of His holy name? Do you find that your own mind is melding ever closer to the thoughts of Jesus in the way you view each given day? Do you feel a little crazed until you're walking in close union with His Holy Spirit; unhinged till your heart is back home with Him?

O Men of God, we cannot *not* preach the Gospel if we're hoping to draw closer to the heart of Jesus. We cannot *not* be about the things that Jesus personally commanded and still expect to be men of God in any reasonable measure. We cannot *not* choose to give our day away to people who desperately need the love of Jesus in their lives. We cannot *not* be unhinged when we're outside of His manifest presence and plan, and yet still belong to Him…

O Man, are you His today? Are you in the center of the action? Can you not *not* do the things He'd call your life to today and rest easy in the providence of His perfect plan? Today will be the answer.

LIVE LIKE MEN

November 25 – Acts 17:18-34

Where will you "immerse" your day?

If you've ever heard a sermon on the subject of this Pauline discourse, you've probably heard some comments like these ones: "Pay attention to how Paul makes use of popular Greek poetry to mark the central theme of this] sermon." Or: "Notice how well Paul makes uses of irony with his pointing to the overwhelming religiosity of the Athenians." Or: "We ourselves must learn to speak within the contexts of the culture we inhabit just like Paul does so well here..."

Yet within the actual context of all Paul's missionary journeys, this particular discourse is a complete dud. Compared to other greater moments in his drawing of a crowd to Jesus, only "a few men became followers" after this one. Compared with other sermons where he left the crowd amazed with who the Lord is, this one ends "not with a bang but a whimper." Compared with other churches that would spring up from such a teaching in other towns he passed through, Paul simply "left Athens." (Acts 18:1)

Consider this quote from Leroy Eims: "Since your life is so short, don't settle for a small life, immersed in self and sin...There are only three things that last for eternity: God, his word, and the eternal souls of people. If your life is immersed in these, you are involved in eternal issues. Let your life be carried along in the grand sweep of God's will in the world. Be caught up with Jesus Christ and his Great Commission. If you do that, even though your life is short, it won't be little."

Daily "results" didn't seem to matter much to the Apostle Paul because he knew he was entrenched in the middle of God's will for him. He was utterly "caught up" in his Savior and his Lord Jesus Christ and in daily doings of His Great Commission. He "immersed" each day in God Himself, in His word, and "the eternal souls of people," leaving the results up to God. Paul probably woke up on this particular morning with perspective only for that day, and he lived out his personal calling to the full.

O Men, where are you "immersed" today? O Man, where are you "caught up"? May we live today with Paul's complete absorption in the lives of people, in the Word and in God Himself. For we are men of eternal mindset. We are men who'll do His will, no matter the cost.

November 26 – Acts 18:1-5

Only "working" so that we might be His Workers

It isn't by coincidence that we read of Paul taking these occasional personal sojourns *into* the "work-world." And I don't think it's any random-chance occurrence that Paul's trade was what it happened to be, the humble art of "tentmaking." After all, think of the many examples that are given throughout the scriptures for the utilitarianness of tents for God's people. And think, also, of the ways the "tent" is used to speak of life and its inconsequence, its fleeting moveable nature. For example: "Now we know that if the earthly tent we live in is destroyed, we have a building from God, an eternal house in heaven…" (2 Cor. 5:1) Or: "I think it is right to refresh your memory as long as I live in the tent of this body, because I know that I will soon put it aside…" (2 Peter 1:13,14a)

O Men of God, do you see how Paul would utilize his "work" as the *supplement* to the Work he'd been given by the Lord? Do you see his choice to briefly camp within this work of tentmaking (v. 3) so that he might then *de*camp to his actual job (v. 5)? Do you think that Paul placed all his personal value on his original vocation, telling everyone: "I'm a tentmaker"? Or do you think that Paul saw business as the means by which he'd live out his Vocation, his call to "make disciples"?

O Man of God, what do you "do"? What is God's great Calling on your life? Are you living only to excel within your personal vocation to the detriment of His Chosen Vocation for you? Are you so busy with your "work" and your "career" that you're currently losing your perspective on your "earthly tent"? Are you living as if the "tent" that is your body is actually the end of the story; that you'll never "put it aside"?

May we learn to give our hearts so fully to the calling of the Lord that we "devote ourselves exclusively" to the work of Jesus. May we learn that all our strivings must be "set asideable" if the Lord would like to use us elsewhere at any time. May we see our "work" for exactly what it is: The earthly tent where we're currently working for the bread we'll bodily need today. And may we then know how to decamp from every aspect of its hold upon our lives when the Lord wants to call us away…

O Man of God, what do you do? May we learn to answer as Paul might've, back then.

November 27 – Acts 18:7-11

Being still and listening

For many men, the greatest enemy of peace within our lives is the constant rushing motion of our modern inertia. We feel we have to "do, do, do," always answering "I've been busy," or we're not really the man we're supposed to be. We feel that if we keep our motion constant, we'll always stay "ahead," we'll mystically "get ahead" of the "competition." We secretly hope our movement creates a flurry noticeable enough that we might even get that next big promotion we've been yearning for. We aspire that we might move up in our field so that our upward efforts are eventually wound down into "management." We hearken forward to the end of all this work, onward to retirement, where all this onrushing goes to die…

Yet look at Paul's life in this passage, O Man. Look at how Paul lingered on, here. Look at how he heard the word of God to stay precisely where he was; look at how he then set up camp in that location. Look at how he used his own time so that others might hear the mighty word of God; look at how he was so patient for the Kingdom. As a character in Ivan Turgenev's novel *On the Eve* once said: "Our time doesn't belong to us…"

Today, make the time to sit for half an hour (or more!) in perfect silence with the God who spoke to Paul, back then. If we want to hear His voice and direction – as we often say we do! – we must start to actually listen for Him, for His voice. We must slow ourselves till nothing in this world competes for His complete attention; we must actively *un*divide ourselves. We must sit and listen till we feel His Spirit's presence and are ready to be directly instructed by Him *for His purposes*.

Make the time today, O Man. No one else can make it for you.

November 28 – Acts 18:24-28

A schematic for a manly godly life

Although Apollos still had much to learn about the truth of Jesus, we can certainly learn a lot when reading about his life. If you pay attention while reading again through this section, you can see a great schematic for a godly life, well lived:

Some examples: *"Meanwhile a Jew named Apollos, a native of Alexandria, came to Ephesus. He was a learned man* (**enriched his God-given mind**), *with a thorough knowledge of the Scriptures* (**invested great value in the Word of God by investing himself there**). *He had been instructed in the way of the Lord* (**put a premium on being discipled**), *and he spoke with great fervor* (**a man of passion for the truth**) *and taught about Jesus accurately* (**"correctly handles the word of truth"**), *though he knew only the baptism of John* (**"witnessed" only to what he knew, but still bore witness**). *He began to speak boldly in the synagogue* (**"not ashamed of the gospel"**). *When Priscilla and Aquila heard him, they invited him to their home and explained to him the way of God more adequately* (**humble enough to be teachable**).

"When Apollos wanted to go to Achaia (**ready to "go" for the Gospel**), *the brothers encouraged him and wrote to the disciples there to welcome him* (**had clearly made great friendships with these "brothers"**). *On arriving, he was a great help to those who by grace had believed* (**used his life to help and enrich others' lives and faith**). *For he vigorously refuted the Jews in public debate* (**took a strong convicted stand**), *proving from the Scriptures* (**knew the Scriptures**) *that Jesus was the Christ* (**knew how to use the Scriptures to actually show this**).

O Man of God, from these parenthetic portraits of Apollos' many facets, I bet at least one really sticks out to you, personally. I bet one of these descriptions describes something the Lord is currently seeking to sharpen in your life for Him. So, today, pay attention to that part of Apollos. Live with focus on where the Spirit is focusing your heart. Let's become more like Apollos today. Let's live a life that matters deeply.

November 29 – Acts 19:1-10

Discussions that set us aflame

If you've never read Alexander Solzhenitsyn's 1978 Harvard Commencement Speech, you need to find a copy today. You need to read of how a man who was imprisoned, tortured and banished under Communism *also* didn't love our Western culture. You need to read the ways he chose to define rife Western shortcomings; how he pointed to our essential weaknesses. You need to read of where he worried we'd come undone beneath the weight of our thin materialistic veneer, our secularist mentality.

Take a look at his concluding words: "If the world has not come to its end, it has approached a major turn in history, equal in importance to the turn from the Middle Ages to the Renaissance. It will exact from us a spiritual upsurge, we shall have to rise to a new height of vision, to a new level of life where our physical nature will not be cursed as in the Middle Ages, but, even more importantly, our spiritual being will not be trampled upon as in the Modern era. This ascension will be similar to climbing onto the next anthropologic stage. No one on earth has any other way left but – upward."

O Men of God, we can see how God used the twelve to reach the world; how He used their "heights of vision" for His perfect purposes. In this passage, we saw how Paul gave his attention to another twelve; how he saw the Spirit burning in their hearts. When they found such opposition, they were uncowed by these "obstinate" ones; they turned their glances inward – and "upward." They met each day for doses of discussion that consumed their hearts with fire and raised their lives to a "new level." Paul conceded two years and three months of his rapidly waning life to a group whose passion changed a continent forever. In fact, "all the Jews and Greeks who lived in the province of Asia heard the word of the Lord" during this "spiritual upsurge."

Today, gather with some brothers for a time of deep discussion of the Lord: what He's doing; what He's already done. Take the time to let the Holy Spirit work within your hearts to reveal what He'd like you to discuss in your time together. If we want to be the men who are the vanguards of the "next anthropologic stage," we must let the Holy Spirit fill us entirely. We must gather like those men in Tyrannus' lecture hall, back in those days, and let the Spirit's fire set our hearts aflame.

Get time with your brothers in Christ today. And let the Holy Spirit do what He always does best.

November 30 – Acts 19:13-16

You must entirely own your faith

"Some Christians who went around trying to engage in spiritual warfare tried to invoke the name of the Lord Jesus in the midst of the battle. They would say, 'In the name of Jesus, whom my pastor and my associate pastor and my favorite Christian author and my best friend and my wife and my coworker and my children speak of, I stand up to you, Satan.' Millions of men in the Modern Church were doing this. One day, the evil one answered them, 'Jesus I know, and I know about your pastor and your associate pastor and your favorite Christian author and your best friend and your wife and your coworker and your children, but who are you?' Then the evil one jumped on them with doubts and hardships and despair and enfeebled faith, and he overpowered them all. He gave them such a beating that they ran out of the confines of the Church naked and bleeding…"

O Man of God, are you using another person as a crutch or a prop for your personal faith in Jesus Christ? Are you leaning an undue weight upon a middleman whose faith defines your faith; are you playing that dangerous game? Do you know Jesus Christ because of your own personal experience; do you know this Lord of Lords for yourself? Can you stand upon your own two feet and say, "In the name of Jesus, whom I preach, I command you to come out"?

I don't think it's false to say the seven sons of Sceva's fate is illustrative of those faiths that fake their Christ-relationship. I don't think you'll ever be a man whose faith is worth a lick until you learn to know your Lord for yourself. If your faith is just regurgitation of everything you've been told by others, you won't have strength for harsh spiritual battles. You won't be a fit warrior if your weapons aren't your own; you can't fight with someone else's faith on the day of battle.

Today, give some time to contemplation of the other places where you've placed your hope while in pursuance of the Lord. Do you ascribe too much weight to others' ways of following Jesus; do you know this King of Kings for yourself? Where do you gain your knowledge of Him? Is it first- or second-hand? May we become the men who know Him for ourselves; let's be the kind of men whose faith is truly legendary.

December 1 – Acts 19:23-28

Not standing by your false gods

No man sets a course for life with hopes of great inconsequence; plans to live a life of "chasing after the wind." No man dreams of his death with hopes of leaving behind a legacy filled with time-waste and personal smallness. None of us would hope our life ends up looking just like all others' lives; that our days reflect the "patterns of this world." We aren't the sort of men who'll set our eyes upon a gaudy golden wristwatch as the goal of our personal journey through this life. We aren't the ones who'll sell our souls so very cheaply that we only draw disdain from the evil one's armies. You and I are men who'll fight from dawn to dusk, who "delight ourselves in the Lord" and learn of His desires for us…

However, there's no other way that sets a course unto a greater inconsequence than chasing after worldly false gods. No other life is actually closer to a death than living small lives concerned with matters far from God's best for men like us. There's no life as unremarkable as those who worship livelihoods and "patterns" that extol false earthly worships. We can't be the sort of men we're called to be if we're ever holding up the Artemises of this world as being somehow "great." We can't sell our souls as cheaply as other men if we'd mean to represent the Lord who gave His All for us. We can't properly fight each day from dawn to dusk if each day's given task is only "delighting ourselves" in ourselves…

O Man of God, do you have a false god? O Men of God, do we have collective false gods? Do we "lift our eyes unto the hills" but look there only for the rewards bestowed upon us by this current world's ways? Do we stand upon the ramparts of our cities and proclaim the Lord's greatness, or the greatnesses of our false gods? Do our strivings prove we're "of one mind" with Jesus, or that we've become multi-minded because of gods we've personally fashioned?

O Man of God, do you have a false god? O Men of God, be honest: *Do we?* For we mustn't start the day with twofaced hearts and hope to see the day's results as any different from Demetrius'. Today's task: Name the name of your false god(s). And the next: Banish them from your midst at once.

December 2 – Acts 20:13-38

Having knowledge of God's Purpose

Paul possessed an overriding undergirding **Purpose** that defined his every action in how he "lived and moved and had his being." Operating beneath the pattern of the everyday was his perspective that his life was "worth nothing" if he didn't complete this "task."

Do you likewise have a grasp upon the Meaning that's creating both the means *and* end of your life in Jesus? Can you fill-in-the-blanks to explain what your own life is "about": *Are you armed with God's great Purpose for you?*

Let's fill in some blanks together:

I consider my life worth nothing to me, if only I may finish the race and complete the task the Lord has given to me – the task of –

I have not hesitated to proclaim –

The Holy Spirit has made me overseer of –

I am a shepherd to –

I need to be most on my guard against –

In everything I do, I want to show others that by Christ's kind of hard work we must –

O Man of God, Paul stood on the brink of certain death and affirmed that his life's forfeit was absolutely worth it for the Kingdom. Are we men of that stamp today? Do we fear nothing but God Himself?

LIVE LIKE MEN

December 3 – Acts 21:7-14

Fearlessness banishes fear and creates faith

A man who understands the zero-sum nature of discipleship will become a man exactly like Paul became. A man who speaks those words of John the Baptist, "He must become greater; I must become less" is starting to understand the true formula. We must learn to understand that *all* our losses and our hardships and our struggles are to the greater glory of Jesus. We must learn to comprehend that *all* His gains that correspond with our defeats are a great and absolutely worthy cause. We must know that even if we aren't presently prepared for statements like Paul's here, we must work our way toward them. We must give intentional effort to a small and growing steadfastness in our current life so that, someday, we're fully ready for whatever He asks.

From Spurgeon's *Morning and Evening*: "God will give the strength of ripe manhood with the burden allotted to full-grown shoulders." Or, in other words, He will hone today's shoulders until they're strong, ripe and ready for His great future allotted burdens…

O Men of God, does your daily life point toward a future where you're ready to "take up your cross daily"? Does the way you live your life direct your path unto a set of "full-grown shoulders" or a soft weak pew-sitting backside? Do we understand that how we're living our faith today determines the sort of faith we'll have, in actuality, tomorrow? Do we think we'll ever be ready "to die in Jerusalem" if we're having trouble "dying to ourselves" during this particular day? Do you think that Paul would've become <u>THE APOSTLE PAUL</u> without the trials and the struggles and the battles he'd already fought? Don't you think that his shoulders had been growing through the years and now were simply "ripe" for massive burden-taking?

O Man of God, also pay close attention to how Paul's undivided heart for Jesus led to similar results in others' lives: "When he would not be dissuaded, we gave up and said, 'The Lord's will be done'" – his trust taught others how to trust.

Today, may we live with faiths and trusts that shout out, "He is Lord!," not the niggling doubts that shake men's souls. May we offer glimpses of the life of Jesus in the way we live our own lives, so that other men's hearts grow stronger. May we never doubt that He is in complete control of every aspect of our day; that His will *will* always prevail. May we be the men so ready to "take up our cross" today that we're even more ready for it on the morrow.

December 4 – Acts 21:27-22:21

Getting into His kind of trouble

There wasn't any truth in these temple-desecration accusations leveled against the apostle Paul. Paul hadn't taught "all men everywhere against our people and our law and this place," as he was being charged with doing. He hadn't done a thing deserving of the brutal physical treatment he was receiving at the hands of this rabid crowd. He'd only done the work of the Lord among the lost; he was a faithful "witness to all men of what [he had] seen and heard."

Yet he *followed* One who'd similarly been brought up on charges that involved destruction of Solomon's temple (Mark 14:58). He personally *taught* of One who came to sow the seeds of radical change; who'd stirred up all the "people all over Judea" (Luke 23:5). He *lived* for One who didn't do a thing deserving of His death; who'd died that men might have eternal life through Him. Paul *stood* for One who'd come to do the work of the Lord: "that they may have life, and have it to the full" (John 10:10).

O Men of God, when it comes to trial, tribulation, terror and daily trouble, there's only one actual guarantee we've been given: "In this world you will have trouble," said our Savior. "But take heart! I have overcome the world" (John 16:33). We're guaranteed the more and more we give our lives to Him, the more and more our lives will gain more of His brand of trouble. Yet it's our closeness to the One who gave His life that'll gives our lives all the "peace" He personally promises to us.

O Man of God, what do you desire? Do you want only quiet and safety? Do you want to go to bed tonight without a single stroke of hardship being brought against your day today? Do you want to "follow Christ" without the *blessings* that His hardships offer us, or be cursed with soft safety? Do you think a life of daily smooth-sailing lands a man in intimate relation with His Savior – *yes or no?* Would you rather be amidst the thronging crowds of the religiously "faithful," or be Paul upon the steps of these barracks? Would you rather be amidst the vital movements of the Lord, or be "left alone" to live your life quietly, unbothered? You'll only find your real answers when you plant your feet upon the Lord's strength and do what He asks of you today. We'll only be the Lord's kind of men whenever we're acquainting ourselves with trouble: *His kind of trouble.*

December 5 – Acts 23:12-33

Being dangerous to the evil one

For many men, the seminal work of recent Christian male authorship is John Eldredge's book, *Wild at Heart*. In fact, it'd be pretty interesting to know just how many men began a vital part of their spiritual journey through that particular book. It'd be interesting to know how many men have found "recovery and release of [their] man's heart" through its strong honest wisdom. How many men remember reading the words, "dangerous man…in a really good way," and being absolutely set free by them? How many men have rediscovered that their Lord would speak to their manhood; that He'd actually say, "It is good" to them? How many men can point to *Wild at Heart* and thank the Lord for all the hard work John Eldredge must've put into its creation?

That book is very important. It marked a turning point of male Christian history.

Yet, to be honest, I would rather that a "detachment of two hundred soldiers" was needed around me than "to go West" metaphysically. I'd rather be thought dangerous in the battling mind of Satan than by "beauties" of a "captivating" nature who might happen to catch my eye. I'd rather have conspiracies swirling around my living for the Lord than "to rush the fields at Bannockburn" like a modern Wallace. I'd rather be a man of concrete purpose than "a riddle, wrapped in a mystery, inside an enigma" of modern manly metaphors.

O Man of God, if your life even a slight bit "dangerous" when you compare it with the life of the apostle Paul? Is the evil one so bent on harming you that there are "forty men…in ambush" waiting for you every time you turn around? Have you been so vocal with the presentation of the Gospel that the devil's daily ire is drawn out by the way you're living? Have you been so single-minded in obedience that your life was led to places of the Lord's personal persecution?

Today let's contemplate what it might actually take for our lives to be threatened for the sake of Jesus and His Kingdom. If there's not a hint of "danger" about how you're living for Jesus, you'll become the wrong sort of "dangerous" man. Yes, you'll get your kicks by catching cutthroat trout, shooting guns, riding dirtbikes, if you're not Christ-dangerous. You'll fill the void with hearty manly stuff that's just a *shadow* of the danger for which we're actually intended.

LIVE LIKE MEN

Do you want to be wild at heart today? Then simply "Follow me," wherever Jesus leads.

December 6 – Acts 24:10-27

Do your convictions convict?

Paul didn't stand before the governor and his wife with clever defenses for the charges brought against him by the Jews. He didn't mete out any counter-accusations against them even though his cause was worthy, his grounds perfectly righteous. He didn't take the time to speak of how deserving he was for a quick release or an absolutely instantaneous pardon. He didn't raise a single complaint, even when his house arrest was lingering on for more than two years…

No, Paul took every earthly opportunity he was ever afforded to speak of Jesus: His life, His death, His resurrection. Paul fearlessly "discoursed" on his "faith in Christ Jesus"; "on righteousness, self-control and the judgment to come." Paul figured that his personal placement in the life of crooked Felix was a placement that the Lord had sovereignly ordained. He used every chance to speak with mighty conviction and his hearers heard the word of God in its entirety…

Would you say the way you're living your life is speaking to others' hearts "about faith in Christ Jesus" in any way? Would you say that your convictions, spoken well, are actually resulting in some people being made a little "afraid"? Would you say that your life's passion for the Lord is leading others to desire their own passion for the Lord? Are you making the most of every opportunity – *everyday* – with everyone who happens to cross your path?

O Men of God, you and I are the "lights of the world," we're His "cities on a hill"; may we never ever hide ourselves! May our convictions be so fully firmly believed that just our presence is required to convict men's hearts of His eternal presence! May we cease with vocal human judgments when the "aroma of Christ" suffices for conviction of men's thoughts and deeds! May we be like seeds of light that He's planted in the midst of broken, hurting, dying, crooked, wicked men!

And may we shine, O Men, today – *all day*! Let's live that men might have the chance to live!

LIVE LIKE MEN

December 7 – Acts 25:23-26:1

Be wronged and cheated for His sake

We're not allowed to judge our passage through this life against false constructs such as "fairness" and/or "rightness," O Men. After all, if we're following after One who went to trial unfairly, went to death without wrongdoing, what do we expect for ourselves? Do we think we deserve a finer life than He who actually gave His life for men and yet was mistreated by those very men? Do we think our lives should be immune to common hardships when we follow after One who was inured to our hardships? Do we hate to see the great apostle Paul put under subjugation by this pompous fool of a man, King Agrippa? Does it bother us to read of how the greater man is "brought in," almost as if to entertain the lesser?

O Men of God, we must view our lives with greater humble detachment if we don't want to become pompous fools ourselves. We must cease to see our lives as being our own if we want to follow after the One who gave His All for our lives. It's utter idiocy to insist our lives should always be given "fair treatment"; that something done to us isn't "fair" or "right." It isn't manly to pore over little prickings we've received when we're actually supposed to be in the fight of our lives…

As Paul himself wrote: "The very fact that you have lawsuits among you means you have been completely defeated already. *Why not rather be wronged? Why not rather be cheated?*"

O Man of God, are you living life as if your own life matters most; are you living like your "pomp" is fine and dandy? Do you feel as if "my day today", "my work", "my possible promotion" are the only things that take personal precedence? Would you be okay with your life if "life" was totally *un*fair to you; if the Lord required your whole life *and* your pride? Would you "rather be wronged," "rather be cheated," for the name of Jesus, than to be "right" and not cheated for your own?

Today, let's let everyone run absolutely roughshod over our lives for the sake of Him who gave His life for us. Let's not ask for any "fairness" or for what's "right" in our lives, that we might experience more of Jesus' life and death. Let's each of us aspire to let others have their way today; let's be man enough to *not* fight for our rights. We won't understand our Savior till we've learned we "have been crucified with Christ and [we] no longer live…" Let's you and I no longer live today. Let's let Him live through us.

December 8 – Acts 27:1-8

Going absolutely wherever He would send you

Can you picture Paul standing out upon the decks of all these ships, sailing to Rome, for what might've meant his earthly death? Can you feel the wind blowing against his bearded face; feel the painful chafing of the chains around his hands and ankles? Can you lean against the mast and picture all the trials in his near future; imagine the beatings, tortures and, most likely, death? Can you stand beside a man like Paul and somehow still imagine that your "faith" is totally fine "just how it is"? Can you sail off into hardship, hatreds, terror, trial and death with a heart that trusts the Lord's sovereign leading for your life? Are you man enough to follow the "Lamb who was slain" even if it meant the eventual naming of "(your name) who was slain?"

A quote from Jack London that perfectly describes the apostle Paul: "…not that they were unafraid to die, but that they were brave enough to not live at the price of shame…"

O Men of God, will we live our lives with shame because we're scared of sharing something of Jesus' suffering and death? Are we learning personal bravery by actions that dispel all thoughts of living life outside of His costly daily discipleship? Would we rather we were dead than to ever disown destinies to which He's called us; willing to die if He'd count us worthy of that calling? Could we stand aside the mighty peace that dwelt inside of Paul and go anywhere for the sake of Jesus' name?

Where is Jesus calling you today, O Man? And, most importantly, are you going?

December 9 – Acts 27:13-44

You bear the truth amidst the shipwreck of this world

You and I are passengers aboard the "ship" of this broken hurting world, tossed and pitched upon the waves of certain ruin. We are standing on the decks with lost people "in constant suspense," people hoping for a safe landfall soon. You and I are holding all the words proclaiming Life in ourselves; we're the bearers of the only Truth that *is* Life. You and I know how this shipwreck of our world can be arighted through the work of Jesus at work in men's hearts.

Consider Paul's words in this context: "Men, you should not have attempted living life on your own; then you would have spared yourselves this damage and loss. But now I urge you to keep up your courage, because, in Christ, not one of you will be lost; only this earth will be destroyed. Two thousand years ago, the Son of God, the One I serve, came to us and said, 'Do not be afraid, man of God. I have stood trial for you and all the men of this earth; I will graciously save all those who put their hope in me.' So keep up your courage, men, by giving your hope and heart and life to the God who loves you. It will happen just as he told me…"

O Men of God, no place in our modern world is actually any safer than the ruinous confines of Paul's foredamned storm-tossed ship. So if our daily hope is in the things of this world, we're like all of Paul's companions, pointlessly tossing away grain and cargo. If we're ever trying to right the passage of this fallen world without the Lord Jesus, we're feebly "passing ropes under the ship." There will actually *be* a shipwreck in the future for all men, women and children who don't know Him; the question's this: *What are you personally choosing to do about it?* Will you be His presence in the midst of the storm? If you're the only one who knows this One who gives life by His Life, are you choosing to make Him known to others?

I love this thought from Leroy Eims: "Paul knew he was safer on a storm-tossed sea, while living in the will of God, than if he was resting comfortably at home, living disobediently outside the will of God."

Where is your current life, O Man of God? "At home" or "on a storm-tossed sea"?

December 10 – Acts 28:11-16

Go to great lengths to love your brothers

Without a doubt, these men who traveled from "the Forum of Appius and the Three Taverns to meet us" were an encouragement to the apostle Paul. After having nearly died upon the seas, I imagine they brought a dose of comfort by the act of simply showing up to see him. It doesn't matter if they brought him gifts or wonderful words of wisdom or financial assistance; what mattered was their actually coming. What matters to the hearts of godly brothers is the consistent sharing of this Jesus-following life we're living – *together*. What matters is our taking time to make abundantly clear that we love and cherish each other with the gift of time. What matters most is our Lord's admonition that "all men will know that you are my disciples, if you love one another…"

Today, let's you and I "travel" to be with our brother(s). Let's go to great lengths to show our great love. May "all men" be shocked to feel the presence of Jesus within our loving presence in each other's lives throughout this particular day. May we be a source of encouragement by working hard, doing whatever it takes, to truly love each other, O Men of God.

Let's be men of *great* love today.

Let's love our brothers in Christ deeply.

December 11 – Acts 28:17-31

"Woe to me if I do not preach the gospel!"

No one would've thought it strange if Paul had shown up in the capital and then become a quiet, fearful recluse. Not a person would've questioned his love for Jesus if he'd sought some peace before his upcoming trial before the Caesar. It might seem that if a person *ever* earned a spell of personal relaxation, it would've been the apostle Paul, here. One would think it perfectly normal if he'd used these years of house arrest for nothing more than writing and reflection upon his life…

But, no, not this Paul! Not this man who'd once been called Saul! Not this man who'd been the persecuting prosecutor of the Way until the Lord grabbed his heart outside Damascus! Not this man who'd used his every ounce of Jewish education for extrapolation of the Messiah's coming and life-narrative! Not this man who spent his every day of every week of every month of every year proclaiming Jesus' name! Not this man who'd ventured all around the known world, more than once, for the purposes of Christ's Gospel! Not this man who "worked much harder, [was] in prison more frequently, [was] flogged more severely" etc, etc! Not this man who sat upon the edge of his bed within a prison cell and wrote "to live is Christ and to die is gain"!

My brothers, even though he's now awaiting his coming trial and possible death, Paul "preached the kingdom of God" ever boldly. Even though his days were waning before the Caesar might call his case, he "taught about the Lord Jesus Christ" "without hindrance." Paul used his every earthly opportunity – *every single day* – so that he might just bring more "lost sheep" to the "Shepherd." He absolutely meant it when he wrote those words unto the Corinthian church: "Woe to me if I do not preach the gospel!"

O Men of God, are we using every opportunity that presents itself for personally preaching and teaching of Jesus to the world? Even if we are in hardship, do we use our circumstances to be bold and to disciple others "without hindrance"? Even if we are so busy with our "success," are we still using our prime placement for the purposes of God's plan? For there's not a place in the whole of the world, or in the lives of other men, that's not useable for the Lord's good purposes. There are just too many men who use *perceptions* of their place and time as anti-Pauline excuses for *not* doing.

What sort of man are you today, O Man? Is it "woe to *you* if *you* do not preach the gospel"? Are you living under "house arrest" for the sake of Jesus; will you use whatever place He's given you to give Him away to others?

December 12 – Romans 16:23a

A day of great hospitality

For Paul to sit and pen the divinely-inspired epistle we know as "Romans," he needed a scroll and ink to actually write with. He also needed time and space to contemplate his chosen words, a comfortable seat to sit upon and get his work done. He needed food and drink to give him strength and nourishment as he wrote those mighty mystic words that continue to teach us so much. He needed somewhere safe where he could rest his mind for all his future action; for pondering all that God would inspire from his life…

Do you use your personal riches (or your humble means), your house (or your humble apartment) for the Lord's hospitality? Do you see everything you have as something you could actually use for His purposes, for building others up for completion of His work? Do you make use of your own money, food, drink, connections and sway so that others are encouraged and inspired? Have you mastered the art of "having" in order to bless the lives of "have nots," the ones needing Jesus' love?

Today, let's plan a party, plan a dinner, plan a lunch, plan whatever the Lord would ask, in order to bless other's lives. Let's use our worldly "stuff" so someone else is drawn unto our Lord or propelled to greater service for His Kingdom.

Imagine the world without a man named Gaius; imagine it where Paul was unable to write the book of Romans for our reading. "Do not forget to entertain strangers," we are told in Hebrews 13:2, "for by so doing some people have entertained angels…"

Today, be overwhelmingly and incredibly hospitable. A man of God must use his life, and his possessions, well.

December 13 – Galatians 1:11-17

Only God is our refuge

Every single problem in the history of the world can be attributed: *It's sinful man's fault.*

Every single problem in the modern world today is just as easily attributable: *It's sinful man's fault.*

Every single problem throughout the history of the Church is attributable: *It's also sinful man's fault.*

Every single problem in the Modern Church is readily attributable: *It's still sinful man's fault.*

Every single problem in the heart of every man is instantly attributable: *It's sinful man's fault.*

Every single problem in your own human heart is likewise attributable: *It's sinful man's fault.*

O Men of God, if we're aware of where the problem actually lies, why do we always act so stupidly about it? Why, unlike the apostle Paul, do we always seem to find our solace in the sound of man's faulty "wisdom?" Why do we take our cares and struggles first to men, then *eventually* to Jesus, without thinking twice about that course of action? Why do we "go up to Jerusalem to see those who were apostles" before we'd go up to our God…and to Him alone?

As Oswald Chambers wrote: "If there is a sense of being out of touch with God, it is at the peril of your soul you go and ask someone else what you have done wrong."

Today, whatsoever comes along in your life, you must take it first to the Lord; go "immediately into Arabia." Let's go out to the places where the presence of the Lord is mightily manifest and His voice is clearly ready to be heard. May we *not* go to wife or colleague or best friend or any pastor before we've gone directly to the Lord Jesus with it. You and I must seek His face and then seek out His ready wisdom – *every time* – before we give way to any man's thought.

Who do you usually go to, O Man? And, more importantly, who will you go to today?

December 14 – Galatians 2:11-21

It's time for some confrontations

The only thing that's messier than dealing with a church's confrontations is *not* dealing with that church's confrontations. To think that members perfectly coalesce into the Body of Christ without any strife is thinking absolutely idiotically. To think we're not all called to calling out the churchly error around us is to deny membership in Christ's Body entirely. To think you're a man of God without a grain of church-responsibility says you're actually not a man at all!

The apostle Peter was a man among mere boys, yet he let his Jewish background cloud his spiritual judgment, here. He let his fear of dealing with the "circumcision group" begin to make a mockery of the Early Church's holy unity. So Paul, filled with actual righteous indignation, and the Holy Spirit's leading, put his finger up to Peter's chest. He wouldn't let the "awkwardness" of some personal discord, nor "discomfort" of confrontation, hurt the Early Church's progress for the Kingdom…

O Men of God, there are *many* things currently awry with how the Modern Church does business: *What will you do about it?* Will you sit back in your Sunday pew without a thought of "getting too involved" or will you be like Paul was, here? Do you understand that none of us would be where we are today if not for men who stood up for the truth throughout Church history? Do you recognize that we'll never get where we're supposed to be tomorrow if it's not for men like you becoming active about it?

Today, let's gather with some brothers (from your local congregation or not) and discuss the Modern Church's current status. Where are the places where you'd place the Modern Church against the scriptures and find the Modern Church currently lacking? Where are the places you feel led to be "a Paul to a Peter" in the conduct of the Modern Church to the modern world? Where are the places where you're personally called to do something where your *not* doing something will be a churchly sinfulness?

O Man of God, the Modern Church needs you. O Body of Christ, we need more of Jesus.

December 15 – Ephesus 6:21,22

Are we Christ's ambassadors?

The Lord is looking for men whose lives are truly fit for embassy-duty in the service of the coming Kingdom. The Father looks for hearts whose every single beat lines up with how His own heart beats; He wants same-heartedness. The Savior searches high and low for men who'd align their every action with obedience to His stated commandments. The Spirit ranges, looking for the souls of men who'd aspire to be filled, and on fire, with His holy presence. Consider Paul's words as if they were Jesus' words, spoken directly to you: "[Your name], the dear brother and faithful servant of mine, will tell you everything, so that you also may know who I am and what I am doing. I am sending him to the world for this very purpose, that you may know who I AM, and that he may encourage you…"

O Man of God, would you likewise label your own life with the adjective "faithful" in your service to the King of Kings? Do you so adore His holy scriptures that you have the awesome ability to go out and "tell [men] everything" about Him? Do you know the heart of Jesus, and what He's currently doing, so well, that your speaking speaks directly to His heart and actions? Does your life point only upward to the knowledge of I AM; is your ambassadorship an encouragement to all who cross your path?

Tychicus understood the heart and soul of the apostle Paul so well that to send out Tychicus was to send out Paul. The Apostle Paul, for all intents and purposes, was sending out himself on the day when he sent Tychicus out to Ephesus…

Do you and I understand the heart and soul of Jesus Christ so well that to send out *us* is identical to sending Him? For all intents and purposes, when Jesus sends you out, is He sending out His own heart and soul to the lost world?

O Men of God, "we are therefore Christ's ambassadors, as though God were making his appeal through us" to this world. Are our hearts so steeped in the grace and love of Jesus that we represent Him without any fault or blemish?

O Emissary of Christ, what's your mission today? Who will men see living in and through you?

December 16 – Colossians 4:12,13

A session of "wrestling in prayer"

Many of us ascertain the merit of our lives by the measure of the "hard work" we're actively engaged in. There are many men who won't count a workday worthy unless they're exhausted by the toil to be found therein. We all know the daily difference between days filled up with "busyness" and those days filled up with good solid hard work. Whether you're working in the white- or blue-collar side of the working-world, there's something great about actually "working hard."

Now did you notice how Epaphras was commended for his own "working hard"; how he merited Paul's strongest praise? Did you read those words "wrestling in prayer" as the highest form of commendation Paul could possibly muster? Did you think about the implications in the difference between "normal" prayer and this description of a wrestling variety? Do you think your daily "prayer life" ever rises to the point of "wrestling," ever reaches toward a form of blood-sport? Do you think of "working hard" as being synonymous with the way you're hitting your knees in prayer before your Lord? Would you want to be the sort of man whom others would immediately associate with hard-work-praying?

Today you're tasked with carving out some space for earnest "working hard" prayer of the "wrestling" variety, O Man of God. You must spend no less than thirty minutes with the Father, giving Him the honest cares and hurts and needs of your life. You must "wrestle" with the Lord about the issues beyond your personally comprehension; you must absolutely "seek His face." You must strive in your heart for full alignment of your spirit with His Spirit through your time together in the prayer-closet.

O Men of God, let's pray today. And let's pray absolutely mightily. Let's so struggle with the Lord for hard-fought intimacy that it's actually like we're wrestling with Him, all day long. After all, if God was pleased with Jacob's wrestling Him in the desert, He must like a man who's willing to fight to the death. So let's pray with that kind of spirit today, O Men. Let's let nothing stop our prayers.

December 17 – Colossians 4:17

What is the "work" of your life?

You and I were not created for our personal recreation or for creation of some personal wealth, O Men of God. You and I are not so small as only having been built for "providing for our family" etc. We're not the sort of men who'll go down to our graves consumed with worries that we "wasted time" on things and experiences insignificant. We're not the men who'll waste a single moment of this particular day if only we'll keep your eyes affixed to Jesus, the Christ.

O Man of God, who are you? O Man of God, what were you actually made for? O Man of God, do you know the special "work" for which your life was created, "the work you have received"? O Man of God, can another brother ask you for your progress on that "work" and then receive a full progress report? O Man of God, can you hear of Paul's Philemon name for Archippus – "fellow soldier" – and feel absolutely likewise?

O Man of God, speak these words aloud to yourself: "See to it that you complete [your work] you have received in the Lord." O Man of God, what is that particular work? What has God got planned for your life? When you go to your grave, what work will be known as having been your truest work; what is your great calling? What's your Savior wanting you to give your every minute of your every day of your every week of your every month of your every year to? How are you working on your present "work" or giving full-fledged whole-hearted attention to discovering the identity of that special work?

Use the bottom of this page for writing about your work. O Man of God, you were made for something:

December 18 – 2 Timothy 1:16-18

"Search hard" for ways to help another

You can be another Onesiphorus for a brother who's needing refreshment of his spirit in the Lord, today. You can be Onesiphorus in the way that "he searched hard" for Paul, making sure his daily needs were fully met. You can be Onesiphorus since we're all called to be encouragers, called to "build up" Christ's Body for the work of the Kingdom. So will you choose to be Onesiphorus in the way you live your day today: *Will you personally reach out to a brother in need?* Will you see a one who's "hungry and you gave me something to eat," one who's "thirsty and you gave me something to drink"? Will you make an invitation to a total stranger or clothe a naked one or care for the sick or visit the imprisoned? Will you have no shame about spending your life with ones in chains today, whether those chains are real, imagined, spiritual or material? Will you, as "God's workmanship," carry out the work of God today through the way you live out its individual details?

May this be another person's prayer tonight: "May the Lord show mercy to the household of [your name], because he refreshed me today and was not ashamed of my circumstances. On the contrary, as he lived his day today, he searched high and low to be a help and a servant to me. May the Lord grant that he will find mercy from the Lord on that day! I know very well in how many ways he helped my life today, simply by his showing up."

O Man of God, who will pray that prayer tonight? Let's supply the answer with gladness today!

December 19 – Philemon 1-17

Searching for "useful" lives

We should never feel angered or personally diminished by the idea that our "usefulness" is of great importance to the Lord. You and I were made by God with unique characteristics best expressed when they're united with His greatest possible use for us. You'll start to feel joyful and excited once you've actually found the way you'll best be used, temporally and spiritually. Yet you'll always feel frustrated and futile as long as you're refusing to search for and discover your best and most proper usage....

So how will we find our highest usages, O Men? How do we know when our best use is really found? How do we parse our personal best for the Lord's eternal purposes, both in "work" and in our working for His coming Kingdom? How can we find that perfect place where we're uniting our spiritual use with the conduct of our passing days' labors?

Consider this quotation from James Joyce: "To discover the mode of life or of art whereby your spirit could express itself is unfettered freedom." And also this one from Thomas Merton: "It is a tremendous thing, the economy of the Holy Ghost! When the Spirit of God finds a soul in which He can work, He uses that soul for any number of purposes: opens out before its eyes a hundred new directions, multiplying its works and its opportunities for the apostolate almost beyond belief and certainly far beyond the ordinary strength of a human being."

O Man of God, is your current "mode of life" allowing expression of your spirit *and* the Spirit of the Lord? Can you say without a doubt that you're personally "useful" to the Kingdom of God: "multiplying its works and its opportunities"? Is your bond-service to Jesus making a man of you "far beyond the ordinary strength of a human being" in actuality? Is your spiritual life one of "unfettered freedom" because you're learning to be useful in the temporal earthly realm?

"You have been set free from sin and have become slaves to God," like the apostle Paul's "dear brother," Onesimus. The "benefit you reap leads to holiness," making you ever more useful to the Master of your heart and soul. May we live today in "modes of life" united with "the economy of the Holy Ghost," truly limitless and free! May we be those men whose slavery to sin has been replaced with great service to the King of Kings! Let's you and I be like Onesimus today. Let's make our lives absolutely useful.

December 20 – 3 John 1-4

Pursuing the good health of our souls

Imagine if we men of God gave attention to our "soul health" in the same way we give such energy to our body's health. Imagine if we pushed and strained and strived and pumped our souls with the very same passion that our muscles receive at the gym or on the trail. Imagine if the time we invested in staying personally fit was equally invested in the upkeep of our eternal God-given souls. Imagine how the Church would look and function if all men demanded of their souls equal performance with what they expect from their bodies.

From his wording, it would seem that John regarded bodily health as being clearly secondary to Gaius' personal "soul-health." When he says "even as your soul is getting along well," John seems to imply that his good health should follow after that. John hoped that Gaius paid enough attention to the status of his soul that it was a precursor to his daily bodily health. He could "have no greater joy than to hear that my children are walking in truth" because Gaius must've already known the formula…

Do you know that formula, O Man? Is your own soul "well," this day? Have you taken stock of where your soul is currently finding rest; whether your own soul is feeling well or sickly? Have you, in the last short while, experienced such intimacy with your God that it made your soul feel fully alive and perfectly functional? Do you feel "close to God" or "distant from Him" right now; have you given Jesus the time to draw you closer to Himself?

O Men of God, each of us is as "close" or as "distant" with our Savior as our souls are well or sick during the course of the day. We'll be of use to Him – *or not of use* – in direct correlation to the way our souls receive daily personal care from us. Do you need to make some space today for deferred soul-maintenance; for drawing close to your Savior's heart once again? Do you need to drop all else that's competing with the "upward call" of Jesus and retreat into His Presence? Have you ceased to see your soul's health as actually being everything; how its wellness is the only thing that really matters? Have we slacked off in our caring for the only part of us that's actually eternal for the benefit of the temporal?

How's your soul doing today, O Man of God? Is your soul "well" or not?

December 21 – Revelation 1:9

Living with John's sort of spirit

Oftentimes we take for granted John's three-year discipleship with Jesus; the fact that he'd followed Him *every day* of those three years. We take for granted his alignment within that innermost "inner three," that he'd gotten the closest teaching possible from Jesus. We take for granted that he'd stood beneath the cross and then been given charge of taking care of Jesus' own mother. We take for granted that he'd stood with all the disciples on that mountain and received the Great Commission as his own personal calling. We take for granted that John actually lived out the Great Commission with his every breath of every day bestowed on him. We take for granted that he, too, became a witness "in Jerusalem, and in all Judea and Samaria, and to the ends of the earth." How quickly I forget that his providential planting "on the island of Patmos" was actually an honor for the apostle John! For would we have the chance to sit and sample this Revelation if our brother John had not been so faithful to His Master?

O Man of God, you and I are on your own personal "island of Patmos" for the sake of Jesus's Gospel today. You've been placed within an exile of great hardship, or a season of security, for His perfect heavenly purposes. Are you thankful for your identity as a "companion in the suffering and kingdom and patient endurance" of your Savior, Jesus? Is your life resolved toward thoroughgoing joy because you're counted worthy to be known as His personal chosen friend? Did you wake up to this day with a sense of John's exhilarated spirit that His Holy Spirit is within you? Will you make use of this day for Him, whether it's met with His Revelation *to* you or your revelation *of* Him?

I believe we take for granted that our earthly lives will never "measure up" against the life of someone like John. I believe we think John's life was somehow inevitable, as if everyday he didn't make the *choice* for joy and obedience to Jesus. But what might you and I accomplish if we'd also strive for lives that have the savor and strength shown by John's life? Who might we be if we would make the choice, every single day, to follow Jesus, to be likewise obedient?

Your life today is your Patmos-placement, O Man. Now do you want His Revelation?

LIVE LIKE MEN

December 22 – Revelation 1:10-20

O, the magnificent Christ!

"In the Spirit," John was graced with seeing the face of his Best Friend in the glory of His wondrous heavenly Self. Jesus allowed that John might look upon His radiant glowing all-powerful Form and know an absolute godly fear. Even though he knew that this was really Jesus, John "fell at his feet as though dead," terribly terrified of his Master. Even though he was "the disciple whom Jesus loved," John was mortified to be within His pure holy unfiltered Presence.

Today, I'd ask that we would locate, purchase or download, and then listen to the beautiful modern hymn *In Christ Alone*. I'd ask you to listen to it, while meditating upon its lovely words that are written down for you, down below. I'd ask us each to personally make the invitation to His Holy Spirit to be present in our meditations upon these words. I pray that you might feel His glory, experiencing His manifest presence, knowing this mighty One who is your Lord and Savior presently:

In Christ alone, my hope is found

He is my light, my strength, my song

This cornerstone, this solid ground

Firm through the fiercest drought and storm

What heights of love, what depths of peace

When fears are stilled, when strivings cease

My comforter, my all in all

Her in the love of Christ I stand

In Christ alone, who took on flesh

Fullness of God in helpless Babe

This gift of love and righteousness

Scorned by the ones He came to save

'Til on that cross as Jesus died
The wrath of God was satisfied
For ev'ry sin on Him was laid
Here in the death of Christ I live

There in the ground, His body lay
Light of the world by darkness slain
Then, bursting forth, in glorious day
Up from the grave, He rose again

And as He stands in victory
Sin's curse has lost its grip on me
For I am His and he is mine
Bought with the precious blood of Christ

No guilt in life, no fear in death
This is the pow'r of Christ in me
From life's first cry to final breath
Jesus commands my destiny

No pow'r of hell, no scheme of man
Can ever pluck me from His hand
'Til He returns or calls me home
Here in the pow'r of Christ I'll stand.

December 23 – Revelation 4

Worshipping in preparation for eternal worship

Would you say this everlasting giving of "glory, honor and thanks to him" sounds personally appetizing as your certain future? Do you relish in the thought of forever falling before the throne of God in worship of "him who lives for ever and ever"? Is there *any* part of you that reads these descriptions with discomfort at the absolute "ongoingness" of this worship format? Do you read about the twenty-four elders' occupation and sometimes wonder if you're up for *that* sort of heaven?

O Men of God, we will always be uncomfortable with "that sort of heaven" until our hearts have been consumed with the very thought of Jesus. Until we ascribe our human hearts to constant worship of Jesus now, we'll be disturbed by that eventual future. We'll only think about the "streets of gold" if we're only giving today's thoughts to the world's gold in our present lives. We'll only start to reconcile our restive hearts unto eternal worship of the King when we give Him worship *right now*.

O Man of God, will you worship Jesus today? Will your heart be filled with bowing-down moments? Will your spirit intertwine, in peace and power, with His Holy Spirit given as a "deposit" on your eternal future? Will you live today like worshipping the Lord for all eternity is the single greatest hope of your imagination? Will you unite the way you're living your day today with thoughts of everlasting worship and be absolutely glad in it?

Today, O Men of God, let's worship Him mightily. Let's not wait for heaven to give Him His due.

December 24 – Revelation 5

Our Christian Dualism

You and I have already "triumphed" through the victory of the Lion; we're victors over both death and the evil one. We're unvanquished by the onslaughts of the enemy even if he keeps on coming with his hard-fought plans and attacks. We aren't afraid of any scenario that the world or life or culture or mankind would think is daunting, terrifying or fearful. We aren't the men who'd run from any fight to which we're called; we will stand and fight with the Lion, wherever He asks.

Yet we men of God must *also* understand that we're co-heirs of everything that has been done to the Lamb of God. You and I are men who'll be mistreated and slaughtered every day that we're living with the heart of our Savior, Jesus. We won't raise a single complaint whenever Satan undermines our livelihoods; when he tries to kill our love for Jesus. We won't be the men who'll run away from any death to which we're called; we will stand and die with the Lamb, wherever He asks.

O Man of God, do you understand this daily dualism that *must* define our living for this Savior, Jesus? Do you know that you and I are called to live with His triumphant Spirit and yet also called to daily "lay down your life"? Have you started understanding that His calls unto obedience are a call to daily death in His name? Do you know that we're victorious *only* when we tie our lives and hearts directly to His heart for this fallen world?

May we concentrate our minds and hearts and spirits on a life that's lived with a triumphant attitude toward all we face for Him, today. We serve the Lion who "triumphed" over sin and death; we're men whose final victory is one fully assured. Yet may we also live with humble-hearted knowledge that "we always carry around in our body the death of Jesus." We're brothers with a Brother who let Himself be slain so that all men might have the chance for life and salvation and eternity.

O Men of God, we're men with a dual nature. May we give our hearts to both sides of Christ's coin.

December 25 – Revelation 6:12-17

The baby is the conqueror-God

After you've gathered around this morning's warm fuzzy Christmas tree, come right back to Jesus in His almighty wrath. After you've opened your myriad presents and brimming stockings, reacquaint yourself with One who'll blot out both the sun and moon. Be reminded that the One who came within the baby's body is also the One who eventually rains down rocks and mountains. He who "lay down His sweet head" is also the God whose wrath will lay low everything that's of the realm of death and sin. All the "kings of the earth, the princes, the generals, the rich, the mighty" will be absolutely terrified at His second earthly coming. "Every slave and every free man" will go running when they hear of His righteous indignation upon the fallen earth. May we look upon the baby in the manger with an eye unto eternity: *This is the all-conquering King!* May we sing about a "Silent Night" with ears *un*stopped to future desolation of the evil one's warring armies!

O Men of God, let's give your Christmas-contemplations to the One who came so humbly for the sake of our hearts. But may we not, for a single second, underestimate the power of He who stooped so low that we might reach so high! Let's not let the lights and trees distract our thoughts from He who *was* the Light and personally *died* upon a Tree for our sake. Don't forget that He whose First Coming was so very humble is the same One who'll someday come with almighty power. Let not our thinking about His first birthday's weakness be the *only* picture that we have of this blessed Savior. May we know that He's coming again – *maybe today!* – and that He'll tear apart the fabric of all we know and understand.

Do you know that One, O Man of God?

And what are you doing in preparation for Him today?

December 26 – Revelation 7:9-17

Aware of the Future while acting Today

I won't waste your time with talk of Pre- or Post-Tribulation; too many men have already wasted too much time on that! Too many men have sacrificed their whole lives to semantic backs-and-forths that could've been used for Jesus' actual Great Commission. Too many men are sitting on their righteous "theologically correct" backsides arguing over "signs" and "times" right this very minute. Too few men are doing much beyond ever saying, "Lord, Lord"; too many assume that their whole lives aren't actually required.

But we won't be those sort of men, will we? We won't waste time we don't possess, am I right? We won't "worry about tomorrow" when we know that all eternity is comprised within this very day that's before us. We won't fold our hands and let another man do the work required from our own lives in Jesus, will we? We won't relegate our "faith" to someday-status; we will fight today so men might know this Savior of our lives…

O Man of God, I believe the apostle John *actually saw **your** face among this white-robed multitude in heaven!* I believe your future shines with all the glory accorded to the ones who've "washed their robes" in Jesus' shed blood! I believe that you and I will meet our Savior – *and each other* – in the middle of this vast sea of rejoicing! I believe we're assured of everything that's promised to us men by the very words of Jesus Himself, the Christ!

So, O Man of God, you're already "in" with Jesus! "Your life is now hidden with Christ in God"!

Now what will you do about that today, O Man? Today's your whole life in Him; let's actually live!

December 27 – Revelation 10:1-7

The "mystery" is in you

Do you understand that fearsome angels like the one in this passage only act as *servants* of the Savior who came for you? Do you know that this particular "mighty angel" bellowing with "the roar of a lion" is your fellow servant before the Lord? Do you understand the incomparable incomprehensibility of the One who gave His life for our hearts and our lives? Can't you see that if His servant is so large as straddling across sea and land, *nothing will ever be too big for our Lord!*

Jesus Christ "is the image of the invisible God, the firstborn over all creation. For by him all things were created: things in heaven an on earth, visible and invisible, whether thrones or powers or rulers or authorities; all things were created by him and for him. He is before all things, and in him all things hold together. And he is the head of the body, the church; he is the beginning and the firstborn from among the dead, so that in everything he might have the supremacy. For God was pleased to have all his fullness dwell in him, and through him to reconcile to himself all things, whether things on earth or things in heaven, by making peace through his blood, shed on the cross." And just like the mighty angel's "mystery," we're bearers of the greatest "mystery" ever known: "Now I rejoice in what was suffered for you, and I fill up in my flesh what is still lacking in regard to Christ's afflictions, for the sake of his body, which is the church. I have become its servant by the commission God gave me to present to you the word of God in its fullness – the *mystery* that has been kept hidden for ages and generations, but is now disclosed to the saints. To them God has chosen to make known among the Gentiles the glorious riches of this *mystery*, which is *Christ in you*, the hope of glory…"

O Man of God, throughout human history men have yearned and fought and hungered for the mystery now alive in **you**. This very day, you and I are bearing in our chest the power of the One who was the Creator of all we see around us. You're a fellow servant with all the angels, prophets and Apostles who bore the Spirit of the Lord within their spirits. May we live today unconquerably in preparation for this Conquering King *who already lives within our hearts, right now!* Today's the day, O Man of God. As always, today is the only day.

December 28 – Revelation 14:1-5

We will "follow the Lamb wherever he goes"

The commendation given to this hundred-and-forty-four-thousand men is our own personal aim for this particular day. If "they follow the Lamb wherever he goes," we must be the modern men who follow the Lamb wherever He's going right now! We must live today without a single thought for human time and daily schedules and life's false machinations! We must be so fast and loose with following Jesus that our day will pulse with heartbeats of our Savior's very own heart!

Here are your two tools for this day, O Man of God: *His holy Word and His Holy Spirit living in your manly chest.* May we fall asleep tonight *without* our normal day-end thoughts; let's live our lives today with a totally precarious lifestyle. May we live so close to Jesus that we'd know "wherever he goes" and be following close behind Him, all the way. May we hearken after the quiet-beating drumbeats that are whispers of His Holy Spirit, no matter what it costs us.

May today feel totally wild, O Men of God. For that's "life to the full" as Jesus intended it.

LIVE LIKE MEN

December 29 – Revelation 19:11-16

"We are more than conquerors"

You and I must never wonder if the Lord is "strong enough" to provide for, protect and purify our earthly lives. We must be the men whose mornings are replete with awed excitement that our lives actually already belong to Him. We must read of He who's coming with a passion that provokes our hearts to making His Kingdom's paths constantly ready. We must have the mindset that Today is part of His eternal plan for the world; we're truly warriors in His conquering army…

"And we know that in all things God works for the good of those who love him, who have been called according to his purpose. For those God foreknew he also predestined to be conformed to the likeness of his Son, that he might be the firstborn among many brothers. And those he predestined, he also called; those he called, he also justified; those he justified, he also glorified.

"What, then, shall we say in response? If God (the "rider called Faithful and True," the One with eyes "like blazing fire," the Savior in the "robe dipped in blood," the "KING OF KINGS AND LORD OF LORDS") *is for us, who can be against us? He who did not spare his own Son, but gave him up for us all – how will he not also, along with him, graciously give us all things? Who will bring any charge against those whom God has chosen? It is God who justifies. Who is he that condemns? Christ Jesus, who died – more than that, who was raised to life – is at the right hand of God and is also interceding for us. Who shall separate us from the love of Christ? Shall trouble or hardship or persecution or famine or nakedness or danger or sword? As it is written: 'For your sake we face death all day long; we are considered as sheep to be slaughtered.' No, in all these things we are more than conquerors through him who loved us. For I am convinced that neither death nor life, neither angels nor demons, neither the present nor the future, nor any powers, neither height nor depth, nor anything else in all creation, will be able to separate us from the love of God that is in Christ Jesus our Lord."*

O Man of God, **this** is your identity in Jesus! May we live as the unconquerable ones today!

December 30 – Revelation 21:1-7

Has the old gone and the new come?

Then I saw new men and new lives, for the old men and their old lives had passed away, and there was no longer any fear. I saw the Holy Spirit, the Counselor, who had come down from heaven, making all these men alive. And I heard a loud voice from the throne saying, "Now the dwelling of God is with men, and he will live with them. They will be his men, and God himself will be with them and be their God. He will wipe every tear from their eyes. There will be no more fear of death or fear of anything, for the old order of things has passed away."

He who was seated on the throne of our hearts said, "I am making everything new!" Then he said, "Write these words on 'tablets of your human hearts,' for these words are trustworthy and true."

He said to us: "It is done. I am the Alpha and the Omega, the Beginning and the End. To him who is thirsty I will give to drink without cost from the spring of the water of life. He who overcomes will inherit all this, and I will be his God and he will be my son…"

O Man of God, is the "old you" dead; has your "old life" passed away; are you living life without any hint of fear? Do you feel the presence of His promised Holy Spirit living within you, giving peace, giving power for your daily living? Do you have the "mind of Christ" giving you wisdom and direction: Is the Lord alive in your thoughts all throughout the day? Are you letting Him make everything about you totally "new" as He promised in this unbelievably powerful passage?

As we ready our hearts and minds for starting out another New Year, are we truly new already in Jesus Christ? Have we journeyed through the scriptures, seen the life of God in men's lives, and been made anew through Him? Are you ready to begin another chapter of this life that you've been given – *by* Him – *for* Him? Will we give our hearts to ever-growing obedience to His ever-present Spirit and be glad that we're of practical use?

O Man of God, "I am making everything new!" Let's be made new again today!

December 31 – Revelation 22:1-5

The End and the Beginning

In many ways, the plan of God for Adam still remains the daily plan for a man after His own heart. After all, it wasn't the heart of God that changed during the course of this year, it was the changeable heart of Jesus' brother – *you!* God has placed you in a perfect setting: provided for; presiding over; alive in your full and fruitful manhood. Yet, more importantly, you've actually had the chance to walk in God's manifest presence, totally unashamed, fully alive through Jesus. You were formed from the dust of the ground, breath breathed by your God; your relationship is one of perfect harmony. God's call for Adam's life remains the call upon the whole of your life: full-hearted manhood in His perfect plan. You're now standing as His man within this world; a master over its beauty, its fruit, its profuse perfection. God has only asked you for a single thing: a single-minded obedience to one simple straightforward task…

The call of God to you during this past year has revolved around a daily dose of one simple question, O Man: Would you today – and tomorrow – and the day after tomorrow – *all year* – be obedient to Jesus? Would you bask within the ever-present glow of His ever-available presence first thing every single morning? Would you realize His provisionary promises for those who "seek His kingdom" are abundantly true for you? Would you *not* seek first to make yourself like Him in His perfect knowledge, to hunger for the fruit of His knowledge of good and evil? Instead, would you "hunger and thirst for righteousness" and taste deeply of the tree and the river of life?

O Man of God, did you actually follow through in your becoming a disciple of the God you desire to serve? Did you live this year from the fullness of the manhood you were actually created for, O holy Son of Adam? Did you live the bulk of every single day seeking to obey all the commandments spoken to you by His Holy Spirit? Were you open to be challenged by the wonderful life of God at work in the lives of His chosen men?

O Men of God, we're right back where we started! We're standing next to His Tree! May His Holy Spirit, and His Holy Word, guide and direct the way you launch into your next New Year.

God bless you, my brother. May we one day meet in His Kingdom.

ABOUT THE AUTHOR

Eugene lives in Colorado with his wife and children. If you'd like to talk or even meet in person, please feel free to contact him by email at eugeneluning@gmail.com

Made in the USA
Columbia, SC
02 May 2018